Cross-Cultural Management

Essential Concepts

Third Edition

David C. Thomas
University of New South Wales

&

Mark F. Peterson
Florida Atlantic University
Maastricht University

Los Angeles | London | New Delhi
Singapore | Washington DC

Los Angeles | London | New Delhi
Singapore | Washington DC

FOR INFORMATION:

SAGE Publications, Inc.
2455 Teller Road
Thousand Oaks, California 91320
E-mail: order@sagepub.com

SAGE Publications Ltd.
1 Oliver's Yard
55 City Road
London EC1Y 1SP
United Kingdom

SAGE Publications India Pvt. Ltd.
B 1/I 1 Mohan Cooperative Industrial Area
Mathura Road, New Delhi 110 044
India

SAGE Publications Asia-Pacific Pte. Ltd.
3 Church Street
#10-04 Samsung Hub
Singapore 049483

Copyright © 2015 by David C. Thomas

Printed in the United States of America

Library of Congress Cataloging-in-Publication Data

Thomas, David C. (David Clinton), 1947-

Cross-cultural management : essential concepts / David C. Thomas, University of New South Wales & Mark F. Peterson, Florida Atlantic University. — Third Edition.

pages cm
Includes bibliographical references and index.

ISBN 978-1-4522-5750-1 (alk. paper)

1. International business enterprises—Management. 2. International business enterprises—Management—Cross-cultural studies. 3. Management—Cross-cultural studies. 4. Intercultural communication. 5. Communication in management—Cross-cultural studies. I. Peterson, Mark F. II. Thomas, David C. (David Clinton), 1947- Essentials of international management. III. Title.

HD62.4.T488 2014
658′.049—dc23   2013051164

Acquisitions Editor: Patricia Quinlin
Editorial Assistant: Dori Zweig
Production Editor: Olivia Weber-Stenis
Copy Editor: Karin Rathert
Typesetter: C&M Digitals (P) Ltd.
Proofreader: Carole Quandt
Indexer: Michael Ferreira
Cover Designer: Karine Hovsepian
Marketing Manager: Liz Thornton

SFI label applies to text stock

14 15 16 17 18 10 9 8 7 6 5 4 3 2 1

Brief Contents

Detailed Contents

List of Tables and Figures

List of Tables

List of Figures

Preface

This new edition continues the tradition of previous volumes in that it extracts key concepts on management from a cross-cultural perspective and condenses them into a concise volume. Therefore, the amount of description and number of examples given for a particular concept are limited. However, we have updated each topic area with the most current research. The complexity of cross-cultural management is recognized, and care has been taken not to speculate when evidence supporting a particular concept or relationship is limited. And, the book is extensively referenced and indexed so that the interested reader has ready access to the source of the material presented and can easily follow up on the areas of most interest. In this edition, we have added questions for discussion at the end of each chapter.

Designed to present key issues in international management in a concise way, this book allows a number of options for its use in the classroom. It can be used in combination with complementary readings and cases as the core text for an advanced course in international or cross-cultural management with a microfocus, or if combined with more experiential exercises, it can form the basis of short courses for students with some background in organizational behavior or international business. The book may also be a useful supplement in courses with a macro approach to international management. Scholars, particularly those without a deep background in cross-cultural management, will find it a concise reference to key issues and ideas in the field.

Because it is an *essentials* volume, choices had to be made concerning the domain of the topic area and the particular perspective that informed the organization of the material presented. In this book, we examine cross-cultural management issues from a predominantly psychological perspective. As opposed to being country specific, this book focuses on the interactions of people from different cultures in organizational settings. The approach used is to understand the effect of culture in a way that can then be applied to a wide variety of cross-cultural interactions in a number of organizational contexts. Students of organizational behavior, industrial and organizational psychology, and social psychology will find many of the topics familiar. However, the focus of this book is on application of these concepts to global management.

Part I presents four chapters that provide an essential basis for understanding the influence of culture on management. In Chapter 1, we describe the role of the global manager and present the context in which today's manager must function. We briefly explore the major facets of the global management environment (legal, political, economic, and cultural), with the cultural aspect presented as, in many ways, the most challenging dimension. This chapter also recognizes that our understanding of cross-cultural management is only in its infancy and addresses the challenge of continued learning. Therefore, we outline general issues concerning the limitations of current methods and theory in explaining cross-cultural management, classify studies of international management, and present key methodological issues regarding cross-national and cross-cultural research. In Chapter 2, we demystify and define culture in practical terms that can used to explain and predict. We suggest that culture shapes, at the most fundamental level, the way individuals' cognitions are structured. We discuss the reasons that cultures form and persist, and we compare and contrast the influence of culture with the influence of human nature and personality. We also present the central debates surrounding the culture construct. Chapter 3 is devoted to the major frameworks that have been used to describe the systematic variation in cultures. The goal of the chapter is to convey the idea that cultural variation is not random but systematic and can therefore be used to explain and predict behavior. In Chapter 4, we apply the basics of social cognition to the context of cross-cultural interaction. Among the concepts discussed are selective perception, stereotyping, ethnocentrism, differential attributions, behavioral scripts, and cultural differences in self-concept. The message in this chapter is that culture affects managerial behavior through identifiable psychological mechanisms.

Part II contains three chapters that focus on the roles of decision maker, negotiator, and leader that dominate the activities of global managers. In Chapter 5, we review the process of decision making and explore the opportunity for cultural variation in the ways in which managers simplify the complex global decision-making environment. In addition, we discuss the ethical dilemmas presented by decision making in a global context. In Chapter 6, we discuss, in terms of the application of cross-cultural communication, the process and behavioral aspects of negotiation. We present the basics of communication, concepts that transfer meaning across cultures, as grounding for understanding negotiation across cultures. More holistic approaches to understanding negotiation across cultures are also discussed. In Chapter 7, we explore the difficult task of motivating and leading individuals from different cultures. We contrast Western approaches to motivation and leadership with theories indigenous to other cultures and present a cross-cultural model of leadership.

Part III is devoted to some of the challenges that face global managers, which can be informed by a better understanding of intercultural interactions. Chapter 8 presents the first of these challenges, involving multicultural work groups and teams. We identify the fundamental factors affecting performance of all work groups and describe culture as influencing these groups through three interrelated yet distinct mechanisms. We also discuss implications for cross-cultural variation in the rapidly growing phenomenon of global virtual teams. In Chapter 9, we discuss international organizations in terms of both a universal logic to organizing and the influence of culture on organizational structure. We describe the basic dimensions of organizational structure and design and discuss different schools of thought with regard to explaining organizational structure. We present the influence of culture and examples of cross-national variation in both the formal and the informal organization. A discussion of the multinational corporation as a unique organizational form leads to consideration of its influence on managerial roles and the relationship of culturally different individuals to the firm. Chapter 10 looks at the challenges associated with the assignment of individuals overseas from both the perspective of the firm and that of the individual expatriate. In this chapter, we summarize the significant volume of research that has tried to explain the success or failure of overseas employees by examining individual, organizational, and environmental factors. In addition, we discuss the shift in focus that has occurred toward understanding overseas assignments and experience in terms of their longer-term career implications for individuals and in terms of the transfer of knowledge for organizations. Concluding this part, Chapter 11 examines some key environmental trends and attempts to outline some of the future challenges that will be faced by cross-cultural managers. The discontinuous nature of change in the various environments of global business presents organizations and managers with the need to adapt in order to thrive.

The globalization of the business environment that is being driven by technological and economic factors is resulting in an ever-increasing number of cross-cultural interactions in the workplace. Understanding the influence of culture on interpersonal interactions in organizational settings is now a fundamental requirement of effective international management. We hope this book will be an aid to that understanding. As always, we recognize that our own cultural backgrounds influence our ability to be objective, and we would be more than pleased to hear from readers who think our cultural orientations may have caused us to miss or misrepresent things that are obvious to them.

David C. Thomas

Mark F. Peterson

Acknowledgments

We sincerely appreciate the assistance and support of the many people who have contributed to the production of this third edition. We are grateful to SAGE Publications for seeing value in a revised and updated version of the text. As in previous editions it is important to acknowledge the work of Peter B. Smith and Michael Harris Bond, now joined by Ronald Fischer and Vivian Vignoles in their book *Understanding Social Psychology Across Cultures,* which along with its predecessors is part of the intellectual foundation of this volume. We thank Alicia Boisnier, Arpita Joadar, Waheeda Lillevik, Denise Potosky, Susan Sharp, and David Yen who reviewed the previous edition and offered suggestions for this new edition. Your comments were instrumental in helping us craft this new version. Any errors or omissions are of course our responsibility alone. Aycan Kara and Echo Yuan Liao provided research assistance to make sure this edition is as current and up to date as possible. Maaja Vadi and the Ph.D. seminar students at Tartu University provided helpful comments on some of the final revisions. We are grateful for their help. Karin Rathert did her usual superb job in copyediting the manuscript. She is the best! We thank our university homes that allow us the latitude in our work to engage in projects of this type. The University of New South Wales, Simon Fraser University, Florida Atlantic University, Maastricht University and Tartu University have been generous in their support. The work of our colleagues in the International Organizations Network is widely represented in this volume and they provide a continual source of intellectual inspiration. And, they are fun!

Part I

Management and Culture

Introduction:
The Challenging
Role of the
Global Manager

It is generally agreed that planning, organizing, coordinating and controlling are basic activities of management.

Henri Fayol (1916, as cited in Gray, 1987)

Growing interconnections brought about by the globalization process require that both managers and organizations expand repertoires of roles.

Barbara Parker (2005)

The world of international management is no longer limited to jet-setting corporate troubleshooters or seasoned expatriate managers. Virtually all business conducted today is influenced by a cross-border transaction of some kind. Twenty years ago, even geographically isolated cotton farmers in West Texas who grew short-fiber cotton for making clothing, such as blue jeans, were worried about crop failure from hail or lack of rain. They now have the added worry about the success of the cotton crop in faraway China. Likewise, international responsibilities and contact with other cultures are commonplace and often do not require leaving the office. Dramatic shifts in economics, politics, and technology shape the role of the international manager. These shifts are often encapsulated in the term *globalization*. This chapter explores the economic, legal, political, technological, and cultural environments in which today's global managers must function, by examining the changes that define globalization. Each of these environmental factors is influential; however, the most difficult to understand and the one most often neglected by managers can be the influence of culture. Culture's significance for all aspects of what managers do becomes clear when international management is defined by the structure and content of managerial roles, as opposed to the functions of management. The roles that managers play share certain features across cultures but are best understood within their cultural context. By focusing on these roles, the importance of the manager's interactions with individuals from different cultures becomes apparent. Although economics, politics, and technology can define the playing field of international management, it is a game of cross-cultural interactions being played. This chapter also provides some guidance for evaluating international and cross-cultural management research, such as the studies referred to in this book.

Globalization

The term globalization is omnipresent in contemporary writing about management. However, definitions and descriptions of globalization vary widely. In order to understand what it means to be a global manager, we must first define the term globalization. Globalization has been described as the "crystallization of the world as a single place" (Robertson, 1995, p. 38), the overlapping of the interests of business and society (Renesch, 1992) or "an increase in the impact on human activities of forces that span national boundaries" (Goldin & Reinert, 2012, p. 2). Parker (2005, p. 5) provides a useful general definition when she describes globalization as "a process whereby worldwide interconnections in virtually every sphere of activity are growing. Some of these interconnections lead to integration/unity worldwide; others do not." This increase in interconnections is the result of shifts that have taken place in technological, political, and economic spheres. The following four categories of change illustrate the process of globalization.

Growing Economic Interconnectedness

The economic interconnections among countries were dramatically increased with the advent of free-trade areas in the 1990s. The number of regional trade agreements ballooned to more than 300 in January 2012, up from 100 at the end of the millennium and about 45 a decade earlier (World Trade Organization, 1999, 2013). The three largest trade groups, the European Union (EU), the North American Free Trade Agreement (NAFTA), and the Asia-Pacific Economic Cooperation (APEC), account for about one-half of the world's trade, with the strongest recent growth occurring in Asia and the Commonwealth of Independent States (World Trade Organization, 2005). In addition, the World Trade Organization (WTO), formed in 1995 as a result of the Uruguay round of the General Agreement on Tariffs and Trade (GATT) with the goal of reducing tariffs and liberalizing trade across the board, now has 157 member-nations. The result of these agreements is to create a greater degree of interconnectedness among the world's economies. Therefore, local economic conditions are no longer the result of purely domestic influence.

The gap between regional GDP growth rates of the fastest growing and least dynamic regions of the world has begun to narrow. Although the developed world continues to show GDP growth rates at approximately the world average, GDP in other economies, mainly in Africa and the former Russian republics, had output growth rates of 7 to 15 percent in 2012 (World Trade Organization, 2013). Economic growth in even the more prosperous nations of Europe (Germany, the United Kingdom) has slowed since 2010 to about 1.5 percent as of 2012.

The level of foreign direct investment (FDI) also has a globalizing effect. FDI, as a percentage of world gross domestic product (GDP), doubled between 1985 and 1994 (UN Conference on Trade and Development, 2013). The decline in flows that was observed in the early 2000s, after the Internet bubble was reversed in 2004, peaked in 2007. Since the great recession began, flows have stabilized at approximately their 2000 levels. The inward flow of FDI now accounts for about one-third of the GDP of developing countries compared to about 10 percent in 1980 (UN Conference on Trade and Development, 2005), with China the world's second largest recipient (Deresky, 2006). The result of these changes in trade and FDI flows is a shift in the economic center of the universe away from North America and Western Europe. Global economic turmoil during the past decade indicates that the effects of globalization not only have the potential to favor developed market economies and a small number of large emerging economies but are not even consistently positive in developed economies (Goldin & Reinert, 2012; Stiglitz, 2007, 2008).

Organizational boundaries are also affected by globalization. In modern multinational corporations (MNCs), production, sales and marketing, and distribution might all be located in different countries to capitalize on certain location-specific advantages (see Leung & Peterson, 2011 for a discussion). UN Conference on Trade and Development (2005) reports that now about one-third of global trade is intra-firm. Moreover, conventional organizational forms are giving way to networks of less hierarchical relationships (Kogut, 1989) and cooperative strategic alliances with other firms (Jarillo, 1988). An additional aspect of changing organizational boundaries is the emergence of virtual organizations in which employees do not meet face-to-face but are linked by computer technology (Maznevski & Athanassiou, 2006).

Multinational firms now manufacture and sell on a global basis on an unprecedented scale, and the expansion of international production continues to gather momentum. And the world's economies are interdependent as never before. Thus economic globalization connects countries and organizations in a network of international linkages that shape the environment in which global managers must function.

More Complex and Dynamic Work Environment

Related to the increased interconnectedness of economies and organizations are changes that affect the stability of the work environment within organizations. These include downsizing, privatization, and movement toward team-based management.

For example, globalization means that layoffs can occur in Milan or Seattle because of cheaper labor in Mexico or Malaysia. Increased rates of mergers and acquisitions, because of efforts to remain competitive in a more difficult environment, result in workforce reductions. These workforce changes have an effect on those who remain in the company as well as on those who leave (Offerman & Gowing, 1990).

Additionally, the number of permanent migrants is changing the composition of the workforce in numerous countries. As boundaries to migration become more permeable, migration resulting from economic, political and social factors increases. The current magnitude of migration is very large indeed. According to the Global Commission on Migration (GCIM, 2005) there were nearly 200 million migrants in 2005, counting only those who have lived outside their country for a year or more. This is equivalent to the population of the world's fifth largest country—Brazil. Table 1.1 shows the countries that are the largest recipients of migrants.

Two recent trends in migration are worth noting. First, the number of women migrants is increasing. In 1976 fewer than 15 percent of migrants were women, while in 2005, women accounted for 70 percent (GCIM, 2005). Second, the traditional migration pattern following World War II was low-skilled workers from less developed to more developed countries. While economic factors continue to be a major pull, today's migrant is much more likely to be highly skilled (Carr, Inkson, & Thorn, 2005). For example, up to 20 percent of the total population of New Zealand has migrated to live and work outside their country (Bryant & Law, 2004).

A third factor influencing the work environment in many firms is privatization. Governments in both developed and developing countries are selling state-owned business to private investors at an increasing rate ("Privatization," 1997). Privatization

Table 1.1	Migrants as a Percentage of Total Population (Countries With at Least 20 Million Inhabitants)

Country	Percentage of Population
Saudi Arabia	26%
Australia	20%
Canada	19%
Ukraine	15%
United States	13%
Germany	12%
France	11%
Spain	11%

SOURCE: Population Division of the United Nations Secretariat (2005).

enables formerly government-controlled enterprises to be available for purchase by foreign firms, thus reducing boundaries. In addition, because these enterprises have often been noncompetitive, privatization has a dramatic effect on the work life and management in these firms. Major changes in technology, workforce size, and management are often required to meet global standards of quality and efficiency. The privatization of government-run enterprise in the former Soviet Union, where over 12,000 state-owned companies were sold ("Russia's State Sell Off," 1994), is perhaps just the most obvious example of this worldwide trend (e.g., Sanderson & Hayes, 1990).

Finally, organizations around the globe are increasingly looking toward the formation of teams of workers as a solution to productivity problems (Hoerr, 1989). Concurrently demographic shifts in the workforce have been occurring in many countries. Demographic changes, including increasing cultural diversity because of ease of movement of workers of all skill levels across borders, the rising average age of employees, and the addition of more women to the workforce predicted for the year 2000 (Johnston, 1991), have now been realized. Introducing teams in these increasingly multicultural workplaces is a complex affair involving changing work methods, compensation systems, level of employee involvement, and the role of the first-line supervisor (Thomas, Ravlin, & Barry, 2000). These changes, resulting from downsizing, privatization, international migration and team-based management, contribute to create a more complex and dynamic work environment for firms around the world.

Increased Use and Sophistication of Information Technology

The most significant force toward globalization, the one with the most potential to shape the international management landscape, might be the dramatic advances in information technology (Naisbitt, 1994). The rate of change in communications and computing technology is staggering. Multinational firms can now communicate all types of information (e.g., voice, data, text, graphics) throughout their geographically dispersed enterprise instantaneously. In addition, access to information, resources, products, and markets is influenced by improved information technology. With computer technology, it is now possible to establish a business that is almost entirely unconcerned with traditional boundaries and barriers, including barriers with regard to economies of scale and scope (Cairncross, 2001; Govindarajan & Gupta, 2001). The decreasing price and increased sophistication of computing systems has placed in the hands of small business capabilities that a few years ago were available only to large multinationals. Information technology breakthroughs that affect almost all areas of human endeavor seem to be occurring on an almost daily basis. Some authors warn that this technological change will render physical place irrelevant for so-called virtual firms and ultimately be the undoing of the nation-state (e.g., Knoke, 1996). Other authors suggest that the psychological influence of being a physical presence when communicating with someone limits the influence of electronic communication technologies (Leung & Peterson, 2011). At a minimum, the likely effect is that the work roles of employees and managers will need to be adjusted to reflect an increasingly information-driven environment (Leung & Peterson, 2011).

More and Different Players on the Global Stage

Some authors suggest that globalization, as defined by increased interconnectedness, is nothing new (see Parker, 2005). This view stems in part from the fact that trade in terms of a percentage of gross world product was only slightly higher at the end of the 20th century than it was before 1914 (Farnham, 1994). From this perspective, it is possible to argue that globalization is just business as usual. However, it seems impossible to ignore the numbers of new entrants to the international business arena in recent years. Although cross-border commerce has been conducted since ancient times, the most rapid expansion of international business occurred in the latter half of the 20th century (Leung & Peterson, 2011). The players on the international business stage were originally the firm and its foreign constituency but were soon joined by home- and host-country governments and, more recently, by special interest groups, international agencies, and economic alliances (Robinson, 1984). In addition, the characteristics of these actors have changed over time. U.S. multinational firms dominated the postwar period, but in 2011, as shown in Table 1.2, Tokyo and Beijing were home to most of the *Fortune* magazine's Global 500.

As noted previously, technology is facilitating the entry of small business into the international arena. For example, in the mid 1990s, 25 percent of all exporting firms

Table 1.2　Host Cities: Global *Fortune* 500 in 2011

Rank	City	Country	Number of Global 500 Companies (City)	Global 500 Revenues $ Millions (City)
1	Tokyo	Japan	47	$2,268,640
2	Beijing	China	41	$2,222,366
3	Paris	France	23	$1,285,432
4	London	United Kingdom	18	$1,170,270
5	New York	United States	18	$955,291
6	Seoul	South Korea	12	$640,586
7	Osaka	Japan	8	$376,607
8	Toronto	Canada	7	$197,294
9	Houston	United States	6	$377,702
9	Moscow	Russia	6	$348,084
9	Madrid	Spain	6	$323,345
9	Zurich	Switzerland	6	$221,818
9	Mumbai	India	6	$207,156

SOURCE: Host Cities, Global *Fortune* 500 (2011).

had fewer than 100 employees (Aharoni, 1994). In 1996, small and medium-size enterprises accounted for 80 percent of all the MNCs in Sweden, 60 percent of these firms in Italy, and over 50 percent of the new foreign affiliates established by Japanese firms in that year (UN Conference on Trade and Development, 1999). In addition, the service sector of the global economy is increasing rapidly, with as much as 70 percent of advanced economies (80 percent in the U.S.) contained in this sector and with trade in services now about 20 percent of world exports (Parker, 2005). A growing percentage of international managers are involved in industries, such as travel, transportation, entertainment, advertising, and telecommunications.

Often omitted from discussions of the players on the global stage are international gangs and terrorists. Global gangs based in Russia, China, Hong Kong, Japan, Colombia, Italy, and the United States manufacture and transport illegal drugs around the world, trade in human cargo, and use the international banking system to launder billions of dollars (Parker, 2005). Worldwide trade in human beings is valued in the billions of dollars, and INTERPOL estimates that illegal drug sales account for about US$400 billion annually. The acts of terrorists were once perceived as isolated local events. However, events such as the attack on the World Trade Center on September 11, 2001, violence in the "Arab spring" movements, and train bombings in Spain have clearly had a global impact. While the world may have been changing for some time, the repercussions of these dramatic events have made the reality of global interconnectedness apparent.

In summary, the players encountered on the global stage are now more likely to include firms headquartered outside of the United States. Increasingly, they could be small to medium-size businesses and are more likely than ever to be a part of the service sector. Finally, global managers must recognize that the increased permeability of boundaries associated with globalization also applies to illegal and terrorist activities. Some might argue that globalization has a single cause, such as technology or trade liberalization. However, it is sometimes difficult to disentangle the causes of globalization from its effects. What seems clear is that the environment in which global managers must function is undergoing changes that influence traditional boundaries. One key result of globalization is that global managers face an external environment far more complex, more dynamic, more uncertain, and more competitive than ever before.

Environment of Global Management

The elements of the global manager's environment can be divided into four categories: economic, legal, political, and cultural. Making managerial decisions on a global basis requires an understanding of the economic strategies of countries in (or with) which one is conducting business. Also, some of the complexity of global management arises from the variety of laws and regulations that exist throughout the world. And political systems are the structures and processes by which a nation integrates the parts of society into a functioning unit and forms part of the framework in which management activity takes place.

These three aspects of the global business environment (economic, legal, and political) provide the backdrop against which global managers must function. In the remainder of this book, although recognizing the importance of these aspects of the environment, the focus is on the effect of culture on management. Culture is singled out as uniquely important to international management for three reasons. First, to a great extent, the economic, legal, and political characteristics of a country are a manifestation of a nation's culture. That is, these systems are derived from a country's culture and history. Even in cases where a single person or a small number of people dictates these systems and maintains them through force, history and culture can contribute to their development. As discussed in more detail in Chapter 2, culture stems from the fundamental ways in which a society learns to interact with its environment. The economic, legal, and political systems that have developed over time are the visible elements of a more fundamental set of shared meanings. And the extent to which individuals share beliefs about the world around them is an indication that they share a culture (Rohner, 1984). Culture also affects the goals of the institutions of society, the way the institutions operate, and the attributions their members make for policies and behavior (Schwartz, 1992). Second, unlike economic, legal, and political aspects of a country, which are observable, culture is largely invisible. That is, the influence of culture is difficult to detect, and managers therefore often overlook it. Although culture might or might not be the most important influence on the practice of management, it is the aspect of the management context most often neglected. Finally, as argued in the next section, the practice of management largely focuses on interpersonal interactions. One of the distinct characteristics of global management is that these interactions occur with individuals who are culturally different. For many "global" managers, the global nature of their environment can consist largely of working with a multicultural workforce in their own country. This perspective on global management, that management is what managers do as compared to what functions they serve, emphasizes the importance of interpersonal interactions across cultures.

What Global Managers Do

Most management textbooks describe management in terms of some derivation of Henri Fayol's 1916 definition that "to manage is to plan, organize, coordinate, command, and control" (as cited in Gray, 1987, p. 13). However, these functions of management are difficult to observe; they do not operate in any sequential way, and there are some managerial activities that do not fit neatly into any of these categories. Dissatisfaction with this description of management has led a number of scholars to seek alternative ways to describe what managers do. The best known of these studies was conducted by Henry Mintzberg in the late 1960s (Mintzberg, 1973). He suggested that managers have formal authority over their organizational unit and that this status divides their activities into interpersonal, informational, and decisional role categories. Contrary to earlier beliefs that managerial work was systematic and rational, Mintzberg demonstrated that it was more accurately characterized by brevity, variety, and fragmentation, with a high degree of interpersonal interaction (1973). Notable is the extent to which what managers do involves interactions with other people.

To some extent, these findings underlie the organization of subsequent chapters of this book around the leadership, decision-making, and communication and negotiation roles that form the key components of the global manager's job. Regardless of the labels given to the categories, there seems to be at least some moderate agreement about the common behaviors associated with managerial work. Clearly, however, interpersonal interactions are at the core of management.

How Global Managers Carry Out Their Role: Sources of Guidance

Managers throughout the world report that they rely heavily on their own judgment shaped by their experience and training to understand and make decisions about their work activities (Peterson & Smith, 2008). However, managers also rely on other people, their *role set*, and *norms* in order to understand how to carry out their job. Role set members include colleagues, superiors, and subordinates, as well as staff departments, internal and external consultants, and sometimes even friends and family members. Norms include explicit organizational rules and procedures as well as governmental laws, and also implicit norms about "how we do things around here" that are well known and typically followed in an organization or society. Role set members and norms provide sources of ideas, principles, and other ways of thinking that managers use to guide their understanding of the events, issues, and problems that they encounter in their work and to help them make decisions. As discussed ahead in Chapter 3, each of these sources of guidance is more heavily used in some parts of the world than in others. Being aware of the sources that organization members tend to rely on most heavily in a particular part of the world can inform an international manager about the ways of having a constructive influence in an unfamiliar society.

Organizational Context, Culture, and Managerial Roles

Despite the emphasis on describing the similarities among managers, some research has tried to systematically account for differences in the work of managers. Of particular interest is the extent to which the global context of international management might affect the manager's role.

From the previous discussion of the environment faced by global managers, it is clear that they face demands and constraints that are both quantitatively and qualitatively distinct. Although empirical research has generally found more similarities than differences in managerial roles (Hales, 1986), some studies demonstrate the effect of contextual factors, such as environmental and technological complexity (Gibbs, 1994), the size of the firm (Choran, 1969), the amount of uncertainty in the environment (Leifer & Huber, 1977), and the organization's structure (Aldrich & Herker, 1977; Hales & Tamangani, 1996) on managerial roles. For example, in one study, environmental complexity increased the frequency of informational roles, whereas complexity and dynamism increased the frequency of decisional roles (Gibbs, 1994). In another, managers in more centralized organizations spent more time in downward communication in contrast to those in decentralized organizations, who emphasized upward communication (Hales & Tamangani, 1996). In summary, the manager's role relates directly to the constraints and demands of the national and organizational environment and involves choices in which roles are emphasized.

Consistent with the choices that managers have in their roles, research finds that managers can have jobs with similar demands and constraints and still differ in what roles they choose to emphasize (Graen, 1976; Stewart, 1982). One very apparent difference involves the choices that managers from different cultures make about their roles. For example, differences in the activities that managers emphasize have been found for Germans as compared with British managers (Stewart, Barsoux, Kieser, Ganter, & Walgenbach, 1994) and among Chinese, Japanese, Korean, and U.S. managers (Doktor, 1990). Therefore, the roles and work behaviors of managers are the result of both the national and organizational context, which establishes demands and constraints on the choices they make. The direct effect of culture on a manager's responsibilities is the focus of much of the remainder of this book. However, it is important to emphasize that culture also affects the roles and behavior of managers indirectly, such as in the choice of informational, interpersonal, or decisional roles as well as on sources of guidance. Culture has its indirect influence by shaping the context in which managers must perform. For example, in a study of Chinese managers, Boisot and Xing (1992) found that although Chinese managers share many behavioral characteristics with their U.S. counterparts, they do so in an institutional setting that places different demands and constraints on their behavior. Specifically, because of the strong hierarchical organization, Chinese managers spent about the same amount of time in downward communication as U.S. managers but about four times as much time in communication with superiors and only about one-half as much time in communicating with outsiders and peers. Similarly, Stewart et al. (1994) found differences in German and British firms that gave rise to specific differences in roles for managers. For example, German organizations were flatter and more integrated and placed a greater emphasis on technical as opposed to interpersonal controls than did British firms. This resulted in German managerial jobs that involved less concern over gaining cooperation, less awareness of organizational constraints, less choice over job roles, more involvement in the technical aspects of tasks, less direct supervision, fewer meetings and networking, but more desk work than the jobs of British managers. In these cases, national cultural differences influenced managerial jobs indirectly. That is, culture shapes the context of managerial work, which in turn influences managerial roles.

The practice of management is anything but static. As globalization increases the amount of intercultural contact in organizational settings, the inadequacy of our present understanding of management to explain and predict behavior in these settings becomes more apparent.

Evaluating Cross-Cultural Management Studies

For practicing managers and management scholars to continue to enhance their understanding of management in this dynamic environment, it is imperative that systematic study of management across cultures continues to improve. Failure to do so reinforces the lack of relevance of which management research is often accused. The type of exploration needed is not easy for those conducting international studies, and understanding the findings and their implications is often not straightforward for consumers of this research. In the following section, general issues about the limitations of current management theory to explain global management are outlined. Then, studies of international management are classified by the types of questions they can answer. Finally, key methodological issues regarding cross-national and cross-cultural research are presented, both as a reminder for scholars and a consumer's guide for managers.

Limitations in Present Management Studies

As will be evident in this book, research has identified myriad differences among management practices around the world. However, to try to understand what is happening in practice in various countries, management scholars are often relegated to rely on theory and findings from the United States and a small number of other developed countries. As scholars construct theory, they are searching to understand the world that they perceive around them (Doktor, Tung, & Von Glinow, 1991). If, as is the case in much management research, that world is the United States, their theory reflects it. This bias in theory development is not the result of an inherent belief in the superiority of U.S. management but of parochialism—a lack of awareness of alternative contexts, models, research, and values (Boyacigiller & Adler, 1991; Gelfand, Leslie, & Fehr, 2008). This parochialism is understandable and can be better considered in our evaluation of management research if we review its origins.

First, the questions to which management scholars seek answers are a product of the time in which they are studied (Abrahamson & Fairchild, 1999; Lawrence, 1987). Much of contemporary management knowledge was defined in the United States following World War II. As the only economic power left intact, the United States dominated the world economy for the next 20 years. It was during this period of U.S. economic dominance that the field of management studies began to emerge and was thus marked with a U.S. orientation (Boyacigiller & Adler, 1991; Gelfand, Leslie, & Fehr, 2008). Under the assumption that the underlying influence of the economic success of the United States was U.S. management practices, U.S. firms were studied and their practices were held up as models for the world (Beechler & Pucik, 1989; Hofstede, 1983). Whether or not it was actually management practice, or as argued by some (Ouchi, 1984; Thurow, 1984), a benevolent environment that accounted for U.S. success, the study of management has an indelible U.S. imprint. While the first few years of the 21st century have seen a dramatic increase in international and cross-cultural management studies (Kirkman & Law, 2005), these historical factors have served to perpetuate parochialism in management studies.

A U.S. orientation on management theory is important because the activity it purports to describe, management and organizing, does not appear to be universal. The preponderance of evidence, as limited as it is in some areas, indicates substantial cultural variation in management and organizational practices. Therefore, it is important to recognize the unique cultural orientation that a U.S. perspective has brought to the study of management and organizations. Like all national cultures, the United States has deeply embedded values that influence the way scholars from the United States perceive and think about the world they are investigating. The lack of universality of "made in America" theories is described to some extent in later chapters. However, Boyacigiller and Adler (1991), suggest three particularly pervasive aspects of the U.S. perspective that limit the ability of U.S. management theories in explaining organizational phenomenon in cultures with contrasting orientations. These are (a) extreme individualism, (b) a belief that individuals are in control of their own circumstances and can, to a great degree, influence their environment and future events (or free will), and (c) low-context communication (discussed in detail in Chapter 6), where most of the meaning of a message is contained in the explicit communication as opposed to the context surrounding the information exchange. Unfortunately, theories indigenous to other cultures, which might show what is being missed by applying U.S. approaches abroad, are rare (Smith, Fischer, Vignoles, & Bond, 2013). In the best case, theoretical relationships could be tested simultaneously in several different cultures based on concepts that are meaningful in each. Then the results are compared for possible convergence. However, this approach is not typical, and most cross-cultural research must be carefully evaluated with the recognition of the limitations presented by the cultures involved and the method used.

Types of International Management Research

Global (international) management research can take a number of forms, each with a distinct purpose and characteristic. The types of studies have been categorized in a number of ways by different authors (e.g. Adler, 1983; Drenth & Wilpert, 1980; Earley & Singh, 1995; Peterson, 2001; van de Vijver & Leung, 1997). The typology presented here incorporates elements of these previous approaches to arrive at six categories of research studies. The six different types of studies shown in Table 1.3 differ in terms of the assumptions they make about culture, about the universality of management theory, and in the types of questions they address. Each type also has specific methodological issues that must be confronted.

Domestic Research. Domestic research is defined here as those management studies designed and conducted within a single country without regard for the boundary conditions set by the cultural orientation of the country. These studies assume the universal applicability of the constructs and relationships they test. The vast majority of this type of research originated in the United States and suffers from the parochialism mentioned previously. Before such research can be applied to a culture other than the one in which it originated, its generalizability across cultures must be proven.

Replication Research. These studies attempt to replicate research results first found in one country, typically the United States, by repeating the research in other countries. That is, they anticipate that the concepts being measured will have the same meaning to the participants in the new culture as they did in the culture in which the study was conceived. They then use a combination of translation and statistical procedures to adjust the measures to the new context and evaluate how successful measures were in

Table 1.3 Types of Cross-Cultural Management Studies

Category	Description	Cultural Assumptions	Research Questions
Domestic	Management studies in a single country	Culture is ignored, or universality of theory is assumed.	How can we explain and predict the behavior of people in organizations?
Replication	Management study repeated in another country	Universality is questioned; there is no theory available to predict the effect of culture.	Does this theory that applies in culture *A* also apply in culture *B*?
Indigenous	Individual management studies conceived and executed in one or many cultures	Cultural differences are assumed to exist; indigenous theory is needed to explain behavior.	How can we explain and predict the behavior of people in organizations in country *X*?
Comparative	Management study conducted in two or more countries	Similarities and differences exist; there may or may not be a theory available to predict the effect of culture.	What similarities and differences exist in the behavior of people in organizations? Is this theory universal?
International	Studies of multinational organizations	Similarities and differences exist, or culture is ignored.	How do organizations that operate in multiple countries function?
Intercultural	Studies of intercultural interactions in organizations	Specific aspects of culture are part of the theoretical framework underlying the study.	How is this theory influenced by cultural differences, and how is it universal?

their new application. The goal of such research is to compare the responses in the two cultures as closely as possible. The advantages of such work are to evaluate the assumption that research findings that have been reported in one cultural context will apply in another. Among the major limitations are that the adjustments made to the measures through the translation and measure adjustment process can change the meaning of the measures and that other better or more important concepts could be developed from the new context. While some well-known U.S. studies have been replicated, the assumption of equivalence where it may not exist is probably the reason that many studies fail to replicate in other cultures (Smith, Fischer, Vignoles, & Bond, 2013). Many of the studies reported in this book are examples of replication research.

Indigenous Research. This research focuses on the different and varied ways in which managers behave and organizations are run in a specific cultural setting in a way that highlights something that is expected to be unique. Like domestic research, indigenous studies are conducted within a single country. However, they differ in that they assume cultural differences (and in extreme cases, that cultures are unique, Berry, 1969) and require locally generated theory to explain and predict behavior within a culture. Examples of indigenous approaches are the concept of *simpatía* central to understanding interpersonal interactions in Hispanic cultures (Triandis, Marin, Lisansky, & Betancourt, 1984; Levine, Norenzayan, Philbrick, 2001), *amae* (indulgent dependence) as an important element in superior-subordinate relationships in Japan (Doi, 1973; Yamaguchi, 2004), and *guanxi* (relationships) as a fundamental building block for Chinese businesses (Wu, 1999; Chen, Chen, & Xin, 2004). Like domestic research, these concepts and the relationships they support are only applicable within their own cultural context until generality is proven. Some analysts argue that many supposedly unique cultural characteristics turn out to be locally nuanced versions of broadly known ideas (Smith, 2008).

Comparative Research. Comparative studies seek to find both the similarities and differences that exist across cultures regarding a particular management issue. Therefore, both the ways in which a theory is universal and the ways in which it is culturally limited are key questions. Comparative research accepts the challenge to incorporate multiple cultural standpoints by obtaining substantial guidance from colleagues in multiple countries while the research is being designed (Peterson, 2001). Descriptive comparative studies document the similarities and differences found across cultures, such as differences in leadership preferences (House et al., 2004). Predictive comparative studies test relationships suggested by theory, including a theory predicting the expected cross-cultural differences. For example, Smith et al. (2011) predict specific kinds of cultural differences in the relationship between relying on leaders or rules on the one hand and satisfaction on the other. Numerous examples of comparative research are found in this book.

International Research. This category of research captures those studies that focus attention on the multinational enterprise (MNE). Although these studies recognize that both similarities and differences exist across cultures, the cultural context does not figure prominently in the conceptualization or execution of the study. For example, studies of the human resource policies of MNEs that affect expatriate managers fall into this category, as would studies of how expatiates adjust in their foreign assignment (see Chapter 10). These studies are not concerned with comparing the cultural context in each of the countries the firm might operate, except as it applies to the organization as a whole.

Intercultural Research. A great deal of research provides information about similarities and differences between countries and societies, but understanding interactions between parties from different societies requires knowing about more than just their similarities and differences. Intercultural research seeks to understand the interactions between culturally different individuals in organizational settings. Therefore, the mechanisms responsible for the influence of culture (as discussed in Chapter 4) are an integral part of these studies. Intercultural research considers the culture of both (all) parties in the interaction as well as contextual explanations for observed similarities and differences. These types of studies are represented in studies of cross-cultural negotiation (e.g., Rosette, Brett, Barsness, & Lytle, 2012), in studies of the interactions among members of multicultural work groups (e.g., Thomas, 1999; Thomas et al., 1996), and in studies of leader-follower interactions across cultures (e.g., Thomas & Ravlin, 1995; Ah Chong & Thomas, 1997).

Both managers and researchers can benefit by recognizing the cultural assumptions and purpose of the research on which they depend for theoretical development or practical application. Each of the six categories of studies outlined here has specific characteristics that define the boundaries of its applicability. However, these limitations are not always made explicit in the presentation of the research itself. Therefore, it is important for the consumer of this research to recognize the boundary conditions that might be associated with a cross-cultural study and that affect its applicability.

Methodological Issues in Cross-Cultural Research

As noted previously, not all studies that might interest global managers involve more than one culture. For example, descriptions of the characteristics of Chinese family business (Chapter 9) can be very important for managers interested in doing business in China. However, much of the focus of this book is on the behavioral aspects of management, which highlights the similarities and differences in behavior across cultures. Studies that involve two or more cultures share several common methodological issues that are not present in purely domestic research (Peterson, 2009). These are discussed under the broad headings of equivalence, sampling, and data collection.

Equivalence. Perhaps the most important issue in cross-national or cross-cultural research is equivalence. Cross-cultural equivalence cannot be assumed at any stage of a cross-cultural study. In fact, it must be established at three key points: the conceptualization of the theoretical constructs, the study design, and the data analysis (Leung, 2008; Peterson, 2009; van de Vijver & Leung, 1997). *Conceptual or construct equivalence* relates to the extent to which concepts have the same meaning in different countries. As we noted previously, many concepts taught in general management courses are assumed without documentation to be universally meaningful, and some indigenous concepts are expected to have locally unique meanings. The involvement of researchers from different cultures in the development of a study is one indication that thought was given to the need for conceptual equivalence (Peterson, 2001). *Method equivalence* relates to similarities and differences in the way to which the cultural groups being studied respond to measurement instruments in general. Threats to this type of equivalence include acquiescence and extremity bias. Acquiescence is the tendency for some cultural groups to agree (or disagree) with all or most questions asked. Extremity bias has to do with the extent to which cultural groups systematically choose the extreme points or the middle points on rating scales (e.g., Smith, 2004). In addition, different levels of familiarity with the construct being studied, the physical conditions surrounding data collection, and communication between the researcher and participants can contribute to this type of nonequivalence. Finally, *metric equivalence* refers to the extent that questions (survey items) have similar measurement properties across different groups. For example, the hypothetical statement "My work is my life" might be highly correlated with other questions about commitment to one's organization in the United States but be difficult to translate and hence unrelated to other commitment questions elsewhere. Nonequivalence can result from poor item translation, complex item wording, and culture-specific aspects of the way questions are phrased. In addition, different levels of familiarity with the construct being studied, the physical conditions surrounding data collection, and communication between the researcher and participants can contribute to this type of nonequivalence.

The opportunity for bias because of cultural differences in values, attitudes, and normative behavior is staggering. Given cultural differences, unmodified instruments will rarely be equivalent across cultures. This does not mean that replication research or research based on concepts developed in one country such as the United States cannot be done. Statistical adjustments can be made for acquiescence and extremity bias when data are being analyzed. The success of translation and data collection equivalence can be statistically checked and decisions made about how to treat specific questions that are used to create a measure. Equivalence challenges do mean that the instrument development process and data collection strategy play a large role in research across national boundaries.

Sampling. The goal of sampling is to conduct research with a small number of participants who accurately represent a clearly identifiable population. If samples differ in important ways between countries (e.g., if most of the data is from accountants in some countries and marketing managers in others), then distinguishing country differences from other sample characteristics can be very difficult. Since few if any studies represent the entire populations of multiple countries, the ability to generalize the results from one study to groups other than those from which the data were collected needs to be evaluated. Similarly, to firmly document the universality of any phenomenon would require a random sample of countries. There are only about 200 countries, and the logistics and statistical requirements of random sampling argue against anything but an approximation of random sampling of countries.

In cross-cultural research, selecting an appropriate international research sample is closely tied to conceptual and instrument development. For example, questions about virtual teams will mean something different to managers who have worked on them than to other managers. Much domestic research is conducted with organizations with which a researcher has some personal association or with a group of working students or trainees to which a researcher has access. The ability to select matching samples from multiple nations is especially difficult unless a researcher happens to be on good terms with senior managers of a multinational organization that has operations in multiple countries. Consequently, cross-cultural studies are often based on samples of people who are either from only roughly similar organizations in multiple nations, groups of working students or trainees, or from mail surveys or phone interviews done under conditions in which only a very small proportion of people respond. Research is increasingly being done using samples arranged by companies that specialize in paying people who will respond to on-line surveys. To the extent that country samples are heterogeneous in demographic characteristics, researchers attempt to statistically adjust for sample differences after the data have been collected (Peterson, 2009). Even with optimal access to data, sample comparability is usually compromised by differences in the social implications of many sample characteristics. For example, including an equal proportion of women in a study of local bank managers in Jamaica, where many such employees are female, with local bank managers in Japan, where few are female, would have an element of nonequivalence. Not only gender but age, marital status, and even occupation (e.g., being a McDonald's employee in China in 1990 was a relatively high status position) can have culturally different implications among countries that can influence international comparative studies.

Several approaches to assessing the effects of sample differences have been taken in recent years. One has been to document relationships between different studies that measure similar concepts that are designed to be similar but that are based on different samples gathered at different times. For example, as discussed ahead in Chapter 3, four studies using concepts related to a society's views about power differences and emphasis on hierarchy show high correlations between similar measures (Hofstede, 2001; House et al., 2004; Smith, Peterson, & Schwartz, 2002). A second approach has been to document within-country differences in the cultural characteristics of subgroups so that those differences can be taken into account in studies that compare the countries (e.g., Lenartowicz & Johnson, 2003).

Data Collection. The most common methods of data collection in cross-cultural research are questionnaires, followed by interviews (Peng, Peterson, & Shyi, 1991). This is not surprising because U.S.-trained organizational researchers conduct most international research. People in different cultures differ in how familiar they are with particular research methods and in how ready they are to participate. Such differences come up most strikingly with the self-administered questionnaires so popular in international management research. Some factors, such as variation in literacy rates, are reasonably obvious. However, other more subtle effects are also typical. In many countries, a researcher's purpose is suspect (Napier & Thomas, 2001). Participants can view the researcher as an agent of management, a union, or even the government. This perception can be hard for researchers to avoid if those groups control access to participants. In these cases, concern about response bias emerges. Also, respondents may not have a frame of reference with which to respond to questions. For example, people in the United States are used to responding to hypothetical questions. Asking such hypothetical questions of respondents who do not think in conditional terms can result in unreliable responses (Bulmer & Warwick, 1983).

Whereas questionnaires are the most common *quantitative* method, interviews are the most common *qualitative* method used in international and cross-cultural research. While interviews have many advantages, a key disadvantage is the possible interaction between interviewer and respondent. For example, characteristics of the interviewer (age, gender, personal appearance) can influence respondent answers; the interviewer's technique (e.g., question phrasing, tone of voice) can bias responses; and the interviewer can selectively perceive or anticipate the respondent's answers. When the interviewer and respondent are culturally different, the opportunity for error is heightened. For example, a Chinese person may give very different responses to a Malay than to another Chinese, and Saudis do not feel comfortable with the possibility of having to explain their behavior implied in the interview process (Usunier, 1998). The sort of ethnographic qualitative research especially prevalent in anthropology, in which a person spends an extended period living in a culture to document, interpret, and explain its characteristics, also sometimes appears in cultural studies about management. This research has been useful for documenting the unique characteristics of many specific locations and groups as well as for showing the process of learning about a cultural context.

Critiques of International and Cross-Cultural Research

A number of critical reviews of the state of international and cross-cultural research have been conducted (e.g., Adler, 1983; Bhagat & McQuaid, 1982; Peng & Peterson, 1993). The following is representative of the types of criticism often leveled at this field of study:

Questionable Theoretical Base. Cross cultural studies are often criticized as relying too heavily on a very small set of dimensions about a society's cultural values that do not capture a broad enough view of culture or within-society variation. And cross-cultural studies have been criticized for emphasizing the differences among nations as opposed to testing management theory in a cross-cultural context (Sullivan, 1997).

Parochialism. As noted previously, culture is often ignored in management research, and what are really domestic conclusions are assumed to be universal. Even when an international perspective is included, an assumption that organizations and management behavior in other cultures should be compared to a Western industrial model dominates (Boyacigiller & Adler, 1991; Gelfand, Leslie, & Fehr, 2008).

Samples That Assume Country Homogeneity. Samples need to be interpretable such that variables, including organization type, hierarchical level, and demographic characteristics, and so on need to be taken into account by matching or by using statistical controls. Each sample's representation of known within-nation subcultures should be documented.

Lack of Relevance. The critical question consuming scholars and managers in the United States might not be viewed as important at all abroad (Napier & Thomas, 2001). International research puts relevance sharply into focus.

Reliance on a Single Method. The vast majority of international and cross-cultural research has relied on responses to questionnaires gathered at a single point in time. Both the temporal aspect of cultural influence as well as the richness provided by alternative methods is largely absent from this body of research (Osland & Osland, 2001).

Bias Toward Studying Large Companies. The vast majority of international and cross-cultural studies have been conducted in the organizational context of large firms.

Reliance on a Single Organizational Level. Most international or cross-cultural studies rely on responses from a single level (managers or skilled-production and service workers) to draw conclusions about cultural differences. Rarely are samples drawn from multiple positions in the organizational hierarchy (Peng & Peterson, 1993).

Limited to a Small Number of Locations. Reviews of cross-cultural research show that most studies were done in a small number of western European countries, Japan, and more recently China. We know very little about the forgotten locations of Eastern Europe, the Middle East, Africa, and Latin America (Thomas, 1996).

The preceding section is not meant as an indictment of cross-cultural research, nor is it a comprehensive guide to conducting such research. Instead, it is intended to sensitize the reader to methodological issues associated with these complex research projects and the steps being taken to address them. Having been so sensitized, it is hoped that instead of accepting the findings of these studies uncritically, readers will interpret studies involving culture with the identified limitations and boundaries in mind. Many of the limitations of the existing body of knowledge about managing across cultures are in the process of being remedied as more scholars recognize the increased demand for relevance of research to managers whose jobs are increasingly global in scope.

Summary

Globalization is affecting the environment in which managers must function. Rapid change is occurring with regard to economic alliances, the work environment, trade and investment, and the players on the international stage. And all of this change is being facilitated by a revolution in information technology. Therefore, today's global manager faces an environment that is more complex, more dynamic, more uncertain, and more competitive than ever before. The challenges presented by economic, legal, and political aspects of the international business environment are formidable. However, it is the influence of culture on management that can be the most difficult with which to deal, because culture has a broad influence on behavior, on other environmental factors, and because cultural effects are difficult to observe.

While management can be defined both in terms of managerial roles and what functions they perform, focusing on "what managers do" emphasizes the importance of the interpersonal aspects of the manager's job. All managers, regardless of their environment, share a significant degree of similarity in their roles. In subsequent chapters of this book, the leadership, communications and negotiation, and decision-making roles of global managers are explored in detail. As will be apparent, important aspects of these roles and their associated behaviors differ around the world. These differences are the result of both a direct effect of culture on management behavior and a more indirect effect of culture on the organizational context. Thus, by defining management in terms of managerial roles, which must be played out in a dynamic global environment, the pervasive effect of culture on management is revealed.

Questions for Discussion

1. How have globalization forces affected global managers?

2. How would you describe the environment and roles of global managers?

3. What are the pros and cons of different types of cross-cultural research?

4. How do researchers deal with the methods problems of cross-cultural research?

2

Describing Culture: What It Is and Where It Comes From

Deep cultural undercurrents structure life in subtle but highly consistent ways that are not consciously formulated. Like the invisible jet streams in the skies that determine the course of a storm, these currents shape our lives; yet, their influence is only beginning to be identified.

Edward T. Hall (1976)

Chapter 1 suggests that culture has a broad influence on how international managers see their world, on what international managers do, and on what others expect of international managers. To understand more specifically how culture affects the practice of management, we first need a clear definition of culture. Anthropologists Kroeber and Kluckhohn (1952) identify over 160 different definitions of the term *culture*. Clyde Kluckhohn (1961) presents a widely accepted definition that integrates many of these perspectives: "Culture consists of patterned ways of thinking, feeling and reacting, acquired and transmitted mainly by symbols, constituting the distinctive achievement of human groups, including their embodiment in artifacts; the essential core of culture consists of traditional (i.e., historically derived and selected) ideas and especially their attached values" (p. 73). From a more psychological perspective, Triandis (1972) presents culture as the subjective perception of the human-made part of the environment. This includes the categorization of social stimuli, associations, beliefs, attitudes, roles, and values that individuals in a society share. A complimentary view is that of Hofstede (1980), who suggests that culture consists of shared mental programs that control individuals' response to their environment.

Features of Culture

These various definitions have implications for understanding the relationship between cultural issues and global management. Three characteristics of culture provide a basis for the definition that we use in this book: Culture is shared, culture is transmitted between generations, and culture is systematic and organized.

Culture Is Shared

Culture is something shared by members of a particular group. Hofstede (1991) makes this point well when he describes culture as mental programming that lies between universal human nature on one side and unique personalities on the other. As shown in Figure 2.1, individuals carry in their mind three levels of programming about how they interact with their environment.

At the broadest level, all human beings share certain biological reactions. We eat when we are hungry, for example. At the narrowest level are the personality characteristics that are unique to each of us as individuals. Culture occurs at an intermediate level based on shared experiences within a particular society. Individuals within a society share an intuition for many of these cultural understandings not shared by outsiders (Peterson & Wood, 2008). Members of any society will be more

Figure 2.1 Three Levels of Mental Programming

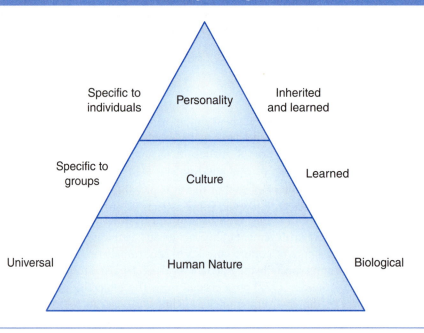

SOURCE: Adapted from Hofstede (1980).

familiar with values and understandings that are epitomized by its heroes than they will be with stories surrounding the heroes of other societies. For example, people in the United States know that the story of George Washington's life demonstrated honesty because of his willingness to accept the consequences of a childhood misdeed (chopping down a cherry tree) by confessing it. People in Saudi Arabia know to be kind to spiders, because they protected the Muslim Prophet by hiding him from his enemies. People in China know to honor their teachers on the anniversary of the birth of Confucius on September 29.

These examples illustrate two main points about culture that are easily missed. One point is that individuals living in a society have very little personal choice about whether or not they are thoroughly familiar with the central cultural qualities of their society. The other point is that individuals can differ quite widely in what they personally like and dislike about the cultural characteristics of their society. For example, people in the United States vary in the value they place on honesty, those in Saudi Arabia have varied feelings about spiders, and those in China differ in the honor they show towards their teachers. While individuals in a society can differ widely in their attitudes about their societies' heroes and stories, it is unusual to be a member of a society without having a deep understanding of its values. Thus, culture is a collective phenomenon that is about elements of our mental programming that we share with others in a society.

Culture Is Learned

A second feature of culture present in many definitions is that culture is transmitted through the process of learning and interacting with the social environment (Peterson & Wood, 2008). Over time, the people in a society develop patterned ways of interacting with their environment. That is, language, systems of government, forms of marriage, and religious systems are all functioning when we are born into a society. Although these institutions gradually change, these patterns are transmitted to the new entrants as they learn the culturally acceptable range of responses to situations that occur in their society. For example, guidance about behavior that is considered appropriate in a particular culture is often contained in the stories that parents tell their children, such as those described previously about societal heroes (Howard, 1991). Learning through stories implies not only that children can learn about their own culture but that it is possible to learn about the cultural patterns of another society. However, some aspects of an unfamiliar culture are likely to seem strange, and for an adult to develop a deep understanding of a new culture can be similar to the challenge of learning to speak a new language without the accent of one's first language.

Culture Is Systematic and Organized

A third important element is that cultures are integrated coherent systems, the parts of which are interrelated. Culture is more than a random assortment of customs. It is an organized system of values, attitudes, beliefs, and behavioral meanings related to each other, to a cultural group's physical environment, and to other cultural groups. To understand a particular facet of a culture, it is necessary to understand the cultural context. For example, most U.S. citizens have difficulty identifying with the marital practice of polygamy (Ferraro, 2006). A number of contextual factors support this general lack of comfort with the practice in U.S. culture. First, it is illegal. Second, it is counterproductive in a cash economy in which more partners means a need for more money to support them and their children. However, for the Kikuyu of East Africa, polygamy is a viable marital alternative. Kikuyu society is based on subsistence agriculture, and more wives and children enhance the economic well-being of the household because they produce more than they consume. Moreover, social status is based on the size of one's household and particularly on the number of male kinspeople in one's social unit. More wives mean more sons. In addition, because Kikuyu religion is fundamentally ancestor worship, larger families mean a bigger religious following. Therefore, not only are cultural beliefs about polygamy not viewed as immoral in Kikuyu society, they fit other aspects of the Kikuyu and are logical when considered in that cultural context.

Culture: A Working Definition

At the most general level, a working definition that is useful in considering the effects of culture on global management practice is as follows: *Culture is a set of knowledge structures consisting of systems of values, norms, attitudes, beliefs, and behavioral meanings that are shared by members of a social group (society) and that are learned from previous generations.* As discussed ahead in Chapter 3, average levels of the values that a society's members express are often good indicators of societal culture characteristics. While a society's cultural characteristics are generally well known among its members, some cultural values, attitudes, and beliefs will be accepted more widely than will others. Culture is most directly about behavioral meanings and societal norms and only indirectly about patterns of behavior or personally held values.

Consistent with our working definition of culture, Schein (1985) describes three levels of culture: artifacts and creations, values, and basic assumptions. Figure 2.2 depicts the relationship among these three levels of culture, which can be likened to an iceberg with only a small percentage being visible above the surface of the water. Figure 2.2 shows that above the surface are cultural artifacts, which include all the visible features of a culture, such as the architecture of its physical environment, language, technology, clothing, manners, dress, and so on. Just below the surface are the espoused values of the culture. These values are *consciously* held in the sense that they are explanations for the observable artifactual features of culture. Deep below the surface are the basic underlying assumptions shared by the culture, which are the ultimate source of values and action. These basic ways of structuring reactions to the world shape beliefs, perceptions, thoughts, and feelings at an *unconscious* level and are taken for granted by members of a cultural group. As pointed out in Chapter 1,

Figure 2.2 Levels of Culture

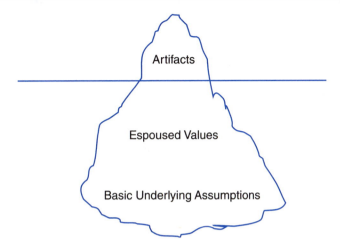

Artifacts

Espoused Values

Basic Underlying Assumptions

SOURCE: Adapted from Schein (1985).

because they are unconscious and taken for granted, the effects of culture are often not apparent to a society's members and are therefore often overlooked by global managers.

Why Cultures Differ and Persist

Armed with a working definition of culture as a set of knowledge structures shared in a society, it is now possible to examine elements of the environmental context that give rise to and reinforce cultural differences. It is not possible to evaluate all possible contributors to cultural variation. However, anthropologists have derived a set of assumptions about how cultures interact with the environment, which relate to how societies confront and solve the common problems of existence. These characteristics are summarized in Box 2.1.

Based on these assumptions, elements of culture evolve in terms of different solutions to common environmental problems. This is not to say that a particular ecological or environmental context will always result in similar cultural characteristics (see Cohen, 2001). For example, while developing methods of producing warm clothing is more useful to cultural groups in semi-arctic climates than in tropical climates, groups in the chillier parts of the world have developed many alternative kinds of warm clothing and ways of producing it. However, understanding something about how cultures emerge, are maintained, and are changed can help international managers to anticipate ways in which the parts of the world in which they are working are likely to react to globalizing technological, social, and economic conditions.

Box 2.1 Assumptions About a Society's Interactions With the Environment

There are a limited number of common human problems for which all peoples at all times must find solutions. (For example, every society must decide how to feed, clothe, house, and educate its people.)

There are a limited number of alternatives for dealing with these problems.

All alternatives are present in a society at all times, but some are preferred over others.

Each society has a dominant profile or value orientation but also has numerous variations or alternative profiles.

In both the dominant profile and the variations there is a rank order preference for alternatives.

In societies undergoing change, the ordering of preferences may not be clear.

SOURCE: Adapted from Kluckhohn, C., & Strodtbeck, K. (1961). *Variations in value orientations.* Westport, CT: Greenwood, as presented in Adler (1997).

Survival (and the Emergence of Social Institutions)

Many cultural characteristics, such as the development of systems to produce warm clothing, originally developed to aid the survival of groups in their environment. For example, people in many Western cultures shake hands with their right hand as a form of greeting. Initially, this was probably an indication that no weapon was being held or about to be drawn with the dominant right hand. Similarly, the Maori of New Zealand have an elaborate challenge ceremony or *wero*, which is now reserved for greeting dignitaries (Barlow, 1991). Originally, this challenge, which involves sending forth warriors who challenge the visiting party by prancing about and brandishing fighting weapons followed by presenting a token on the ground to their leader, was to determine the intentions of visitors. If they come in peace, the leader will pick up the token, and the warriors will lead the visitors onto the *marae* (community meeting place). Having determined the intent of a visitor, there was no need in this culture to display an empty right hand as a form of friendly greeting. As a sign of peace, the Maori greeting among individuals is to press noses or *hongi* (Barlow, 1991). As another example, people in different climates seem to have different attitudes toward time. For example, the lack of urgency often observed in tropical climates might have originally reflected the lack of seasonality in agriculture. That is, because crops can be grown year-round, they do not need to be planted and harvested at certain times. Consequently, such societies tended to develop little regard for deadlines.

Ways of dealing with societal problems, such as determining the friendly or hostile intent of visitors or coordinating the use of time with agricultural demands, come to be built into a society's *institutions*. Institutions are the structures and activities that provide stability to a society; they consist of the family, education, economics, religious, and political systems. Institutions that support a society's cultural orientation typically include some governing group that rewards desired behavior and punishes socially unacceptable behavior as well as organizations that teach and promote desirable behaviors. Children learn the concepts that their society has institutionalized in terms of beliefs about right or wrong, good or bad, ugly or beautiful, and so on. Cultural concepts that have their foundation in ancient beliefs about survival and that have become fundamental beliefs about right and wrong are likely *programmed* at a very deep unconsciousness level (Hofstede, 1991; Schein, 1985). Their meaning might not be apparent to the outsider and can even be obscured to members of the cultural group. And, evolutionary theorists (e.g. Rozin, 1998) have demonstrated the importance of so-called *initial conditions* on the persistence of patterns of thinking over time. That is, once a cultural pattern is established it is very resistant to change even when surrounding circumstances change.

Language

Language plays a particularly prominent role in the way cultural characteristics have spread throughout the world and how they are maintained within a society (Hall, 1966). One long-standing view is that because people encode things in memory in terms of a particular language, language defines the way they view the world (Whorf, 1956). That is, language determines the range of possibilities that a society provides its members to mentally represent their environment. Although language is influenced by the environment and reflects the concerns of society, linguists disagree about the degree of control that language exerts over people (Bonvillian, 1993). For example, the Inuit language of the indigenous people of the northern part of North America contains numerous words describing snow. Apparently, however, the existence of many more terms for snow does not necessarily indicate the ability to distinguish types of snow any better than with fewer terms (Pinker, 1994). Some argue that language does not constrain thought. For example, when we do not have a word for something, we invent or borrow one. However, because we use language for interaction with others, it has a powerful role in shaping behavior and in perpetuating beliefs and habitual patterns of interaction (Berger & Luckman, 1966), hence, culture. Recent research (Nisbett, Peng, Choi, & Norenzayan, 2001) suggests that some features of language, such as whether it is based on pictorial representations (e.g., Chinese characters) or phonetic scripts, is related to how people view the world. By identifying the location in the brain where different kinds of memories are stored, neuropsychologists suggest that our first language has a more basic role in structuring how we think than do languages learned later in life. Language, therefore, is an artifact of culture that helps to perpetuate its values, attitudes, beliefs, and behavioral routines. The fierce protection of the French language by francophone Canadians is an example of the recognition of the powerful effect of language in perpetuating culture.

Religion (and Ideology)

Religions and ideologies reflect beliefs and behaviors shared by groups of people that cannot be verified by empirical tests (Terpstra & David, 1985). Religious traditions are closely related to cultural values (Inglehart & Baker, 2000) and can have a cultural influence through the *content* of their belief systems, the *structure* of their beliefs and rituals, and the *identities* that they promote. For example, the content or specific teachings of many religious traditions promote a strong work ethic, not just among their adherents but throughout the societies where the religious groups have been especially influential (Niles, 1999). Reliance on authoritative texts or on a succession of authoritative leaders can influence a society's structure even when the content of the teachings change. For example, the reliance on written texts as a basis of authority has contributed to the written language unity and an emphasis on education of Chinese societies, even as authority has changed from Confucian teaching to Maoist teaching to more eclectic sources of information (Marginson, 2011). Religious groups have long competed with nation states as a basis for social identities that shape with whom people are most willing to work, trade, or fight. The extent to which religion influences the cultural profile of a society depends on the extent to which a particular religion is dominant or state sanctioned, the importance that society places on religion, the degree of religious homogeneity in the society, and the degree of tolerance for religious diversity that exists in the society (Mendenhall, Punnett, & Ricks, 1995). Some evidence suggests that religious devotion is related to particular cultural values, such as tradition, conformity, and benevolence (Huismans, 1994) and/or future orientation and collectivism (House et al., 2004). Additional evidence suggests that devoutly religious individuals are more likely to endorse the dominant cultural profile of a society (Burris, Branscombe, & Jackson, 2000). As societies shift from agrarian to industrial, and survival is taken for granted, traditional religious beliefs tend to decline. However, while attendance at religious services has declined, spirituality is on the rise, and deep differences along religious lines remain (Inglehart & Baker, 2000).

Although Christianity currently has the largest number of adherents worldwide, its percentage of followers is projected to be relatively stable in the near future, with Islamic religions and Hindus representing an increasing percentage of the world population (due in part to differences in birth rates) (Barrett, Kurian, & Johnson, 2001). Table 2.1 shows the approximate geographic distribution of the major religions around the world.

Of course, religions are not evenly distributed across the planet, with some religions concentrated in specific geographic regions. For example, Islam is largely concentrated in Asia and Africa, and Shinto exists almost exclusively in Japan. Obviously, therefore, specific religions have a greater influence in some cultures than in others. Religions and ideologies have to do with explanations for things that cannot be empirically demonstrated, as the definition of religion suggests. Therefore, research issues discussed in Chapter 1 have special significance with regard to assessing the effect of religion. A great deal that people believe about what is valuable and what actions will have what consequences is difficult to demonstrate empirically. Societies can support very rigid values and beliefs that shape the politics of how they

Table 2.1	Distribution of Religions Around the World (Thousands of Adherents)						
Religion	Africa	Asia	Europe	Latin America	North America	Oceania	Total
Bahaism	1,929	3,639	146	813	847	122	7,496
Buddhism	148	369,394	1,634	699	3,063	493	375,431
Chinese folk religions	35	400,718	266	200	713	133	402,065
Christianity	401,717	341,337	553,689	510,131	273,941	26,147	2,106,962
Confucianism	300	6,379	17	0.8	0	51	6,748
Ethnic religions	105,251	141,589	1,238	3,109	1,263	319	252,769
Hinduism	2,604	844,593	1,467	766	1,444	417	851,291
Judaism	224	5,317	1,985	1,206	6,154	104	14,990
Islam	350,453	892,440	33,290	1,724	5,109	408	1,283,424
Shinto	0	2,717	0	7	60	0	2,784
Sikhism	58	24,085	238	0	583	25	24,989
Other religions	164	102,718	517	12,197	1,502	67	117,165
None	5,912	601,478	108,674	15,939	31,286	3,895	767,184
Atheism	585	122,870	22,048	2,756	1,997	400	150,656

SOURCE: Adapted from *World Almanac and Book of Facts* (2006).

should operate and ethnocentric views that their members take for granted about the self-evident truth of their beliefs or the goodness of their practices.

Other Factors

Numerous other factors can be suggested as contributors to cultural variation and persistence. For example, Smith and Peterson (1997) identify the following factors in addition to those mentioned previously:

- *Climate, topography and the indigenous economy* affect traditions and behavior in the primitive heritage of modern societies.
- *Proximity and topography* affect the exchange of culture among societies, because barriers, such as mountains and oceans, limit the potential for cross-cultural interaction.

- *Economic systems and technology* affect the exchanges between cultures and hence the transfer of culture.
- *Political boundaries* (also discussed ahead) define areas where there is more or less interaction among cultures.

Debates Surrounding the Concept of Culture

In part, because of the ambiguity of the culture concept, a number of debates regarding culture have emerged in the literature. The issues raised are important because they influence the utility of the concept of culture for explaining and predicting behavior in organizations. These issues are the concept of a national culture, the convergence or divergence of cultures, the concept of an organizational culture, and the effects of acculturation.

National Culture

A key question to identifying culture, so that its effect on management can be assessed, is the extent to which a nation has a distinctive culture. In fact, much of the research in this book reports little more than the nation in which respondents lived. It should be apparent that based on the definition of culture presented previously, this could be misleading. That is, multiple cultures can exist within national borders and the same cultural group can span many nations (Lenartowicz & Johnson, 2003). For example, Canada is the home to both Anglophones and Francophones, each having distinctive cultures. Yet both are Canadian in their unique appreciation for the dynamics between these two specific subcultures. And the First Nations peoples of North America span the borders of the United States and Canada, and any major North American city will have pockets of many distinct cultures that also exist elsewhere. However, the 19th and 20th centuries saw the emergence of nation-states that in many cases were a political expression of cultural similarity (or a carefully forged economic and political alliance between a small number of culturally different subgroups). The dynamic between cultural fragmentation and national unity raises the question of the appropriateness of the concept of a national culture.

Hofstede (1983) makes a powerful argument in favor of national culture. He argues that because nations are political entities, they vary in their forms of government, legal systems, educational systems, labor, and employment relations systems, all of which reflect a working cultural consensus. In addition, most nations are characterized by one or a small number of official languages, which may be in addition to the one inhabitants learned from birth. Many nations are small enough to have relatively similar geographical and ecological conditions that may promote cultural homogeneity (Smith, 2006). These institutional and geographical factors influence the way in which people interact with their environment and each other and thereby condition the way they think—their *mental programming*. That is, nations are social systems and therefore can have cultures. In addition, Hofstede (1983) suggests that nationality has a symbolic value to citizens that influences how we perceive ourselves. Thus, we all derive our self-identity, in part, from our nationality (Tajfel, 1982).

For managers, the activities of firms are governed by laws and regulations of sovereign nations. Therefore, from an international business perspective, national culture is probably the most logical level of analysis from which to begin to understand the cultural environment. If, for practical purposes, the concept of national culture is adopted, two major issues must be recognized (Smith, Fischer, Vignoles, & Bond, 2013). First, by comparing national cultures, the large number of subcultures that exist within some nations is at risk of being ignored. We must remember that differences of the magnitude observed between any two countries might also be found between selected subcultures within a country (Lenartowicz & Johnson, 2003). Within any country, cultural differences that are not obvious to the outside observer are often much more apparent to local nationals. Second, we risk ignoring the variation, conflict, and dissent that exist within national cultures. Not only do countries have subcultures, but each individual has unique life experiences with various local and global cultural groups that contribute to diversity within a national culture. Finding agreement on the defining elements of a complex concept, such as culture, is not easy. The search for a common language to describe cultural variation is discussed in Chapter 3.

Convergence, Divergence, or Equilibrium

An additional consideration to identifying culture is the extent to which cultures around the world are becoming more similar or more different. The fact that national culture is related to other societal factors, such as political, legal, educational, and labor relations systems, leads some authors to suggest that the rapid technological and economic development around the world (characteristic of globalization) will have a homogenizing effect on culture (Dunphy, 1987; Webber, 1969). Scholars who emphasize processes that maintain cultural stability, however, argue that cultural diversity will persist or even expand as societies with different cultural traditions respond to rapid technological development (Huntington, 1996). Stability, it is argued, is fostered by the large number of complex links between the various elements having a long history that make up a culture (Goldstein, 1999).

The argument for convergence of cultures hinges on the fact that nations are not static entities but develop over time. This development of nations is evident in changes, such as the expansion of education, increased occupational diversity, urban intensification, and development of mass communication (Yang, 1988). Proponents of the convergence perspective suggest that this modernization results from a common economic orientation (Eisenhardt, 1973) and eventually leads to a common society where differences in ideology (values) will cease to exist (Kerr, Dunlop, Harbison, & Myers, 1960). That is, given enough time, cultures will converge to the point that no difference in values, attitudes, beliefs, and behavior exists. Furthermore, because, until recently, economic development was equated with Western capitalistic economic orientations, convergence suggests adopting the ideological values of the West (Ralston, Holt, Terpstra, & Yu, 1997). Some support for the convergence hypothesis is also provided by Inglehart's (Inglehart, 1977; 1990; Inglehart & Baker, 2000) survey of values in 65 countries. He identified two value orientations (materialist and postmaterialist) related to a country's wealth. As wealth increased, so did endorsement of postmaterialist values. A steady year-by-year increase in the endorsement of postmaterialist values was found in economically developed countries in three administrations (1981/1982, 1990/1991, 1995/1998) of the World Values Survey (Inglehart & Baker, 2000). This sort of empirical finding supports the notion that as wealth gradually increases in a country, cultural differences diminish and people become more similar.

In addition, sociologists suggest that to participate effectively in a modern society, people must possess a core set of psychological characteristics (Kahl, 1968). That is, preindustrial life is depicted as a game against the forces of nature, industrial life a game against the fabricated nature of the technical, mechanical, rationalized, and bureaucratic world directed toward dominating the environment, and postindustrial life, which centers on services, becomes a game between persons (Bell, 1973). In modern, postindustrial societies, most people spend their productive time interacting with people and symbols, with a growing emphasis on self-expression and autonomous decision making. Yang (1988), in a review of the literature on modernization, found a high degree of agreement on the characteristics of a modern person regardless of culture. These are summarized in Box 2.2.

Box 2.2 The Profile of a Modern Person

- A sense of personal efficacy (antifatalism)
- Low social integration with relatives
- Egalitarian attitudes toward others
- Openness to innovation and change
- A belief in sex equality
- High achievement motivation
- Independence or self-reliance
- Active participation in social organizations
- Tolerance of and respect for others
- Cognitive and behavioral flexibility
- Strong future orientation
- Empathetic capacity
- A high need for information
- The propensity to take risks in life
- Secularization in religious belief
- A preference for urban life
- An individualistic orientation toward others
- Psychological differentiation
- A nonlocal orientation

SOURCE: Yang, K.-S. (1988). "The Cross Cultural Link," from *The Cross-Cultural Challenge to Social Psychology*. Thousand Oaks, CA: Sage. Reprinted with permission.

This profile of a modern person is conceptually similar to key concepts in descriptions of *Western* culture. Smith and colleagues (2013) point out an interesting reaction in developing countries to the idea of cultural convergence. As arguments for cultural convergence are popularized, many developing countries take action to distinguish themselves from the West and assert their cultural uniqueness. Political leaders in these countries are often concerned with the growth in self-centeredness and erosion of civil harmony associated with Western-style modernization (Smith et al., 2013). In addition to technological and economic pressures, an additional force toward cultural homogeneity is an increasing awareness of the interdependence of humanity (Smith et al., 2013). Humankind's pursuit of personal and national wealth leads to the depletion of energy resources, overharvesting of the oceans, erosion of the atmosphere, destruction of rain forests, and depletion of agricultural land. This results in a common dilemma (Dawes, 1980), the maintenance of the systems that support life on earth. One result of this common threat is the development of *world mindedness* or internationalism, which implies a common set of attitudes and behaviors toward people of different races, nations, and cultures. Some preliminary empirical support for a growth in internationalism (or what might be termed by some as globalization) around the world has been found (Der-Karabetian, 1992). The long-term effect, of course, would be to reduce variability of differences among national cultures.

Despite the logic of arguments in favor of cultural convergence, upon close examination they are somewhat less compelling. Although Inglehart (1990) found a shift toward postmaterialist values related to economic development, this finding does not hold for other elements of culture (see Inglehart & Baker, 2000). That is, culture is more than just holding post-materialist values, and other variations in national culture that have nothing to do with modernization are probably related to social behavior in much the same way (Smith et al., 2013). The case of the McDonaldization of the world provides another example. That is, the seemingly identical McDonalds restaurants that exist almost everywhere actually have different meanings and fulfill different social functions in different parts of the world (Watson, 1997). Although the physical facilities are similar, eating in a McDonalds is a very different social experience in Japan or China or the United States or France. And, while some convergence toward Western managerial values is evident in firms in transition economies, the form of this convergence is not uniform nor is the effect on managerial behavior (Alexashin & Blenkinsopp, 2005). Moreover, modernization is probably not the linear uniform process that it is sometimes presented to be. Studies of modernization reveal that countries can modernize in different ways, at different rates, and with different outcomes (Sack, 1973). Smith and colleagues (2013) argue that because of the unique origins and complexity of cultures, cultures will evolve in different and unpredictable ways, making the idea of convergence toward some common end point highly unlikely. This type of cultural change is called path dependence (Inglehart & Baker, 2000). That is, while economic development brings pervasive cultural changes, the historically basis for a society has an enduring effect on the character of this development. In addition, cultural systems might be able to combine traditional and modern elements in unique ways. For example, Hong Kong Chinese seem to be able to retain their traditional respect for authority while rejecting its fatalism and adopting modern competitiveness but rejecting modern views toward sexual promiscuity (Bond & King, 1985).

At the level of organizations, the convergence argument centers on convergence toward common organizational practices in different countries because of technological determinism. This was a popular line of thinking, particularly regarding the economic resurgence of Japanese industry, during the late 1970s and early 1980s (Ouchi, 1981). However, research results indicate that similar general technology could be operated differently by different social systems (Dunphy, 1987). For example, although Japan adopted Western technology, distinctive practices that related to national culture persisted (Whitehill & Takezawa, 1978). Despite technological changes toward *American* methods over a 15-year period, Japanese workers maintained many traditional attitudes toward their work environment, such as the commitment to the company and its productivity goals and a norm for workplace harmony.

The debate over cultural convergence versus divergence has resulted in a number of compromise proposals concerning organizations. Child (1981), in a review of organizational studies, suggested that cultural convergence-divergence was a matter of level of analysis. His study concludes that studies of macrolevel issues of organizational structure and technology often indicate cultural convergence, whereas research-concluding divergence was typically involved with the more microlevel issues of the behavior of individuals within organizations. Yang (1988) suggests convergence in only those cultural characteristics that relate specifically to functioning more easily in a technological environment. That is, certain behaviors and attitudes are necessary to adapt to the imperatives of an industrial society, but others have no functional relationship to industrialization. They are, therefore, not influenced by modernization. Ralston and colleagues (Ralston, 1993; Ralston et al., 1997) attempted to accommodate the middle ground by coining the term *crossvergence* to refer to the incorporation by individuals of influences from both national culture and economic ideology.

A final perspective on cultural variation is provided by Cohen (2001). He argues that while different environments produce different social systems, different environments can produce similar systems and that similar environments can produce vastly different cultures. This results because cultures reach (multiple) stable equilibriums depending on their interaction with not only the physical but also the social, intercultural and intracultural aspects of their context. While the physical environment provides a starting place, the social nature of humans leads to multiple possible solutions to environmental issues, and these equilibrium conditions take place within the context of other surrounding cultures. And finally, any change must consider current cultural conditions.

None of these compromise approaches is likely to be entirely satisfactory to proponents of extreme convergence or divergence perspectives. However, they offer the opportunity to understand the present cultural variability that exists in the world while also allowing for growth and change within cultures.

Organizational Versus National Culture

In the early 1980s, managers became aware that the social characteristics of organizations in some ways resemble the cultural characteristics of societies (Smircich & Calas, 1986). This awareness came partly because something about Japanese culture seemed to be promoting the competitive success of Japanese organizations. Managers and business scholars hoped that the keys to that success could be imitated (Peterson, 2011). The notion that it might be useful to think of an organization as having its own culture raises two questions about the conceptualization of culture and its influence. First, how are national culture and organizational culture related? How are they similar or different? Second, to what extent does an organizational culture moderate or negate the effect of national culture?

The term *organizational culture* was imported into the management literature from anthropology. However, the definition of culture is not synonymous in the two fields (Smircich, 1983). In particular, traditional anthropological views of culture, as we have described earlier in this chapter, emphasize the very strong and fundamental influence that a society has in shaping the way that children view the world. Organizations, however, have culture-like qualities mainly to the extent that they can (1) attract and select a subset of a society's members who have already adopted the organization's values and (2) socialize members into the organization's way of doing things (Feldman, 1976). Organizational culture has been variously defined as stable attitudes, beliefs, and values held in common by organization members (Williams, Dobson, & Walters, 1993); shared normative beliefs and behavioral expectations (Cooke & Szumal, 1993; 2000); or a set of goal-directed values, beliefs, and behaviors (Eldridge & Crombie, 1974). While there is little in the way of consensus as to the definition of the term, many authors describe it as an internal attribute of the organization that is socially constructed, historically determined, holistic, and difficult to change (Hofstede, Neuijen, Ohayv, & Sanders, 1990). Much of the literature on organizational culture focuses on what Schein (1985) describes as consciously held values about an organization's strategies, goals, and philosophies.

Hofstede et al. (1990) have made perhaps the clearest distinction between the constructs of corporate and national culture. They provide evidence that organizational culture and national culture are composed of different elements. Although the culture (values) of founders and key leaders shape organizational cultures, the way these cultures affect organizational members is through the routinized practices of the organization. These practices, as Hofstede refers to them, include organizational programs like human resources procedures and informal ways of doing things. The reason proposed for this distinction is that people enter organizations after their national cultural values, attitudes, and fundamental beliefs are well developed, whereas organizational practices are learned through workplace socialization (Hofstede et al., 1990). Organizational practices, like goal-setting programs or going out together after work, have different implications depending on the national culture where they occur. This focus on behavioral norms as the fundamental element of organizational culture amplifies the distinction between organizational culture and societal culture. Norms tell people how they should behave in a particular situation, whereas culture tells them the inherent meaning of the situation (D'Andrade, 1989). The effect of organizational culture is probably very weak in comparison to national culture and has limited lasting impact (Triandis, 1995). For example, Hofstede's (1980) classic study, discussed in more detail in Chapter 3, found striking cultural differences within a single MNC (IBM) that is often described as having a *strong* corporate culture. Individuals are only partly involved with their organizations, although they are totally immersed in their national culture. Membership in an organization is conditional and based on a relatively focused exchange relationship that depends on both the person and the firm meeting certain conditions to continue the relationship (Thomas, Au, & Ravlin, 2003). Membership in a national culture, however, is much broader in scope and unconditional. Table 2.2 outlines the characteristic differences between national and organizational culture.

Another avenue for the possible effect of organizational culture is in its compatibility with national culture. Research suggests that national or societal-level culture influences the relationship of organizational culture to organizational outcomes (England, 1983; Joiner, 2001). For example, attempts to transfer organizational practices, such as diversity management programs (Ferner, Almond, & Colling, 2005), across cultures can produce intercultural stresses if their meaning and application cannot be adapted to local conditions. A more complete discussion of this compatibility issue is presented in Chapter 9, in which organization structure is discussed. Culture may also influence the type of local organizational culture that evolves within a single firm. In one recent study (van der Vegt, van de Vliert, & Huang, 2005) the cultural dimension of Power Distance (see Chapter 3) moderated the effect of demographic diversity on an innovative organizational climate in different local operations of a single MNC. Therefore, it is important to note that the implications of specific organizational norms, rules, procedures, and even climate, might need to be evaluated in relation to societal culture.

The idea of organizational culture remains central to the way many managers think and feel about their organizational experiences and continues to draw scholarly attention (Alvesson, 2011). The early expectation of the positive effects of a strong

Table 2.2 Comparison of Organizational and National Culture

National Culture	Organizational Culture
Shared meanings	Shared behaviors
Unconditional relationship	Conditional relationship
Born into it	Socialized into it
Totally immersed	Partly involved

organizational culture in which organization members can depend on one another to do the right thing has not been supported in most studies (Sackmann, 2011). However, analyses of overall organizational culture have spawned separate subfields that consider its specific components. For example, scholars now often find that the strength of norms emphasizing specific outcomes, such as safety, production quality, or service quality, often predict organizational performance (Schneider, Ehrhart, & Macey, 2011; Sackmann, 2011). Also, whereas early organizational culture research showed the tendency noted in Chapter 1 to be done in the United States, the majority of such studies since 2000 have been done in other parts of the world (Sackmann, 2011). In fact, whereas early organizational culture research was stimulated by the interest in how to transfer Japanese-like practices to the United States, recent organizational culture research has been especially prominent in nations such as China as they seek to optimally use and appropriately adjust practices developed elsewhere (Denison, Xin, Guidroz, & Zhang, 2011; Peterson, 2011).

In summary, organizational culture is a somewhat different construct and is composed of different elements than is national culture. In addition, entry to and transmittal of organizational culture occur in different ways and at different times from national culture. Moreover, individuals are only partly involved with an organizational culture as compared to totally immersed in their national culture. However, the influence of organizational norms must be considered in concert with societal culture in understanding the causes of behavior in organizations.

Acculturation and Biculturalism

Acculturation concerns the psychological and behavioral changes that occur in people because of contact with different cultures. Most often, it is used to describe the changes in people who relocate from one culture to another. Acculturation, however, can also occur on a larger collective scale. In collective acculturation, the whole group (e.g. the large group of Turkish immigrants in the Netherlands or the nation of Japan when controlled by the United States after WWII), as opposed to the individual, changes (Triandis, 1995). The gradual process of psychological acculturation that occurs during immigration results in changes in individual behavior, identity, values, and attitudes (Berry, 1990). For example, in a study of Italian and Greek immigrants to Canada, first-generation immigrants exhibited a stronger ethnic identification than did their children (Lalonde & Cameron, 1993). That is, over time the identification of people with their new country becomes stronger. However, some evidence suggests that these changes might take generations. Boski (1991), in a study of two generations of Polish immigrants to Canada, found that after two generations, participants' values were still more closely allied to prototypical Polish than to Canadian value profiles.

The acculturation patterns of individuals and groups can be influenced by a number of individual difference and situational factors. The entry status of individuals (Berry, 1997), their facility in communication in the local language (Elkholy, 1981), their personality (Padilla & Perez, 2003), and whether the immigrants forge relationships on entry with host country nationals or coethnics (Kosic, Kruglanski, Pierro, &

Mannetti, 2004) all influence acculturation patterns. For example, Kosic et al. (2004) found that for individuals with a high need for cognitive closure (the desire for definitive answers as opposed to uncertainty or ambiguity), those who formed initial close relationships with coethnics had a strong tendency to adhere to their culture of origin, while those who formed initial close relationships with host nationals showed a stronger tendency to adapt to the new culture.

Finally, some individuals with experience living in multiple cultures acculturate to the extent that they demonstrate the ability to function very effectively in more than one culture. These so-called bicultural individuals (see Brislin, 1993 and also Chapter 11) have, through time living in another culture or through intensive daily interaction with culturally different others, developed cultural flexibility so that they can adjust their behavior based on the cultural context of the situation (Bhawuk & Brislin, 1992). Research indicates that biculturals do not just superficially adapt their behavior but that they are able to hold different conceptions of themselves reflecting two different cultures. For example, they can define themselves as simultaneously independent of others and interdependent with others (Yamada & Singelis, 1999), which are characteristic of individualism and collectivism, respectively (discussed ahead in Chapter 3).

The concept of culture, as presented in this book, suggests that a society's culture is resistant to change and that this resistance is typically too strong for a work organization to overcome. However, this is not meant to suggest that cultures are static (Kara & Peterson, 2012). One way that cultures change is through the process of acculturation, as large groups migrate from one society to another and mutual adjustment occurs.

Culture and Social Groups

A key aspect of culture as presented in this chapter is that culture is associated with a specific group of people. Identifying ourselves with a particular social group places boundaries around our group (in-group) and defines nonmembers as an out-group. The in-group/out-group distinction is useful in describing attitudes and behavior both within and across cultural-group boundaries. An important premise is that identifying a social group serves no purpose if no one is excluded from the group. That is, groups are about differentiation. For example, anthropologists report that those cultural groups that exist in isolation do not have characteristics (e.g., tribal name or unique symbols) that indicate a strong group identity (Mead, 1937). Treating culture as associated with social groups further illuminates two important considerations of cultural groups. First, while groups have systems of norms and role structures that give them stability despite changes in their membership, the characteristics of groups can in fact change as key members or large numbers of members come and go. For example, concerns about *brain drain* from developing nations suggest that both the sending and receiving societies are changed by the migration of people who have special abilities. Second, our membership in a cultural group helps to determine how we perceive ourselves—our self-identity—as well as how others perceive us (Peterson & Thomas, 2007). The mere categorization of individuals into different groups results in a number of assumptions about both the in-group and out-group members. The assumptions about group members that arise from categorizing ourselves and others as members of certain groups can lead to different beliefs about, attitudes toward, and behavior directed at different cultural groups. When categorized as a group, individuals are thought to be relatively more similar in their beliefs and behavior, their behavior is thought to convey less information about them as individuals, and the group is believed to be a more important cause of their behavior than are individual characteristics (Wilder, 1986). The in-group/out-group boundary that results from categorization has several implications for the way individuals select, structure, and process social information. The way in which social categorization influences the process of culture's influence on management behavior is developed more fully in Chapter 4. In brief, however, this categorization results in a comparison of our own group with other cultural groups resulting in intergroup bias. Intergroup bias can be either positive or negative but most often favors our own group.

In-Group Bias and Prejudice

The universal bias in favor of one's own group is related to the role of our cultural group in defining who we are. We derive our sense of self, in part, from our identification with the groups to which we belong, including our cultural group (Tajfel, 1981). To maintain our self-image, we favorably compare the attributes of our own group with those of out-groups (Tajfel & Turner, 1986). Therefore, we consistently discriminate in favor of the group(s) with which we identify. Prejudicial judgments about members of out-groups relate to beliefs about the character of these groups. These, often negative, attitudes toward out-group members are based solely on their membership in a particular group. Prejudice translates to discrimination when action is taken for or more frequently against members of this out-group. The extent to which prejudicial attitudes result in discriminatory behavior depends on both personal and cultural factors (Smith et al., 2013). However, in-group favoritism is a consistent consequence of social categorization that occurs across gender, age, and nationalities (Wilder, 1986). Numerous, management-related examples of this bias exist, including reports of the so-called country-of-origin effect (Peterson & Jolibert, 1995). That is, although there may be some global country-of-origin biases to prefer special products from special countries, such as perfume if it comes from France, products described as coming from a person's own country are typically rated higher in quality than the same products coming from another country.

Ethnocentrism

In much of the cross-cultural management literature, the attitude that reflects the categorization of cultural groups is encapsulated under the term *ethnocentrism*. Ethnocentrism is described as an attitude that one's own cultural group is the center of everything and all other groups are evaluated with reference to it (Sumner, 1940). Although related to a narrow or provincial perspective of not even recognizing that cultural differences exist that is often labeled *parochialism*, ethnocentrism is a universal tendency resulting from social categorization that has broad implications. Triandis (1994) identifies the following characteristic of ethnocentrism:

- What goes on in our culture is seen as "natural and correct," and what goes on in other cultures is perceived as "unnatural and incorrect."
- We perceive our own in-group customs as universally valid.
- We unquestionably think that in-group norms, roles, and values are correct.
- We believe that it is natural to help and cooperate with members of our in-group, to favor our in-group, to feel proud of our in-group, and to be distrustful of and even hostile toward out-group members. (pp. 251–252)

Examples of ethnocentric attitudes in management include beliefs that the way business is conducted in one's own country is the only way to be effective, that people of one's own culture are naturally better suited to almost any management job, and the role of women in management is only correct as it exists at home.

Summary

This chapter presented the concept of culture as a set of shared mental representations that, in the most fundamental way, shape the way in which managers interact with their world. Therefore, it is responsible for the way in which management is conceptualized and the way in which managers enact their various roles. Culture is not inherited but is developed over time by the way societies interact with their physical environment, their social context, and with other societies. It is learned by each new generation. Culture is presented as a characteristic that can be associated with any social group. Thinking of culture in this way places boundaries around our cultural group and differentiates us from other groups. This perspective provides a basis in social cognition for understanding the influence of culture as something that influences the values that a society's members deeply understand even more than the values that they consciously support.

In addition, the concept of a national culture is presented as an appropriate starting place for understanding cultural influences on international management. Managers are concerned with the legal and political characteristics of countries, which are derived from a country's history and culture. Culture can be thought of as the most fundamental characteristics of a society, even though some aspects of culture will be more widely shared than others. National culture can be seen as distinct from organizational culture both in terms of its constituent elements and its influence on behavior. Although national cultures are relatively stable, they do change over time, and individuals can identify with a new culture through the process of acculturation. Some can even identify with more than one culture. While arguments can be presented for convergence, divergence, or multiple stable equilibrium perspectives on national cultures, the reality probably occupies some middle ground. That is, some aspects of cultures could be converging because of globalization, but other aspects of culture are selectively affected or unaffected by global technological and economic changes.

Questions for Discussion

1. What are the main features of culture?

2. Why do cultures differ and persist?

3. What are the debates about what culture is and whether it matters?

4. How does culture affect behavior by social groups?

Comparing Cultures: Systematically Describing Cultural Differences

For the strength of the Pack is the Wolf, and the strength of the Wolf is the Pack.

Rudyard Kipling

Culture is expressed in the complex interactions of values, attitudes, and behavioral assumptions of a society, which are reflected in its institutions and well understood by its members. However, for culture to be a useful concept in management studies, we must find some way to talk about specific aspects of culture rather than just the overall culture concept (Schwartz, 1994). Although alternative definitions and theoretical perspectives are as numerous as the disciplines that analyze culture, much of our understanding of cultural variation has been achieved by focusing on the study of values. As discussed in this chapter, analyzing a society's values provides a way to understand many coherent patterns in how a society deals with basic social problems. As noted in Chapter 2, value differences arise from the solutions that different social groups have devised for dealing with the fundamental problems that all societies face. Because there are a limited number of ways in which a society can manage these problems (Kluckhohn & Strodtbeck, 1961), it is possible to develop a system that categorizes and compares societies on this basis. By examining the choices that social groups make, we can infer their preferences for such fundamental human issues as their relationships to their environment and to each other. This provides the ability to categorize a social group according to these shared assumptions about the way things ought to be or the way one should behave. Having considered a society's cultural values, we can then analyze how cultural values are reflected in the way that the individual people with whom managers need to work think about their world. As introduced in this chapter and developed further in Chapter 4, culture shapes individuals by influencing the content and structure of the basic mental representations that members of particular social groups share.

This chapter reviews the major frameworks that have been devised for categorizing and comparing cultures and how these frameworks have been used to understand cultural distance. Despite being conducted at widely different times and using different methods, these frameworks have identified some very similar sets of cultural dimensions, such as individualism and collectivism. This similarity leads to a more in-depth description of individualism and collectivism and their relationship to other elements of the sociocultural system. Finally, recent alternatives to a values-based view of cultural variation are reviewed, as are the uses that managers can make of the systematic descriptions of culture.

Kluckhohn and Strodtbeck Framework

Several lines of early work in comparative anthropology produce frameworks for identifying the problems for which societies need to find cultural solutions (Inkeles & Levinson, 1969; Malinowski, 1939). One framework that has significantly influenced the way the management literature has conceptualized cultural variation identified six problems that all societies face (Kluckhohn & Strodtbeck, 1961; Maznevski, DiStefano, & Nason, 1993). Societies place different emphases on three alternative ways of handling each of these problems:

- *Relationships to nature*: People have a need-duty to control or master nature (domination), to submit to nature (subjugation), or to work together with nature to maintain harmony and balance (harmony).
- *Beliefs about human nature*: People are inherently good, evil, or a mixture of good and evil.
- *Relationships among people*: The greatest concern and responsibility is for one's self and immediate family (individualist), for one's own group that is defined in different ways (collateral), or for one's groups that are arranged in a rigid hierarchy (hierarchical).
- *Nature of human activity*: People should concentrate on living for the moment (being), striving for goals (achieving), or reflecting (thinking).
- *Conception of space*: The physical space we use is private or public or a mixture of public and private.
- *Orientation to time*: People should make decisions with respect to traditions or events in the past, events in the present, or events in the future.

Figure 3.1 shows the variation in preferences that cultures exhibited on these six dimensions. Because many readers will be familiar with the U.S. culture, this preference pattern is highlighted in the figure.

In this conceptualization of cultural variation, the six value orientations are not bipolar dimensions. That is, a high preference for one assumption does not necessarily imply a low preference for the other two assumptions in the same value orientation. All preferences can be represented in a society, but with a rank order of the preferred alternatives. For example, in the case of orientation to time, people from the United States might exhibit a preference for a present time orientation, but a future orientation might be a close second choice.

Although this framework was well supported in extensive field research (Kluckhohn & Strodtbeck, 1961) and has obvious management behavior implications (e.g., a *doing* orientation suggests that employees would be motivated to achieve goals, whereas a *being* orientation suggests that employees would only work as much as needed to support their lifestyle), very few management studies have directly used it. Instead, its important insights about basic societal issues have been incorporated into other frameworks.

Figure 3.1   Cultural Variation in Value Orientations

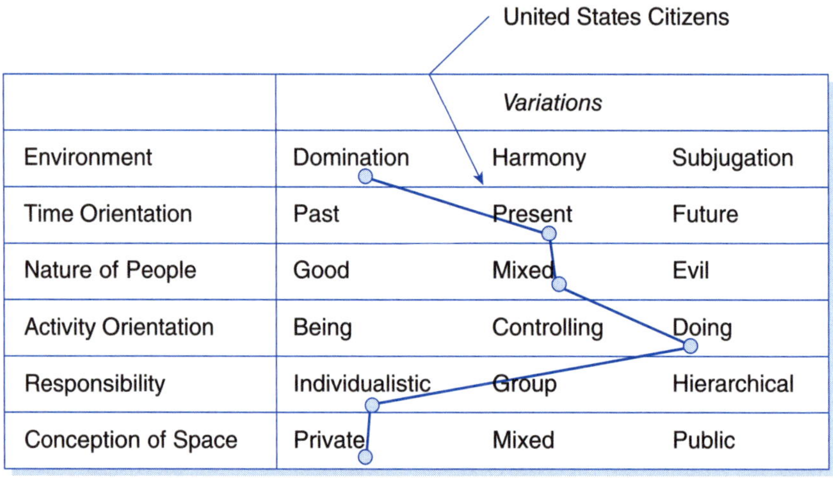

		Variations	
Environment	Domination	Harmony	Subjugation
Time Orientation	Past	Present	Future
Nature of People	Good	Mixed	Evil
Activity Orientation	Being	Controlling	Doing
Responsibility	Individualistic	Group	Hierarchical
Conception of Space	Private	Mixed	Public

SOURCE: Adapted from Kluckhohn & Strodtbeck (1961).

Hofstede's Study

A framework that has received a great deal of research attention is Hofstede's (1980, 2001) now-classic study of work values. Based on questionnaire surveys of 117,000 IBM nonmanagerial sales and service employees, Hofstede developed four dimensions to classify countries. These dimensions were named *individualism–collectivism, power distance, uncertainty avoidance,* and *masculinity-femininity.* He named and interpreted these dimensions based on a way of understanding societal problems that was developed from an extensive review of anthropological and psychological studies of national culture during the first half of the 20th century (Inkeles & Levinson, 1969).

Individualism–collectivism is the extent to which the self-identity of a society's members depends on individual characteristics or the characteristics of the groups to which the individual belongs on a permanent basis and the extent to which individual or group interests dominate. Although people can enjoy and work well together in groups in both individualist and collectivist societies, collectivist societies distinguish between in-groups and out-groups more sharply and more permanently than do individualist societies. Power distance refers to the extent that power differences are accepted and sanctioned in a society. Uncertainty avoidance is the extent to which societies focus on ways to reduce uncertainty and create stability. Unlike the sort of risk in games of chance that have clear probabilities, accepting uncertainty means being accustomed to acting without basing choices on known probabilities. Masculinity-femininity refers to the extent to which *traditional* male orientations of ambition, acquisition and achievement are emphasized over *traditional* female orientations of nurturance and interpersonal harmony. By giving each of the 40 countries a score, ranging from 0 to 100 on each of the four dimensions, Hofstede derived a classification of national cultures. The original sample was later expanded to include 53 countries and world regions. The scores given to the countries are shown in Table 3.1. More recently, Hofstede, Hofstede and Minkov (2010) have updated these scores by drawing from follow-up research since the IBM study to provide scores for 73 nations. Other scholars suggest ways to refine the scores by adjusting for changes since the IBM study in economic conditions that are associated with culture (Tang & Koveos, 2008).

A number of advances continue to be made to improve culture dimension measures within the Hofstede tradition, while alternative approaches to understanding societal culture have also been proposed. We first consider some advances closely related to Hofstede's original dimensions and then some alternatives.

Long-Term Orientation

The omission of a culture dimension having to do with the way in which a society dealt with the problem of time as the Kluckhohn and Strodtbeck (1961) model suggests was an obvious limitation of Hofstede's (1980) original set of culture dimensions. Subsequently, Hofstede found a way to represent time orientation in a study done in collaboration with a scholar who was studying Confucian cultural traditions. That dimension was initially labeled Confucian Work Dynamism (Chinese Culture Connection, 1987) and later renamed long-term orientation. It included supporting the values of relationships based on status, thrift, persistence, and a sense of shame and rejecting the values of steadiness and stability, face, tradition, and reciprocating gifts. Long-term orientation was shown to be related to a society's economic growth (Hofstede & Bond, 1988). However, since culture dimension scores were only available for 23 countries and the scores were based on surveys of undergraduates, this dimension received little attention. More recently, Minkov and Hofstede (2012) used data

Table 3.1 Hofstede's Rankings

Country	Power Distance	Individualism	Masculinity	Uncertainty Avoidance
Argentina	49	46	56	86
Australia	36	90	61	51
Austria	11	55	79	70
Belgium	65	75	54	94
Brazil	69	38	49	76
Canada	39	80	52	48
Chile	63	23	28	86
Colombia	67	13	64	80
Costa Rica	35	15	21	86
Denmark	18	74	16	23
Ecuador	78	8	63	67
Finland	33	63	26	59
France	68	71	43	86
Germany (F.R.)	35	67	66	65
Great Britain	35	89	66	35
Greece	60	35	57	112
Guatemala	95	6	37	101
Hong Kong	68	25	57	29
India	77	48	56	40
Indonesia	78	14	46	48
Iran	58	41	43	59
Ireland	28	70	68	35
Israel	13	54	47	81
Italy	50	76	70	75
Jamaica	45	39	68	13
Japan	54	46	95	92
Korea (S.)	60	18	39	85
Malaysia	104	26	50	36
Mexico	81	30	69	82
Netherlands	38	80	14	53
New Zealand	22	79	58	49
Norway	31	69	8	50

Country	Power Distance	Individualism	Masculinity	Uncertainty Avoidance
Pakistan	55	14	50	70
Panama	95	11	44	86
Peru	64	16	42	87
Philippines	94	32	64	44
Portugal	63	27	31	104
Salvador	66	19	40	94
Singapore	74	20	48	8
South Africa	49	65	63	49
Spain	57	51	42	86
Sweden	31	71	5	29
Switzerland	34	68	70	58
Taiwan	58	17	45	69
Thailand	64	20	34	64
Turkey	66	37	45	85
United States	40	91	62	46
Uruguay	61	36	38	100
Venezuela	81	12	73	76
Yugoslavia	76	27	21	88
Regions:				
East Africa	64	27	41	52
West Africa	77	20	46	54
Arab countries	80	38	53	68

SOURCE: Adapted from Hofstede, G. (1991). *Culture and organisations: Software of the mind.* London: McGraw-Hill.

obtained from 38 countries, mainly from the late 1990s, that were collected in another large-scale survey study, the World Values Survey (WVS). They identify long-term orientation as a set of values that place low importance on service to others and high importance on thrift and perseverance. They also found that this long-term orientation measure is both highly correlated with the Hofstede and Bond (1988) measure and, like that measure, with economic growth.

Indulgence Versus Restraint

An additional culture dimension based on WVS data that has become part of the Hofstede tradition and which is quite different from the other five is *indulgence versus restraint*. Indulgent societies have a relatively large proportion of citizens who say that they are very happy, believe that they are in control of their lives, and place a very high importance on leisure. The implications of this dimension for managers have been studied less than for other culture dimensions, but initial studies indicate that it has marketing implications. Indulgent societies show higher birthrates, less cardiovascular disease, higher importance of friends, more support for casual sex, and more obesity in developed nations (Hofstede, Hofstede, & Minkov, 2010). Many of these and other findings have implications for the markets for various products in different parts of the world. Knowing that a society places high emphasis on indulgence also suggests possible implications for cultural differences in how best to motivate employees.

Measures derived from the WVS have the potential to increase the number of countries for which basic culture characteristics can be analyzed. As the WVS will likely continue to be administered once or twice every decade, additional updates, refinements, and supplements to Hofstede's original dimensions may occur.

Schwartz Value Survey

Since Hofstede's study was first published in 1980, several other large-scale surveys of values have been conducted. Each of these studies adds something new to our understanding of cultural differences. The first of these is the Schwartz Value Survey. Based on a review of previous theory and research, Shalom Schwartz and his colleagues (Sagiv & Schwartz, 1995; Schwartz, 1992, 1994; Schwartz & Bilsky, 1990) conducted a series of studies about the content and structure of human values. The content of values refers to the various criteria that people use to evaluate events and select courses of action. Structure refers to the organization of these values based on their similarities and differences. Initially, Schwartz and his colleagues identified three universal human requirements similar to the kind of societal problems that Kluckhohn and Strodtbeck had considered. The first issue is the nature of the relationship between the individual and the group. The second issue is the preservation of the society itself, and the final problem is the relationship of people to the natural world. They used this set of requirements to organize and add to a set of values that had previously been identified by Rokeach (1973) and derived 56 values that reflected various ways of meeting these three requirements. University students and secondary school teachers in 20 (later an additional 40) countries were asked the extent to which each value was a guiding principle in their lives.

For purposes of identifying value orientations at the level of cultural groups, Schwartz and colleagues first calculated the average response to each value question for the people in each group (Sagiv & Schwartz, 1995; Schwartz, 1992, 1994; Schwartz & Bilsky, 1990; Schwartz, 2009; Sagiv, Schwartz, & Arieli, 2011). They then performed a multidimensional scaling analysis on the correlations between the average ratings of the 45 items that they had found to represent universal values in a number of different samples in 63 countries (Sagiv & Schwartz, 2000). This analysis yielded seven value orientations that were labeled as the following:

- *Egalitarianism*: recognition of people as moral equals
- *Harmony*: fitting in harmoniously with the environment
- *Embeddedness*: people as embedded in the collective
- *Hierarchy*: unequal distribution of power is legitimate
- *Mastery*: exploitation of the natural or social environment
- *Affective autonomy*: pursuit of positive experiences
- *Intellectual autonomy*: independent pursuit of own ideas

Having defined these dimensions of national culture, they went on to compare samples from 57 countries on this profile of values. Then, using a technique called a co-plot, they constructed a profile of differences between all pairs of countries in the sample. This procedure generates a two-dimensional graphic representation of the relationship of countries to each other on all seven dimensions simultaneously (see Sagiv & Schwartz, 2000). An example of a comparison of samples of teachers is shown in Figure 3.2.

As shown in Figure 3.2, the location of country samples along the seven value vectors indicates their relationship to each other. The direction of the vector indicates the increasing importance of the value type in relationship to the center of the diagram marked by the X. For example, the line drawn on Figure 3.2 indicates the importance that each sample attributes to *intellectual autonomy*. To locate a country sample on this dimension, a perpendicular is drawn from the position of the country to the vector. The lines drawn on the figure indicate that this dimension is very important in France, less so in Norway, India, and Singapore, and very unimportant in Ghana. Because the co-plot summarizes the position of countries on seven value types on only two dimensions, the graphic location of each country is not perfect. Overall, however, it generally provides an accurate representation of the relationship of countries to each other (Sagiv & Schwartz, 2000), and studies with other samples have shown very similar patterns of relationships (Schwartz, 1992; Sagiv, Schwartz, & Arieli, 2011).

Trompenaars's Dimensions

Another broad-based study of value orientations was conducted by Fons Trompenaars. During a 10-year period, he administered a values questionnaire to over 15,000 managers in 28 countries. Subsequently, it was used in a much larger number of countries (Trompenaars, 1993) and includes a number of former Soviet-bloc countries not included in previous studies of values. His seven value dimensions were derived primarily from the prior work of North American sociologists and anthropologists (Kluckhohn & Strodtbeck, 1961; Parsons & Shils, 1951). The first five of these dimensions concerned relationships among people.

Figure 3.2 Co-Plot of Value Dimensions Across 57 National Cultures

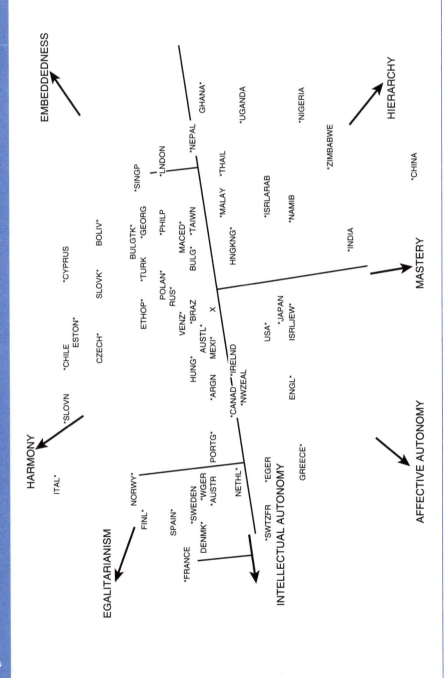

SOURCE: Sagiv & Schwartz (2000). Reprinted with permission of SAGE Publications, Inc.

- *Universalism–particularism*: Universalism is a belief that what is true and good can be discovered and applied universally, whereas particularism is a belief that unique circumstances determine what is right or good.
- *Individualism–collectivism*: Similar to Hofstede's definition, this dimension concerns the extent to which people plan their actions with reference to individual benefits versus those of the group.
- *Neutral–affective*: In neutral cultures, emotion should be held in check, and maintaining an appearance of self-control is important, whereas in affective cultures, it is natural to express emotions.
- *Specific–diffuse*: This dimension refers to the extent to which individuals are willing to allow access to their inner selves to others. In specific cultures, people separate the private part of their lives from the public, whereas in diffuse cultures, these aspects of the individual overlap.
- *Achievement–ascription*: This dimension is about how status and power are determined in a society. In an ascription society, status is based on who a person is, whereas in an achievement society, status is based on what a person does.

The final two dimensions are similar to Kluckhohn and Strodtbeck's (1961) categorization and are about orientations toward time and the environment:

- *Time*: This dimension is about past versus future orientations but also with the extent to which time is viewed as linear versus holistic and integrative with past and present together with future possibilities.
- *Environment*: This dimension refers to the extent to which individuals feel that they themselves are the primary influence on their lives. Alternatively, the environment is seen as more powerful than they, and people should strive to achieve harmony with it.

A subsequent analysis of Trompenaars's data yielded two main dimensions of cultural variation at the national level (Smith, Dugan, & Trompenaars, 1996). These were the following:

- *Loyal involvement-utilitarian involvement*: representing varying orientations toward group members
- *Conservatism-egalitarian commitment*: representing orientations toward obligations of social relationships

These two dimensions can be seen as extensions and refinements of Hofstede's (1980) individualism–collectivism and power distance dimensions, respectively. This refinement is also consistent with the relationship found between the Schwartz Value Survey (SVS) and Hofstede's dimensions. That is, the most important relationships that exist between the SVS value types and the Hofstede dimensions are for the dimensions of individualism–collectivism and power distance (Schwartz, 1994).

The GLOBE Study

Another major study of cultural differences in value orientations was undertaken as a part of the Global Leadership and Organizational Behavior Effectiveness (GLOBE) program (House, Hanges, Javidan, Dorfman, & Gupta, 2004). GLOBE involved 170 researchers working in 62 different societies and collected data from approximately 17,000 middle managers in 951 organizations. One of the outcomes of the GLOBE research was the construction of nine dimensions of cultural variation. The first four of these dimensions are described as direct extensions of Hofstede's (1980) work, with the exception that GLOBE proposes two dimensions of collectivism, with in-group collectivism being the most highly correlated with the Hofstede individualism–collectivism dimension. And, the GLOBE uncertainty avoidance dimension focuses more specifically on the use of explicit procedures to handle uncertainty than does its counterpart in the Hofstede scheme. These four dimensions are the following:

- *Institutional collectivism*: The degree to which organizational and societal institutional practices encourage and reward collective distribution of resources and collective action
- *In-group collectivism*: The degree to which individuals express pride, loyalty, and cohesiveness in their organizations or families
- *Power distance*: The degree to which members of a collective expect power to be distributed equally
- *Uncertainty avoidance*: The extent to which a society, organization, or group relies on social norms, rules, and procedures to alleviate unpredictability of future events

The next two dimensions can be seen as reconceptualizations of Hofstede's masculinity-femininity dimension. They are the following:

- *Gender egalitarianism*: The degree to which a collective minimizes gender inequality
- *Assertiveness*: The degree to which individuals are assertive, confrontational, and aggressive in their relationships with others

The next two dimensions have their origins in the work of Kluckhohn & Strotdbeck (1961) on the *nature of people* and *time orientation* presented previously and are as follows:

- *Humane orientation*: The degree to which a collective encourages and rewards individuals for being fair, altruistic, generous, caring, and kind to others
- *Future orientation*: The extent to which individuals engage in future-oriented behaviors, such as delayed gratification, planning, and investing in the future

The final dimension is described by the GLOBE authors (House et al., 2004) as derived from McClelland's (1961) work on achievement motivation. However, linkages to Hofstede's (2001) masculinity construct can also be found (Peterson, 2004). This dimension is

- *Performance orientation*: the degree to which a collective encourages and rewards group members for performance improvement and excellence.

In addition to the fact that the GLOBE data were collected from middle managers in the country in which the firms were headquartered, several other aspects of this study are worth noting. Most interesting, perhaps, is that the cultural dimensions were measured both as *practices* (the way things are) and *values* (the way things should be). And, for some of the dimensions these two kinds of measures were negatively correlated. This raises some interesting questions about the attitudes of middle managers in some countries toward society (Peterson, 2004). At present, the GLOBE study may best be viewed as complimentary to Hofstede's (1980; 2001) work, its most closely linked predecessor (Peterson, 2004).

As discussed, the results of the major studies of national variation in value orientations have some remarkable similarity, despite being conducted at widely different times, with different samples, and using different methods. They are also closely connected to a broad range of social and economic indicators (House et al., 2004; Hofstede, Hofstede, & Minkov, 2010). This consistency of findings and the association with other societal characteristics besides just values lends validity to this approach to describing cultural variation. In addition, however, because they appear in some form in all of the frameworks, individualism–collectivism and power distance are perhaps especially important to understanding cultural variation. Indeed, these dimensions relate to two of the fundamental societal problems to which each of the theories of such problems point. The first has to do with boundaries between individuals and groups and the second with the preservation of order in society.

Individualism and Collectivism

Individualism and collectivism are perhaps the most useful and certainly the most frequently studied dimensions of cultural variation in explaining a diverse array of social behavior. In addition to their inclusion in most studies of multiple culture dimensions (Kirkman, Lowe, & Gibson, 2006), a major line of cross-cultural study has focused specifically on individualism and collectivism (Triandis, 1995; Triandis & Suh, 2002). As a societal characteristic, individualism refers to the tendency to view each person as independent of others and to be more concerned about the consequences of a person's actions for that person alone. Alternatively, collectivism refers to the tendency of a society to view people as interdependent with selected others who are part of stable groups, such as a kinship group. Collectivist societies tend to be concerned about the consequences of behavior for each person's reference group and expect people to be more willing to sacrifice personal interests for the good of their group. However, individualism–collectivism should not be depicted as simply a dichotomy of self-interest and a generalized concern for all of society. That is, collectivism does not equate with socialism. For example, people in collectivist societies can pursue self-interests as well as group interests as long as priority is given to the group (Erez & Earley, 1993), and self-interests can be instrumental in attaining group interests. In addition, as noted in Chapter 2, people from both individualistic and collectivistic societies both derive a sense of self, in part, from the groups with which they identify, their in-groups. Although people who grow up in individualistic and collectivistic societies probably have similar views about members of their in-group, they differ in the way in which they designate who is a member of this group. That is, collectivist societies tend to have very few of these groups, but the groups are broad in scope, encompassing many interrelated activities. For business, this quality of collectivist societies means that people may like to work and do business with other extended family members or friends of long standing. By contrast, individualistic societies are organized around many groups with which they identify, but the groups tend to have specific functions and have rapidly changing membership. In contrast to collectivist societies, people's extended family, their business associates, and their friends are likely to be unacquainted with one another.

Ideas related to individualism and collectivism often have been used both to understand the psychology of individuals as well as the cultural characteristics of societies. Although research about socialization suggests that people are more likely to prefer their nation's cultural orientation to that of other nations, individuals still differ substantially in how much their individual values reflect aspects of their country's culture, as discussed in Box 3.1.

Box 3.1 Cultural Values and Personal Values of Individuals

It is particularly important to emphasize that societal culture reflects the context that a society's members know intimately, but it does not necessarily reflect the values that any individual prefers. All of the culture dimension scores discussed in this chapter are based on the *average* score for all participants in each cultural group to a set of questions. Therefore, it is not appropriate to infer that because two countries have different mean scores on a survey question about a particular value that any two individuals from those countries will differ in the same way. That is, within each nation, individuals vary considerably on how much they agree with, like, or support different aspects of their society's cultural orientation. For example, the following figure shows the hypothetical overlap between individuals' scores for how much they value some specific aspect of individualism–collectivism in a collectivist country (Malaysia) and an individualist country (New Zealand).

The differences in means indicate that it is rare to find an individual in New Zealand who does not have extensive experience with living in an individualistic society. As

Figure 3.3 Hypothetical Distribution of Individualism–Collectivism Scores

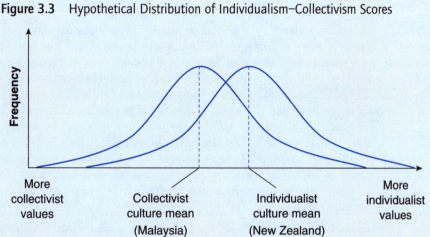

More collectivist values — Collectivist culture mean (Malaysia) — Individualist culture mean (New Zealand) — More individualist values

shown in the figure, however, it is entirely possible to find an individual in New Zealand who values some aspect of their society's individualism less than does someone in Malaysia.

Even the fundamental concept of what a value is can be different in what it implies for a country and what it means for an individual. For example, cultural collectivism for a country implies stable in-group relationships that have broad implications. At the societal level, collectivism may imply that a person has connections to a group from the time of their birth. These connections may be based on their parents' background and choices rather than the person's own choice and are difficult to change. At the societal level, collectivism also may imply that a member's group rather than the particular member or the government has special responsibility for the person's well-being when facing personal problems, like sickness or financial difficulties. Also at the societal level, the dependence of each person on their in-group is likely to imply a reciprocal responsibility that the person must consider the implications that their personal choices have for that in-group. This configuration of characteristics—limited choices about one's in-group, group responsibilities for personal welfare, and dependence on one's group when making decisions—fit logically together for a society. For an individual, however, they may not fit together at all. Any individual who lives in a collectivist culture can personally value one, all, or none of these societal culture characteristics. The same issues apply to differences between the logic that underlies other societal culture value dimensions as compared to the logic of the personal values of individuals.

Consistent with individual differences in support for societal culture characteristics, it is also increasingly clear that the level of endorsement in a society to survey questions about values can vary systematically (Taras, Kirkman, & Steel, 2010). There could be differing degrees of consensus on any particular value orientation. Researchers have measured this intranational consensus, as the opposite of variation, by examining

(Continued)

(Continued)

differences in the standard deviation in measures of value orientations across cultures (e.g., Au, 1999) and norms for conformity (Gelfand et al., 2011). Evidence suggests that value consensus is related to socioeconomic development and democratization of societies (Schwartz & Sagie, 2000). It has implications for organizational behavior similar to those found for other types of heterogeneity (Au, 1999).

In this book, when referring to the cultural orientation of a person, terms such as *individualist* mean someone whose way of thinking or *cognitive structures* reflect deep experience and understanding of the norms and social pressures to conform to these norms in an individualistic society. This use of such terms is based on research, which suggests that important aspects of the way that individuals think are based on their cultural context regardless of whether they personally value all aspects of that context.

Tightness and Complexity

An aspect of individualism–collectivism that has recently received more attention is the idea of cultural tightness and looseness (Triandis, 1995; Gelfand et al., 2011). This research builds on Triandis's recognition (1995) that a society's individualism is closely related to its looseness and complexity, whereas collectivism implies tightness and simplicity. Tightness refers to the extent to which members of a culture agree about what is correct behavior, believe they must behave exactly according to cultural norms, and believe they will receive or should give severe criticism for even small deviations from cultural norms (Gelfand et al., 2011; Pelto, 1968).

Japan is an example of a tight culture, whereas the United States is a loose culture (see for example Chan et al., 1996). Tightness is also associated with homogeneous cultures that often have high population density. Alternatively, loose cultures often have multiple and sometimes conflicting norms about appropriate behavior. Although a culture might be characterized as tight or loose overall, both tightness and looseness can occur in a society in different contexts (Triandis, 1995). For example, a culture can be tight in its political orientation but loose in terms of religion. Cultural complexity refers to the amount of differentiation in the various domains of individuals' lives. The numbers of different roles available to individuals, the size of communities, and the GNP per capita of a country are suggested as measures of cultural complexity. For example, hunter-gatherer societies are less complex than modern societies that have thousands of different possible roles represented. The proposed relationships between tightness, complexity, and individualism–collectivism are presented in Figure 3.4. As suggested in Figure 3.4, collectivism is maximized in tight, simple cultures, such as might be found in the subcultures of the kibbutz in Israel and the Amish of North America, whereas individualism is maximized in loose complex cultures such as metropolitan France and the United States.

Figure 3.4 Relationship Between Tightness, Cultural Complexity, and Individualism–Collectivism

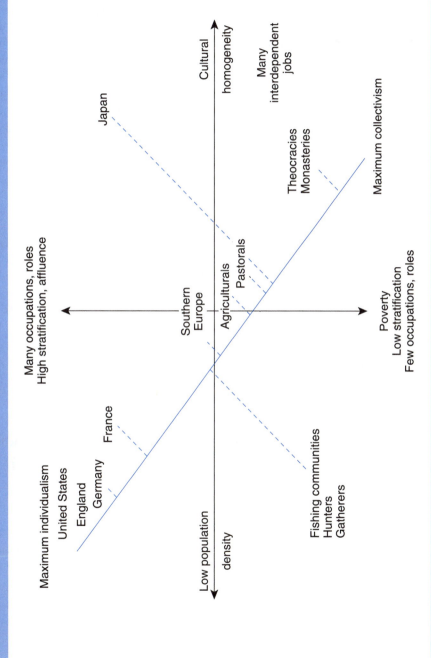

SOURCE: H. C. Triandis, *Culture and Social Behavior* (New York: McGraw-Hill, 1994). Reprinted with permission.

Vertical and Horizontal Dimensions

In addition to the differences in motives and in the specification of reference group members noted previously, a number of other refinements of the individualism–collectivism concept have been suggested (Earley & Gibson, 1998). For example, Triandis (1995) identified more than 60 culture-specific characteristics that differentiate between different kinds of individualism and collectivism. Significant among these are the vertical and horizontal dimensions that relate to the way in which people view their status relationship with others. The vertical dimension is somewhat similar to Hofstede's (1980) power distance dimension and relates to the SVS (Schwartz, 1992) value orientations of hierarchy and harmony. In combination with individualism and collectivism, these dimensions correspond to the four types of self, independent or interdependent (Markus & Kitayama, 1991) and same or different (Triandis, 1995).

Table 3.2 indicates how these different combinations of vertical and horizontal individualism and collectivism correspond to how societies tend to view their members, their value orientations on the Rokeach (1973) dimensions, their dominant political systems, and their typical patterns of social behavior as defined by Fiske (1990). As shown in Table 3.2, this distinction between vertical and horizontal individualism and collectivism results in four different cultural profiles or syndromes. However, the correlation between power distance and collectivism (at $r = .67$, according to Hofstede, 1980) suggests that vertical collectivism and horizontal individualism might be the dominant cultural profiles around the world (Triandis, 1995).

Triandis (1995) offers the following defining attributes of these cultural syndromes. Vertically collective societies view their members as parts of an in-group,

Table 3.2 Culture, Self Orientation, and Politics				
	Vertical		**Horizontal**	
	Collectivism	**Individualism**	**Collectivism**	**Individualism**
Kind of self	Interdependent Different from others	Independent Different from others	Interdependent Same as others	Independent Same as others
Fiske orientation	Communal sharing Authority ranking	Communal sharing Authority ranking	Communal sharing Equality matching	Communal sharing Equality matching
Rokeach values	Low equality Low freedom	Low equality High freedom	High equality Low freedom	High equality High freedom
Political system	Communalism (e.g., Indian village)	Market democracy (e.g., U.S., France)	Communal living (e.g., Israeli kibbutz)	Democratic socialism (e.g., Sweden, British Labour party)

SOURCE: Triandis, H. C. (1995). *Individualism and collectivism*. Boulder, CO: Westview Press, a member of Perseus Book Group.

but members of the in-group differ in terms of status, and different in-groups are also likely to have varying status. The traditional caste system of India is an example. These cultures are characterized by patterns of social relationships that emphasize communal sharing according to need and authority ranking or the distribution of resources according to rank (Fiske, 1990). They typically have social systems that do not reflect the values of individual freedom or equity (Rokeach, 1973). Inequality is the accepted norm, and serving and sacrificing for the in-group feature prominently. In horizontal individualistic societies, the self is autonomous and people are generally equal. These cultures typically show patterns of social behavior that emphasize equity in resource sharing according to contribution and distribution of resources equally among members (Fiske, 1990). They have social systems that emphasize both the values of equality and individual freedom (Rokeach, 1973). What these two dominant syndromes suggest is that verticality serves to reinforce collectivism, and horizontalness reinforces individualism. For example, although the United States might be more vertical than, say, New Zealand or Canada, individualistic cultures relative to collectivist cultures tend to be horizontal.

Social Axioms

As the previous discussion indicates, societal value orientations have taken center stage in analyses of cultural variation. This can easily lead to a mistaken view that societal culture is only about value orientations. In keeping with the definition of culture at the beginning of this chapter, value orientations are also coming to be understood as useful simplifications indicating typical ways that a society's members think and organize the society's institutions. In addition to considering values, researchers (Leung et al., 2002) have recently proposed that general beliefs or *social axioms* provide a complementary way to understand societal cultures. Social axioms are basic truths or premises (hence the term *axiom*, as in mathematics) or generalized expectancies that relate to a wide range of social behaviors across different contexts (Bond et al., 2004). The formal definition by Leung and colleagues (2002, p. 289) is as follows:

> Social axioms are generalized beliefs about oneself, the social and physical environment, or the spiritual world, and are in the form of an assertion about the relationship between two entities or concepts.

Unlike values, social axioms do not have an evaluative or "ought" component, as in "Good health is important," which is a value statement. Instead, a typical social axiom has the structure "A is related to B," and the relationship can be correlational or causal, as in "Good health leads to success." This social axiom might be endorsed to a greater or lesser degree in different societies (Leung et al., 2002).

Based on a literature review, interviews and content analysis of newspapers, books, popular songs, folklore, and so on, Leung et al. (2002) identified many thousands of social axioms. Based on their fit with the four categories of *psychological attributes, orientation toward the social world*, *social interaction*, and the *environment* the items were reduced to 182 axioms. Based on survey results in Hong Kong and Venezuela and then later in Japan, Germany, and the United States, the number of items was further reduced to 60.

In a study with 7672 university students in 41 cultural groups, Bond and colleagues (2004) derived a cultural level structure of social axioms. At the cultural level, one strong factor was labeled *dynamic externality*, because it represented a cluster of beliefs that focused around religiosity and a belief that effort would ultimately lead to justice (Smith et al., 2006). A second factor labeled *social cynicism* was composed almost entirely of items that reflected a cynical view of people—a negative view of human nature, a biased view against some groups of people, a mistrust of social institutions, and a disregard of ethical means of achieving an end. A comparison of these generalized beliefs with previous values-based assessments of cultural variation found that dynamic externality was closely related to but not identical with cultural collectivism. However, social cynicism appears to be a new cultural dimension in that it correlates only moderately with dimensions from previous studies of cultural variation (Bond et al., 2004).

Culture as Sources of Guidance

Another line of research seeks to understand cultural differences based on characteristics of the *role structures* typical in organizations in a society. This research considers the extent to which individuals (middle managers) in different nations rely on others in different roles and on rules and norms to deal with their daily work situations (Smith & Peterson, 1988; Smith, Peterson, & Schwartz, 2002). Specifically, it analyzes how societies differ in the extent to which managers consider eight sources of guidance for handling the work situations that they face. These sources are (1) organization rules and procedures, (2) their superiors, (3) their colleagues, (4) their subordinates, (5) staff experts (such as internal consultants), (6) their organization's norms, (7) their society's norms, and (8) their own experience and training. All of these sources provide managers with guidance about how to deal with all kinds of work situations, such as how best to reward a subordinate or how to resolve a conflict with another department. Managers use these different sources to formulate their preferences about what actions to advocate to their colleagues and bosses and to inform their choices when they need to personally make a decision.

Smith, Peterson, and colleagues have collected survey responses from 7,701 middle managers in 59 countries (Peterson & Smith, 2008; Smith et al., 2011). Summaries of the scores for examples of the countries studied are shown in Table 3.3. Each score is based on the average response (calculated after first subtracting the manager's average response to all of the questions) about the extent to which the managers say that they use each source of guidance to handle eight different work problems.

As shown in Table 3.3, the positive numbers in the *own experience* column mean that managers almost everywhere indicate that they rely the most on their own experience

	Formal	**Unwritten**					**Own**	**Widespread**
Country	**Rules**	**Rules**	**Subordinates**	**Specialists**	**Colleagues**	**Superiors**	**Experience**	**Beliefs**
Argentina	−08	05	−07	−43	−07	32	61	−44
Australia	47	07	−23	−53	−36	50	70	−62
Brazil	42	04	−27	−35	−23	42	68	−69
Canada	22	07	−03	−48	−05	42	59	−78
China	36	−28	−36	−28	−23	56	27	−04
India	33	00	−07	−60	−17	30	36	−14
Japan	38	−23	01	−56	−29	42	61	−34
Nigeria	55	−13	−12	−35	−16	35	19	−36
Saudi Arabia	38	17	11	−40	03	−15	31	−50
Turkey	12	18	−21	−78	−12	84	49	−52
Ukraine	−04	−21	−06	−39	−15	88	59	−62
USA	26	02	−10	−61	−16	58	54	−56

SOURCE: Adapted from Peterson & Smith (2008).

and training. The negative numbers in the *widespread beliefs* column indicate that managers report that they rely the least on their society's norms (or widespread beliefs) for dealing with work situations. Despite this overall trend, as shown in Table 3.3, societies differ widely in the relative emphasis that managers say that they place on all of these sources of guidance. For example, managers from Nigeria report making more use of their organization's rules and procedures relative to other sources of guidance than do managers in the other nations listed. Those countries where rules are used most heavily include many countries where managers sometimes work to improve the quality of and accountability of rules and at other times work diligently to find ways around them. Such dynamics produce cultural differences between countries in whether or not using rules heavily is associated with managers' evaluations of how well work situations are handled (Smith et al., 2011). At the country level, questions about relying on superiors and on rules are somewhat positively correlated with one another and negatively correlated with relying on self and subordinates. Supported by these modest correlations, these four measures have sometimes been combined into an overall measure of the use of vertical sources of guidance (Smith, Peterson, & Schwartz, 2002).

The previous discussion has identified the main attempts that have been made to identify dimensions along which cultures can be systematically described and compared. Each is deficient in some regard, but taken as a whole, they begin to paint a reasonably clear picture that cultural variability is systematic and that cultural characteristics can be identified and described.

Cultural Distance

One of the benefits of quantitative measures of cultural dimensions is the ability to construct indexes of *cultural distance* between countries. This sort of an index draws an analogy with physical distance to consider how culturally different national cultures are from each other based on the value orientations measured. For example, by using Hofstede's four cultural dimensions, a composite index of national cultural distance was developed (Kogut & Singh, 1988). The index is corrected for differences in the variances of each dimension and then arithmetically averaged. The algebraic formula for the index is as follows:

$$\text{Cultural Distance} = \sum_{i=1}^{4} [(I_{ij} - I_{iu})^2 / V_i] / 4$$

I_{ij} = index for the ith cultural dimension for the jth country

I_{iu} = index for the ith cultural dimension for the uth country

V_i = variance for the ith cultural dimension

This index represents the relative distance of nations from each other based on a combination of these four cultural dimensions. As such, it transcends the specific value orientations of the cultures represented to indicate the overall degree of similarity-dissimilarity between different nationalities. For example, using this index, the cultural distance between the United States and Japan is 2.63, whereas the cultural distance between the United States and Canada is 0.25. In practice, a large degree of cultural distance between a negotiating team from one country and the team from another country might suggest that both teams would face a large amount of uncertainty when working with one another (Kogut & Singh, 1988). Also, a small degree of cultural distance suggests that managers from two nations might find it easier to develop trusting relationships with one another than with managers from culturally distant countries (Doney, Cannon, & Mullen, 1998). Although cultural distance indices can provide some degree of help in anticipating how cultural relationships may develop, care must be taken in their interpretation. They are only meaningful as a very broad comparison at the national level and thus are subject to all the caveats associated with culturally different groups within nations, the degree to which managers are familiar with the other culture or with culture in general, and the influence of legal systems, economic considerations, and many other factors that enter in to international business relationships (Zaheer, Schomaker, & Nachum, 2012; Usunier, 1998).

Limitations of Country Culture Research

Analyzing the cultures of many countries based on a finite number of dimensions was a major advance over earlier research about culture (Peterson, 2007). Studies before Hofstede's (1980) tended to consider only a few countries and typically considered unrelated aspects of culture. Numerous studies have shown that the dimensions developed by Hofstede, Schwartz, and the GLOBE study among others explain a broad range of differences in the economic and social characteristics of countries (Hofstede, 2001; House et al., 2004; Peterson & Soendergaard, 2011; Sagiv, Schwartz, & Arielli, 2011). Corresponding measures from these studies, notably measures of individualism and collectivism and of power relationships, tend to correlate with one another.

Research about societal culture dimensions, however, is not without critics (e.g., McSweeney, 2009). Many of the criticisms of societal-culture research in general or of the specific research projects described in this chapter are based on the challenges to doing cross-cultural research as described in Chapter 1. The results in these studies have the potential to be influenced by the nature of the samples used, and survey results have the potential to be limited by the nature of the questions asked (Dorfman & Howell, 1988). Some of the surveys were not developed from any unifying theoretical base but extracted from a broader survey (e.g., Hofstede, 1991), and others used theories to guide the design that might have distorted the results to correspond to the researchers' biases (Hofstede, 2006; Javidan et al., 2006). Criticisms that culture is not well represented by only Hofstede's early set of four dimensions encouraged him and his colleagues to develop additional dimensions and encouraged others to propose some of the alternative culture dimension schemes described in this chapter. Country culture research has also been criticized on the grounds that countries have major geographic subcultures as well as cultural groups that are unrelated to country boundaries (Sackmann & Phillips, 2004). These concerns have encouraged research into various sorts of subcultures (Hofstede et al., 2010; Lenartowicz & Johnson, 2003; Peterson & van Iterson, in press). Other methodological criticisms associated with these studies are that even in those using the largest number of countries, the number of countries studied is quite small for sophisticated data analysis techniques. And, studies of societal culture face ongoing questions about whether or not the dimensions they describe are clearly distinct from one another (Dorfman & Howell, 1988; Maznevski et al., 1993). For example, Hofstede's power distance and individualism measures have large, negative correlations; the 18 GLOBE measures have a complex pattern of correlations that is hard to interpret; the Schwartz measures are sometimes presented as seven and sometimes as two or three orientations. Despite these limitations and differences in the way in which the studies were designed and conducted, there is overall support for these approaches.

One of the important limitations to models of cultural values is that they generally are not appropriate for understanding the personal values of individuals. As indicated in Box 3.1, country averages of people's answers to survey questions provide the basis for measures of country cultural values, which are good indicators of many aspects of the contexts that shape the way that individuals think. However, managers should avoid losing sight of the unique personal values that each individual in a society adopts. For example, personal values are likely to be especially important in situations where managers carefully think about their own values when they seek to make important decisions. Several measures of the personal values of individuals appear in the culture literature. These measures have been developed using the Kluckhohn and Strodtbeck framework and are regularly used for management training (Maznevski, DiStefano, Gomez, Noorderhaven, & Wu, 2002). Many measures of personal-value dimensions have been inspired by Hofstede's country culture dimensions (Kirkman, Lowe, & Gibson, 2006; Farh, Hackett, Liang, 2007). These personal-value dimensions tend to emphasize one or another aspect of the country culture characteristics from which they are named. Hofstede's societal-culture dimensions have also been found to be correlated with country means derived from the questions used to form the major *Big Five* dimensions of personality (Hofstede & McCrae, 2004). Also, the Schwartz Value Survey was originally presented as representing 10 domains of personal values (Schwartz & Bilsky, 1990) until data from enough countries became available to create valid country culture scores. These original 10 measures of personal values are now often reduced to two personal-value dimensions for most research and application in management (Brett, 2007; Fischer Vauclair, Fontaine, & Schwartz, 2010), in part because of the relatively low reliability of the 10 domains when used to create separate measures (Ralston, Egri et al., 2011). Also, the questions used to develop the two social axioms dimensions for describing countries that are described in this chapter are used to develop five axioms for analyzing personal values (Leung, Bond, et al., 2002). In the sources of guidance project, the same eight sources can be used to understand the sources that individual managers use as well as the sources that are most emphasized in different countries (Smith et al., 2011). However, at the individual level they are more clearly distinct from one another (less strongly intercorrelated) than they are at the country level. Whereas individualism and collectivism are often found to be at the extremes of one dimension at the country level for reasons described in Box 3.1, a larger range of measures is often distinguishable at the individual level (Triandis, 1995). In subsequent chapters, we draw on cognitive psychology to understand the influence that societal culture has on managers and the individuals with whom managers work.

Use of the Frameworks

The significance of being able to systematically define cultural variations is that it then provides a first rough approximation for explaining and predicting behavior on a comparative basis. However, the ability to profile national cultures along a limited number of dimensions also opens up the possibility for a dramatic oversimplification of the effect of culture. The scholars who designed these studies do not suggest that knowledge of culture dimensions is sufficient for a manager to function fully in an unfamiliar society (Hofstede, 2006; House et al., 2004). Because of the practical limitations in being able to solve all of the research design challenges to cross-cultural research that are described in Chapter 1, much cross-cultural management research relies on overly simplistic models of the effect of culture. This oversimplification sometimes results in stating that people from this particular type of culture behave this way, whereas those from that other type of culture behave like that. Often, this is done by referring to an existing typology of attributes of national culture. In effect, instead of using cultural dimensions as a constructive starting point for understanding other cultures, they can be misused to construct so-called *sophisticated* stereotypes of a culture that are substituted for the complex reality that exists (Osland & Bird, 2000). In this way they can have the opposite effect of constraining the way in which managers regard the individuals they encounter from another culture. For example, we run the risk of thinking of all Japanese people as personally accepting value orientations that are high on *masculinity* and *uncertainty avoidance*, low on *individualism*, and moderate on *power distance*. Although Japanese people will have extensive experience living in a society that has these characteristics, they may or may not personally value some or all aspects of their society. The fallacy of making personal value attributions based on societal values is apparent to anyone who has encountered behavior in members of another culture that is inconsistent with the picture painted by the profile. These seeming paradoxes between cultural patterns and individual characteristics can often be explained when the situational context or cultural history of a particular country is considered (Osland & Bird, 2000).

Subsequent chapters of this book present a more sophisticated way of thinking about cultural influences on individuals. However, these problems do not render the systematic description of cultural variation useless. On the contrary, they can be valuable in selecting national cultures to compare when trying to assess the degree of similarity or difference on responses to particular management questions. In addition, they are useful tools, both for researchers and managers, as long as their limitations are understood. The following conditions are a concise summary of the care that should be taken when using descriptions of cultures based on a limited number of dimensions, so-called cultural stereotypes:

- They should be consciously held, that is, we recognize that we are dealing with limited information.
- They should be limited to describing members of the other cultural group and not contain an evaluative component.
- They should provide an accurate description of the behavioral norm of the cultural group.
- They should be used as a first best guess about the behavior of a cultural group prior to developing direct information about individuals in the group.
- They should be modified based on additional information gained about the group through observation or experience. (Adler, 1997)

The underlying rationale for these simple *rules of thumb* becomes more apparent as a more sophisticated understanding of the influence of culture in relation to the characteristics of individuals is developed.

Summary

This chapter presents the main attempts at systematically describing variations in national culture. However, other interesting ways of characterizing cultures can be found in books designed to be helpful to managers. For example, Gannon and Pillai (2010) present a qualitative rather than statistical analysis of different societies based on central cultural metaphors such as "the Turkish coffeehouse" and "the Brazilian samba." Our understanding of cultural differences is influenced largely by studies of national differences in values and a high degree of consistency is found in the structure of values across cultures. Each of the frameworks presented in this chapter offers useful ways to systematically describe the ways that national cultures might differ. The most frequently studied is individualism versus collectivism. Refinements of this dimension, such as consideration of vertical and horizontal elements, might make it more useful in defining the dominant cultural profiles in the world. Improved measures of some dimensions, such as long-term orientation and ways of updating potentially outdated country scores, are being developed. Research programs are emerging to provide culture dimension scores for within-nation regions and subcultures to refine country culture dimension scores (Gironda & Peterson, in press; Peterson & Van Iterson, in press). Recent research, involving generalized beliefs (social axioms) and role relationships, promises to broaden the array of conceptual tools available to assess cultural variation. Our ability to systematically describe cultural variation is a necessary but limited first step in understanding the effect of culture on management behavior.

Questions for Discussion

1. Discuss the similarities and differences of the major dimensional approaches to societal culture as described by Kluckhohn and Strodtbeck, Hofstede, the Schwartz Value Survey, and Trompenaars.

2. How do the ideas of social axioms and culture as a source of guidance help us understand national culture beyond cultural value dimensions?

3. How does cultural tightness or looseness relate to the concepts of individualism and collectivism?

4. Explain the concept of cultural distance.

5. How should the cultural frameworks be used?

4

How Culture Works: Fundamentals of Cross-Cultural Interaction

"What kind of bird are you, if you can't sing?" chirped the bird.
"What kind of bird are you, if you can't swim?" quacked the duck.

Prokofiev in "Peter and the Wolf"

As described in Chapter 3, much of the written work about international management identifies variations in national culture and then describes the implications of this cultural variation for a wide range of behaviors and organizational issues. Identifying cultural variation is important, especially when making strategic plans and managing large groups. For example, it can help predict whether large groups such as employees of a foreign manufacturing plant are likely to respond to a management practice in the same way as employees in the country where the practice was developed. When working with other individuals, it also can help a manager anticipate what aspects of culture a foreign colleague is likely to take for granted and what aspects the manager himself or herself is likely to misunderstand when working abroad. To understand how best to work with other individuals, however, societal culture dimensions provide only a first step. This approach alone does not do justice to the influence of culture because it does not identify precisely how *awareness* of cultural differences and *knowledge* about another particular culture affect the interactions between people from different societies. In this book we suggest that culture manifests its influence through a number of intermediate psychological and interpersonal mechanisms. These mechanisms involve how managers think about, evaluate, and respond to people who are culturally different.

Sometimes societal culture characteristics are linked to individuals by analyzing the personal values that individuals endorse and suggesting that these personal values reflect societal cultures (as well as other personal experiences of the individual). This treats individual values as similar to personality traits or attitudes. Consistent with the discussion in Chapter 1 that roles and role relationships are at the core of a manager's job, the focus of the approach in this book is different. Rather than focus on the value characteristics of individuals, in this chapter we explore the mechanisms through which culture influences managers and their work relationships. We do so by examining how people think about their interactions, their *social cognition*, when they work with others from cultures different from their own. These mechanisms are then summarized in a general model of cultural influence on management behavior. In addition, this chapter examines how culturally based self-concepts influence the motives of individuals from different societies. The goal of the chapter is to outline a framework for cultural influence that can then be applied to a range of cross-cultural management issues.

Social Cognition

Our understanding of how culture influences behavior in organizations is grounded in the idea of social cognition. Social cognition explains how we develop mental representations and how our mental representations influence the way we process information about people and social events. Stored in these mental representations are the specific features that define an object, event, or situation and the rules defining their interrelationships (Markus & Zajonc, 1985). These representations are called *schemas* when they define a category or *scripts* when they contain a behavioral sequence. These cognitive structures are derived from our past experiences and are simple representations of the complex concepts that they represent. They help us reduce the complexity of our environment to a manageable number of categories. For example, *fish* defines the category that contains *salmon*, but it does not perfectly describe a salmon. Once formed, these categories are used in future information processing. That is, we *chunk* information in order to facilitate later recall (Miller, 1956). For example, our knowledge of the features of the category *fish* can be used to infer information about all kinds of fish.

In international management, we are most concerned with the effect of the categorization of persons, particularly regarding their culture. The categorization of persons operates in the same way as the categorization of other aspects of the environment and occurs because of our inability to process all the complexity presented by our surroundings (Wilder, 1978). Box 4.1 provides an example of the basic categorization process.

Box 4.1 Basic Categorization Process

People develop cognitive structures that help them organize and process information efficiently. These structures consist of categories (called schemas) that develop slowly over time through repeated experiences with objects, people, and situations. Schemas are like pigeonholes into which mail is sorted in a nonautomated post office. Each hole might be labeled with the last three digits of a postal code. As letters are sorted, the post office worker does not have to read the name or street address on the letter or even look at the city of the address. The sorter need only glance at the last three digits of the code, and the letter can be sorted into the appropriate pigeonhole. The information processing demands on the sorters are greatly reduced, and letters can be sorted more quickly. Letters that do not have postal codes or whose last three digits don't match any of the pigeonhole labels are likely to be thrown into the dead letter bin or placed into a special location, where they are dealt with later.

SOURCE: Adapted from Shaw, J. B. (1990). A cognitive categorization model for the study of intercultural management. *Academy of Management Review, 15*(4), 626–645.

Cultural Schemas

Schemas shape what people associate with everything from simple everyday aspects of life, such as the image that the word fish brings to mind, to social groups, such as a family, and even to abstract ideas, such as quality music. These schemas are affected by culture (Smith & Peterson, 1988). For example, the idea of a fish to people in a fishing society will be accompanied by a complex set of mental pictures of different kinds of fish and fishing situations.

One kind of schema that is particularly helpful for understanding intercultural interactions is the self-schema (Markus, 1977). Individuals have an inner or private self that consists of thoughts and feelings that cannot be directly known by others (Markus & Kitayama, 1991). The characteristics that people associate with the inner self can include personally significant personality traits like competent, attractive, irritable, or conscientious. Self-schemas also include memories associated with personal experiences that people see as having shaped who they are as individuals. Self-schemas are quite detailed, since all people have extensive experience with themselves. However, even self-schemas are simplifications, since we are only partially aware of everything about ourselves. Some aspects of the inner self are probably universal (e.g., I am hungry), but others can be specific to different cultures (e.g., my soul will be reincarnated) because of a culturally shared understanding of what it means to be human (Triandis, 1989).

People in all cultures develop an understanding of themselves as physically distinct and separate from others (Hallowell, 1955), but some characteristics of the inner self differ between societies in ways that influence cross-cultural interactions.

Notable among these is the extent to which people regard themselves as independent or separate from others or as interdependent or connected with others (Markus & Kitayama, 1991). An *independent self-schema* is typical in Western cultures in which people are expected to think and act as autonomous individuals with unique attributes. In such societies, a person's behavior is expected to be organized and made meaningful based on the person's own internal thoughts and feelings. As noted in Chapter 3, this concept of self is typical of people who are brought up in individualistic cultures (Triandis, 1995). In contrast, for people who have adopted an *interdependent self-schema*, their individuality is less differentiated and more connected to a particular group of other people. For such individuals, behavior is influenced by, contingent on, and to a large extent, organized by their perception of the thoughts, feelings, and actions of others in some larger social unit (Markus & Kitayama, 1991). An interdependent self-schema is typical of people raised in collectivist cultures. For example, the word for self in Japanese, *jibun,* refers to one's share of the life space (Hamaguchi, 1985).

A number of culturally specific conceptions of self can exist partly because interdependent self-schemas can be based on different reference groups (e.g., extended family, neighborhood, school friends, nation). As with definitions of the cultural value orientations of societies, it is a convenient simplification to think of people as maintaining one of two types of self-schemas: independent and interdependent. Certainly, some people raised in individualistic societies wish for a sense of community, while some people in collectivist societies find themselves overwhelmed by their social obligations. Adopting an independent or interdependent self-schema, however, is not simply a matter of personal choice that is readily changed. Brain imaging research suggests that particular sections of the brain are activated differently by some tasks and social situations depending on whether a person has been socialized in a culture that supports independent or interdependent self-schemas (Kitayama & Uskul, 2011). Perhaps in the future we will understand the process that a person goes through to develop the schemas and scripts needed to successfully do business in a broad variety of cultures.

Cultural Identity

As in the post office example in Box 4.1, we often sort ourselves and others into groups that separate members from nonmembers (Turner, 1987). We categorize ourselves and others in terms of characteristics that group members share, such as physical appearance, religion, political views, lifestyle, and country of origin. These schemas also include information about the attitudes and behaviors associated with their members. The total of the social categories that people use to describe themselves is their social identity. Individuals differ in the relative importance of the different components of their social identity. As noted in Chapter 3, people from individualist and collectivist societies can differ in how firmly they distinguish between who is and who is not a member of their group. However, for all of us, one of the groups that forms part of who we are, our social identity, is our cultural group.

Through the assignment of a set of characteristics to a particular national culture label, we create a schema for that nationality. To the extent that culture is consistent with these more directly observable characteristics, we are also categorizing them according to their cultural group. The systematic description of national cultures described in Chapter 3 is one such form of categorization. However, the most important aspect of categorizing others can be whether or not they belong to our own cultural group. This categorization of others and ourselves results in a sense of who we are and how we should act toward others (Tajfel, 1981). It is this categorization of our social environment into *them* and *us* that underlies much of the discussion in this chapter.

Cultural Scripts and Norms

Scripts are largely unconscious mental representations that shape how we think and act in a given situation (Abelson, 1981; Gioia & Poole, 1984). Unlike schemas, scripts are concerned with how a sequence of events will unfold and how we adjust our actions appropriately (Lord & Kernan, 1987; Markus & Zajonc, 1985). People rely on scripts to guide behavior when some new situation matches similar situations with which they have had extensive prior experience. Each person's scripts are based on the experiences that they have had in the cultures with which they have had the most involvement. Consequently, scripts can create confusion in cross-cultural interactions because people often take for granted the scripts that they have formed from experience with different cultures.

Evidence for the influence of culturally based scripts has been found in work group interactions (Thomas, Ravlin, & Wallace, 1996) and negotiator behavior (Brett, 2007) but likely exist for numerous business situations. For example, managers from the U.S. culture might have a script for attending a business meeting that includes arriving on time (or a little early), engaging in brief pleasantries with others before rapidly getting down to business, pressing one's point of view during the meeting, and arriving at a decision. For U.S. people, attending a business meeting invokes the behavioral sequence just described without much active thought. For members of other cultures, attending a business meeting might evoke a very different sequence of behaviors.

When individuals find themselves in these familiar situations, they follow an action plan or behavioral sequence more or less automatically, but careful attention is needed when something interferes with scripted behavior. In the meeting example, when people having different cultural backgrounds work together, differences in the scripts that they follow can create confusion about the sequence of events, the duration of each phase of the meeting, and the cues about switching from one stage of the meeting to the next. Cultural differences in scripts mean that unexpected events will occur that will require all those attending the meeting to make thoughtful rather than spontaneous adjustments.

Schemas and scripts influence each another. The categorization of one's self and others into groups and identifying with a group influences the scripts that are applied. One result of identifying with a particular cultural group is consciously seeking to adopt its norms. Cultural norms, like other norms, are acceptable standards of behavior that are shared by members of our cultural group. Norms tell us what to expect from others and what is expected of us in certain situations. Although individuals can vary in the extent to which they adopt them, the norms of groups with which we identify have a powerful influence on our behavior (Asch, 1951). In fact, continued acceptance as a member in our cultural group often requires that we exhibit socially acceptable or at least politically correct behavior. For example, the somewhat derogatory terms *Oreo*[1] or *banana* are sometimes used by blacks or Asians to describe a person as black or yellow on the outside but white on the inside. This reflects a belief that these people hold attitudes or exhibit behavior inconsistent with the norms of their ethnic group and therefore do not really belong.

As discussed in Chapter 3, cultures vary along identifiable dimensions that reflect the value orientations of society. These cultural value orientations provide a generalized way of thinking about a much larger number of specific societal norms that are helpful for knowing what to expect and how to behave in a given society. Just understanding the norms of a society, however, is insufficient to explain and predict cross-cultural interactions. Not all societal norms are enforced in all situations, and part of a manager's role is to judge when different norms are most relevant for their actions. Social groups only enforce norms if and when they perform one of the following functions:

- *Facilitate the group's survival, for example, by protecting them from other groups*
- *Increase the predictability of group member's behavior*
- *Reduce embarrassment for group members*
- *Express the central values of the group, that is, clarify the group's identity* (Goodman, Ravlin, & Schminke, 1987)

Therefore, an individual's behavior is influenced by the cultural norms of society but only to the extent that a norm exists for a particular situation and for which societal sanctions for noncompliance exist. Also, societal norms having different historical origins can be applied in different situations within the same society. For example, the very high level of charitable giving that is characteristic of people in the United States seems inconsistent with their norm for self-reliance. Although self-reliance might be a central value, the cultural history of the United States as a pioneer society also suggests a norm for helping others in community projects and emergencies (see Osland & Bird, 2000). In addition, as discussed ahead in more detail, norms can be more important predictors of behavior in collectivist than in individualist cultures.

We should expect cultural differences in the content of behavioral scripts for a particular situation because they can be guided by culturally differing norms (Miller, 1994). Because scripts are learned, members of one's cultural group can pass them on and reinforce them. An example of a culturally based normative script is that most Chinese are strongly influenced to be respectful and obedient to superiors *when* they are present or even indirectly involved in a work situation (Liu, 1986). That is, the situational cue of the involvement of superiors automatically invokes respectful and obedient behavior. Therefore, much of our behavior and the behavior that we observe in others is a semireflexive response to the situation influenced by cultural norms. How we respond to this behavior depends, in part, on our ability to perceive it.

Selective Perception

Perception is the process by which individuals interpret the messages received from their senses and thereby give meaning to their environment. As suggested previously, at any one time, the environment presents us with much more information than we can effectively deal with. Therefore, we screen out much of what is presented to us by our senses. What is perceived and what is screened out are influenced by the characteristics of the perceiver, the person (or object) being perceived, and the situation. A perceiver has goals that focus attention on information that will help meet those goals. For example, subordinates awaiting instructions attend to the words of their superior. A perceiver also can be distracted by cues to which they are not attending. For example, fire alarms (at least momentarily) catch everyone's attention. Objects that are in some sense extreme or distracting receive attention. Being in the work place prepares people for work-related information that they might disregard in the home setting. Those aspects of the environment that a person perceives are shaped by the schemas and scripts that they habitually use.

Research on perception has consistently found that different people can be presented with the same stimulus and perceive it differently (e.g., Dearborn & Simon, 1958). Of particular importance to international management are differences in the way people from different cultures perceive events and each other. Does culture influence which stimulus receives attention and which does not? Different priorities for what stimuli we should attend to are formed by the gradual internalization of prevailing cultural patterns (Markus & Kitayama, 1991; Miller, Bersoff, & Harwood, 1990). As we are socialized into a particular cultural group, we learn how to perceive. We share certain expectations and understandings of situations. For example, Mexican and U.S. children, when presented simultaneously (using a tachioscope) with pictures of a bullfight and a baseball game, perceived the event differently. The Mexican children recalled only the bullfight, whereas the U.S. children recalled only the baseball game (Bagby, 1957). These two cultural groups had *learned* to attend to particular stimuli. Anyone observing an unfamiliar sporting event for the first time can attest to selective perception. Unless you are Australian, Aussie rules football is probably a mystery to you, and people from other than the United States have more difficulty picking out the many subtleties of a baseball game. This selective perception also extends to social situations. For example, Forgas and Bond (1985) reported that Chinese and Australian participants were found to differ in their perceptions of 27 identical social episodes (a recurring interaction sequence about which people generally agree, such as meeting someone for lunch or visiting a doctor).

When we perceive people as opposed to objects or events, a key element of our perception is whether a person is categorized as a member of our in-group or an out-group member. A number of factors seem to influence the extent to which we categorize others as a member of our group or not (Smith et al., 2013).

- First, certain category indicators, such as race and gender, may be universal indicators of group membership.

- Second, the distinctiveness of the category indicator against the social field may be a primary categorization factor if, for example, the number of distinctively different others is small. For example, Anglo-Europeans are obvious in rural Japan.
- Third, the extent to which a person is prototypical of a particular group influences categorization into that group. Atypical persons are harder to categorize.
- Fourth, deviations from normal speech in terms of accent, syntax, or grammar are particularly salient cues for group membership. The most dramatic speech difference is, of course, the use of a foreign language.
- Finally, a history of interactions with another group will enhance the ability to categorize them. For example, our attention is heightened with groups with whom we have had a history of conflict.

An important effect of categorization of others as out-group members is that once categorized they are subsequently perceived as being more similar to each other than are in-group members (Linville, Fischer, & Salovey, 1989). We see the individual variation that occurs in our own cultural group but perceive other cultures as homogeneous. For example, to non-Japanese, all Japanese people might seem very similar in appearance and behavior.

Selective perception also depends on the characteristics of what is being perceived. We tend to pay more attention to information that is distinctive (Rubin, 1915) or somehow inconsistent with our expectations (McGuire & Padawer-Singer, 1976). Behavior somehow "out of place" or uncharacteristic of the other culture will be recalled more accurately. Still another way in which information presented by our environment is filtered is through *selective avoidance*. When confronted with information contrary to our existing views, we "tune it out" by diverting our attention elsewhere (Kavanaugh, 1991).

Therefore, as discussed previously, cultural differences can influence perception in several ways. First, we are socialized by our culture to perceive things in a particular way. Second, we tend to have better recall of information inconsistent with our culturally based expectations but also tend to filter out this information if it is incompatible with our views. Finally, we perceive members of other cultures to be more similar to each other than members of our own cultural group.

Perceived Similarity and Attraction

The perceptual bias about our own versus other cultural groups, noted previously, has an additional implication for cross-cultural interactions. Perceptions of similarity lead to interpersonal attraction (Byrne, 1971). Essentially, we are attracted to people whom we perceive to be similar to us, because this similarity validates our view of the world and the way it should be. We look to others to obtain what is called consensual validation (Festinger, 1957). When someone agrees with us, this agreement validates our view and provides *evidence* that we are correct. Disagreement has just the opposite effect. Several decades of research supports the idea that similarity, particularly attitude and status similarity, leads to interpersonal attraction.

Other aspects of similarity, such as communication style (Lee & Gudykunst, 2001), religion and race (Kandel, 1978), national culture (Thomas & Ravlin, 1995), age (Ellis, Rogoff, & Cramer, 1981), and even the preference for particular activities (Lydon, Jamieson, & Zanna, 1988) can also predict interpersonal attraction. In fact, we might be biologically programmed to respond positively to similarity of all kinds (Rushton, 1989).

Similarity can also influence other aspects of interpersonal interaction. For example, demographic similarity is related to increased frequency of communication and friendship ties (Lincoln & Miller, 1979) and frequency of technical communication (Zenger & Lawrence, 1989). Therefore, regardless of our other perceptual biases, the extent to which other individuals are perceived as similar to us influences our attitudes and behavior toward them. Essentially, other things being equal, perceptions of similarity predict more positive interactions.

The mechanisms that lead to selectively perceiving others are based on learning to perceive in a certain way because of socialization in a culture. However, these mechanisms also rely on some expectation of how people outside our own culture will behave. As discussed in the following section, these expectations about culturally different others are often based on very limited information.

Stereotypic Expectations

Stereotypes are closely related to the idea of schemas and are a categorization of the characteristics and behavior of a set of individuals (Ashmore & Del Boca, 1981). That is, stereotypic expectations of a cultural group are a result of the natural cognitive process of social categorization described earlier. These expectations are based on simplifying the plethora of information provided by our environment. Stereotypes need not be negative or noxious, although the term *stereotype* often conjures up negative images because of its linkage to prejudice (Allport, 1954) and the fact that stereotypes invariably include feelings about the cultural group as well as expected behavior.

National Stereotypes

Early research on stereotypes indicated that people could hold intense stereotypes about other national cultures even though they had never met a person from that culture (Katz & Braly, 1933). However, these cultural stereotypes are often associated with other groups with which one's culture has had a long history (often a negative history) of association. One has only to observe the fans at a soccer match between England and Scotland or at a rugby game between New Zealand and Australia to get a sense of the intensity of feelings associated with national stereotypes. The rest of the world might see Australia and New Zealand or Scotland and England as similar to each other. However, nationals of those countries will be quick to point out significant differences. The suggestion, made in previous chapters, that we can categorize cultures based on a limited number of dimensions is a form of national stereotyping. This presents us with a simple, some would say overly simple, representation of a cultural group. However, as noted at the conclusion of Chapter 3, these *on average* cultural expectations can be useful if we are aware of the influence of stereotyping.

Stereotypes are based on very limited information about others. We use very basic physical or social evidence (i.e., skin tone or country of birth) to categorize people and to organize information about them (Taylor, 1981). And once this categorization has occurred, we apply the stereotype to the same degree to each individual in the category (Allport, 1954). For example, if I have had little or no contact with Chinese people, my stereotype might consist almost entirely of information gained from secondary sources, such as films or television. And, I expect all Chinese people to behave in this way. The opportunity for inaccuracy in my expectation of typical Chinese behavior, as shown in Figure 4.1, is obvious.

Resistance to New Information

As noted previously, once we categorize an individual as a member of a category, such as a culture, the associated information about the category is applied to them. And once formed, these stereotypic expectations of others tend to become self-perpetuating (Snyder, 1981). We reconstruct information about the social category (culture) to be consistent with our stereotype and behave toward members of the culture in ways that confirm our expectations. New information about a member of the culture is often discounted as not representative, thereby maintaining the stereotype (Hamilton, 1979). For example, when confronted with a Japanese businessperson who exhibits a very Western behavior of using an informal greeting, we discount this individual as being atypical and still maintain our stereotypic expectation that Japanese businesspeople are formal.

Stereotype Complexity and Evaluation

Because stereotypes are learned, we tend to have more complex (more and better-organized information) stereotypes about social categories with which we have more

---

Figure 4.1   Stereotypic Expectations

SOURCE: Larry Feign. Copyright © 1985. Used with permission.

familiarity (Fiske & Taylor, 1984). Therefore, because we have the most familiarity with our own culture, we have more complex mental pictures of that culture than we do of other cultures (Peterson & Wood, 2008). This leads to the expectation of more variability in behavior in our own culture than in others, as previously noted. However, it also results in differences in our evaluation of new information about that culture. New information about a social group for which we have a very simple stereotype (e.g., another culture) is evaluated more extremely (more positively if the information is positive and more negatively if the information is negative) than for groups for which we have a more complex picture. For example, in a study of identically qualified law students of two different ethnic groups, members of the evaluator's own ethnic group were evaluated less extremely (Linville & Jones, 1980). Therefore, the more information we have about a cultural group, the more likely we are to accept (evaluate accurately) new information about them. Interestingly, bicultural individuals (see Chapters 2 and 11) seem to have more complex cultural representations of both their cultures, as compared to monocultural individuals in each (Benet-Martínez, Lee, & Leu, 2006). This suggests that significant exposure to another culture may increase an individual's ability to detect, process, and organize cultural information in general.

Social Dominance

National stereotypes might also ascribe to what is called social dominance theory (Sidanius, 1993; Smith et al., 2013). Social dominance theory suggests that within every complex society certain groups are dominant over others and enjoy a disproportionate amount of privilege. Similarly at a global level, there might be a generally accepted hierarchy of nationalities based on status. High status can be attached to a particular nation because of economic dominance or other desirable characteristics. According to this idea, the extent to which my national group is high status will influence the attitude of others toward it and my attachment to it. For example, nationals of less developed countries might hold U.S. nationals in high esteem because of the level of economic development of the United States, or people from countries plagued by ethnic violence might accord high status to Canadians because of Canada's reputation for tolerance.

As discussed previously, the usefulness of stereotypic expectations about members of another culture is thus limited by the following:

- The extent to which these mental pictures contain accurate information
- Our recognition that either positive or negative feelings about the cultural group are invariably attached to the stereotype
- Our ability to adjust our expectations based on new information about the group

An example of an effective use of a stereotype in international business is presented in Box 4.2.

Box 4.2 Use of Cultural Stereotypes

In meetings between U.S. and Mexican businessmen, each had an accurate stereotypic expectation about the other's orientation toward time. Both agreed that Mexicans were *polychronic* or had a *mañana* orientation, with a flexible perspective on time. Both also agreed that Americans were *monochronic* (take time constraints and deadlines seriously). This agreement allowed the groups to reach a compromise on how to manage time, but only after they understood why each group held the expectation that they did.

SOURCE: Lee & Duenas, "Stereotype Accuracy in Multicultural Business," in *Stereotype Accuracy: Toward Appreciating Group Differences*. Copyright © 1995, American Psychological Association. Reprinted with permission of the American Psychological Association.

In this example, accurate stereotypes were helpful but not sufficient to achieve an effective intercultural interaction. It was also important to understand why the cultural groups behaved as they did. That is, they needed to make a judgment as to the cause of the behavior. As discussed ahead, social categorization of cultural groups also influences the way in which the causes of behavior are evaluated.

Differential Attributions

Attribution helps us to understand and react to our environment by linking the observation of an event to its causes. The search for and assignment of cause for behavior seems to be a mental process that operates in much the same way across cultures (Schuster, Fosterlung, & Weiner, 1989). Any number of causes might be assigned to behavior we observe. However, the central distinction is between factors that are internal to the individual (personality, cultural values) and factors external to the individual (Trope, 1986). Internally caused behaviors are those under the control of the individual, and externally controlled behaviors are forced on the person by the situation. In order to attribute behavior, we rely on cues from the situation that indicate the extent to which individuals are in control, such as whether or not the behavior is distinctive to a situation, consistent over time, and if the same behavior is displayed in similar situations (Kelley, 1972).

Inconclusive Information

Sometimes, however, the situational cues that we rely on to make attributions are inconclusive. Not all behavior is unambiguous about its cause. In cases in which our observations do not clearly indicate to us the cause of behavior, we rely on information we already have about the individual to make a judgment (Darley & Fazio, 1980). In cross-cultural interactions, we might rely on our stereotypic expectations of another culture to fill in the gaps (e.g., people from the United States will behave in their own self-interest). In other cases, we can project our own behavior on the situation (e.g., what would cause *me* to behave that way). In either case, cultural differences influence the process. In the first case, our cultural-based expectations of an out-group member influence our attribution. In the second, our own culturally based behavioral norms or scripts influence our judgment of causality. Box 4.3 provides an example of making an inappropriate attribution for the behavior of a member of another culture.

Box 4.3 Attribution to Internal Cause

Helen Conner had been working in a Japanese company involved in marketing cameras for 2 years and was well respected by her colleagues. In fact, she was so respected that she was often asked to work with new employees of the firm as these younger employees learned the ropes. Recently, one young employee, Hideo Tanaka, was assigned to develop a marketing scheme for a new model camera. He worked quite hard on it, but the scheme was not accepted by his superiors because of industry-wide economic conditions. Helen and Hideo happened to be working at desks near each other when the company executive transmitted the news of the scheme's nonacceptance. Hideo said very little at that point. That evening, however, Helen and Hideo happened to be at the same bar. Hideo had been drinking, and he vigorously criticized his superiors at work. Helen concluded that Hideo was a very aggressive Japanese male and that she would have difficulty working with him again in the future.

SOURCE: Cushner & Brislin (1996). Reprinted with permission of SAGE Publications, Inc.

In this case, Helen has made an attribution (to his character) for Hideo's behavior based on information she held in memory (the projection of her own society's norms for behavior under the same circumstances) because the situation did not clearly indicate to her the cause of his behavior.

Attribution Error

Attribution of the cause of behavior is also influenced by whether or not the behavior is being exhibited by a member of our own cultural group. Again, the social categorization of our environment is at work. Because we derive part of our self-identity from our association with our cultural group, we are favorably biased toward that group. Therefore, we are more likely to attribute desirable behaviors by members of our in-group to internal causes but more likely to attribute desirable behaviors of out-group members to transient external causes (Hewstone, 1990). If members of our cultural group exhibit positive behavior (perform well on a task for example) we are more likely to attribute that behavior to their ability or effort. In contrast, when we observe the same behavior by members of another cultural group, we are more likely to attribute it to luck or other favorable circumstances. Research with several different cultural groups has supported this group-serving bias in attributions (e.g., Al-Zahrani & Kaplowitz, 1993; Taylor & Jaggi, 1974), which is called "the ultimate attribution error" (Pettigrew, 1979). Biased belief systems about members of one's own national culture are pervasive and extend, for example, to favoritism for products coming from one's own country, the so-called country-of-origin effect (Peterson & Jolibert, 1995) mentioned in Chapter 2.

Cultural Differences in Attribution Bias

Until recently, psychologists thought that the general tendency of people to attribute any behavior to characteristics about the individual and underestimate the effects of the situation, the so-called *fundamental attribution error* (Ross, 1977), was consistent across cultures. However, this effect is much more difficult to find in Asian as compared to North American or European populations (Choi, Nisbett, & Norenzayan, 1999). For example, Miller (1984) found that Indians preferred to explain life events in terms of the situational context while Americans were more likely to explain the same events in terms of individual characteristics. And, Chinese people have been found to be more likely to explain murders in terms of situational or societal factors, whereas Americans were more likely to explain murders in terms of characteristics of the perpetrators (Morris & Peng, 1994). This is not to say that Asians do not attribute behavior to individuals, but they may be less likely to be biased in that regard.

Also, despite the strong evidence in support of a universal in-group bias effect discussed previously, some variation across cultures may exist. For example, in some cases, it might not be possible for a group to find a positive basis on which to compare itself with others (Tajfel, 1981). Also, in cultures characterized by vertical collectivism, disadvantaged groups might accept as legitimate the higher status of other groups (Smith & Bond, 1999). In addition, people from individualist and collectivist societies may not engage in inter-group comparisons to the same degree (Hinkle & Brown, 1990). Collectivists might not be as interested in comparing themselves with out-groups and instead focus on their in-group (Triandis, 1994). Individualists, by contrast, might make more comparisons but also make a distinction between groups with which they do and do not compare themselves (Smith et al., 2013).

As outlined previously, our interactions with culturally different others depend, in part, on how we attribute the cause of their behavior. Cultural differences influence this attribution through the meaning that we give to the situational cues presented and the expectations that we have for behavior in the other culture. In most cases, we can expect differences in the attributions for the behavior of members of our own culture versus members of other cultures.

Cross-Cultural Interaction Model

In the preceding section, several mechanisms through which culture can be seen to influence behavior were identified. To suggest more specifically how this influence occurs, it is helpful to examine the actions and reactions that might comprise a cross-cultural encounter. The following interaction sequence is typical of those that occur regularly in international management contexts. It highlights the effect of cultural differences on an interpersonal interaction. Inferences about the processes through which culture influences behavior can be made at each step of the interaction sequence.

The interaction presented in Figure 4.2 assumes as a starting point some behavior of a person from another culture. The person might behave according to some culturally based script for the situation or, because of some expectation about how their behavior will be perceived, adjusts their behavior. There are an almost infinite number of situations in which a cross-cultural interaction might take place. However, many situations in business settings will be familiar. Situational cues determine the extent to which the situation evokes a preexisting behavioral sequence, a script. If a script does not exist for the situation, the individual will give more thought as to how to behave and how such behavior might be perceived.

Next, the person perceiving the behavior interprets the meaning of these actions. This interpretation consists of two stages. The first is the identification of the behavior.

Figure 4.2 Cross-Cultural Interaction

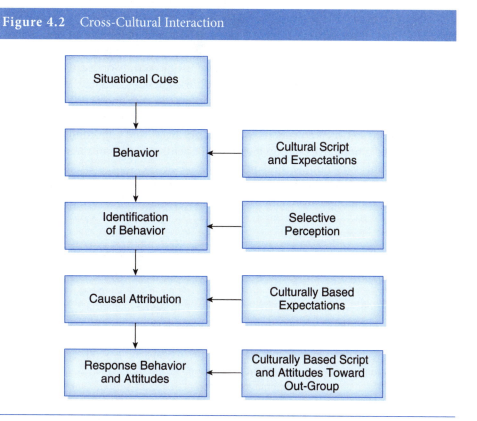

SOURCES: Based on Shaw (1990) and Thomas (1992).

This identification can, as discussed in this chapter, be influenced by culturally biased selective perception. An important part of the identification of behavior is categorizing the other person as a member of another culture (out-group). This categorization is influenced by the extent to which the behavior being exhibited matches a preexisting expectation. Behavior consistent with expectations will result in an automatic categorization, whereas inconsistent information must be processed more thoroughly.

The second part of the function is attributing the behavior to a cause. This attribution is influenced by the culturally based expectations that the perceiver has for members of the other culture. The extent to which situational cues about the cause of the behavior exist and the relative development of the perceiver's mental representation of the other culture both influence the accuracy of the attribution. Individuals with very well-developed prior conceptions of another culture are likely to be less extreme and more accurate in their evaluation of behavior. In situations where the cues are ambiguous or provide little information, individuals will rely more heavily on information they already have to make a judgment. They must rely on stereotypic expectations of the other culture.

Finally, the perceiver's attitudes and behavioral response depend on how the behavior is attributed. To the extent that the attributions made are attributed to a familiar cause, the response behavior itself can be scripted. If, however, the behavior does not fit an existing category, the person might be unable to use an existing script to guide behavior and invent a new one. The reactive behavior starts another interaction sequence. The ability of people to adjust old scripts or create new ones is a significant part of having a successful cross-cultural encounter (Shaw, 1990) and becoming more competent in future cross-cultural interactions (Thomas, 2006).

This behavioral sequence plays itself out day after day in international organizations between coworkers, between managers and subordinates, between negotiators, and among work-group members. The situational context and the status of the participants vary, but the fundamentals of the interaction remain the same. Box 4.4 provides an example of how such a cross-cultural interaction sequence might proceed in an encounter between a manager and subordinate.

Box 4.4 Cross-Cultural Interaction Sequence

Todd works for an American company in Korea. Sometimes he wonders why he ever accepted a position overseas—there seems to be so much that he just doesn't understand. One incident in particular occurred the previous Friday when his secretary, Chungmin, made a mistake and forgot to type a letter. Todd considered this a small error but made sure to mention it when he saw her during lunch in the company cafeteria. Ever since then, Chungmin has been acting a bit strange and distant. When she walks out of his office, she closes the door more loudly than usual. She will not even look him in the eye, and she has been acting very moody. She even took a few days of sick leave, which she has not done in many years. Todd has no idea how to understand her behavior. Perhaps she really is ill or feels a bit overworked.

When Chungmin returns to work the following Wednesday, Todd calls her into his office. "Is there a problem?" he asks. "Because if there is, we need to talk about it. It's affecting your performance. Is something wrong? Why don't you tell me, it's okay."

At this, Chungmin looks quite distressed. She admits the problem has something to do with her mistake the previous Friday, and Todd explains that it was no big deal. "Forget it," he says, feeling satisfied with himself for working this out. "In the future, just make sure to tell me if something is wrong." But over the next few weeks, Chungmin takes 6 more sick days and does not speak to Todd once.

SOURCE: Cushner & Brislin (1996). Reprinted with permission of SAGE Publications, Inc.

The interaction in Box 4.4 is an example of misattributions by both parties and a subsequent escalation of the problem as one behavior sequence builds on the previous one. Todd's first mistake was in relying on a U.S.-based behavioral script for dealing with a Korean employee. Chungmin considered being reprimanded in public very rude and attributed this behavior to Todd's thoughtlessness. She responds by relying on a Korean script for expressing her displeasure through subtle cues. Todd fails to perceive these cues accurately (because he lacks a well-developed schema for Korean culture) and has difficulty making an attribution for Chungmin's behavior. He tries to solve the problem by having an open and frank discussion with Chungmin, another Western script that is not well received. Chungmin responds with more subtle cues.

The model presented in Figure 4.2 is, of course, a simplification that does not take into account other important aspects of an interpersonal interaction, such as the motives of the participants involved and other information-processing demands of the situation. This simplification allows the effect of culture through social cognition to be demonstrated.

Self-Schemas and Motivation

Motivation involves the reasons that people take or persist in a particular action as described in more detail in Chapter 7. Here we discuss the influence of differing self-schemas for motivation across cultures. Western explanations of motivation (e.g., equity theory, Adams, 1965; expectancy theory, Vroom, 1964) depend on the assumption that people will act in their own self-interest. However, culture guides choices by giving meaning and ascribing value to motivational variables. A society's cultural values both reflect an individual's needs and prescribe the behavior required to satisfy those needs (Erez & Earley, 1993). Therefore, we should expect that members of different cultures would respond to different motivating factors in their intercultural interactions. For example, for people from the United States, individual rewards might be central motivating factors, whereas this reward practice would have a negative effect in a culture that values equality and cooperation. Central to understanding the nature of motivation in different cultures is the way in which people define themselves, their self-concept.

The distinction between independent and interdependent self-schemas described at the beginning of the chapter has several motivational implications. First, those people with independent self-schemas will be motivated to express internal needs, rights, and the capacity to withstand undue social pressure (Janis & Mann, 1977). In contrast, those with interdependent self-schemas will be motivated to be receptive to others, to adjust to their needs, and to restrain their inner needs or desires (Markus & Kitayama, 1991). Moreover, people with interdependent (compared to those with independent self-schemas) report that their behavior is more influenced by contextual factors including norms (Singelis & Brown, 1995; Trafimow & Finlay, 1996). Consistent with this finding, social norms are found to be a more important determinant of behavior for people from collectivistic than from individualistic societies (Gelfand et al., 2011; Triandis, 1995).

One study of the motives of Chinese people (from collectivist societies) found high levels for the need to comply, socially oriented achievement, change, endurance, nurturance, and order; moderate levels for autonomy, deference, and dominance; and low levels of individually oriented achievement, aggression, exhibition, and power (Bond & Hwang, 1986). That is, the interdependent self-schemas of the Chinese were reflected in the average level of needs that people in these societies expressed. It can also be argued that differences in the self-schema lead to differences in the extent to which the reduction of cognitive conflict or dissonance is a motivator. Dissonance occurs when one says or acts one way in public but feels quite differently in private (Festinger, 1957). Such dissonance is often disturbing enough to people that they may reconsider their values to resolve it (Rokeach, 1968). If, as is the case for people with an interdependent self, one's internal attitudes and opinions are not a significant defining aspect of the self, there is little need to make these internal attitudes consistent with external behavior. For example, Americans have been found to be much more concerned with consistency between feelings and behavior than are Japanese (Doi, 1986). Furthermore, and as noted previously, these internal feelings should be regulated as required by the situation.

Finally, motives linked to the self, such as self-enhancement or self-verification, can assume a different form depending on the concept of self being enhanced or verified (Markus & Kitayama, 1991). The motive to maintain a positive self-image is probably universal. However, what constitutes a positive view of self depends on how the self is construed. For those with independent selves, feeling good about oneself means being unique and expressing one's inner attributes. For those with an interdependent self, a positive self-image is derived from belonging, fitting in, occupying one's proper place, engaging in appropriate action, and maintaining harmony.

In summary, cultural differences might be expected in motivation based on an individual's internal representation of self. Although all people might be motivated by self-interest, a fundamental difference is the role that others play in how people define themselves. That is, individuals are differentially motivated depending on whether they view themselves as independent of or interdependent with others. In intercultural interactions, this motivational difference influences behavior throughout the interaction sequence just described.

Summary

This chapter presented a more sophisticated approach to specifying the effects of culture on the behavior of individual managers that extends beyond the simple projection of cultural stereotypes. The basics of social cognition were applied to the context of cross-cultural interactions that are fundamental to management across cultures. By doing this, a number of mechanisms or conduits through which culture manifests its influence were identified. In addition to the effect that variations in national culture have on the normative behavior of individuals in that culture, several other influence mechanisms exist. These include the development of scripts for particular situations, culturally based selective perception of the behavior of others, and differential attributions for behavior founded in culturally based expectations. These mechanisms can be seen to operate in a basic interaction sequence that underlies the interpersonal interaction between culturally different individuals in a variety of organizational settings. This sequence of behavior-perception-attribution reaction is central to our understanding of intercultural interactions. However, it is important to recognize that motivational differences based on differing conceptualizations of the self can influence behavior throughout the interaction sequence. By understanding the basic mechanisms presented in this chapter, it is possible to develop a deeper understanding of the possible effect of culture on the wide variety of interpersonal interactions in which managers may be involved.

Questions for Discussion

1. What is social cognition? How are its main components affected by culture?

2. How do culturally stereotypic expectations affect other aspects of thought and behavior?

3. How do attribution differences associated with culture affect the way people draw conclusions?

4. How does culture affect each of the steps between noticing an event and responding to it?

5. Why are cultural differences in self-concept so important to motivation?

Note

1. An *Oreo* is a type of cookie (biscuit) with a white confectionary center sandwiched between two chocolate layers.

Part II

Roles of the Global Manager

5

The Manager as Decision Maker: Cross-Cultural Dimensions of Decision Making

The organizational and social environment in which the decision maker finds himself determines what consequences he will anticipate, what ones he will not; what alternatives he will consider, what ones he will ignore.

—J. March & H. Simon (1958, p. 139)

International managers face a variety of decisions every day. Resources must be allocated, employees selected, and the attractiveness of joint venture partners evaluated; all must be done in a highly complex international environment. All decisions involve choices between alternatives. Many of these choices are made almost automatically because of culturally based scripts that individual managers have for the situation. However, when confronted with a new or very important decision, managers can invoke a more thorough consideration of differently weighted alternatives.

This chapter reviews the process of individual decision making and explores the opportunity for cultural variation in the ways managers simplify complex decision-making processes. In addition, this chapter discusses the ethical dilemmas presented by decision making in an international context.

Rational Decision Making

The study of managerial decision making is typically divided into prescriptive approaches (what managers should do) and descriptive approaches (what managers actually do). On the prescriptive side, the rational model of decision making is based on a set of assumptions that indicates how a decision should be made. The goal of the rational decision maker is to make an optimal choice between specific and clearly defined alternatives (Simon, 1955). In order to optimize a particular outcome, people must progress either implicitly or explicitly through six steps in the decision-making process. These steps are described in Box 5.1.

As shown in Box 5.1, the rational decision maker has a clear goal and a comprehensive set of alternatives from which to choose, which are themselves weighted according to known criteria and preferences, and can choose the alternative that has the highest score.

Box 5.1 Steps in the Rational Decision Process

Problem definition. First, managers must recognize that a decision is needed and identify the problem to be solved. A problem is typically a difference between the actual situation and what is desired. However, managers often act without understanding the problem to be solved or define the problem in terms of a proposed solution or in terms of its symptoms (Bazerman, 1998; Kahneman, 2011). For example, in response to employee complaints about salaries being too low (a symptom), managers might define the problem as a comparison of salaries to industry averages. However, the more fundamental problem could be that the total compensation package, including benefits, does not suit the demographic characteristics of the firm's employees.

Identify decision criteria. Decisions often entail the consideration of more than one objective. For example, in selecting a manager for an overseas operation you may want to maximize his or her ability to adapt to the new culture, maximize the level of technical skill he or she has, and minimize the cost of the assignment. To be completely rational, a decision maker must identify all the criteria that should be considered.

Weight the criteria. The criteria identified in the previous step may not be of equal importance to the decision maker. In order to be prioritized, they must be assigned weights. A rational decision maker will know his or her preference for certain criteria and assign relative weights accordingly (e.g., cost of the assignment versus technical skills in the previous example).

Generate the alternatives. This step requires the rational decision maker to identify all possible alternatives that will satisfy the decision criteria. No attempt is made at this step to evaluate the alternatives.

(Continued)

(Continued)

Evaluate the alternatives. Each alternative must now be evaluated against the weighted criteria. This is often the most difficult part of the decision-making process, because it requires the decision maker to predict the future outcomes of each choice. However, the rational decision maker is able to assess the consequences of each alternative.

Select the optimal solution. The optimal solution is computed by simply multiplying the expected effectiveness of each alternative on each criterion times the weighting of each criterion for each solution. The sum of these scores is an evaluation of each alternative against the weighted decision criteria. The optimal alternative should then be selected.

Cultural Differences in the Optimization Model

The rational or optimizing model is best thought of as a prescriptive or normative approach that demonstrates how managerial decisions should be made. While management theorists have long recognized that managers always have limited time or resources that put boundaries on rationality, it is also useful to consider *cultural* variation in this normative framework.

For example, the Kluckhohn and Strodtbeck (1961) model of cultural variation in preferences for certain modes of behavior (Chapter 3), suggests cultural differences in the rational model. Specifically, at the problem definition step, the activity orientation of the culture might influence when a situation is defined as a problem. Managers from cultures with a *doing* or problem-solving orientation, such as the United States, might be more prone to identify a situation as a problem to be solved than will managers from *being* or situation-accepting cultures, such as Indonesia and Malaysia (Kluckhohn & Strodtbeck, 1961). Research also indicates that the amount of information one considers before making a final decision is culture bound. For example, East Asians have a more holistic approach to decisions and consider more information than do Americans (Choi, Dalal, Kim-Prieto, & Park, 2003).

The identification and weighting of criteria can also be affected by culturally different value orientations. For example, when asked to identify and rank criteria regarding a desirable acquisition target, U.S. and Korean managers had different opinions, as shown in Box 5.2. An examination of Box 5.2 reveals the cultural variation in decision criteria consistent with what we might expect, based on the cultural orientations of the two sets of managers. With the exception of the fourth item in the U.S. list, all of the criteria relate to short-term financial measures consistent with U.S. short-term orientation (Chung & Lee, 1989). In contrast, with the exception of the second item in the Korean managers' list, all of the criteria relate to long-term growth-oriented measures.

Cultural variation can also be anticipated in the generation and evaluation of alternatives. For example, harmony- as compared to mastery-oriented cultures are

Box 5.2 Desirable Characteristics of an Acquisition Target

United States Managers

1. Demand for target's products
2. Discounted cash flow
3. Return on investment
4. Attractiveness of industry
5. Management talent

Korean Managers

1. Attractiveness of industry
2. Sales revenue
3. Market structure
4. Manufacturing capabilities
5. Research and development capabilities

SOURCE: K. H. Chung & H. C. Lee. "Korean Managerial Dynamics" © 1989. Reproduced with permission of Greenwood Publishing Group, Inc., Westport, CT.

likely to place more emphasis on alternative solutions that support natural environmental concerns (Sagiv & Schwartz, 2000). Research also indicates cultural differences in the extent to which people vary in the choice rules they use in making decisions (Kim & Drolet, 2003). For example, people from individualist cultures, in which feeling unique is a common goal, are more likely to use a variety of different choice rules as compared to individuals from collectivist cultures. In addition, motivational differences (related to differences in self-concept, discussed in Chapter 4) can influence the weighting of alternatives, for example, in favor of the alternatives that have the most highly valued outcomes for individuals or for a collective.

Finally, who makes the choice and how long the decision process takes can be culture bound. Vertical individualist cultures, such as the United States and France, are likely to have decision-making authority vested in only a few high-ranking individuals (Heller & Wilpert, 1981), with superiors being a culturally important source of guidance for making decisions in such settings (Smith, Peterson, & Schwartz, 2002). In contrast, horizontal collectivist cultures (e.g., Israeli kibbutzim) are likely to push decision making well down in the organizational structure and involve large numbers of people. In addition, a culture's orientation toward time might influence the pace of decision making. For example, the longer time orientation of Arab cultures is reflected in a more deliberate pace of decision making than is found in North America, where being decisive means making choices quickly (Morrison, Conaway, & Borden, 1994). And, some evidence suggests that decision making in the Russian context exemplifies an extreme level of cultural cynicism (Bond et al., 2004) in which organization members are inclined to place very limited confidence in whether decisions that are announced actually can be implemented as planned (Puffer, 1994).

Research on the decision-making structures of organizations in different countries tends to support the kind of cultural variation in normative decision-making processes proposed previously. For example, in a very comprehensive study of this type (IDE Research Group, 1993), the level at which major decisions were made and the degree of employee involvement in decision making varied significantly across the 10 European countries surveyed. And for a variety of managerial decisions, as described in Chapter 3, the use of different roles, rules, and norms varies substantially across countries (Peterson & Smith, 2008). The decision structures in organizations are likely to reflect a culturally based view of a rational decision process. For example, the *ringi-sei* decision-making process characteristic of Japanese organizations (Misumi, 1984) is consistent with cultural orientations of both collectivism and high power distance (verticality). In this system, decisions are made using a participative procedure in which a subordinate submits a tentative solution that often reflects guidance from a superior (Nakane, 1970). The idea is then cleared through successive levels of the organization, where it is altered and approved by the people who must implement it. The final decision is the result of a managed form of participation that maintains the existing status hierarchy (Earley, 1999).

Limits to Rationality

Regardless of the type of normative cultural variation previously suggested, the optimization model assumes that decision makers can

- accurately define the problem,
- identify all decision criteria,
- accurately weigh the criteria according to known preferences,
- be aware of all available alternatives, and
- accurately assess each alternative.

Although decision makers might attempt to follow a rational model consistent with their cultural norms, they are limited in their ability to do so. Individual judgment is restricted or *bounded* in its ability to be rational (Simon, 1955). These boundaries exist because decision makers often must deal with incomplete information about the problem, the decision criteria, and even their own preferences. The cognitive limitations mentioned in Chapter 4 apply. Decision makers can handle only a small portion of the information available to them, and their perceptions are not always accurate.

An alternative to the rational model of decision making that recognizes these limitations is the *satisficing* model (March & Simon, 1958; Simon, 1955). Essentially, it suggests that decision makers forgo optimal solutions for ones that are acceptable. They do not evaluate all possible alternatives but search for a solution that meets a minimally satisfactory set of criteria. If a particular alternative meets these criteria, the search ends. If it does not, they continue to the next alternative and the next, until a satisfactory solution is found. Because of limits to rationality, decision makers most often satisfice rather than optimize.

Cultural Constraints on Rationality

In addition to the cognitive limits to rationality, the concept of rationality itself may be culture bound. Rationality or being motivated by self-interest, as discussed in Chapter 4, might be defined differently depending on how individuals from different cultures define themselves (interdependent with others versus independent from others). Moreover, even though a manager makes a decision in a less than rational way, it could be more important to appear rational in some cultures than in others.

Conflict models of decision making (Janis & Mann, 1977) suggest that decision makers use one of four decision styles to cope with the psychological stress of making a decision. According to the model, the optimal decision style is *vigilance*, which is a pattern consisting of a careful collection of facts and consideration of alternatives. In contrast are three alternative or maladaptive styles. *Complacency* involves either ignoring the decision completely or simply taking the first available course of action. *Defensive avoidance* is passing the decision off to someone else, putting off the decision, or devaluing the importance of making a decision. Finally, *hypervigilance* is making a hasty, ill-conceived decision, also called panicking. Research using this model with Japanese and other non-Western samples has found significantly greater use of the alternatives to vigilance than in Western (Australia, New Zealand, and United States) samples (Radford, Mann, Ohta, & Nakane, 1989; Mann et al., 1997). This is not to imply that East Asians are less efficient decision makers. On the contrary, what might be presented as less efficient decision processes in the West could be the dominant patterns in other (predominantly collectivist) cultures. Other research in the Japanese culture suggests that they are less likely than are Western cultures to report that they use systematic rational processes in favor of more intuitive decision making (Torrence, 1980). As opposed to focusing on collecting facts, defining the problem, and considering all alternatives, their primary considerations are the impressions of others, feelings and emotions, and intuition (Radford, Mann, Ohta, & Nakane, 1991).

International management decisions are complex and frequent. The concepts of bounded rationality and satisficing suggest that these managerial decisions will rarely conform to a rational model. In fact, an observational study of what managers do indicates that they might actually avoid analytical processes (Mintzberg, 1973). To determine more specifically in what way international managers' decisions might deviate from rationality, we must consider the ways in which they simplify the complex environment surrounding their decisions (Bazerman, 1998). The next section discusses simplifying strategies called heuristics (Tversky & Kahneman, 1974; Kahneman, 2011) that apply to decision making in general. In addition, because managers from different cultures simplify complex realities in different ways, the opportunity for culturally based differences in the application of these heuristics is discussed.

Heuristics

Heuristics are rules of thumb (cognitive tools) that people use to simplify decision making (Bazerman, 1998). Heuristics can result in biases in making decisions, but the increased speed of decision making often outweighs the loss in decision quality. Usually, managers do not consciously make this trade-off between decision quality and speed because they are typically unaware that they are using a heuristic. By becoming aware of the impact of heuristics, however, managers can learn to use them to advantage. The three general heuristics that are used to simplify decision making are availability, representativeness, and anchoring and adjustment.

Availability

Availability is the extent to which instances or occurrences of an event are readily brought to mind. It influences managers' judgments of the frequency, probability, or likely causes of that event (Tversky & Kahneman, 1973). An event that is easily imagined or evokes emotions is more easily recalled than vague or bland events. For example, in a U.S. experiment (Russo & Shoemaker, 1989), participants said that motor vehicle accidents caused more deaths each year than stomach cancer. In fact, stomach cancer caused twice as many deaths. However, vivid and numerous media accounts of motor vehicle deaths have created a bias in U.S. culture that affects the perception of the frequency of the two events. Also, a vivid event temporarily increases the availability of similar events. For example, after the terrorist attack on the World Trade Center, the probability of terrorist attacks on the United States was wildly exaggerated.

Because the availability heuristic is based on life experiences, cultural differences in judgments that result from availability are easily suggested. For example, Thai people are likely to have much higher estimates of the worldwide death rate from being trampled by a water buffalo than are people living in the United States. That is, culturally different individuals might differ systematically in the way they apply their available recollections to larger situations outside their experience.

Representativeness

Managers' assessment of the likelihood that an event will occur is influenced by how similar the occurrence is to their mental representation (stereotype) of similar experiences. They often ignore base rates in favor of how well a particular example matches their expectation. For example, people do not enter prenuptial agreements because they do not believe that the high base rate for divorce applies to them. Representativeness is powerful and can overrule the logic of probability as shown in Box 5.3.

Another example of ignoring probability in favor of the representativeness heuristic involves misconceptions of chance. People often inappropriately expect that random and nonrandom events will even out. That is, after a run of bad outcomes, they believe they are due for a positive result. For example, they might believe that after they hire five poor performers, the chance that the next hire will also perform poorly is lower. In reality, of course, the outcome of a random event is independent of the outcomes of previous events, and the next person hired is just as likely to perform poorly as the previous five.

Box 5.3 The Linda Problem

Linda is thirty-one years old, single, outspoken, and very bright. She majored in philosophy. As a student, she was deeply concerned with issues of discrimination and social justice and also participated in antinuclear demonstrations.

Rank the following in terms of likelihood:

Linda is a teacher in elementary school.

Linda works in a bookstore and takes yoga classes.

Linda is an active feminist.

Linda is a psychiatric social worker.

Linda is a member of the League of Women Voters.

Linda is a bank teller.

Linda is an insurance salesperson.

Linda is a bank teller and an active feminist.

Most people agree that Linda is more likely to be a feminist bank teller than a bank teller (the other options are distractors). However, the probability that Linda is a feminist bank teller *must* be lower than the probability of being a bank teller. The set of feminist bank tellers is contained within the larger set of bank tellers. Because Linda fits the idea of a feminist bank teller so well, representativeness trumps the logic of probability.

SOURCE: Adapted from the classic experiment in Tversky, A., & Kahneman, D. (1982). Judgments of and by representativeness. In D. Kahneman, P. Slovic & A. Tversky (Eds.), *Judgment under uncertainty: Heuristics and biases*. Cambridge, UK: Cambridge University Press.

An extension of this idea that has cross-cultural implications is reflected in the notion that people search for causes that are similar in strength to the effect they observe (Gilovich & Savitsky, 2002). We want to think that big events are the result of big causes and small events stem from small causes. For example, it is difficult for many people to believe that the assassination of U.S. President John F. Kennedy was the work of a lone person, and they continue to search for a cause of higher magnitude (conspiracy theories) for this dramatic event. Because of cultural differences in holistic versus analytic reasoning (Nisbett, Peng, Choi, & Norenzayan, 2001) collectivists and individualists vary in the extent to which they expect similarity in cause and effect and can tolerate contradiction. For example, North Americans have been found to expect that events corresponded in magnitude to their causes to a greater degree than do Chinese (Spina et al., 2010).

Related to representativeness is the confidence a decision maker has in the correctness of the decision. Evidence suggests that once they have made a decision, people from collectivist societies display greater confidence in its correctness (Yates et al., 1989). This greater confidence is probably the result of the tendency of collectivists to view the world and hence categorize decisions in terms of perfect certainty or perfect uncertainty (Wright & Phillips, 1980). In contrast, people from individualist societies might consider more possible negative outcomes of their decision and therefore be less certain. For example, when asked to list possible reasons why their decision might be wrong, Chinese respondents produced far fewer reasons than U.S. respondents (Yates, Lee, & Shinotsuka, 1996). In a related example, Mexicans (collectivists) were more likely to escalate commitment (throw good money after bad) than Americans and had more confidence in the decision to do so (Greer & Stephens, 2001).

Anchoring and Adjustment

Managers often make a judgment by starting from some initial point and then adjusting to yield a final decision, as often occurs in intercultural negotiation (e.g., Brett, 2007). The initial point or anchor can come from the way a problem is framed, from historical factors, or from random information. Even when an anchor is absurd and people recognize it as such, their subsequent judgments are often very close to that starting point (Dawes, 1988). Regardless of the initial anchor point, subsequent adjustments tend to be insufficient (Tversky & Kahneman, 1974). There are numerous examples of bias resulting from anchoring and adjustment. For example, some school systems categorize children into certain performance categories at an early age. Whereas a child anchored in a low-performance group might meet expectations, another child of similar ability but anchored in a higher-performance category could be perceived as being a better performer simply because he or she was categorized as being a high performer. In international negotiation, the anchor is important because it often strongly influences the final outcome of a negotiation (Brett, 2007). Both the source of an anchor and norms for adjustment might vary with cultural experience. For example, the willingness of new migrants from Hong Kong to Vancouver in the 1990s to pay far above market prices for residential property might be explained by this heuristic. The Hong Kong Chinese might have anchored their initial estimate of the cost of housing in Vancouver in their previous experience. Subsequent estimates might still have been higher than reality because of the general tendency to make an insufficient adjustment mentioned earlier and a collectivist norm for avoiding extremes in evaluations.

These three general heuristics represent ways in which managers tend to simplify the decision-making process. As shown, these simplifications can result in specific types of biases. When we consider cultural variation and the role it plays in social cognition, we can anticipate systematic differences in how these heuristics are applied and the resulting biases. In reality, more than one of the heuristics might be used in any single decision. In addition, many other types of biases result from the use of these three heuristics or from rules of thumb. However, a complete discussion of all possible effects of cognitive simplification of the decision-making process is beyond the scope of this book (see Bazerman, 1998; Kahneman, 2011). What is important to note is that in making decisions, managers simplify reality in predictable ways. Additionally, because managers from different cultures perceive the world differently, their subjective realities differ; therefore, so will the ways in which they simplify complex realities.

Motivational Biases in Decision Making

In addition to the cognitive simplification effects previously discussed, many of the decision choices managers make can be influenced by motivational biases. Motivational biases in decision making can be based on the differences in self-concepts described in Chapter 4. First, decision makers with interdependent self-concepts should be more influenced by motives that are social or refer to others, such as deference, affiliation, nurturance, avoidance of blame, and the need to comply. An example of a culturally guided motivational difference specific to decision making is provided in a study of Brazilians (interdependent self) and people from the United States (independent self). In that study, Brazilians were more likely than U.S. people to perform and enjoy performing a behavior costly to themselves (forgoing personal benefit to visit a sick friend; Bontempo, Lobel, & Triandis, 1990). In a similar example, Indian students were found to be more likely to consider a donation of bone marrow to save someone's life to be morally required than were U.S. students (Baron & Miller, 2000).

As suggested in Chapter 4, a culturally based motivational difference might exist in the need for consistency in internal attitudes and external behavior. For example, some authors (Doi, 1986) argue that people from individualistic societies, such as the U.S., are much more likely to be concerned with consistency between feelings and actions than are collectivists, such as the Japanese. The independence of the Japanese expressions *honne* (true feelings privately held) and *tatemae* (the truth that is presented) reflects this lower need for people with interdependent self-concepts to reconcile the inner self with external behavior (Hall & Hall, 1987). Research has verified this more holistic reasoning approach of East Asians and their tendency to take inconsistency and contradiction for granted. For example, Koreans have been shown to be less surprised than were U.S. people when someone's behavior contradicted their expectations (Choi & Nisbett, 2000). Therefore, we should not expect judgments made by those with interdependent self-concepts to be motivated by the same sort of cognitive consistency that drives those with independent notions of self.

A common decision bias relates to an unrealistically positive self-evaluation (Taylor, 1989). For example, studies with U.S. people (independent self) indicate that they often believe that they are far more likely to graduate at the top of their class, get a good job, obtain a high salary, or give birth to a gifted child than reality actually suggests. Research suggests that this optimism bias is stronger in people with an independent self-concept. For example, Canadians (independent self) seem to demonstrate this self-enhancing bias, whereas Japanese (interdependent self) do not (Heine & Lehman, 1995). This overoptimistic view of outcomes can be related to individual self-esteem, which is higher in those with independent self-concepts (Mann, Burnett, Radford, & Ford, 1997).

The previous section introduces several motivational biases in decision making that can vary across cultures. Differences in decision motives can be expected based on the decision maker's internal representation of self. Certainly, other motivational biases exist. However, what is important to recognize is that patterns of decision making that vary from a normative rational model can be the result of the culturally based motivation of the decision maker and the cognitive simplification of the process.

Selection and Reward Allocation Decisions

Two common managerial decisions that are relevant in terms of cross-cultural interactions are the selection of employees and the allocation of rewards. All organizations need to recruit and select new members. Based on the previous discussion, we would expect considerable variation around the world in the procedures used to conduct this important decision-making activity. The research on selection procedures in different cultures is far from complete, but it does demonstrate systematic variation in the decision process. For example, in a survey of the selection processes of 959 companies in 20 nations, a significant pattern of similarities and differences in the selection procedures used was found (Ryan, McFarland, Baron, & Page, 1999). Table 5.1 reports the extent to which companies used a particular technique on a scale of 1 = *never* to 5 = *always or almost always.*

The variation in selection techniques is consistent with the suggestion that cultural differences influence the institutionalization of the selection process. For example, graphology (handwriting analysis) was popular only in France and was never used in many countries, and firms in Hong Kong and Singapore were the most likely to rely on family connections. Similarities also existed in that one-on-one interviews were commonly used across all the firms surveyed. This contrasts with previous research, which found that Chinese firms rarely reported using interviews for selection purposes (Huo & Von Glinow, 1995), with more important selection criteria being the institution from which the person graduated or his or her home province (Redding, Norman, & Schlander, 1994). Despite some convergence toward common practices, an examination of the selection processes in 10 countries using the Best International Human Resource Practices Survey found more differences than similarities in the practices used (Huo, Huang, & Napier, 2002). Thus, it seems that considerable variability continues to exist in the selection decision across cultures.

Related to the selection decision is the development of a potentially qualified pool of applicants from which to choose. Again, cultural variation in the specifications of job requirements used in recruiting candidates is evident. For example, in an analysis of hundreds of newspaper advertisements in eight European countries, 80 percent of

Table 5.1 Selection Methods by Country

Method	Australia	Belgium	Canada	France	Germany	Greece	Hong Kong	Ireland	Italy	Netherlands	New Zealand	Portugal	Singapore	South Africa	Spain	Sweden	U.K.	U.S.	All
Application form	3.59	3.94	3.29	4.09	3.65	2.92	4.75	3.46	4.19	3.55	3.64	3.40	4.67	4.20	3.22	1.19	4.26	4.12	3.53
Education	4.21	3.19	4.31	4.37	4.47	4.32	4.50	4.42	4.08	4.68	4.33	4.91	4.33	4.46	2.43	4.30	4.32	4.47	4.26
Personal references	2.88	2.74	3.00	2.79	3.06	3.44	2.75	3.46	3.04	2.47	3.40	3.14	3.07	3.63	2.91	3.94	3.51	3.18	3.22
Employer references	4.32	2.64	4.05	3.32	2.03	2.30	3.75	4.53	2.69	2.72	4.40	3.14	3.13	4.09	2.43	4.49	4.37	4.02	3.77
Certificate or license	2.52	3.19	3.05	2.25	3.33	2.83	3.88	3.02	2.38	4.23	2.66	4.35	3.47	3.37	3.52	1.89	2.83	2.96	2.95
Family connections	1.30	1.57	1.68	1.56	1.47	1.87	2.00	1.55	1.52	1.50	1.31	1.75	1.80	1.52	1.48	1.22	1.33	1.53	1.46
One-to-one interviews	3.59	4.70	4.35	4.85	4.65	4.92	3.38	3.34	4.93	3.78	4.05	4.77	4.13	4.72	4.70	4.84	3.88	4.78	4.30
Panel interviews	4.08	2.75	3.57	2.06	1.88	2.71	3.63	4.00	1.50	4.30	3.71	3.29	3.47	3.63	2.45	2.82	3.82	3.27	3.36
Questionnaire	2.75	3.73	2.87	2.63	1.74	2.65	2.88	2.98	1.58	3.03	3.45	3.27	2.64	3.44	3.09	3.74	3.41	2.51	3.09
Job trial	2.05	3.05	2.33	2.12	1.56	2.74	1.57	2.71	1.48	3.94	1.59	3.12	2.00	2.06	2.57	1.55	1.87	2.02	2.20
Biodata	1.23	1.52	1.19	1.20	2.77	3.87	1.62	1.18	1.92	1.53	1.35	2.29	1.80	1.41	1.68	1.59	1.23	1.21	1.52
Cognitive ability test	2.39	3.85	2.59	2.29	1.90	2.54	1.83	2.79	1.33	3.76	3.37	3.27	2.83	3.25	3.75	2.86	3.08	2.09	2.98
Physical ability test	1.40	1.04	1.27	1.29	1.00	1.08	1.17	1.15	1.00	1.61	1.12	1.69	1.17	1.26	1.00	1.17	1.18	1.21	1.22

(Continued)

Table 5.1 (Continued)

Method	Australia	Belgium	Canada	France	Germany	Greece	Hong Kong	Ireland	Italy	Netherlands	New Zealand	Portugal	Singapore	South Africa	Spain	Sweden	U.K.	U.S.	All
Foreign language test	1.11	3.02	1.67	2.79	1.60	2.85	2.83	1.58	1.67	1.62	1.19	2.36	1.00	1.33	3.07	2.18	1.37	1.21	1.75
Work sample	1.89	1.40	1.80	1.50	1.50	1.79	1.83	1.39	1.00	1.32	1.49	1.69	1.67	1.71	2.15	1.22	1.84	1.40	1.59
Personality test	2.56	3.75	2.78	3.42	1.70	3.14	2.50	3.17	1.86	3.29	3.59	3.00	2.67	3.66	4.43	3.68	3.46	1.62	3.21
Honesty test	1.16	1.60	1.52	1.00	1.00	1.85	1.33	1.04	1.00	1.69	1.20	1.92	1.67	1.62	2.21	1.11	1.12	1.09	1.33
Vocational interest test	1.51	1.98	1.76	2.33	1.40	2.29	1.50	1.07	1.00	1.65	1.54	2.62	1.33	1.73	2.33	1.53	1.33	1.15	1.61
Simulation exercise	1.58	2.73	2.58	1.82	1.70	1.85	1.50	1.44	1.57	2.82	1.89	2.57	1.33	2.66	2.15	1.72	2.52	1.82	2.14
Situation judgment test	1.35	2.16	2.30	1.33	1.50	1.15	3.00	1.31	1.00	1.82	1.57	2.23	1.67	1.94	2.33	1.64	1.85	1.71	1.78
Video-based test	1.10	1.33	1.15	1.06	1.00	1.15	1.17	1.00	1.00	1.55	1.07	2.00	1.00	1.30	1.33	1.19	1.18	1.26	1.20
Projective techniques	1.12	1.33	1.33	1.69	1.00	1.00	1.00	1.00	1.00	1.68	1.13	2.60	1.00	1.73	1.69	1.77	1.12	1.03	1.32
Drug tests	1.34	1.08	1.55	1.18	1.18	1.15	1.17	1.32	1.00	1.06	1.13	1.93	1.00	1.58	1.00	1.93	1.35	2.21	1.41
Medical screen	3.34	3.50	2.63	1.76	4.45	2.36	3.67	4.31	2.33	4.18	1.95	4.14	3.33	3.77	3.54	3.26	3.91	2.26	3.18
Graphology	1.07	1.56	1.00	3.26	1.00	1.21	1.00	1.00	1.00	1.24	1.02	1.00	1.00	1.45	1.75	1.27	1.10	1.09	1.25

SOURCE: Adapted from Ryan, A. M., McFarland, L., Baron, H., & Page, R. (1999). An international look at selection practices: Nation and culture as explanations of variability in practice. *Personnel Psychology, 52*(2), 359–391.

NOTE: Scores are mean responses on a 5-point scale anchored by 1 = *never use* and 5 = *always use.*

the ads in Scandinavian countries (Sweden, Norway, and Denmark) emphasized the interpersonal skills required, whereas in Germany and the United Kingdom 65 percent emphasized interpersonal skills, and in France, Italy, and Spain, only 50 percent of ads emphasized interpersonal skills. Ads in France, Italy, and Spain emphasized a particular age as a requirement. In the more egalitarian Scandinavian countries, the interpersonal skills needed for collaboration were most important, whereas in higher power distance countries age was more important. These examples provide evidence of cultural differences in both the processes used in the selection decision and the criteria that are most important in the decision.

Another key decision in the management of international organizations is reward allocation. A substantial number of studies have examined reward allocation decisions, and most of these dealt with differences in perceptions of fairness by individualists and collectivists in relation to in-groups and out-groups, but many of these studies may have ignored important contextual factors (Leung, 1997). Recently, it has been recognized that power distance (verticality) or hierarchy may be the best predictor of differences across cultures in reward allocation (Fischer & Smith, 2003).

Reward allocation criteria include equity, equality, need, and seniority. Cultural differences appear to exist in the fairness associated with each of these decision criteria. In hierarchical societies (high power distance), there is a strong preference for equity over equality (Fischer & Smith, 2003). Also, the emphasis on harmony in collectivist cultures suggests that fairness might be perceived to result from equality as opposed to equity in reward allocation. In general, individualists seem to prefer reward allocations based on equity, and collectivists prefer more equal distributions (Kim, Park, & Suzuki, 1990; Leung & Bond, 1982). However, for individualists this preference might be moderated by the expectation of future interaction between work group members (Elliott & Meeker, 1984). In addition, the preference of collectivists for equality rather than equity in reward allocation is affected by whether the reward is to be received by an in-group or out-group member. For example, when allocating rewards to in-group members, Chinese used an equality norm, whereas U.S. people used an equity norm. However, when the allocation was made to out-group members, Chinese adhered more closely to an equity norm than did U.S. people (Leung & Bond, 1984). Collectivists also show a higher propensity to allocate rewards according to need than do individualists (Berman, Murphy-Berman, & Singh, 1985). When present, need seems to override other preferences for reward distribution in all cultures; however, this effect is more pronounced for collectivists. Cultural differences in reward allocation based on seniority also exist. Collectivist logic suggests that this group might be more prone than individualists to see reward allocation based on seniority as fair. In general, this relationship seems to be true (C. C. Chen, 1995) and is more pronounced, as would be expected, for vertical collectivists (Chen, Meindl, & Hunt, 1997). However, it is possible that gender roles specific to a given culture might influence the extent to which a seniority norm for reward allocation is invoked. For example, in one study, male subjects in Taiwan were more likely to use seniority to allocate rewards, whereas in the United States, female subjects used this norm (Rusbult, Insko, & Lin, 1993).

It is important to consider that societal-level cultural and economic factors as well as organizational norms influence reward allocation in organizations. For example, a study across five countries (Fischer et al., 2007) reported that reliance on an equality norm for reward allocation was predicted by organization factors, and reliance on need was predicted by the unemployment rate and the societal value of embeddedness (see Chapter 3). And the perceived fairness of a reward allocation strategy can be affected by a number of factors, including the status of the person making the reward allocation.

In summary, both selection decisions and reward allocation decisions vary across cultures in a systematic fashion. Much of what we know about this variability relies on the cultural dimensions of individualism and collectivism or power distance (verticality) for explanation. Although relying on this limited evidence is far from satisfactory, it does point out that we must be very careful in trying to apply decision models based on Western modes of thought to non-Western cultures. In fact, the cognitive processes involved in decision making seem far from universal (Nisbett et al., 2001).

Ethical Dilemmas in Decision Making

Increasingly, managers around the world are recognizing the ethical dimension of their decisions. Although they generally agree that sound ethics is good for business, they are very skeptical about what they and their peers actually do and about the existence of unethical practices in their industry (Brenner & Molander, 1977). The decisions international managers make cross cultural and geographic boundaries. In the process, the consensus about what is morally correct erodes in the face of differing values and norms. For example, payments that are considered bribes in the United States can be viewed as a perfectly acceptable business practice in some other cultures. Discrimination in employment against women that is reprehensible in one culture is a normal expression of gender-based roles in another. The study of ethical decision making, like decision making in general, has resulted in both normative or prescriptive models and descriptive models. However, because managers are reluctant to have their ethics directly observed or measured, empirical tests are limited (O'Fallen & Butterfield, 2005). In this section we outline the common normative frameworks or moral philosophies for ethical decision making. Then we present a descriptive model based on the cognitive moral development of managers that provides for the effect of culture.

Moral Philosophies

A moral philosophy is a set of principles used to decide what is right or wrong (Ferrell & Fraedrich, 1994). Managers can be guided by one of several moral philosophies when making decisions that present an ethical dilemma. The main categories of moral philosophies that are relevant to international management decisions are teleology or consequential models, deontology or rule-based models, and cultural relativism.

Consequential Models

Consequential models focus on the outcomes or consequences of a decision to determine whether the decision is ethical. A key precept of this principle as a guide for decision making is utilitarianism (Mill, 1863). Utilitarianism is the moral doctrine that we should always act to produce the greatest possible balance of good over harm for everyone affected by our decision (Shaw, 1996). Selecting a decision that considers the interests and maximizes the utility for all individuals and groups affected by a decision is extremely difficult. It becomes even more difficult when the stakeholders affected by a decision have culturally different values and attitudes.

Some philosophers (called rule utilitarians, in contrast to act utilitarians, described previously) espouse the view that, if followed, general moral rules (e.g., religious norms) will maximize the benefits to all and can be used as a shortcut to the complexity of evaluating the utility of each decision (Shaw, 1996). They are guided by the belief that some types of behavior (e.g., refraining from excess profits) will *always* maximize the utility of everyone involved.

Deontological or Rule-Based Models

Deontological principles hold that human beings have certain fundamental rights and that a sense of duty to uphold these rights is the basis of ethical decision making rather than a concern for consequences (Borchert & Stewart, 1986). One of the best known of these rule-based approaches is the categorical imperative of Immanuel Kant (1724–1804). Essentially, the categorical imperative asserts that individuals have the right to be treated as an entity unto themselves and not simply as a means to an end. Unlike utilitarianism, deontology argues that some behaviors exist that are never moral even though they maximize utility. An obvious difficulty with rule-based normative approaches to decision making is achieving wide consensus on which rules (whose values) to base fundamental rights on (Donaldson, 1989). Despite this difficulty, a number of transnational corporate codes have been promulgated that attempt to codify a set of universal guidelines for international managers. By reducing these transnational codes to their key common elements, one can develop guidelines for ethical practices that have some degree of cross-national acceptance (Frederick, 1991). Box 5.4 presents examples of these guidelines that refer to business operations as well as to basic human rights and fundamental freedoms.

It might be possible to gain universal acceptance for a set of fundamental rights if they protect something of great importance in all cultures, if they are under continuous threat, and if all cultures can absorb the cost of protecting them (Donaldson, 1989). However, some research suggests that national culture affects the preference of individuals for consequential versus deontological or rule-based principles in ethical decision making. For example, a comparison of seven countries found a preference for consequential principles in the United States and Australia as compared to Eastern European and Asian countries (Jackson, 2000). More important, perhaps, is that managers in different cultures can subscribe to the same moral philosophy (e.g., utilitarianism or fundamental rights) but still choose to behave in ways that are very different (Phatak & Habib, 1998). This is the problem of cultural relativism.

Box 5.4 Normative Corporate Guidelines

Employment Practices and Policies

MNCs [multinational corporations] should not contravene the manpower policies of host nations (ILO);

MNCs should respect the right of employees to join trade unions and to bargain collectively (ILO, OECD, UDHR);

MNCs should develop nondiscriminatory employment policies and promote equal job opportunities (ILO, OECD, UDHR);

MNCs should provide equal pay for equal work (ILO, UDHR);

MNCs should give advance notice of changes in operations, especially plant closings, and mitigate the adverse effects of these changes (ILO, OECD);

MNCs should provide favorable work conditions, limited working hours, holidays with pay, and protection against unemployment (UDHR);

MNCs should promote job stability and job security, avoiding arbitrary dismissals and providing severance pay for those unemployed (ILO, UDHR);

MNCs should respect local host-country job standards and upgrade the local labor force through training (ILO, OECD);

MNCs should adopt adequate health and safety standards for employees and grant them the right to know about job-related health hazards (ILO);

MNCs should, minimally, pay basic living wages to employees (ILO, UDHR);

MNCs' operations should benefit lower-income groups of the host nation (ILO); and

MNCs should balance job opportunities, work conditions, job training, and living conditions among migrant workers and host-country nationals (Helsinki).

Consumer Protection

MNCs should respect host-country laws and policies regarding the protection of consumers (OECD, TNC Code) and

MNCs should safeguard the health and safety of consumers by various disclosures, safe packaging, proper labeling, and accurate advertising (TNC Code).

Environmental Protection

MNCs should respect host-country laws, goals, and priorities concerning protection of the environment (OECD, INC Code, Helsinki);

MNCs should preserve ecological balance, protect the environment, adopt preventive measures to avoid environmental harm, and rehabilitate environments damaged by operations (OECD, TNC Code, Helsinki);

MNCs should disclose likely environmental harms and minimize risks of accidents that could cause environmental damage (OECD, TNC Code);

MNCs should promote the development of international environmental standards (INC Code, Helsinki);

MNCs should control specific operations that contribute to pollution of air, water, and soils (Helsinki); and

MNCs should develop and use technology that can monitor, protect, and enhance the environment (OECD, Helsinki).

Political Payments and Involvement

MNCs should not pay bribes nor make improper payments to public officials (OECD, TNC Code);

MNCs should avoid improper or illegal involvement or interference in the internal politics of host countries (OECD, TNC Code); and

MNCs should not interfere in intergovernmental relations (TNC Code).

Basic Human Rights and Fundamental Freedoms

MNCs should respect the rights of all persons to life, liberty, security of person, and privacy (UDHR, ECHR, Helsinki, ILO, TNC Code);

MNCs should respect the rights of all persons to equal protection of the law, work, choice of job, just and favorable work conditions, and protection against unemployment and discrimination (UDHR, Helsinki, ILO, TNC Code);

MNCs should respect all persons' freedom of thought, conscience, religion, opinion and expression, communication, peaceful assembly and association, and movement and residence within each state (UDHR, ECHR, Helsinki, ILO, TNC Code).

The United Nations Universal Declaration of Human Rights (UDHR) (1948);

The European Convention on Human Rights (ECHR) (1950); The Helsinki Final Act (Helsinki) (1975);

The OECD Guidelines for Multinational Enterprises (OECD) (1976);

The International Labor Office Tripartite Declaration of Principles Concerning Multinational Enterprises and Social Policy (ILO) (1977); and

The United Nations Code of Conduct on Transnational Corporations (TNC Code) (not yet completed nor promulgated but originating in 1972).

SOURCE: From Frederick, W. C. (1991). The moral authority of transnational corporate codes. *Journal of Business Ethics, 10,* 166–167. Reprinted with kind permission from Kluwer Academic Publishers.

Cultural Relativism

In cultural relativism, moral concepts are legitimate only to the extent that they reflect the habits and attitudes of a given culture (Donaldson, 1989). Ethical standards are specific to a particular culture, and any cross-cultural comparison is meaningless. What is considered unethical in one culture might be quite acceptable in another, even though the same moral principle is being followed. An example of cultural relativism in a selection decision is demonstrated in Box 5.5.

Cultural relativism implies that one should not impose one's own ethical or moral standards on others (a practice particularly characteristic of individualists, according to Triandis [1995]) and that international decisions should be evaluated in the context of differences in legal, political, and cultural systems. However, it also leaves open the opportunity to attribute a wide range of behavior to cultural norms. The use of child labor in Myanmar and China (Beaver, 1995) and discrimination against women in Japan and Saudi Arabia (Mayer & Cava, 1993) are just two examples of conduct that is attributed to cultural relativism. To adopt the concept of cultural relativism in its entirety declares the international decision arena a *moral-free zone* where anything goes (Donaldson, 1989).

For cultural relativism to hold up as a normative model, we must declare that even the most hideous or reprehensible behavior is not objectively wrong but depends on how a culture defines *wrong*. However, most of us can imagine acts that we cannot defend in terms of variation in cultural practice. This gives rise to so-called hypernorms, which reflect principles so fundamental to human existence that they transcend religious, philosophical, or cultural differences (Donaldson & Dunfee, 1994).

These prescriptive or normative models suggest how one should behave in making an ethical decision. However, like all prescriptive models, they tell us little about how managers actually behave (Fritzsche & Becker, 1984). The development of descriptive ethical decision-making models has lagged these prescriptive models. However, one approach that shows promise because it allows for both cultural and situational influence is the idea of stages of cognitive moral development.

Box 5.5 Cultural Relativism in a Selection Decision

Moral principle: Attributes of individuals must not be used for differential treatment of the individuals unless they are clearly connected to the goals and tasks required.

Indian manager: I must hire people whom I know or who belong to my network of friends and relatives because I can trust them to be dependable employees.

American manager: I must hire the best person for the job regardless of class, race, religion, gender, or national origin.

SOURCE: Adapted from Phatak, A., & Habib, M. (1998). How should managers treat ethics in international business? *Thunderbird International Business Review, 40*(2), 101–117.

Cognitive Moral Development

Cognitive moral development is an approach to understanding ethical decision making that focuses on the mental determination of right and wrong based on values and social judgments (Kohlberg, 1984). It is particularly appropriate in understanding managers' responses to ethical dilemmas across cultures. This model suggests that all people pass through stages of moral development and that ethical behavior can be understood by identifying a person's level of moral maturity. As shown in Table 5.2, the six stages of development make up three distinctive levels.

Stages in the model relate to age-based stages in human development. In general, children under the age of nine are at Level One, adolescents and most adults

Table 5.2   Stages of Moral Development

Stage of Moral Development	Social Perspective
Level One: Preconventional	Individual Perspective
Stage One: Obedience and punishment	Sticking to rules to avoid physical punishment. Obedience for its own sake.
Stage Two: Instrumental purpose and exchange	Following rules only when it is in one's immediate interest. Right is an equal exchange, a fair deal.
Level Two: Conventional	Member of Society Perspective
Stage Three: Interpersonal accord, conformity, mutual expectations	Stereotypical "good" behavior. Living up to what is expected by people close to you.
Stage Four: Social accord and system maintenance	Fulfilling duties and obligations to which you have agreed. Upholding laws except in extreme cases where they conflict with fixed social duties. Contributing to the society, group.
Level Three: Postconventional	Principled Perspective
Stage Five: Social contract and individual rights	Being aware that people hold a variety of values; that rules are relative to the group. Upholding rules because they are the social contract. Upholding nonrelative values and rights regardless of majority opinion.
Stage Six: Universal ethical principles	Following self-chosen ethical principles. When laws violate these principles, act in accord with principles.

SOURCE: Adapted from Kohlberg, L. (1984). *Philosophy of moral development.* New York: Harper & Row.

plateau at Level Two, and only a small percentage of people reach Level Three. Level Three is the stage at which people will accept society's rules only if they agree with the moral foundation on which the rules are based (Kohlberg, 1984). However, level of moral development is not exclusively age based and has been found to be related to intelligence, level of education, work experience (Colby, Kohlberg, Gibbs, & Lieberman, 1983), and degree of ethical training (Penn & Collier, 1985). As individuals' cognitive process of moral decision making becomes more complex, they progress to higher stages of moral development. The existence of cognitive development stages has been tested with participants of both sexes, from a range of social classes, and in a number of cultures. There is some evidence that culture is related to moral reasoning as conceived by Kohlberg, because the model rests on an expanding awareness of the impact of decisions on the individual, the in-group, and society (Colby & Kohlberg, 1987). For example, Triandis (1995) suggests that Stage Two is a type of primitive individualism, and Stage Three focuses on morality as a function of the consequences for one's in-group, characteristic of collectivist cultures (Husted, 2000). Although numerous studies find differences in ethical attitudes and behavior across cultures (Treviño, Weaver, & Reynolds, 2006), this evidence fails to show that some cultures are more or less ethical in their decision making than others (O'Fallon & Butterfield, 2005). Stages One through Four of the Kohlberg model have been found to exist in all cultures, and evidence of the principled perspective has been found in both Western and Eastern cultures (Snarey, 1985).

Managers' stage of cognitive moral development determines their mental process of deciding what is right or wrong, and as noted previously, these stages of moral development seem to exist (if not uniformly [Snarey, 1985]) in all cultures. However, both individual and situational factors have the potential to affect the relationship between the assessment of what is right or wrong and actual ethical decision making in organizations (Treviño, 1986). The process of ethical decision making involves four steps—identifying the ethical nature of an issue, making an ethical judgment, establishing ethical intent, and engaging in moral action. In addition, both individual and situational differences as well as the decision-making process may be culture bound (Thorne & Saunders, 2002). Figure 5.1 is a graphic representation of this process.

As shown in Figure 5.1, the model suggests that individual differences can influence the likelihood of people acting on the choice of what they believe to be ethical. For example, individual factors, such as the extent to which one believes that an outcome is the result of one's own efforts (*locus of control* [Rotter, 1966]) and the extent to which people depend on information from external reference points (*field dependence* [Witkin & Goodenough, 1977]), might influence their reliance on their own internal beliefs about what is right or wrong. In this example, decisions by managers with high field dependence and external locus of control can be less consistent in their level of moral judgment than managers with internal locus of control and field independence. Both the expectation about the outcomes of one's actions and the reliance on social information to make decisions are strongly shaped by culture (Leung, Bond, & Schwartz, 1995; Smith & Bond, 1999; Smith, Trompenaars, & Dugan, 1995). In this way, culture might influence the relationship between level of moral development and making an ethical or unethical decision. For example, because their belief about the outcome of their action is shaped by their long-term orientation and collectivist norms, Chinese are more likely to report an unethical act (blow the whistle) by peers than are Canadians (Zhuang, Thomas, & Miller, 2005).

Managers approach an ethical dilemma with a particular level of cognitive moral development. However, decisions made in a social context can be strongly influenced by the situation. Initially of course, the cultural context has a direct effect on the identification of the ethical component of an issue. For example, significant differences were found among Korean, Indian, and U.S. managers as to whether or not specific practices were ethical (Christie, Kwon, Stoeberl, & Baumhart, 2003). However, a person's susceptibility to external influence is related to the stage of moral development, with people at lower levels more susceptible (Treviño, 1986). Situational factors that might be proposed to influence the relationship between stage of moral development and ethical decision making include such factors as the extent to which the environment specifies normative behavior (highly specified in collectivist cultures), whether the social referents in the situation are members of one's in-group or out-group, and the extent to which demands are placed on the decision maker by people in authority. For example, normative behavior regarding sexual harassment might be very easy for U.S. people to recall from memory, whereas for Indonesians appropriate behavior in this situation is more ambiguous. In addition, social information provided by a superior has a more dramatic influence on decisions for vertical collectivists than for horizontal individualists (Liu, 1986). The social context

Figure 5.1 Culture's Influence on Ethical Decision Making

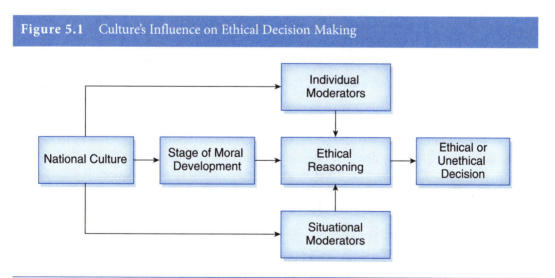

SOURCES: Adapted from Treviño (1986), Rest (1994), Robertson & Fadil (1999).

for managers also includes the organization in which they function. Organizations differ in adopted principles of social responsibility and have processes for social responsiveness (Wood, 1991). In addition, these organizational features can vary across cultures (Donaldson, 1993). These principles and processes can facilitate or impede ethical decision making.

The concepts presented in the model shown in Figure 5.1 have been subjected to only limited empirical tests. For example, an analysis of the ethical judgments of U.S., Eastern European, and Indonesian participants indicated that the type of ethical issue influenced cultural differences. However, after situational characteristics and the cultural background of participants were controlled for, the moral judgments participants made were consistent with their ethical ideology (Davis, Johnson, & Ohmer, 1998). Other research points to the effect of social influence on ethical decision-making. In a comparison of U.S. people and Israelis across a range of ethical issues, the best predictor of ethical judgments was what participants felt peers would do (Izraeli, 1988). And a study of U.S. expatriates supported the moderating effect of cultural context. That is, in the absence of the previously discussed hypernorms, expatriates were likely to adopt the local norms for ethical behavior (Spicer, Dunfee, & Bailey, 2004).

Thus, the limited amount of research on descriptive models of ethical behavior illuminates the importance of the three factors—(1) level of moral development, (2) individual factors, and (3) situational factors—in describing ethical decision making in an international environment. First, the concept of a level of cognitive moral development appears to apply to some extent across cultures. However, it would be naive to believe that managers' decisions are somehow hardwired to their value judgments about what is right or wrong. Therefore, both individual characteristics of the manager, such as culturally based values, and the situational (cultural and organizational) context in which the decision is being made are logical moderators of the relationship between the level of cognitive moral development and ethical behavior.

Summary

The decisions that international managers make are made more complex by an environment that includes stakeholders with potentially very different perspectives on desirable outcomes. Because of limits to rationality, managers rely on heuristics or rules of thumb to guide decision making. These heuristics simplify the decision-making process; because managers from different cultures perceive the world differently, they differ in the way in which they simplify complex realities. In addition to cognitive simplification, the decisions made are influenced by motivational biases, based in part on cultural values, and different definitions of self-interest.

International management decisions are further complicated by legal, political, and cultural boundaries. When these boundaries are crossed, what is moral can be blurred by cultural differences. There is no shortage of prescriptive models on which managers can draw for ethical guidance. However, actual ethical decision making is probably the result of the complex interplay of the level of cognitive moral development of the manager with other individual and situational factors.

Questions for Discussion

1. What does rational decision making mean? How do cognition and culture limit it?

2. What are heuristics and how does culture affect them?

3. How might cultural differences in motivational biases affect selection and reward allocation decisions?

4. What are the different ways in which people make ethical judgments? Give examples about how they affect responses to ethical dilemmas.

5. What are the stages of moral development proposed by Kohlberg? What are the implications of culture for ethical decision making?

The Manager as Negotiator: Communicating and Negotiating Across Cultures

Grammar and pronunciation aren't as important as expressing yourself in a way that matches the way Westerners think, which is very different from our thought process. So when you're in America you must be clear, and when you return to Japan you must be vague. It's more difficult than you can imagine.

—Akio Morita, founder, Sony Corporation

A significant part of every manager's job is the role of negotiator. That negotiator role can involve activity across the boundary of the organization, such as buyer–seller negotiations, or within the company, such as negotiating performance expectations with an employee. Underlying every negotiation that takes place in an international context is the process of cross-cultural communication. This chapter discusses the behavioral aspects of international negotiation. This discussion is grounded in the more general topic of cross-cultural communication.

Cross-Cultural Communication Process

Communication is the act of transmitting messages, including information about the nature of the relationship, to another person who interprets these messages and gives them meaning (Berlo, 1960). Therefore, both the sender and the receiver of the message play an active role in the communication process. Successful communication requires not only that the message is transmitted but also that the meaning of the message is understood. For this understanding to occur, the sender and receiver must share a vast amount of common information called grounding (Clark & Brennan, 1991). This grounding information is based on each individual's field of previous experience but is updated moment by moment during the communication process. Probably all of us have noticed how people who have extensive common information can communicate very effectively with a minimum of distortion. For example, hospital emergency room personnel depend on sharing a great deal of information, such as medical jargon and the seriousness of the situation, in order to communicate complex messages efficiently.

Cross-cultural communication is significantly more demanding than communicating in a single culture, because culturally different individuals have less common information. They have less grounding in common, because of differences in their fields of experience (Ronen, 1986; Schramm, 1980). In this chapter, the term *cultural field* refers to the culturally based elements of a person's background (e.g., education, values, attitudes) that influence communication. The additional complexity that this adds to the basic communication process is presented graphically in Figure 6.1.

Figure 6.1 shows (in simplified linear form) how the communication process involves the meaning that is to be transmitted, the sender of the message, a channel through which the message is transmitted, and the receiver of the message. All of these elements are embedded in their respective cultural fields. The message is encoded (converted to symbolic form) and sent by some means (channel) to the receiver, who

Figure 6.1   Cross-Cultural Communication Process

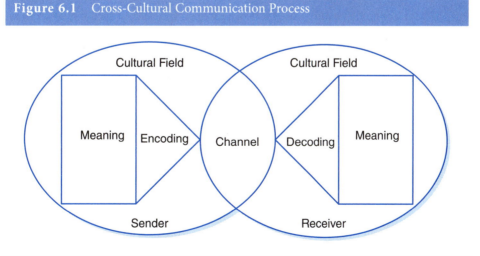

SOURCE: Adapted from Ronen (1986) and Schramm (1980).

then interprets (decodes) the message. The effectiveness of the communication depends on minimizing the distortion that can occur at all the stages of the communication process.

First, the meaning of the message is grounded in the personal field of experience of the sender, which can affect how it is encoded (see Brannen, 2004). Thus, the encoded message can be affected by the communication skills and knowledge of the sender and by the associated cultural field. That is, we cannot communicate what we do not know, and our ability to encode accurately is determined by our skill in the chosen channel (e.g., speaking or writing). In addition, like all behavior, much communication behavior is scripted and proceeds in a routine manner consistent with the cultural field. For example, in North America the response to "How are you today?" is often "Fine, thanks!" without any real consideration being given to one's actual physical condition, and the Chinese response to the common greeting "Have you eaten yet?" is similarly automatic. Without a common field of experience, the correct meaning is not ascribed to these messages (see Ronen, 1986).

Second, the symbols a person uses to express an idea vary with the cultural field. This includes not only the language used but also aspects of communication that transcend language, such as communication style, conventions, and practices. For example, Japanese use different verbs and make different decisions about who should control a conversation based on differences between the communicators in age, gender, and status. We might think that people would choose a different communication channel depending on the goal of the communication: written for task-oriented communications and verbal for relationship-oriented communications, for example. While these differences have been found and countries certainly do differ in the availability and typical use of communication technology (Desai, Fukuda-Parr, Johansson, & Sagasti, 2002; Peterson et al., 2010), the reality seems to be that convenience and skill in the use of the medium can be even more important (Kayany, Wotring, & Forrest, 1996). Today, for example, email and text messaging have come to substitute for a variety of communication channels for those who know how to use them.

Finally, all of the factors that affect the sender also influence the receiver. The symbols must be decoded into a form that can be understood by the receiver. Just like the sender, the receiver must be skilled in the channel in use and also have sufficient knowledge to interpret the message correctly. As in any cross-cultural interaction (Chapter 4), the ability of receivers to accurately perceive the communication behavior is influenced by their cultural field. In addition, the extent to which the cultural fields of individuals overlap reduces the opportunity for distortion in the communication process. That is, the more each party understands the other's situation, perspectives, and culture, the easier it is to use symbols that will be encoded and decoded similarly. For example, during the early 1980s when Sony set up its first U.S. production facility in San Diego, its engineers in the U.S. had an easier time communicating with their counterpart engineers from Tokyo about technical matters about which they shared much common grounding than when they talked with them about social and personal matters.

Language

One obvious consideration in cross-cultural communication is the language being used. Language is a symbolic code of communication consisting of a set of sounds with understood meanings and a set of rules for constructing messages. The meanings attached to any word by a language are completely arbitrary, but cultural conventions control the features of language use (Triandis, 1972). For example, the Japanese word for cat (*neko*) does not look or sound any more like a cat than does the English word. Somewhere during the development of the two languages, these words were chosen to represent the animal. Similarly, the Cantonese word for the number four (*sei*) has the same sound as the word for death, whereas the word for the number eight sounds like *faat* (prosperity). Therefore, some Chinese avoid things numbered four and are attracted to things numbered eight, although there are no such connotations for English speakers.

Although English may have become the lingua franca of international business (Naisbitt & Aburdene, 1990; Neeley, 2012), culturally based conventions create differences even between English speakers. In Britain, a *rubber* is an eraser, to *knock someone up* means to call at their house, and *tabling* an item means to put it on the agenda, not to defer it. Likewise, British people live in flats and might stand in a queue, U.S. people live in apartments and stand in line, and Canadians live in suites and stand in a lineup.

Even when translators know the meaning of words and the grammatical rules for putting them together, effective communication is often not achieved. The following notices written in English and discovered throughout the world illustrate the point:

- In an Austrian ski resort hotel: "Not to perambulate the corridors during the hours of repose in the boots of ascension."
- Outside a Hong Kong tailor shop: "Ladies may have a fit upstairs."
- From a Japanese car rental brochure: "When passenger of foot heave in sight, tootle the horn. Trumpet him melodiously at first, but if he still obstacles your passage then tootle him with vigor."

The diversity of languages in the world means an important issue in cross-cultural communication is finding a common language that both parties can use to work effectively. Practically, this means that at least one of the two parties must use a second language. Because the majority of Westerners in international business are monolingual (Ferraro, 2006) and English is spoken by one quarter of the world (Neeley, 2012), English is often the bridge language. This suggests that the second language in use in international business is most often English.

Many organizations, regardless of their country of origin or where they are based, have adopted English as the common corporate language (Zander et al., 2011). This language standardization is being driven by competitive pressure, the globalization of tasks and resources, as well as cross-border mergers and acquisitions, all of which demand a common language (Neeley, 2012).

> ### Box 6.1 English Only at Rakuten
>
> In March of 2010, Hiroshi Mikitani, CEO of Japan's largest online retailer (Rakuten), mandated that English would be the official company language, affecting some 7,100 Japanese employees. Over 550 million people use English on the Internet, and he believed that this new policy would help Rakuten achieve its goal of becoming the number one Internet services company in the world. Rakuten's growth had been fuelled by mergers and acquisitions in France, Germany, and the United States, and it had established joint ventures throughout Asia. Mikitani demonstrated his seriousness about the change by announcing it to employees in English as opposed to Japanese. By the next day, cafeteria signs, elevator directories, and so on were replaced and employees were told that they must demonstrate competence in English within two years or risk demotion or dismissal. As of 2012, half of Rakuten's Japanese employees could communicate adequately in English, and 25 percent were doing business in English on a regular basis.

The use of a second language has a number of implications for cross-cultural communication. First, using a second language creates cognitive strain (Smith & Bond, 1999). It takes more effort on the part of the second-language user, who could already be contending with other demands of communication or of the task at hand. Over long periods of time, second-language use is exhausting. Second, the greater the fluency of second-language speakers, the more likely they are to be seen as competent in other respects (Hui & Cheng, 1987). Third, first-language speakers in a cross-language interaction tend to respond to lower linguistic competency of their partner by modifying aspects of their speech, such as slowing the rate of speech and reducing sentence complexity (Gass & Varonis, 1985). This simplification of speech can improve communication by removing redundancy of content (Giles & Smith, 1979). However, this type of speech accommodation, called *foreigner speak,* can be perceived as patronizing and might not be well received (Williams, Garrett, & Tennant, 2004). Box 6.2 is an example of a conversation degenerating into foreigner speak.

> ### Box 6.2 Foreigner Speak
>
> | | |
> |---|---|
> | *Manager:* | Mr. Chan, could you take this report up to Mr. Abercrombie ASAP? |
> | *Mr. Chan:* | Sorry, I don't understand. |
> | *Manager:* | (*In a louder voice*) Could you take this report up to Mr. Abercrombie ASAP? |
> | *Mr. Chan:* | You want that I finish report? |
> | *Manager:* | Chan (*pause*) take report (*pause*) Mr. Abercrombie (*pause*) right now! |
> | *Mr. Chan:* | Sorry! |
>
> SOURCE: Adapted from Gallois & Callan (1997).

Finally, if the first-language speaker is unable to recognize signals that indicate lack of understanding or does not work to create an environment in which it is acceptable to check for understanding, the second-language speaker may pretend to understand in order to avoid embarrassment or appear competent (Li, 1994). The end result of these factors is that cross-language communication can be as demanding for the native speaker of the language as for the second-language speaker. Both participants must devote more attention to the communication process in order to achieve an effective transfer of understanding.

Communication Styles

The previous section presented some of the difficulties that language differences pose for the communication process. Primarily, these were issues of translation and second-language use. However, it is also important to consider the aspects of communication that transcend the specific language being spoken. In general, these communication behaviors are logical extensions of the values and norms that managers have internalized from their respective cultures. Culturally based rules govern the style, conventions, and practices of language usage. Many of these are related to the key value orientations of individualism and collectivism.

Explicit Versus Implicit Communication

One way in which cultural norms about communication style vary is in the degree to which they use language itself to communicate a message. For example, in the United States effective verbal communication is expected to be explicit, direct, and unambiguous (Gallois & Callan, 1997). People are expected to say exactly what they mean. In contrast, communication styles in some other cultures, such as Indonesia (Pekerti, 2001), are much more inexact, ambiguous, and implicit. These two styles are characterized by a bipolar typology called high-context and low-context communication styles.

A high-context (HC) communication or message is one in which most of the information is either in the physical context or internalized in the person, while very little is in the coded, explicit, transmitted part of the message. A low-context (LC) communication is just the opposite; the mass of the message is vested in the explicit code (Hall, 1976, p. 79).

On the basis of observation, a number of countries have been classified along the continuum according to whether they are primarily high or low context (Hall, 1976). In low-context cultures, the message is conveyed largely by the words spoken. In high-context cultures, a good deal of the meaning is implicit, and the words convey only a small part of the message. The receiver must fill in the gaps from past knowledge of the speaker, the setting, or other contextual cues. Figure 6.2 shows the relationship of 12 countries along the high-context and low-context continuum.

Researchers have noted that there is a close agreement between the position of countries on this scale and their location on Hofstede's (1980) individualism–collectivism index (Gudykunst, Ting-Toomey, & Chua, 1988; Pekerti, 2001). And

Figure 6.2 High- and Low-Context Cultures

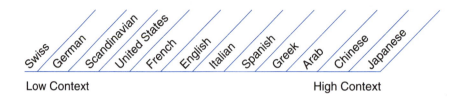

Low Context   High Context

individuals with independent self-concepts (individualists) are more likely to be low-context communicators, and those with interdependent self-concepts (collectivists) are more likely to be high-context communicators (Gudykunst, Gao, & Franklyn-Stokes, 1996). Logically, high context communication would be well suited to societies made up of the sort of stable, long-term groups whose members get to know one another extremely well over many years. Furthermore, high- and low-context communication styles may actually serve to perpetuate collectivism and individualism, respectively. For example, in individualist cultures speech is more focused and briefer, with more reference to *I* and to specific goals. However, in collectivist cultures speech includes more qualifiers, such as *maybe, perhaps, somewhat,* and *probably* (Smith & Bond, 1999). Some support for this idea is found in comparisons of pairs of cultures. Systematic differences in communication styles along the lines suggested here have been found for Jews and Arabs in Israel (Katriel, 1986), for U.S. people and Koreans (Kim, 1994), for Indonesians and New Zealanders (Pekerti, 2001), and for U.S. people and Japanese (Kitayama & Ishii, 2002). Box 6.3 gives an example of how high-context communication might operate in practice.

Box 6.3 High-Context Communication

An Indonesian woman invited the mother of the young man who was courting her daughter to tea. The woman was not pleased with the possibility that her daughter might marry into a family that she viewed as of lower socioeconomic status. During the meeting she never mentioned the relationship of their children, but she served bananas with the tea. The message that her son didn't belong with the woman's daughter any more than bananas go with tea was subtle and implicit but received loud and clear nonetheless.

Direct Versus Indirect Communication

An idea complementary to high-context versus low-context communication styles is the degree of directness of communication. Directness is associated with individualist cultures and indirectness with collectivist cultures (Levine, 1985; Sanchez-Burks et al., 2003). A pertinent example of this difference is expressed in the indirect style in which a collectivist might say no without really saying it, as shown in Box 6.4.

Direct communication is needed at some time in all cultural groups. However, as shown in Box 6.4, directness depends on the social context. The relationship to the social context is evident if we consider the motive for indirectness. In collectivist cultures, politeness and a desire to avoid embarrassment often take precedence over truth, as truth is defined in individualist cultures. For collectivists, truth is not absolute but depends on the social situation. Therefore, the social situation is an important indicator for the appropriate degree of directness or truthfulness. Although making untrue statements to preserve harmony (white lies) is probably universal, the extent of its use is probably higher in collectivist cultures (Smith & Bond, 1999).

Box 6.4 Saying "No" in Response to "Has My Proposal Been Accepted?"

Conditional "yes"	If everything proceeds as planned, the proposal will be approved.
Counterquestion	Have you submitted a copy of your proposal to the ministry of . . . ?
Criticizing the question	Your question is very difficult to answer.
Refusing the question	We cannot answer this question at this time.
Tangential reply	Will you be staying longer than you had originally planned?
Yes, but	Yes, approval looks likely, but. . . .
Delayed answer	You should know shortly.

SOURCE: C. Engholm (1991). "When Business East Meets Business West: The Guide to Practice & Protocol in the Pacific Rim" © 1991. Reprinted by permission of John Wiley & Sons, Inc.

Silence and Verbal Overkill

Just as cultural differences exist in language usage, they also exist in how silence is used in communication. To some extent, collectivist cultures value silence as a way of controlling the communication interaction, whereas individualists value talking in the same way (Giles, Coupland, & Wiemann, 1992). Silence might be thought of as an extreme form of high-context communication (Hasegawa & Gudykunst, 1998). For example, Japanese negotiators allow long periods of silence to develop (or use it strategically) in order to control the negotiation process (Graham, 1985; Morsbach, 1982). These periods of silence are often misunderstood by Westerners, who interpret them as a lack of understanding and try to shorten them with further explanation or by moving on to the next point.

Even among individualist cultures, the use of silence and talking can vary. For example, Australians have a lower tendency to communicate verbally than do people from the United States (Barraclough, Christophel, & McCroskey, 1988), and in Finland silence, is valued as a way of showing encouragement for the speaker to continue (Wiemann, Chen, & Giles, 1986).

Other speech communities have an indirectness and ambiguity similar to those associated with many Asian cultures. However, this indirectness causes them to use speaking and silence in a different way. For example, Arab-language countries engage in what is called *mubalaqha* or exaggeration to make their point (Almaney & Ahwan, 1982). In the Arab language, some common words used at the end of sentences are put there in order to be emphasized; pronouns are repeated, also for emphasis, and highly graphic metaphors and similes are commonly used. It is typical for an Arab speaker to modify a single noun with numerous adjectives for added effect. Research indicates that what would be an assertive statement in North America would probably be viewed as weak and equivocating by an Arab (Prothro, 1955). Smith and Bond (1999) suggest that this might have been at the heart of the Iraqi government's failure to heed the warnings in 1990 of then–U.S. Secretary of State James Baker that an invasion of Kuwait would lead to retaliation. Baker might not have delivered his message with sufficient exaggeration to be taken seriously.

Use of Praise

One additional stylistic element that has a systematic relationship to culture is the use of praise and the response to praise (Triandis, 1978). Several comparative studies have demonstrated stylistic differences about giving and receiving praise. Cultural differences exist in how frequently praise is used, what is praised, and how people respond. For example, U.S. people use praise more frequently and are more apt to praise people to whom they are close, such as friends or family, whereas Japanese are more likely to praise strangers (Barnlund & Araki, 1985). Moreover, U.S. people are more likely to praise physical appearance, whereas Arabs, like Japanese, are more likely to praise skill and work than physical characteristics (Nelson, El Bakary, & Al Batal, 1993). However, consistent with the propensity to exaggerate, Arab praise is typically more elaborate, often containing metaphors. Response to praise also seems to vary across cultures. In cultures such as China, where modesty is a virtue, praise can cause embarrassment. For example, Hong Kong Chinese tend to deflect praise, whereas British people are more likely to politely accept it (Loh, 1993). The cartoon in Figure 6.3 provides an example.

Other Language Considerations

To function effectively in cross-cultural communication, it is important to understand not only the formal structure of the language but also how it is used in certain social situations. We all have a large repertoire of language styles and registers (formality of language) that we adopt depending on the situation. For example, the language U.S. teenagers use with their peers is often quite different from what they would use with teachers or parents. Similarly, a Japanese adult would use very different language to address a superior at work from that used to speak to a child. In our native language,

Figure 6.3   Response to Praise

SOURCE: Feign (1988).

we have a fairly sophisticated grasp of style. However, cultural rules about style and register vary. For example, Chinese and Japanese have a much more complex range of formal styles than does English (Gallois & Callan, 1997). In addition, most languages have nonstandard forms and usage, such as slang, which make understanding this process more difficult.

Slang and Jargon

Many languages change register through the amount of slang they include. Slang is an informal usage of language typically more playful or metaphorical and associated with a particular subgroup. For example, in Australia *shrapnel* is the low denomination coins in one's pocket and a *noah* is rhyming slang for (noah's ark) a shark. Jargon, like slang, is associated with a particular subgroup but is often a very specialized or technical language of people engaged in a similar occupation or activity. In both cases, these specialized forms of language can enhance communications for members of the group with which they are associated but can be almost unintelligible for non-group members. The ability to communicate in the slang or jargon of a particular group helps to define one's membership in that group. For example, the terms *URL, wifi, phishing,* and *gigabyte* are familiar to people who share an interest in computers, and the rough dialect heard by young people on the streets of Paris is still French but serves to identify them as a distinct group.

The use of slang or jargon has three implications for cross-cultural communications. First, the number of possible variations in expression in any particular language group is greater. Second, these nonstandard terms or usage might last for only a few years before disappearing, unless they are incorporated into the standard form of the language. Finally, however, the knowledge of a shared specialized language by culturally different individuals can enhance their communication ability to some extent. For example, engineers or computer technicians from different cultures might share a significant amount of technical jargon that improves their grounding.

Euphemisms

All cultures seem to have words that by tradition or convention are not often used publicly. These prohibited words are often, but not necessarily, associated with sexual relations or bodily functions (Ferraro, 2006). These prohibited words are often handled by substituting a bland or less direct expression, or euphemism. In the United States, people don't die, they *pass away;* they aren't blind but are *visually impaired;* in some Latin American countries, being in an *interesting condition* means a woman is pregnant; and in 1997, Hong Kong was not *handed over* to China, it *returned home.* Obviously, an in-depth knowledge of another culture is needed to understand what topics can be referred to directly and which require a more indirect expression.

Idioms

Every language has unique ways of combining words to express a particular thought. Often, a particular phrase or construction differs from its literal meaning. This poses a particular problem for translation. Box 6.5 compares idiomatic expressions that convey the same meaning in U.S. and French Canadian usage.

Box 6.5 Examples of Idiomatic Expressions

American Expression	French-Canadian Expression
Nothing to sneeze at	Nothing to spit on
A little birdie told me so	My little finger told it to me
To be sitting on the fence	To swim between two streams
To cry in one's beer	To have the sad wine
To make a mountain out of a molehill	To drown in a glass of water
I have a hangover	I have a sore hair

SOURCE: Reprinted with permission of the publisher. From *Blunders in International Business,* by D. A. Ricks. Copyright © 1993. Blackwell. Cambridge, MA. All rights reserved. 1-800-929-2929.

The problem of literal versus idiomatic translation has resulted in a number of humorous (although probably not to those involved) examples of international business blunders. For example, one European firm mistranslated "out of sight, out of mind" to "invisible things are insane" in Thailand (Ricks, 1993).

Proverbs and Maxims

These short sayings express things that are obviously true in a particular culture and often advise people how they should behave. Therefore, they can provide insight into some of a culture's central values. Proverbs are found in all languages, and often the same basic idea can be found in widely different expressions. For example, the maxim "an eye for an eye" is expressed in East Africa as "a goat's hide buys a goat's hide" (Ferraro, 2006). Different cultures rely on proverbs to varying degrees to guide their behavior. Proverbs are often widely understood, if not followed, in a particular culture. For example, not everyone in the United States adheres to the "silence is golden" principle.

Language Pragmatics

In addition to the dimensions of language as a communication medium discussed previously, there are several practical considerations to language usage. These include which language will be used in an intercultural interaction, the effect of linguistic and stylistic accommodation by one speaker, and the effects of second-language ability.

Language Accommodation

Who will accommodate whom in an intercultural communication raises practical questions of language usage in addition to the language fluency of the parties involved. Speech accommodation involves shifting one's speech patterns to achieve greater language similarity. Sometimes, because of a history of antagonism, one language group refuses to speak another group's language (Bourhis, Giles, Leyens, & Tajfel, 1979). However, even when historical relationships between two groups are positive, the issue of who will accommodate whom must be resolved. Who will accommodate whom in an intercultural interaction can be complex and depends on the motives of the parties in the interaction, the identities of the parties, and the situation itself (Gallois & Callan, 1997). A key consideration is what is called the *ethnolinguistic vitality* of the language (Smith et al., 2013). The language that has higher prestige and is widely used in the relevant institutions or settings is more likely to be adopted. In business situations, the default language, because of lack of fluency or cultural conflicts, is often English. In these cases native English speakers are at an advantage because they are able to convey more exact or subtle messages and to demonstrate more variation in personal style. And, the ability of native English speakers to accommodate so-called lingua franca speakers seems to be somewhat limited. Recent studies have found that only a minority of native speakers are able to adjust their language effectively (Sweeney & Hua, 2010). The inability to accommodate nonnative speakers in one's own language is not limited to English. For example, Japanese people tend to believe that it is not possible for foreigners to be really fluent in their language and automatically switch to the foreigner's language (Ross & Shortreed, 1990). In reality, the kind of situation in which only one person

Figure 6.4 Language Accommodation

SOURCE: Feign (1988).

needs to adapt may be fairly uncommon. The effort that one party puts into accommodating the other's language is often appreciated and reciprocated (Giles, Bourhis, & Taylor, 1977). An example of how the role of the participant can influence the choice of language is presented in Figure 6.4.

Stylistic Accommodation

The idea that adapting one's communication style to that of the other culture participant in an intercultural communication will help to bridge cultural distance and improve communication is based on the similarity–attraction paradigm (Byrne, 1971) mentioned in Chapter 4. Stylistic accommodation leads to perceptions of similarity, which in turn lead to positive attitudes toward the member of the other culture. Research has indicated that some linguistic and behavioral accommodation can have a positive effect but that there might be some optimal level of adaptation of the patterns of the other culture beyond which the effects are less positive (Francis, 1991; Giles & Smith, 1979). The extent to which stylistic accommodation is viewed positively seems to depend on the motive to which it is attributed (Thomas & Ravlin, 1995). For example, if speech or behavioral accommodation is perceived as being patronizing or ingratiating, its positive effects are lost. Research indicates that some stylistic accommodation on the part of both parties in the cross-cultural communication can help to overcome communication difficulties (Miller, 1995). However, the optimal level of accommodation can be quite difficult to pinpoint.

Language Fluency

The degree of language fluency creates several problems for the second-language user that extend beyond the user's ability. Higher degrees of language fluency can lead to the second-language user being perceived as having a higher competency in other areas, such as knowledge of cultural norms (Hui & Cheng, 1987). For example, cultural blunders by a foreigner who is not competent in the foreign language might be forgiven as consistent with his or her lack of language skills and hence cultural knowledge. However, the same behavior by a fluent speaker of the language might be perceived negatively, because the person should know better based on his or her level of language fluency. Fluency in a foreign language can also cause a person to be perceived as having beliefs more closely aligned with the foreign language group (Bond, 1985). Additionally, foreign language use can have implications for the attitudes and behavior of the second-language user. For example, individuals have shown differences in attitudes (Guthrie & Azores, 1968) and in linguistic style (Loh, 1993) when responding in a second language. These shifts in attitudes and behavior are generally in the direction of those of the foreign language group (Bond & Yang, 1982).

Nonverbal Communication

Just as important to communication as the verbal components previously discussed are the nonverbal aspects of communication. Nonverbal communications convey important messages and are produced more automatically than are words (Argyle, 1988). They include body movements and gestures, touching, facial expressions and facial gazing, tone of voice, space usage, eye contact, and even scent or smell (Ferraro, 2006). Some researchers suggest that as much as 70 percent of communication between people in the same language group is nonverbal (Nollen, 1984). In cross-cultural communications, it is possible that people rely even more heavily on the nonverbal component (Gallois & Callan, 1997).

Nonverbal communication helps to regulate intercultural interaction by providing information about our feelings and emotional state, adding meaning to our verbal messages, and governing the timing and sequencing of the interaction (Patterson, 1991). Nonverbal behaviors have the same functions across cultures. However, nonverbal systems of communication, like language, have a significant amount of variation around the world. In general, two types of differences exist. First, the same nonverbal behavior can have very different meanings across cultures. For example, sucking in one's breath across the teeth is a sign of interest or admiration in New Zealand but indicates distress or even anger in Japan, and pulling the lower eyelid with the index finger is a sign of disbelief in France but means "I promise" in Iran. Second, different nonverbal cues can be used to mean the same thing in different cultures. For people from the United States and most Europeans, nodding the head up and down indicates agreement. However, this gesture is not universal. For example, in Calcutta rocking the head from side to side has the same meaning (Jensen, 1982).

The systematic study of nonverbal communication across cultures has been hampered by the lack of an underlying theory or framework. Attempts to systematize have included classifying nonverbal cues as conversational, topical, or interactive (Eisenberg & Smith, 1971). Other approaches have focused on the origin of the cues, resulting in many more categories (Condon & Yousef, 1975). There seems to be little agreement on appropriate typologies, and some researchers (Hecht, Andersen, & Ribeau, 1989) have shifted to a functional approach, in which nonverbal behaviors are grouped by the outcomes they achieve as opposed to their origin (e.g., hands, eyes, body, voice). At present, however, the international manager must rely largely on descriptions of the peculiarities of nonverbal communication in various cultures. The following discussion outlines some of the more important categories of nonverbal behaviors (cues) in terms of cross-cultural communication.

Tone of Voice

Along with the words we speak, the way we say them communicates feelings and attitudes (Pittman, 1994). This nonverbal behavior includes pitch, volume, speed, tension, variation, enunciation, and a number of other voice qualities such as breathiness and creakiness (Gallois & Callan, 1997). In addition, these and other features of voice, such as accent, can indicate the cultural identity of the speaker. Cultural norms ascribe different meanings to features and qualities of tone of voice. These meanings can be categorized along the dimensions of dominance, positivity, and arousal (Gallois & Callan, 1997). For example, dominance in the United States is indicated by loud, low-pitched, and fast speech, whereas in Germany dominance is indicated by soft, low-pitched, breathy speech (Scherer, 1979). As in the interpretation of other behavior across cultures, individuals often fall into the trap of using self-referent criteria in explaining tone of voice. They interpret tone of voice as if it were them speaking.

Proxemics

Another nonverbal component of communication that must be considered in cross-cultural interactions is the way in which people use personal space in their interactions with others. The term coined for the study of this dimension of human behavior is *proxemics* (Hall, 1966). People seem to follow predictable patterns when establishing distance between themselves and others that are consistent with cultural norms. For example, based on observation of middle-class North Americans, a typology of distances has been formulated (Hall, 1966) and is shown in Box 6.6.

Because cultural norms influence the appropriateness of a particular spatial relationship, what is an appropriate distance in one culture might seem unusual or even offensive in another. For example, in a study of five different cultures, the appropriate *conversational distance* (between two people without regard for topic or their relationship) was greatest for Scots, followed by Swedes, U.S. people, Italians, and Greeks, in that order (Little, 1968). Whereas North Americans might prefer a conversational distance of, say, 20 inches, Greeks might be more comfortable at about 9 or 10 inches and Arabs even closer. The opportunities for misunderstandings in an intercultural interaction are obvious as each party tries to establish a comfortable distance.

Box 6.6 Typology of Distances

Intimate distance	Contact–18 inches, a distance reserved for comforting, protecting, and love making
Personal distance	18 inches–4 feet, a bubble of personal space the size of which depends on the relationship to the other person
Social distance	4–12 feet, used by acquaintances and strangers in more formal settings
Public distance	12–25 feet, distance at which the recognition of others is not required

SOURCE: Adapted from Hall, E. T. (1966). *The hidden dimension.* New York: Doubleday.

Although much of the evidence for cultural-based proximity norms in conversation is anecdotal, the few studies that have been conducted support their existence. In general, people in colder climates seem to prefer larger physical distance in communication than people in warmer climates (Sussman & Rosenfeld, 1982). For example, in a study of students who were friends, Arabs sat closer, talked more loudly, and touched each other more often than people from the United States (Watson & Graves, 1966). In other research (Watson, 1970), South Americans, Asians, and Indians chose spatial distances midway between that of Arabs and Europeans (including U.S. people and Australians). In yet another study, Japanese chose larger spatial distances than did Venezuelans, with people from the United States choosing a distance in between the two (Shuter, 1977). These findings are for individuals engaged in an interaction. Where there is no requirement for interaction, the findings are somewhat less clear. As is often the case in nonverbal communication, the cultural rules can be different from one situation to the next.

At one extreme of the proximity scale is touching. People touch in a variety of ways depending on purpose (e.g., hand to arm to show guidance, kissing the cheek to show affection). Cultures vary widely in the meanings associated with the various forms of touching and with who can touch whom and on what part of the body in what circumstances. For example, in North America it is typical for two men to show friendliness by shaking hands. However, if these same two men held hands while walking down the street in the United States, a behavior common in Thailand (Warren, Black, & Rangsit, 1985), this would be less conventional.

Cultures have been classified as high touch versus low touch, with Mediterranean cultures, Eastern Europeans, and Arabs and Jews as high touch and English, Germans, northern European, and Asian cultures as low touch (Montagu, 1972). However, as with any classification scheme this broad, it is important not to overgeneralize. Touching behavior in any culture is likely to depend on a number of factors, including age, gender, and social status as well as the situation (Shuter, 1977). For example, a light touch on the back is usually initiated by people of power in the United States as a signal of dominance (Henley, 1977). However, in cultures where touch is common, such as Latin America, such touches might not even be noticed. And gender differences are especially prominent with regard to the use of touch as an expression of dominance in different cultures (Diabiase & Gunnoe, 2004).

Proxemics has some additional implications for the international manager. For example, cultures use office space differently, and this can influence cross-cultural communication. Many North Americans close their office doors only for private conferences, whereas Germans are likely to keep their office doors closed at all times. In Japan, offices are often shared by a number of managers. Meetings are held in separate meeting rooms, whereas in the United States private offices or partitions between workstations are the norm. Hall (1966) reported that one German executive was so protective of his personal space that he had the visitor's chair in his office bolted to the floor in the proper place to keep his U.S. visitors from adjusting it to their preferred distance. These patterns of spatial orientations are important in part because they are subtle channels for communicating a significant amount of information and are often overlooked. For example, one recent study investigated the use of space to establish dominance and found that Chinese were more likely to use this tactic than were Canadians (Semnani-Azad & Adair, 2011).

Body Position and Gestures

Unlike languages, which are generally well documented in structure and meaning, the descriptions of nonverbal elements of communication are usually incomplete and somewhat superficial. The way people position their body conveys information in all cultures. However, people learn which body position is appropriate in a given situation in the same way that they internalize other aspects of culture. The vast array of possible body positions is difficult to categorize in any systematic way. For example, in the United States people stand up to show respect, whereas in Samoa they sit down, and showing the sole of your shoe in a Muslim society is a sign of great disrespect (Morrison et al., 1994).

One suggestion is that body positions that make one appear smaller indicate submissiveness and that rounded body postures communicate friendliness, whereas angular postures communicate threat or hostility (Aronoff, Woike, & Hyman, 1992). People from high-power distance cultures might show more bodily tension as a way of indicating submissiveness or deference (Andersen & Bowman, 1985). For example, bowing is a subtle lowering of the body to show deference to a person of higher status. Bowing is so pervasive in Japan that some department store employees are hired to bow to customers at escalators, and many Japanese bow to their unseen partners in a telephone conversation (Morsbach, 1982). Bowing in Japan is an intricate process, which is determined by the relative social status of the parties and, like many subtle nonverbal elements, is difficult for outsiders to master.

Hand gestures are used both intentionally and unintentionally in communication. Hand gestures used as a substitute for words are called emblems. Because the hand can be configured in numerous ways and with great precision, the number of possible hand gestures is enormous. However, one study has documented the major hand gestures used in Western Europe (Morris, Collett, Marsh, & O'Shaugnessy, 1979). Upon examination, the vast array of alternative hand gestures to indicate the same idea is revealed. For example, this research identified more than a dozen different gestures that men used in different countries to show appreciation for an attractive woman.

Further complicating matters, the same hand gesture can have different meanings in different parts of the world. For example, repeatedly crooking the index finger with the palm up beckons another person to come closer in North America. However, the same gesture is obscene in some cultures. An example of cultural misinterpretation is provided in Box 6.7. Emblems such as these are often quite explicit and can be learned by watching what people do and do not do. Although being able to distinguish the meaning of gestures in a culture seems to be an indicator of cultural competence (Molinsky, Krabbenhoft, Ambady, & Choi, 2005), trying to learn all the hand gestures that exist across cultures would be impossible. Therefore, probably the best advice is to avoid gestures until one is very sure what they mean.

Box 6.7 Bush "Satan Salute" Shocks Norway

U.S. president George W. Bush's (and his family's) "hook 'em Horns" salute, to the University of Texas Longhorns marching band as it passed during the inauguration parade, got lost in translation in Norway. Shocked people there interpreted the hand gesture as a salute to Satan.

In Norway, that's what it means when you throw up the right hand with only the index and little finger raised. "Shock greeting from Bush daughter," read the headlines of the Norwegian online newspaper *Nettavisen*.

SOURCE: Associated Press.

Facial Expression

Facial expression is a key source of information, particularly about underlying emotional states, which seem to be closely linked to facial expression. In addition, people tend to be more accurate in making judgments about emotional state based on facial expressions than based on body movement (Ekman, 1982). Early research indicated that the same facial expressions were associated with certain emotions in all cultures (Ekman, Friesen, & Ellsworth, 1972). Indeed, it appears that six basic emotions of anger, fear, sadness, disgust, happiness, and surprise are evident in facial expressions around the world from a very early age (Izard, 1991). Recent research has shown that the recognition of basic emotions is evident even when one is viewing continuously changing (morphing) facial features (Wang et al., 2006). The three main parts of the face, (a) the forehead and eyebrows, (b) eyes, and (c) mouth, express emotions in roughly the following ways (Gallois & Callan, 1997, p. 57):

- *Happiness*: smiling mouth, puffed lower eyelids, smooth brow and forehead
- *Surprise*: raised eyebrows, wide-open eyes, open mouth
- *Disgust*: brow lowered and drawn inward, upper lip raised, which sometimes causes the nose to wrinkle
- *Fear*: brow raised, furrowed, and drawn inward, wide open eyes, mouth open with lips drawn back
- *Anger*: lowered brow, staring (sometimes narrowed) eyes, jaw clenched, mouth either closed or open with teeth bared
- *Sadness*: brow lowered (sometimes drawn inward), inside corners of eyelid raised, corners of the mouth pulled down

The link between facial expressions and emotions is a direct one that operates without conscious thought (DePaulo, 1992). However, people often deliberately seek to override the linkage between their emotions and their facial expression. In this way, culture can influence facial expression. Very soon after an emotion occurs, facial expressions are influenced by a person's culturally learned display rules (Levenson, Ekman, Heider, & Friesen, 1992). For example, the situation in which Olympic medal winners won and received their medals determined their initial facial expressions. However, slightly later, their cultural background showed an influence (Matsumoto & Willingham, 2006). An examination of smiling behavior provides another example. In one study, people from the United States and Japan both found a smiling face to be more sociable (Matsumoto & Kudoh, 1993), consistent with the universal association of smiling with happiness. However, in Japan smiling can also be used to hide displeasure, sorrow, or anger (Morsbach, 1982), and in China smiling is often associated with a lack of self-control and calmness (Albright, Malloy, Dong, Kenny, & Fang, 1997). Therefore, although all people smile, the meaning of this and other facial expressions can vary across cultures to the extent that people are controlling their facial display.

Some researchers have suggested that cultures can be classified regarding emotional expression rules as either affective or neutral (Trompenaars, 1993). For example, in collectivist cultures, in which people have more interdependent self-concepts, the expression of emotion in public is often suppressed in order to maintain harmony (Ekman, 1982). This may be a reason why Japanese and Chinese people often appear inscrutable to Europeans. Research indicates that it is much harder to guess how a Japanese person feels from facial expression than it is for British or Italians (Shimoda, Argyle, & Ricci-Bitti, 1984).

Eye Contact (Gaze)

Sixteen centuries ago Saint Jerome (374–419 A.D.) said, "The face is the mirror of the mind, and eyes without speaking confess the secrets of the heart." All cultures use gaze (eye contact) in nonverbal communication. Both maintaining eye contact and avoiding eye contact communicate important messages. In North America, a high level of gazing from another is typically interpreted as a sign of friendliness (Kleinke, 1986), unless it persists regardless of the person's response. Then, it can be interpreted as hostile or aggressive (Ellsworth & Carlsmith, 1973). Avoidance of eye contact often suggests shyness, unfriendliness, or insincerity to North Americans (Zimbardo, 1977). Extensive research also indicates that people avert their gaze when thinking (McCarthy, Lee, Itakura, & Muir, 2006). However, societies have various norms regarding where and for how long one should look at another person during social interaction (Knapp & Hall, 2002).

Cultural differences in gaze patterns seem to be fixed fairly early in life and persist regardless of subsequent cross-cultural experiences (Watson, 1970). For example, Arabs, Latins, Indians, and Pakistanis maintain a significantly higher level of eye contact in normal conversation than do North Americans. Conversely, Africans and East Asians interpret high levels of eye contact as conveying anger or insubordination and hence avoid it. In Japan, for example, rather than looking a person in the eyes, one gazes downward toward the neck region (Morsbach, 1982). The appropriate level of eye contact in conversation can also vary according to the relative status of the individuals involved, and appropriate eye contact in public space also varies across cultures (Davis, 1971).

The previous discussion of nonverbal communication behavior must be treated with some caution. First, it is not possible to rely on uniformity even within a single culture because other factors, such as education, occupation, religion, and the relative status of the people involved, can have a significant impact on nonverbal behavior. Second, not all nonverbal behaviors are of equal importance even within a culture. Finally, as noted previously, there are both similarities and differences in nonverbal communication across cultures.

Negotiation and Conflict Resolution Across Cultures

An important application of cross-cultural communication for the international manager is face-to-face negotiation. All negotiations share some universal characteristics. They involve two or more parties who have conflicting interests but a common need to reach an agreement, the content of which is not clearly defined at the outset (Hofstede & Usunier, 1996). A substantial body of literature exists about the effects of both contextual and individual factors on the negotiation process and on outcomes (Neale & Northcraft, 1991). However, the extent to which these findings generalize across cultures is just beginning to be understood.

The study of cross-cultural business negotiation has produced a number of analytical models that identify the antecedents to effective negotiation (e.g., Brett, 2007; Graham, 1987; Tung, 1988; Weiss, 1993). Consistent among them is that the outcomes of negotiation are thought to be contingent on (a) factors associated with the behavior of people involved in the negotiation, (b) factors associated with the process of negotiation, and (c) factors associated with the negotiation situation. In general, culture probably has an indirect (contextual) effect on the outcome of negotiations by influencing all these contingency variables (Brett, 2007; Usunier, 1996).

Efforts to understand cross-cultural negotiation fall into one of three types. The first type is descriptive approaches, which are characteristic of much early study of cross-cultural negotiation. These studies involve documenting differences in negotiation processes and behaviors in different cultures. The second might be called the cultural dimensions approach (Brett & Crotty, 2008), in which the cultural effects are attributed to the cultural values and norms of the participants. The third is a more holistic approach that considers both the knowledge structures of the participants and the social context in which the negotiation takes place (e.g., Gelfand & McCusker, 2002).

Descriptions: Negotiating Process and Behavior

A number of efforts have been made to describe the stages of the negotiation process. The number of stages suggested ranges from three (Salacuse, 1991) to 12 (Gulliver, 1979), with the most widely used of these consisting of four (Graham, 1987) or five (McCall & Warrington, 1990) stages. Although the idea of a sequential, phased structure to negotiations might be a peculiarly Western notion (Weiss, 1993), the concept is nevertheless appealing from a comparative standpoint. The Graham four-stage model seems to have the most elements in common with the other popular models. Essentially, the model suggests that all business negotiations proceed through four stages:

1. Nontask sounding or relationship building

2. Task-related exchange of information

3. Persuasion

4. Making concessions and reaching agreement

Graham (1987) suggests that the content, duration, and importance of each of these stages can be seen to differ across cultures. The internalized cultural values and norms of the negotiator influence which aspect of the process is emphasized. Although no direct tests of the model exist, descriptions of the negotiation process in different cultures (e.g., Pye, 1982; Tung, 1984) support the notion that different aspects of the negotiation process are emphasized in different cultures. For example, Japanese negotiators spend more time in non-task sounding or relationship building than U.S. people, and they also emphasize an exchange of information as opposed to the persuasion tactics preferred by people from the United States (Graham, 1987). These differences are reflected in descriptions of the behavioral styles of negotiators discussed next.

Numerous studies have documented the negotiating styles of people from different cultures. Differences have been recorded in styles of persuasion, conflict resolution preferences, and initial bargaining positions and concession patterns (Leung & Wu, 1990). Regarding styles of persuasion, one early study (Glenn, Witmeyer, & Stevenson, 1977) analyzed the transcripts of the United Nations Security Council meetings during disarmament negotiations and illustrated cultural differences in the styles of persuasion used by the U.S. and Syrian representatives. The factual–inductive style of the U.S. representatives, which relied on appeals to logic, contrasted dramatically with the more affective–intuitive style of the Syrians, which relied on emotional appeals. The same study documented the persuasion style of Russian negotiators, which relied on references to ideology. These three styles of persuasion were labeled rational, affective, and ideological.

Culture also seems to influence the preference that individuals have for a particular conflict resolution style. For example, some cultures prefer confrontation in the negotiation process, whereas others prefer a more subtle form of bargaining in which balance and restraint are important. France, Brazil, and the United States are typically competitive, whereas Japanese and Malaysian negotiators are characterized by their politeness, ambiguous objections, and restraint (Leung & Wu, 1990). In addition, Indians can be even more competitive in negotiations than people from the United States (Druckman, Benton, Ali, & Bagur, 1976). Tinsley (1998) found systematic differences between Japanese, German, and U.S. managers in their preference for a particular conflict resolution model. Japanese managers preferred a status power model in which conflicts are resolved by a higher authority. Germans preferred a regulations model in which preexisting procedures or rules resolve problems. People from the United States preferred an interest model that focuses on discovering and resolving the underlying concerns of the other party to make it worthwhile to reach an agreement.

Culture also seems to influence the initial offers and concession patterns of negotiators. Some cultural groups use very extreme initial offers, such as Russians, Arabs (Glenn et al., 1977), and Chinese (Pye, 1982), whereas others, such as people from the United States, are more moderate in their initial positions. Similarly, cultural differences exist in the willingness of negotiators to make concessions. Russians, for example, seem to view concessions as a weakness, whereas other groups, such as North Americans, Arabs, and Norwegians, are more likely to make concessions and to reciprocate an opponent's concessions (Glenn et al., 1977; Maxwell & Schmitt, 1975).

A series of studies by Graham and his colleagues (Graham, 1983, 1985; Graham, Kim, Lin, & Robinson, 1988; Graham, Mintu, & Rodgers, 1994) documented differences in the tactics used by negotiators from a number of different countries. For example, the differences in both verbal and nonverbal behaviors of negotiators from Japan, the United States, and Brazil are presented in Table 6.1.

Other cross-cultural comparisons of negotiator behavior include the influence of assertiveness on negotiator outcomes (Ma & Jaeger, 2010), the effect of displaying anger on the negotiation strategies across cultures (Liu, 2009), and the display of dominant nonverbal cues (relaxed posture, use of space, and facial display) on cross-cultural negotiation (Semnani-Azad & Adair, 2011).

These descriptions are informative and indicate that negotiator behavior is highly variable across cultures. However, they provide little information about why these differences occur. The consistency they show with what is known about communication styles and with underlying cultural value orientations has led to a consideration of the effect of cultural dimensions on negotiation.

Table 6.1 Negotiator Behavior in Three Cultures

	Individual Tactics as a Percentage of Total Tactics		
	Japanese (N = 6)	American (N = 6)	Brazilian (N = 6)
Promise	7	8	3
Threat	4	4	2
Recommendation	7	4	5
Warning	2	1	1
Reward	1	2	2
Punishment	1	3	3
Positive normative appeal	1	1	0
Negative normative appeal	3	1	1
Commitment	15	13	8
Self-disclosure	34	36	39
Question	20	20	22
Command	8	6	14
	Occurrences in a 30-Minute Bargaining Session		
Number of times word "no" used	5.7	9.0	83.4
Silent periods of 10 seconds or more	5.5	3.5	0
Conversational overlaps (interruptions)	12.6	10.3	28.6
Gazing (minutes per random 10-minute period)	1.3 minutes	3.3 minutes	5.2 minutes
Touching	0	0	4.7

SOURCE: From Graham, J. L. (1985). The influence of culture on the process of business negotiations: An exploratory study. *Journal of International Business Studies, 16,* 81–96.

Cultural Dimensions and Negotiation

Research that relates dimensions of cultures, such as individualism–collectivism or power distance, to negotiation improves our ability to explain and predict the effect of culture. For example, the cultural dimensions of individualism and collectivism can be predictive of a preference for a particular style of conflict resolution. In one study

(Gabrielidis, Stephen, Ybarra, Dos Santos Pearson, & Villareal, 1997), collectivists (Mexicans) preferred conflict resolution styles that showed greater concern for others than did individualist (U.S.) participants. In another study, collectivists preferred bargaining and mediation as conflict resolution strategies, whereas individualists preferred adversarial adjudicative procedures in which arguments are developed and positions are presented by the parties to the dispute (Leung, 1987). The rationale for this difference is that collectivists might actually perceive an adversarial procedure to be desirable, but the confrontation and competitiveness inherent in the procedure reduce their preference for it (Bond, Leung, & Schwartz, 1992; Leung & Lind, 1986). Similarly, Tinsley (1998) found that characteristics of Japanese (social inequity), German (explicit contracting), and U.S. (polychronicity) cultures were linked to conflict resolution preferences for use of authorities, external regulations, and integrating conflicts, respectively.

Cultural dimensions have also been related to differences in cognitive processes related to negotiation. For example, Gelfand et al. (2001) found that Japanese and U.S. participants differed in their perceptions of conflict based on cultural differences in the need to preserve harmony during negotiations. And individualist and collectivist cultures have been found to differ with regard to self-serving bias (called egocentric perceptions of fairness) (Gelfand et al., 2002; Tinsley & Pillutla, 1998).

Negotiation processes can be understood from a cultural dimension perspective as well. For example, negotiators from low-context cultures have been found to engage in more direct information sharing, throughout the stages of the negotiation, whereas negotiators from high-context cultures engaged in direct information exchange in the earlier phases of negotiation (Brett & Crotty, 2008). Recent research suggests that the need to gain information, consistent with Japanese culture, was the reason for early initial offers by Japanese negotiators. Japanese negotiators interpreted offers that they received as indicating the priorities of their negotiating partners. They would then exchange offers in order to learn about one another's priorities. Negotiators from individualistic societies, in contrast, typically interpreted offers as attempts to complete the negotiation process and reach an agreement (Adair, Weingart, & Brett, 2007).

Cultural dimensions also relate to the outcomes of negotiation. Most often this has been studied in terms of distributive (win–lose) or integrative (win–win) outcomes. For example, Natlandsmyr and Rognes (1995) found that Norwegians had more integrative outcomes than Mexicans, based on the cultural profile of Norway that includes low masculinity, weak uncertainty avoidance, and low power distance. And Brett and Okumura (1998) reported that, consistent with their society's hierarchical cultural values, Japanese achieved a lower level of joint gains in intercultural dyads.

The cultural dimensions approach has shed additional light on the effect of culture on negotiations. However, an additional complication is that negotiators may change their behavior when negotiating with someone from another culture. Cultural differences have been reported in how often negotiators change tactics during a negotiation, with negotiators from Spain the most flexible, followed in order by the United Kingdom, Switzerland, Denmark, and Sweden (Porat, 1970). In addition, research found that Japanese in negotiation with Canadians used different types of influence tactics (more assertiveness, threats, appeals to reason, and appeals to a higher authority) than when interacting with members of their own culture (Rao & Hashimoto, 1996). Chinese, when trying to resolve a disagreement, used tactics designed to embarrass a Chinese counterpart but tried to resolve the situation and preserve the relationship with people from the United States (Weldon et al., 1996, cited in Smith & Bond, 1999). However, contrary findings about the extent to which negotiators change their behavior in intercultural interactions exist. For example, in a study of Canadian and Chinese executives, neither group altered its negotiation strategy when negotiating across cultures (Tse, Francis, & Walls, 1994). These contradictory findings suggest that contextual differences can influence the extent to which culturally based preferences for negotiation behavior are altered in cross-cultural interactions.

Holistic Approaches to Negotiation

In order to understand the social context of negotiation, recent approaches have taken a more holistic view of the negotiation process that recognizes that negotiator behavior can vary within the same culture, depending on the context of a negotiation and the people involved (Gelfand & Cai, 2004). For example, a negotiating context in which negotiators believe they are accountable for the negotiation outcomes makes negotiators behave more competitively. However, some research has found that accountability caused negotiators to conform more closely to their culture's norms (Gelfand & Realo, 1999)—that is, be more cooperative in collectivist cultures and more competitive in individualist. Also, the extent to which negotiators who have personality traits causing them to feel the need to bring negotiations to a conclusion quickly (need for closure) moderates cultural influence. Individuals with a high need for closure exhibit more culturally prototypical behavior than do those low in this need because of a stronger desire for external (consensual) validation for their actions (Fu, Morris et al., 2007). And the hierarchical relationship between individuals can influence the extent to which culture influences conflict resolution behavior. For example, in one study cultural norms for resolving a dispute were influenced by whether or not the decision maker was the superior or peer of disputants for Chinese but not for Japanese or U.S. people (Brett, Tinsley, Shapiro, & Okumura, 2007).

One way in which the complex influence of culture and context on negotiation has been studied is by trying to understand negotiation through the metaphors that people use to make sense of the process (see Gelfand & McCusker, 2002). The content of the metaphors tends to be culturally specific, whereas the process being described is universal. Metaphors for negotiation are individuals' subjective realities of the social interaction, which guide the behavior of the participants. They reflect broad cultural themes but are not necessarily stable across all people and situations. Specifically, metaphors identify the tasks to be performed (problem), the norms for interaction (scripts), and the outcomes of the interaction (feelings). An example of culturally based metaphors for negotiation in U.S. and Japanese culture is presented in Table 6.2.

Table 6.2   Cultural Differences in Negotiation Metaphors

	U.S: Sports	**Japan: Household**
Problems	Task oriented.	Relationally oriented.
	Conflict is normal and overt.	Conflict is avoided and covert.
	Discrete activity (beginning and end, events separate).	Continuous activity (no beginning or end, contexts overlap).
Scripts	Universalistic rules.	Particularistic rules.
	Reciprocity (turn taking).	Status dictates action.
	Aggressive behavior.	Face saving is critical.
	Person and task separate.	Person inseparable from task.
Feelings	Outcomes by skill, explicit.	Outcome by roles, implicit.
	Satisfaction from winning.	Satisfaction from role fulfillment.

SOURCE: Adapted from Gelfand, M. J., & McCusker, C. (2002). Metaphor and the cultural construction of negotiation: A paradigm for research and practice. In M. J. Gannon & K. L. Newman (Eds.), *Handbook of cross-cultural management* (pp. 292–314). Malden, MA: Blackwell.

Metaphors may be a useful tool in that they help negotiators understand their own culture and how it shapes the reality they impose on the negotiation situation. This is potentially a first step in helping negotiators restructure their thinking in such a way that complementary or shared metaphors that bridge cultural differences can be created (Schön, 1993). Recent research has supported the idea that an ability to make psychological and behavioral adjustments to intercultural conditions may be a critical factor in reaching consensus in cross-cultural negotiations (Liu, Friedman, Barry, Gelfand, & Zhang, 2012).

Summary

This chapter presented the behavioral aspects of international negotiation and its foundation in cross-cultural communication. Communication across cultures presents additional opportunities for messages to be misunderstood because of a lack of common grounding. In addition, cross-cultural communication is significantly more demanding on both the sender and receiver of the message. Negotiation is a communication in which the parties have a need to reach an agreement but have potentially conflicting interests.

Consistent with cultural variation in communication behavior, negotiators exhibit characteristic differences in their preferred negotiating style, conflict resolution preferences, and persuasion styles. Some evidence suggests that their behavior changes depending on whether the negotiation is within or across cultures and that the context of the negotiation influences cultural effects. The lack of definitive research in this area suggests that prescriptions for improving negotiation across cultures must be treated with some caution. More holistic approaches may yield a better understanding of this complex intercultural interaction.

Questions for Discussion

1. How do the cultural field and language affect the five steps in communicating? Give examples.

2. How do communication styles tend to differ between cultures?

3. What are some of the other aspects of language that interfere with intercultural communication?

4. What are some of the pragmatic ways of dealing with language differences?

5. Describe the nonverbal messages that are part of communication.

6. How does culture affect behavior during different negotiation stages and negotiation in general?

7

The Manager as Leader: Motivation and Leadership Across Cultures

Japanese and American management is 95% the same and differs in all important respects.

—Takeo Fujisawa, cofounder, Honda Motor Company

One of the most difficult tasks that international managers face is the need to motivate and lead individuals from different cultures. Individual motivation is at the core of understanding the behavior of individuals in organizations. And leadership is perhaps the most studied yet least understood topic in management. This chapter examines motivation and leadership in a cross-cultural context. Concepts developed in Western cultures, including the design of motivating jobs, are examined for their applicability across cultures, and non-Western approaches are presented. Finally, this chapter presents a cross-cultural model of leadership that synthesizes some of the current thinking on the topic. This model is consistent with the influence of social cognition in an intercultural interaction, as presented in earlier chapters.

Motivation Across Cultures

Motivation is typically described as the willingness of individuals to exert effort toward a goal. The study of work motivation has often been divided into content theories and process theories. The applicability of both has been examined across cultures.

Content Thories

Content theories explain motivation as the needs that people seek to satisfy. Unsatisfied needs create tension that individuals are motivated to reduce through their behavior. For example, Maslow (1954) suggested that needs motivate individuals in a sequential hierarchy from basic (physiological, safety, belongingness) to growth (self-esteem, self-actualization) needs. Early tests of Maslow's theory suggested systematic differences in need strength across cultures (Haire, Ghiselli, & Porter, 1966). However, other studies have found need structures similar to Maslow's hierarchy in a variety of cultures (see Steers & Sánchez-Runde, 2002). A potential limitation of need theories is that individual needs are given primacy (placed at the bottom of the hierarchy), which may be less appropriate in a collectivist society in which relational needs are more basic (Peterson & Wood, 2008).

A second content theory of motivation that has received a good deal of attention across cultures is McClelland's (1961) focus on the three needs of achievement, affiliation, and power (dominance), which vary among individuals. Research about differences among individuals in the United States indicates that people high in need for achievement strive for personal success, whereas successful managerial (leadership) performance requires individuals high in the need for power and low in the need for affiliation. The cross-cultural study based on this theory focused on societal differences in achievement motivation that can be inferred from a country's children's literature. The basic result was that literature containing a great deal of achievement motivation imagery was related to a nation's subsequent economic growth. As a result, McClelland suggested that achievement motivation training would promote the economic advance of less developed countries. The likelihood is that the relationship between achievement motivation and economic success on a national level is far more complex than originally proposed (see Bhagat & McQuaid, 1982). This line of research has stimulated considerable attention to ways in which the motivational aspects of the societal culture indicators discussed in Chapter 3 predict national economic performance.

The majority of cross-cultural research on content theories has focused on higher-order needs, such as achievement or self-actualization, while ignoring lower-order needs (Steers & Sánchez-Runde, 2002). However, most people, even in the developed world, may be concerned primarily with meeting lower-order needs, not developing satisfying social relationships, seeking personal achievement, or pursuing self-actualization. Societal stratification in many societies affects the dominant needs of individuals (Ravlin, Thomas, & Ilsev, 2000). Thus, the things that motivate people in different strata of society might be quite different across cultures (Peterson & Wood, 2008).

Process Theories

Process theories of motivation explain the choices that people make about their behavior. Examples of these theories are equity theory (Adams, 1965), expectancy theory (Porter & Lawler, 1968; Vroom, 1964), and goal setting theory (Locke & Latham, 1984).

Although these theories derive from U.S.-based research efforts, some studies have been conducted outside the United Sates to evaluate their validity in other cultures.

Equity Theory

Equity theory recognizes that we all are aware of what we contribute and what we receive in return from our roles in work and in life and that we also compare this ratio of our inputs and outcomes with that of other people. There are motivational consequences if people experience an imbalance in which the ratio of their inputs to outcomes is perceived to be unfair compared to what other people receive. For example, I might accept that someone should be more highly paid than am I only if I believe that person contributes more than I contribute. Otherwise, this sense of inequity causes individuals to try to restore balance by doing things such as reducing inputs or changing their point of comparison. If I believe I am underpaid in comparison to a coworker performing equal work, I might reduce my work effort or decide that this other worker is not really a valid comparison for some reason. A considerable amount of research supports the basic equity principle in Western societies, particularly as it relates to being underrewarded.

The application of equity theory across cultures has received mixed results, but it is only recently that researchers have begun to systematically explore the reasons for this variation (Bolino & Turnley, 2008). Some early studies suggested that the equity norm generalized across cultures (e.g., Kim et al., 1990). However, numerous examples have been reported of the failure of pay inequity to lead to the type of remedial behavior predicted by the theory (e.g., Chung, Lee, & Jung, 1997). And studies of reward allocation norms have generally found differences across cultures on the preference for equity (e.g., Chen, 1995; Deutsch, 1975). Recently, it has become fairly clear that the preference for equity in reward allocation is related to the extent of hierarchy (power distance) in society (Fischer & Smith, 2003). More egalitarian societies have a preference for equality over equity. All of the elements of equity theory, the perception of contributions (inputs), receipts from the exchange (outcomes), the choice of a referent other, and the motivation to reduce inequity can be seen to be sensitive to variations in culture (Fadil, Williams, Limpaphayom, & Smatt, 2005).

An extension of equity theory is the idea that some individuals are more equity sensitive than others. Iindividuals can be classified as equity sensitives, benevolents, and entitleds (Huseman, Hatfield, & Miles, 1987). Equity sensitives, consistent with equity theory, prefer to be in a condition of balance between inputs and outcomes they receive. Benevolents are more tolerant of situations in which they are underrewarded, and entitleds experience less dissonance when overrewarded than when under-rewarded. Early cross-national investigations found differences in the extent to which particular nationalities fell into each of the three categories (Mueller & Clarke, 1998; Renard, Tracy, Ostrow, & Chah, 1997). Some recent evidence suggests that individual differences in equity sensitivity are related to cultural values (Allen, Takeda, & White, 2005; Wheeler, 2002). These findings are consistent with observations of acceptance of inequity among individuals in some societies (e.g., Asia and the Middle East) in order to maintain a state of social harmony (Steers & Sánchez-Runde, 2002).

Expectancy Theory

Expectancy theory (Vroom, 1964) suggests that motivation is the result of the combination of the expectation that effort (E) will lead to performance and that this performance will be instrumental (I) in reaching certain outcomes. It also recognizes that individuals can place different value (V) on any outcome. That is, Effort = $V \times I \times E$. In this formulation, employees will only be motivated to put effort into their work if they (1) believe that if they work hard they will accomplish their task, (2) believe that task accomplishment will lead to a reward by their employer, and (3) value the outcomes that they are offered.

On its face, expectancy theory seems to lend itself very well to cross-cultural comparisons, and some support for the basic tenets of the theory in other cultures outside the United States such as Israel (Eden, 1975) and Japan (Matsui & Terai, 1979) has been found. However, other research has found significant differences in both expectancies and valences across cultures (Dubinsky, Kotabe, Lim, & Michaels, 1994). A problem seems to be that some of the core assumptions of expectancy theory make it difficult to transport across cultures. For example, it assumes that individuals have control over their performance and the outcomes for which they will work and that their employer has the ability to identify and provide valued rewards (Steers & Sánchez-Runde, 2002). All of these factors can vary across cultures. The idea that we are in control of our own destiny is not universally held, as suggested by the social axioms research discussed in Chapter 3.

Goal Setting

Models of goal setting involve the responses of individuals to the existence of goals and the manner in which the goals were set. The basic principles of goal setting are as follows: (a) specific difficult (but achievable) goals consistently lead to better performance than specific easy goals, general (do your best) goals, or no goals; and (b) goal setting is most effective when there is feedback showing progress toward the goal (Locke, 1996; Locke & Latham, 1984). The relationship between goal difficulty and performance assumes that the individual accepts the goal and has the ability to achieve it. Research with regard to cultural variation in goal setting has focused on the way in which commitment to goals is achieved, particularly the effect of participation in setting the goal. One study compared U.S. and Israeli participants and found that participation led to higher levels of goal acceptance and performance in both cultures, except for extremely difficult goals. In this case, goal acceptance was related to performance for assigned goals only in the Israeli sample (Erez & Earley, 1987). These findings indicate that prevailing work norms may influence the extent to which participation in goal setting may be effective in a particular culture. For example, participation in the determination of work goals in parts of Europe is institutionalized in political systems that stress egalitarian values (Locke & Schweiger, 1979). And in Norway, individual participation in goal setting is shunned in favor of participation through union representatives (French, Israel, & As, 1960).

Research has consistently found support for goal setting across a wide range of cultures (Locke & Latham, 1990). However, the indiscriminate use of goal setting as a motivational technique in organizations has recently received some criticism, suggesting that goal setting can have harmful effects (for a discussion see Ordóñez, Schweitzer, Galinsky, & Bazerman, 2009). When an MNC's headquarters imposes goal-setting programs that are inconsistent with the culture of a national subsidiary, organization members can show creative ways to appear to comply without actually engaging as the headquarters intended (Mezias, Chen & Murphy, 1999).

Process theories of motivation have been criticized for depicting the individual as a rational information processor seeking to maximize personal gain (Boyacigiller & Adler, 1991). Although the type of rational processing proposed by these theories can certainly occur, it is probably limited to situations with important outcomes and where one's prior experience is limited (Peterson & Wood, 2008). As suggested in Chapter 4, much individual behavior proceeds in a semiautomatic manner based on information stored in memory (scripts), which was learned in a particular cultural context. Thus, culture may affect what motivates people more than the process through which people are motivated.

Meaning of Work

Individual work motivation is influenced by why people engage in work and what they value in their work. A major research project conducted in seven industrialized countries addressed these questions (Meaning of Work International Research Team, 1987). This research indicated some consistency across countries in what people perceive as the functions of work. For example, when asked to divide 100 points across 11 purposes that work serves, approximately 70 percent was accounted for by three purposes in all cultures:(a) needed income, (b) an interesting and satisfying experience, and (c) contact with people. However, respondents from different countries placed different levels of importance on these purposes. For example, Japanese gave nearly twice as many points to needed income as did respondents from the Netherlands, and Israelis assigned the most points to an interesting and satisfying experience (Meaning of Work International Research Team, 1987). Another aspect of the meaning of work is the extent to which work is central to individuals' lives. An index of work centrality for the seven countries measured is shown in Figure 7.1.

As an example of work centrality, the Meaning of Work International Research Team (1987) asked respondents whether they would continue work after winning a significant amount of money. The percentage who replied that they would ranged from 93 percent in Japan to 69 percent in the United Kingdom, indicating significant variation in the centrality of work. However, even a 69 percent response indicates the high level of importance that people attach to work. Studies in other parts of the world have found similarly high levels of work centrality, indicating the importance of nonfinancial aspects of work motivation (Smith & Bond, 1999).

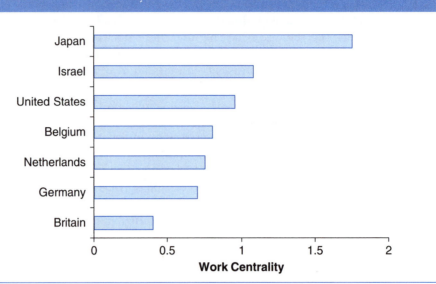

Figure 7.1 Work Centrality Across Seven Countries

SOURCE: Adapted from Meaning of Work International Research Team (1987).

In analyzing the goals that people hope to achieve from work (as opposed to why people have to work, just discussed), the Meaning of Work International Research Team (1987) discovered an interesting pattern, as shown in Table 7.1.

Although a significant amount of variation in the importance of work goals was found, the most important work goal across cultures was that of interesting work (work that you really like). Respondents in four countries (Belgium, Britain, Israel, and the United States) ranked this goal as most important, and the remaining three countries ranked it second or third. This finding suggests that there is some consistency across cultures (at least as represented by these four countries) about what people are looking for in their job. The importance of interesting work across cultures has a number of implications, not the least of which is for the design of jobs.

Designing Motivating Jobs

Although the initial focus of work design was to improve worker efficiency (Taylor, 1911), more contemporary perspectives have focused on how the characteristics of the job affect worker motivation. Three approaches to job design emanating from three different cultures are presented: the job characteristics model, sociotechnical systems, and quality control circles.

One of the most influential models of work design is the job characteristics model (Hackman & Oldham, 1980), developed in the United States. Essentially, the model suggests that any job can be defined in terms of the following five job characteristics:

Table 7.1	Rank Order of Work Goals Across Seven Countries						
Work Goals	**Belgium**	**Britain**	**Germany**	**Israel**	**Japan**	**Netherlands**	**U.S.**
Opportunity	7	8	9	5	7	9	5
Interpersonal relations	5	4	4	2	6	3	7
Opportunity for promotion	10	11	10	8	11	11	10
Convenient work hours	9	5	6	7	8	8	9
Variety	6	7	6	11	9	4	6
Interesting work	1	1	3	1	2	2	1
Job security	3	3	2	10	4	7	3
Match between person and job	8	6	5	6	1	6	4
Pay	2	2	1	3	5	5	2
Working conditions	11	9	11	9	10	10	11
Autonomy	4	10	8	4	3	1	8

SOURCE: Adapted from Harpaz (1990).

- *Skill variety*: Consists of different activities requiring different abilities
- *Task identity*: Requires the completion of a whole and identifiable piece of work
- *Task significance*: Has a substantial effect on other people
- *Autonomy*: Has substantial freedom, independence, and discretion
- *Feedback*: The activities of the job provide direct and clear information on performance.

These characteristics combine to influence the psychological states that are critical to worker motivation. To be motivating, a job must be perceived as *meaningful,* the worker must feel *responsible for outcomes,* and the worker must *know the actual results of work activities.* The motivating potential of the job depends on the extent to which individuals have a strong need for personal growth. Individuals with high growth needs are more likely to experience the psychological states, and they will respond more positively to these psychological states. Considerable research has been conducted on the job characteristics model, which generally supports the idea that there is a set of identifiable job characteristics that influence employees' behavior (Loher, Noe, Moeller, & Fitzgerald, 1980). However, alternative approaches to work characteristics suggest that people respond to socially induced perceptions of their job as opposed to objective characteristics of the job (Salancik & Pfeffer, 1978). Based on the previous discussion of cultural differences in the meaning of work, the opportunity for culturally based differences in these socially induced perceptions of job characteristics is obvious. For example, it seems that increased job autonomy would be more likely to increase the motivating potential of a job in the Netherlands than it would in Britain. In addition, however, job characteristic approaches were developed in an individualistic culture and designed primarily for individual employees. Therefore, the application of this approach in more collectivistic cultures might require modification.

An approach to job design that, although still considering increasing the motivational potential of the job, was developed and applied in societies that emphasize social goals (feminine societies in Hofstede's terms) is sociotechnical systems (Trist, 1981). This approach focuses on integrating the social and technical aspects of the work system. Individual workers are seen as part of a social system that must mesh with the technology of the workplace (Cummings, 1978). Sociotechnical job designs almost always involve autonomous work groups, which have almost complete responsibility for a significant task. The most famous sociotechnical systems application was in the Volvo automobile factories at Kalmar and Uddevalla, Sweden. At the Kalmar plant, the work was organized for teams, and each team had responsibility for a particular portion of the automobile, such as doors, interior, or electrical system. In this approach, the team becomes the focus of job design as opposed to the individual. The team develops task identity by having responsibility for an identifiable portion of the car, team members develop multiple skills that allow them to perform a variety of tasks, and self-inspection of product quality provides feedback (Erez, 1997). Based on measures such as employee morale, employee turnover, and product quality, the experiment at Kalmar was a success. However, the number of hours spent on each car was considerably higher than at U.S. and Japanese manufacturers, suggesting that the teams could have been operating at less than their full capacity (Erez, 1997).

A final example of job design is the quality circles based on the belief that workers understand their own work better than anyone else and can therefore contribute to its improvement. Quality circles are small groups that voluntarily and continuously conduct quality control activities (Onglatco, 1988). In Japan, quality circles have significantly improved quality, reduced costs, and contributed to innovation. However, they have had very limited success when transplanted to the United States (Cole, 1980). Erez and Earley (1993) suggest that this failure results from an expectation of employee participation that cannot be fulfilled by the more individualistic U.S. management philosophy. Quality circles are consistent with the expectation that Japanese employees have for their relationship with their employer but raise unrealistic expectations in U.S. workers.

In summary, the development of individualist job design approaches in the United States, autonomous work groups in northern Europe, and quality circles in Japan are congruent with the value orientations of the three regions. The development of work characteristics that are consistent with the motivational requirements of different cultures is not coincidental (Erez & Earley, 1993). Therefore, the choice of job design might be best informed by cultural dimensions that relate to the way in which the characteristics of the job fulfill culturally based expectations of what work is about.

Leadership

Although the word *leadership* is a relatively new addition to the English language, evidence exists that the concept of leadership has existed throughout recorded history (Dorfman, 1996; 2004). Descriptions of great leaders are present in such culturally diverse manuscripts as Homer's *Iliad,* the Bible, and the writings of Confucius. Despite the thousands of research articles and books written on this subject, no generally accepted definition of leadership exists (Bass, 1990). Western definitions, consistent with motivation theories discussed previously, tend to focus on the ability of individuals to influence organization members toward the accomplishment of goals (Yukl, 1994b), and some international consensus seems to be building toward this definition (Dorfman & House, 2004). However, based on the discussion of systematic variations in values, attitudes, beliefs, and behavior across cultures presented previously in this book, it seems likely that the meaning and importance of leadership vary across cultures.

Box 7.1 What Makes a Good Leader?

In 2011, following the earthquake and tsunami that resulted in the failure of the Fukushima Daiichi power plant, Masataka Shimizu, leader of the Japanese utility Tokyo Electric Power Company (TEPCO) that operated the plant, resigned. While he clearly had no direct role in the accident, he is reported as saying, "I take responsibility for this accident, which has undermined trust in nuclear safety and brought much grief and fear to society . . ." (Tabuchi, 2011). Contrast this with the behavior of BP's CEO Tony Hayward following the oil spill in the Gulf of Mexico in 2010, who eventually stepped down but only after resisting for some time and never fully accepting responsibility; or with Lloyd Blakfein of Goldman Sachs who did not feel the obligation to step down following the 2008 financial meltdown in the United States. Clearly the expectation of appropriate top leader behavior in Japan differs from that in the more individualist West.

SOURCE: Adapted from Dickson, Cataño, Magomaeva, & Den Hartog (2012).

In examining leadership across cultures, several questions need to be addressed:

- Is leadership a global concept?
- Is there a comprehensive set of leader behaviors and styles that are universally important?
- To what extent are universally recognized leader behaviors conceptually and functionally equivalent?
- To what extent are specific leadership characteristics and behaviors enacted differently? (Aycan, 2008; Peterson & Hunt, 1997)

The following section first examines leadership theories developed in the West and their application across cultures. Then non-Western leadership theories are presented, followed by an integrated model of cross-cultural leadership.

Western Leadership Theory

Leadership theory is often described as having progressed through four distinct periods, each with a dominant theoretical approach. These approaches are trait, behavioral, contingency, and implicit theories, and culture plays a different role in each.

Trait Theories

Because the world has been greatly influenced by outstanding individuals, it is not surprising that the study of leadership began as a search for the personality characteristics possessed by great leaders. These so-called great man theories of the early 1900s failed to stand up to scientific tests because of their inability to consistently identify traits that are necessary and sufficient for leadership success (Stogdill, 1948). The inherent difficulty with predicting leadership success from such traits, coupled with the fact that these theories ignore both followers and the effects of differing situations, led researchers in other directions in search of explanations of leadership.

Behavioral Theories

Deficiencies in trait theories first led researchers to shift their focus from what leaders are to what they actually do on the job. It also indicated a change in the assumption that leaders are born to the notion that leaders could be developed. A series of studies identified two dimensions of leader behavior (e.g., Bowers & Seashore, 1966; Fleishman, 1953). These were labeled *initiating structure (production oriented or task)* and *consideration (employee or relationship oriented)* behaviors. Initiating structure included such leader behaviors as assigning tasks to subordinates, coordinating activities, emphasizing deadlines, and evaluating subordinates' work. Consideration behaviors were those that showed concern for subordinates, such as showing regard for their feelings, respecting their ideas, and being friendly and supportive.

A number of cross-cultural studies have found that the two dimensions of leader behavior are important across cultures (e.g., Ah Chong & Thomas, 1997; Ayman & Chemers, 1983; Tscheulin, 1973). Studies using the two-dimensional approach have been conducted in dozens of different countries with the usual and unsurprising result that relationship-oriented leaders increase subordinates' satisfaction (Aycan, 2008; Dorfman, 1996). However, the influence of task orientation is more complex across cultures and is not so simply explained. The sometime-conflicting results found in different cultures for this dimension (e.g., Kakar, 1971; Kenis, 1977) suggest a culture-specific interpretation of task-oriented leadership (e.g., Ah Chong & Thomas, 1997; Howell, Dorfman, Hibino, Lee, & Tate, 1994). Although subordinates' responses to relationship-oriented leadership might be somewhat consistent across cultures, responses to task-oriented behavior seem likely to be more highly variable, depending on what cultures are involved. This finding, coupled with the fact that behavioral theories ignore the influence of subordinates and the situation, probably renders this approach much too simplistic to explain leader behavior in cross-cultural context. The notion that to be effective leaders must adapt their behavior to the situation and the needs of their followers (Yukl & Van Fleet, 1992) can be even more important in cross-cultural situations.

Contingency Theories

Contingency theories were developed in order to reconcile differences between the findings of behavioral studies of leadership. The first and most widely researched contingency model of leadership is Fiedler's (1967) contingency model. The basic idea presented in this model is that a leader's personality influences the leader's behavior style (task or relationship oriented) and that the situation moderates the relationship between the leader's style and effectiveness. Considerable criticism has been leveled at this theory, both for how it is conceptualized (Schriesheim & Kerr, 1977) and for inconsistent findings (Yukl, 1989). However, there is a suggestion that by appropriately including cultural differences as part of the theory, it could prove to be universally applicable (Triandis, 1993). A number of cross-cultural tests of the theory have been conducted. According to Fiedler (1966), initial tests of the theory in Holland and Belgium were very supportive of the model. The possible moderating role of culture was demonstrated in a study by Bennett (1977) in which high-performing Filipino managers were more task oriented and high-performing Chinese managers were more relationship oriented. Tests of the theory in Japan (Misumi, 1985; Misumi & Peterson, 1987) failed to find the proposed relationships between leadership types and leader personality, and somewhat mixed support for the theory was found in a study in Mexico (Ayman & Chemers, 1991) by including self-monitoring as an additional leader characteristic.

Another significant development in response to conflicting results from behavioral approaches was path–goal theory (House, 1971; House & Mitchell, 1974). Path–goal theory was designed to describe how leadership could influence different aspects of motivation described by expectancy theory. It identifies four leader behaviors and specifies a number of situational and follower characteristics that can increase or reduce the relationship of leader style to follower satisfaction and performance. Research has generally shown good support for the predictability of the theory, but some predictions have not been supported (Indvik, 1986). Regardless, it provides a good basis for considering a number of moderators in the study of leadership (Yukl, 1994a). Because culture might sometimes be a key situational moderator, path–goal theory could serve as a platform for considering the moderating effect of culture on the relationship between leader behavior and outcomes (Triandis, 1993).

An idea related to path–goal theory is that the attributes of situations and the characteristics of subordinates could enhance, neutralize, or substitute for some leadership behaviors. So-called leadership substitutes theory (Howell, Dorfman, & Kerr,

1986; Kerr & Jermier, 1978) suggests, for example, that characteristics of subordinates, such as their professionalism, can act as substitutes for such leader behavior as being *directive* while actually enhancing the effect of other types of leader behavior, such as being *supportive* (Dorfman, 1996). Some support exists for the main propositions of the theory (Yukl, 1994b). In addition, it seems that some leader substitutes, such as workers' professionalism and their work experience, are applicable in a number of countries (Howell et al., 1994). However, contradictory results have also been found, and the cross-cultural applicability of the idea of substitutes for leadership has yet to be fully tested (Misumi & Peterson, 1985).

Implicit Theories

Implicit theories of leadership have been concerned with the way in which the sorts of scripts, schemas, and other cognitive characteristics discussed in Chapter 4 influence how subordinates perceive and react to a leader (Lord & Maher, 1991). The implicit leadership theory perspective suggests that followers develop mental representations or prototypes of leaders through exposure to social situations and interactions with others (Lord, Foti, & DeVader, 1984). As we have suggested, culture tends to exert an even stronger influence on mental representations than on the values that individuals endorse. After the formation of a leader prototype, individuals are perceived as leaders by the extent to which their behavior matches the behavior expected of a prototypical leader. Specific leader behaviors do not make a person a leader unless that person is perceived as a leader by followers. A number of laboratory studies supported the notion that leaders who meet the expectations of followers for leader behavior were more likely to be described as leaders (Lord et al., 1984; Lord & Maher, 1991). This idea has been extended across cultures to show that individuals from different cultures can have different leader prototypes (Ah Chong & Thomas, 1997; O'Connell, Lord, & O'Connell, 1990) and that meeting followers' expectations of leader behavior can result in higher perceptions of trust and leader effectiveness (Thomas & Ravlin, 1995). Although these results suggest culturally specific expectations of leadership, it is also possible that there are some universally endorsed attributes and behaviors that comprise implicit leadership. An example of this possibility is charismatic or transformational theories of leadership (Bass, 1985; Burns, 1978; Conger & Kanungo, 1988; House, 1977). Charismatic or transformational leaders are those who are able to inspire their followers to transcend their own self-interests for the good of the organization. As noted at the beginning of this chapter, examples of these leaders are to be found in all cultures. They have an extraordinary effect on followers, which garners the followers' admiration, respect, trust, commitment, dedication, and loyalty. In order to have this effect, followers must attribute extraordinary leadership abilities to people who exhibit certain behaviors. Several studies have tried to identify the traits or behaviors that are characteristic of charismatic leaders (Bennis, 1984; Conger & Kanungo, 1987; House, 1977). They concluded that charismatic leaders are self-confident, have an idealized goal or vision, are very committed to that goal, and are perceived as unconventional and agents of radical change.

Proponents of these theories (e.g., Bass, 1991; House, 1991) argue that charismatic leaders are more effective than noncharismatic leaders regardless of culture. Indeed, a number of studies show a nearly universal relationship for charismatic leadership across cultures (Dorfman, 1996; 2004). However, a few studies suggest that culture does influence the charismatic leadership process. For example, results from the Dominican Republic (Echavarria & Davis, 1994), the Netherlands (Den Hartog, Van Muijen, & Koopman, 1994), and Singapore (Koh, 1990) suggest that although the concept of a charismatic leader might be universal, the way such a leader is described by followers can differ markedly. Other evidence suggests that this model of leadership might not hold for some unique cultures such as Japan (Bass, 1991; Howell et al., 1994). In addition, the effect of charismatic leadership has been found to be stronger for people from the United States than for Mexicans (Howell & Dorfman, 1988), indicating that cultural differences might influence the effectiveness of the transformational or charismatic approach as demonstrated in the following large-scale study.

Project GLOBE

The Global Leadership and Organizational Behavior Effectiveness (GLOBE) research program (House et al., 2004), although much more extensive, is a recent extension of implicit leadership theory. Involving 17,000 respondents in 951 organizations in 62 societies, GLOBE researchers asked what attributes caused individuals to accept and respond to others as leaders. Among the 112 items measured were 22 leadership attributes that were universally desirable (e.g., trustworthy, just, honest, having foresight, encouraging) and eight that were universally undesirable (e.g., asocial, noncooperative, irritable, dictatorial), with the remainder being culturally contingent (e.g., individualistic, status conscious, risk taker). From these items, six dimensions of leadership, described as culturally based shared conceptions of leadership (House et al., 2004), were derived and compared across the 10 cultural clusters defined according to the GLOBE cultural dimensions described in Chapter 3:

- *Charismatic/value based*: The ability to inspire, motivate, and expect high performance from others on the basis of firmly held core beliefs. Generally reported to facilitate leadership. Highest in Anglo countries and lowest in the Middle East.
- *Team oriented*: Emphasizes team building and implementation of a common purpose or goal among team members. Generally reported to facilitate leadership. Highest in Latin America and lowest in the Middle East.
- *Participative*: Reflects the degree to which managers involve others in making and implementing decisions. Reported to facilitate leadership but with significant differences across country clusters. Highest in Germanic Europe and lowest in the Middle East.
- *Humane oriented*: Reflects supportive and considerate leadership, including compassion and generosity. Ranges from almost neutral in some societies to a moderate facilitator of leadership. Highest in South Asia and lowest in Nordic Europe.

- *Autonomous*: Independent and individualistic leadership. Ranges from impeding leadership to slightly facilitating. Highest in Eastern Europe and lowest in Latin America.
- *Self-protective*: Focuses on ensuring safety and security of the individual; self-centered and face saving. Generally reported to impede leadership. Highest in South Asia and lowest in Nordic Europe.

A number of the GLOBE cultural dimensions (Chapter 3) were reported to be related to these leadership dimensions, consistent with the prediction that culture influences the leader attributes and behaviors most frequently enacted, accepted, and effective in a society (House et al., 2004).

Non-Western Theories of Leadership

An alternative to trying to determine the boundaries or contingencies associated with Western leadership theories is to examine leadership theories that are not indigenous to Western cultures. The following section describes three such theories of leadership.

Performance–Maintenance Theory

Descriptions of Japanese management practices abound. However, the systematic evaluation of leadership behavior in this culture, which is governed more by group norms than individual direction, is rare. An exception is a theory influenced by Western conceptions of leadership but developed over 40 years of extensive research in Japan (Misumi & Peterson, 1985). Misumi's (1985) performance–maintenance (PM) theory identifies four types of leadership based on two basic dimensions: performance and maintenance. These dimensions are viewed as functions that a leader needs to fulfill rather than as a specific set of behaviors that a leader needs to carry out. The specific behaviors that a leader needs to carry out to fulfill each function differ among industries and levels of hierarchy. The performance dimension (P) describes behavior directed toward achieving group goals and includes pressure-type and planning-type behavior. Pressure-type behavior is described by Misumi (1985, pp. 34–35) as "supervisory behavior regarding strict observance of regulations and pressure for production," whereas planning-type behaviors "concern the planning and processing of work." The maintenance dimension (M) relates to behavior directed at maintaining individual well-being and preserving social relationships in a group. These dimensions are conceptually similar to the task-oriented and relationship-oriented dimensions found in Western theories of leadership. However, the theory differs in some significant ways from traditional leadership theory (Peterson, 1988). The P and M dimensions are concerned with behavior as experienced by followers and can therefore differ according to the context in which the behavior takes place. Certain factors that represent M in Japan would seem inappropriate to followers in a

Western culture, such as the United States. For example, discussing an employee's personal problems with other organization members in that employee's absence is consistent with a Japanese manager who would be highly rated on the maintenance factor (Smith, Misumi, Tayeb, Peterson, & Bond, 1989). Also, some P-type behaviors, such as "your supervisor is strict about the work you do," "your supervisor is strict about observing regulations," and "your supervisor makes you work to your maximum capacity," might carry less positive connotations outside Japanese culture (Dorfman, 1996). Misumi's (1985) theory also treats the two leadership dimensions as complementary. To be effective, Japanese managers must emphasize both P and M, such that a manager rated by followers as high on both (PM) would be more effective than a manager rated high on one behavior and low on the other (Pm or pM) or low on both (pm). For example, a P-type behavior exhibited by a manager rated high on M would be perceived by followers as reflecting *planning*. The same behavior performed by a manager who was low on M would be perceived as *pressure*. It is possible that leaders who emphasize both P- and M-type behaviors are effective in some Asian cultures because the M gives followers the feeling that they are members of the leader's in-group, and the P behaviors lead to high performance that results in rewards and resources from superiors and other outside parties that are beneficial to all group members (Hui, 1990).

Tests of PM theory outside Japan lend support to the idea that both culture-free and culture-specific leadership behaviors can exist (e.g., Peterson, Smith, & Tayeb, 1993). Although the broad dimensions of performance and maintenance seem to be applicable across cultures (Smith, Peterson, Bond, & Misumi, 1992), the specific leader behaviors perceived by followers to indicate these dimensions seem, at least to some extent, to vary across cultures. Additional research indicates that the performance (P) or task-oriented dimension is the most susceptible to the influence of a specific cultural interpretation (Ah Chong & Thomas, 1997; Peterson et al., 1993).

Leadership in the Arab World

Leadership behavior in Arab societies is strongly influenced by the Islamic religion and tribal traditions as well as by contact with Western culture (Ali, 1990). The tribal influence is evident because managers are expected to behave like fathers. Their roles include protecting and caring for employees as well as having overall responsibility for the business. Overlaying this tribal influence is the legacy of a rigid bureaucracy introduced during rule by the Ottoman Empire (late 13th century until the end of World War I) and Europeans. The combination of these tribal norms with bureaucratic structures resulted in an authoritarian and patriarchal approach to leadership called *sheikocracy* (Al-Kubaisy, 1985). This style is characterized by hierarchical authority, subordination of efficacy to human relations and personal connections, and conformity to rules and regulations based on the personality and power of those who made them. The combination of this leadership style with influences from Western management practices has produced a *duality* in Arab managers who want to be modern by adopting Western practices but simultaneously wish to maintain tradition. According to Ali (1990), this duality results in leadership behaviors such as creating numerous rules and regulations without making any attempt to implement them, creating selection and promotion systems based on performance but selecting and promoting based on personal relationships and family and social ties, and paying people from powerful families who are not required to report for work. The *prophetic–caliphal* model of leadership developed by Khadra (1990) typifies this duality of relationships prevalent in Arab culture. The model specifies two distinctly different leadership types that can emerge to fill the leadership vacuum created by the lack of institutionalism prevalent in Arab society. According to the theory, the very existence of the rational bureaucratic procedures of institutions is undermined by the prevalence of two societal characteristics called individualism and personalism. Individualism, in this case, is the tendency to make decisions without considering the opinions of others. Personalism involves viewing one's relationship to others from an egocentric perspective in which one's own set of needs dominates. There is a strong predisposition in Arab society for a great man or *prophetic* leader to emerge to fill the leadership vacuum. If such a prophetic leader emerges, indicated by the ability to accomplish some great feat, he will garner feelings of love, unity of purpose, and voluntary submission to authority by followers. However, if an ordinary or *caliphal* leader emerges, conflict and strife will result, and he must use coercion and fear in order to maintain his status as a leader. Although the prophetic–caliphal model has yet to be broadly tested, Khadra (1990) presents substantial evidence that the basic premise of the model makes sense to Arab managers. In addition, this model appears to have many consistencies with the notions of charismatic leadership developed in the West.

Paternalism

A recent development with regard to leadership approaches that are unique to a specific cultural context is that of paternalistic leadership. Paternalistic leadership involves a hierarchical relationship between the leader and followers in which the leader, like a parent, provides direction in both the professional and private lives of subordinates in exchange for loyalty and deference (Aycan, 2006). Paternalistic leadership is based in traditional values of familism, Confucian ideology, and feudalism and is common in cultures with large power distance, where superior–subordinate relationships are hierarchical, interdependent, and emotional. Examples can be found in Pacific Asian societies, Africa, and Russia (Aycan, 2008). Aycan (2006) defines five dimensions of paternalistic leadership:

- Creating a family atmosphere at work
- Establishing close and individualized relationships with subordinates
- Involvement in nonwork lives of subordinates
- Expecting loyalty from subordinates
- Expecting deference from subordinates

Paternalistic leadership as measured along these dimensions has been associated with positive employee attitudes in collectivistic and large power distance cultures (Aycan, 2006; Pellegrini & Scandura, 2007). In addition some aspects of paternalistic leadership, in particular the relationship between paternalism and organizational commitment, may generalize across cultures (Pellegrini, Scandura, & Jayaraman, 2010).

Box 7.2 Servant Leadership

Recently, several new perspectives on leadership have emerged as a result of the many scandals and leadership failures that have occurred in the business world. These include ethical leadership (Brown, Treviño, & Harrison, 2005) and authentic leadership (Avolio & Gardner, 2005), both of which emphasize an internalized moral perspective on leadership. A related idea that has received some attention across cultures is the idea of servant leadership (Greenleaf, 1970). Current models of servant leadership are based on the human motive to bond with others and contribute to the betterment of society—to serve (Mittal & Dorfman, 2012). Comparative studies of servant leadership across societies have been conducted in Ghana and the United States (Hale & Fields, 2007), the Philippines and the United States (West and Bocarnea, 2008) and Australia and Indonesia (Pekerti & Sendaya, 2010). The pattern of results that emerges from these investigations is that, while the concept of servant leadership seems to be viewed as universally important for effective leadership, cultural differences exist in the extent to which certain dimensions are emphasised. For example Mittal and Dorfman (2012) found that empathy and humility were aspects that were more strongly endorsed in Asian cultures than in European cultures, and egalitarianism and empowering were endorsed more strongly in Nordic/European cultures than in Asia. Similarly, Pekerti and Sendaya (2010) found that Australians were more likely to endorse a concept of authentic self (strong sense of who we are) than Indonesians, while Indonesians were higher on responsible morality (reflective moral reasoning) and transforming influence (articulation and implementation of a shared vision) than were Australians. While the investigation of servant leadership across cultures is still in its infancy, it may emerge as an important idea in a world where abuse of power, unethical practices, and alienation in the workplace seem to be increasingly common.

The preceding sections indicate that there is certainly no lack of theories of leadership from which to choose. Both traditional and indigenous theories provide useful insights into the process of leadership in a cross-cultural context. Several attempts have been made to define a theoretical perspective that is adequate to explain and predict the complexities of leadership in the international context (e.g., Aycan, 2008, Dorfman, 1996; 2004, Erez & Earley, 1993; House et al., 2004). The following section presents a model that synthesizes much of what we know about cross-cultural leadership to derive implications for today's manager.

Integrated Cross-Cultural Model of Leadership

The model of leadership presented in Figure 7.2 is grounded in work by Dorfman (1996; 2004), Erez and Earley (1993), and Yukl (1989) and is consistent with the emphasis on social cognition taken in this book.

It has as its basis a cognitive information processing approach to leadership. This approach is similar to the implicit theories presented previously in that the ability of the leader to influence others is largely dependent on presenting an image consistent with followers' expectations of a leader. The three key elements of the theory—leader's image, individual and group processes, and substitutes for leadership—are all affected by cultural variation. Culture is considered an all-encompassing or enveloping influence on leadership processes (Dorfman, 1996). For example, cultural differences influence the conceptions that people have of an ideal leader. This culturally determined image defines the behavior required to be perceived as a leader by followers. For example, Pacific Islanders expect leaders to give specific instructions and orders and to insist on adherence to rules and regulations, whereas these same behaviors would not portray an ideal image in Anglo-European culture (Ah Chong & Thomas, 1997). In addition, consistent with the model presented in Chapter 4, the interpersonal interactions between the leader and followers are subject to cultural influence. For example, paternalistic leadership approaches are likely to be more acceptable in large power distance cultures, and the relationship of the leader to the group will likely vary along the cultural dimensions of individualism and collectivism. Situational moderators of various types act as substitutes for particular leadership

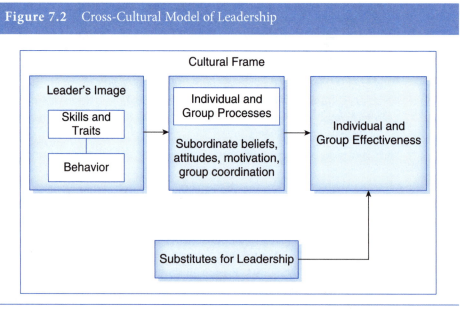

Figure 7.2   Cross-Cultural Model of Leadership

SOURCES: Adapted from Dorfman (1996; 2004), Erez & Earley (1993), and Yukl (1989).

behavior in a number of cultures (Howell et al., 1994). As discussed earlier, culture can be viewed as an underlying factor that determines the nature of the situational characteristics that will act as effective substitutes for leadership. For example, the technical expertise of followers is in part a result of the orientation of a particular society toward education. Finally, the outcomes of leadership are also embedded in a cultural context, in that the evaluation of leader effectiveness can be based primarily on the performance of either individuals or groups. For example, in collectivist cultures individual performance that does not contribute to group harmony and cohesiveness might not be evaluated positively (Dorfman, 1996; 2004).

This model highlights one of the most important but rarely addressed aspects of leadership: the question of how to best manage the interaction between leaders and managers who are culturally different. Very little research exists to address this question, which is a very salient issue for managers faced with a culturally diverse workforce. The few studies conducted (Ah Chong & Thomas, 1997; Peterson, Brannen, & Smith, 1994; Thomas & Ravlin, 1995) suggest two important considerations. First, followers are likely to have an expectation of leadership behavior based on the leader's culture. For example, some research indicates that U.S. subordinates of Japanese managers expect the Japanese managers to be strongly task oriented (Smith et al., 1992). Second, like communication and negotiation behavior, adapting leader behavior to be more like that typical of the followers' culture is risky. For example, Thomas and Ravlin (1995) found that such adaptation of behaviors characteristic of the followers' culture was effective only to the extent that this behavior was perceived as genuine by followers. Therefore, one might adapt too much to the followers' culture. The logical conclusion from this limited evidence is that managers seeking to be favorably perceived need to exercise care in choosing which leader behaviors of a culture to emulate.

Implications for the Practice of Leadership

Despite the wide variation in models of leadership, a number of important implications for managers can be drawn from the preceding discussion. The following ideas are based on the cross-cultural model presented previously and the empirical evidence presented earlier in this chapter.

Universal Leadership Functions

The general functions of leadership are probably universal across cultures. Substantial evidence in a variety of cultures supports the idea of two dimensions of leadership. Leadership in a number of cultures is categorized as concerned with the task, with the relationship with members, or both (e.g., Ah Chong & Thomas, 1997; Smith et al., 1989). In a study of 12 different countries, Bass, Burger, Doktor, and Barrett (1979) found that managers, regardless of culture, indicated a desire to get things done while using less authority. Smith and Peterson (1994) found that managers in 25 countries reported more satisfaction for activities in which they had higher discretion. And, the GLOBE study indicates that middle managers in 63 countries endorse various aspects of integrity, visionary charisma, and inspirational charisma as positive leader attributes (Dorfman, Hanges & Brodbeck, 2004). It seems, therefore, that leaders in all cultures have certain characteristics or exhibit certain behaviors that allow them to be regarded as leaders by their followers. However, as discussed ahead, it is likely that the specific behaviors that are appropriate for different cultures will be highly variable.

Culture-Specific Leader Behaviors

Culture seems to affect the type of leader behavior accepted and effective in a given society. In general, research has indicated that the leadership styles across cultures are consistent with the dominant cultural values of the country (House et al., 2004; Jackofsky, Slocum, & McQuaid, 1988). In this chapter, examples of indigenous approaches to leadership were presented. The integrated model shown in Figure 7.2 suggests that leader behavior consistent with what followers expect will be more likely to result in an individual being perceived as a leader and therefore make that individual more effective. Considerable evidence suggests that being perceived as a leader and meeting followers' expectations result in greater leader effectiveness (e.g., Lord, Foti, & DeVader, 1984; Thomas & Ravlin, 1995). For example, the direct assertive behavior of John F. Kennedy and Martin Luther King Jr. was very different from the quiet, nonaggressive styles of Mahatma Gandhi and Nelson Mandela. However, all could properly be categorized as effective leaders in their respective cultures. In addition, recent research indicates that the specific behaviors that indicate a particular leadership dimension are contingent on culture (e.g., House et al., 2004). For example, specific behaviors considered either task or relationship oriented by followers differ in ways consistent with the cultural setting. Being perceived as treating people fairly is an important leadership characteristic in both Polynesian and Anglo-European culture. However, the specific behavior that indicates fair treatment can be very different for each cultural group (Ah Chong & Thomas, 1997; Aycan, 2006). Therefore, regardless of whether a more traditional behavioral or newer implicit approach to understanding leadership is taken, it seems that differences in the cultural setting must be taken into account in determining who is likely to be perceived as a leader and what leader behavior is most likely to be effective.

Situational Moderators

The characteristics of the situation influence, to varying degrees, the extent to which leadership can make a difference. A number of the theoretical approaches reviewed in this chapter recognize that leadership is situation specific. Under certain circumstances, the characteristics of the situation might constrain the leader's ability to have very much of an effect on followers. Leaders are always under pressure to conform to the social situation in which they must operate. As noted in Chapter 1, the behavior that managers exhibit is determined in part by the expectations for managerial behavior and thinking that are sent by their superiors, their peers, and their followers (Peterson & Smith, 2008). In addition, many of the factors that influence the performance of followers, such as organizational policies and procedures, are outside a manager's control. For example, research on charismatic leaders (Conger & Kanungo, 1988) indicates this type of leader is most likely to emerge during periods of rapid growth, change, or crisis. In addition, different cultures tend to place different degrees of importance on the role of leadership. In the United States, leaders in corporations are often paid many times the salary of those in non-leadership roles, indicating a belief that leaders do indeed make a difference. However, Dutch people place much less value on leadership in their egalitarian society (Hofstede, 1993), and Japanese tend to credit employees and teams rather than leaders for corporate success (Bass & Yokochi, 1991).

Summary

This chapter addressed the difficult task that international managers face in motivating and leading individuals from different cultures. Theories of individual motivation developed in the West have only limited applicability across cultures. However, some insight as to a potentially universal process of motivation can be gained from them. The development of work characteristics in different cultures seems to be consistent with their motivational requirements. Therefore, the choice of job designs is probably best informed by cultural dimensions that relate to the way in which the characteristics of the job fulfill culturally based expectations of what work is about. Finally, leadership theories with a Western imprint are of limited use in cross-cultural context. However, when combined with knowledge of cross-cultural interactions drawn from social cognition, they can be useful in drawing important implications for managers about appropriate leader behaviors.

Questions for Discussion

1. How might culture affect the application of the main content theories of motivation?

2. How might culture affect the application of the main process theories of motivation?

3. How does job design motivate? Cultural variation?

4. How might culture affect the application of the main Western leadership theories?

5. What are the main points of the Integrated Cross-Cultural Model of Leadership?

6. What are the concluding implications about culture and leadership?

Part III

Global Management Challenges

The Challenge of Multicultural Work Groups and Teams

When you have a very diverse team—people of different backgrounds, different culture, different gender, different age, you are going to get a more creative team—probably getting better solutions, and enforcing them in a very innovative way and with a very limited number of preconceived ideas.

Carlos Ghosn
Chairman and CEO, Renault; Chairman and
CEO, Nissan; Chairman and CEO, Renault-Nissan Alliance

Groups are a part of almost every organization, and as jobs become more complex, groups will accomplish more of the world's work. Group behavior is more than the sum total of individuals acting in their own separate ways. When people must work together in groups to perform a task, the cultural differences among group members often become more apparent. Even within a single country, the reality of a multicultural workforce in most industrialized countries means that managers are now more than ever faced with the task of managing work groups composed of culturally different members. In addition, as collaboration across geographic boundaries becomes increasingly important in business, managers are finding themselves involved in work groups composed of culturally different members, which often function with little, if any, face-to-face contact (Leung & Peterson, 2010). This chapter explores the influence of cultural diversity on the way that work groups function and the role that managers can play in getting the most from both managing and being members of these groups.

Work Groups

The types of work groups that are of most concern to managers have four distinctive characteristics (Cartwright & Zander, 1968; Hackman, 1991). First, work groups are social systems that have boundaries with members who have different roles and are dependent on each other (Alderfer, 1977). Both people within the group and those on the outside will recognize the group's existence and which individuals are members and which are not. Second, these groups have a task to perform. Third, work groups need to deal with the relationship between individuals and the group so that members contribute to the group and remain members. Finally, work groups function within and as part of a larger organization.

A useful categorization of work group types by Arrow and McGrath (1995) distinguishes among three primary types of work groups—namely, task forces, crews, and teams. Task forces focus on the completion of a specific project, typically within a limited time frame. The group comes together for the length of time required, and members are selected based on the task-related skills required by the group. A group of bankers who specialize in different national markets designing a new investment fund is an example. Crews, in contrast, focus on the tools required to perform a task, and the appropriate interaction with or use of a tool specifies the interaction among group members. Tools are defined broadly to include a wide variety of task-related implements or devices. For example, airline flight deck crews interact with each other in a very regimented way as dictated by the requirements of effectively operating the aircraft. The flight crew of one jumbo jet will behave in very much the same way as any other crew during routine operations. By contrast, organizational teams focus on the interrelationships among the group members. Teams are sets of people with specific skills and abilities who are provided with tools and procedures to address certain sets of tasks over a long period of time. Executives working for an international pharmaceutical company who are specialists in the economic situations of different parts of the world operate as a team when they work together on corporate financing strategies.

These differences in work group types highlight the need to recognize the structure of a work group when managing or working in intercultural organizational groups. However, as discussed in the following section, to understand and promote work group effectiveness, group structure must be considered in concert with other group characteristics. This is especially true when the group is composed of members from different cultures.

Work Group Effectiveness

Narrowly defined, the effectiveness of a work group depends on how well the group uses its resources to accomplish its task. However, not all organizational tasks have clearly defined correct or even best answers. The long-term effectiveness of a work group might not be assessed accurately by considering only how it is performing at a single point in time. Therefore, a broader definition of work group effectiveness that more accurately portrays whether a work group is functioning well in an organization is suggested (Hackman, 1991).

- First, the output of the group must meet the quantity, quality, and timeliness standards of the organization.
- Second, the processes employed by the group should enhance the ability of the group members to work together.
- Finally, the group experience should contribute to the growth and personal well-being of the group members.

This broader definition encourages a longer-term view of work group effectiveness consistent with the requirement that work groups function within the confines of the larger organization. For example, in the late 1970s and early 1980s, a Japanese company would sometimes assign a group of production managers to run a facility in the United States or Europe more to learn how to operate in and adjust corporate practices to a particular part of the world than to promote immediate company profitability (Liker, Fruin & Adler, 1999).

To understand the relationship of culture to group effectiveness, it is first necessary to identify the underlying dynamics of work groups. Group dynamics are complex, and research has produced a number of group process models. Here, a model (shown in Figure 8.1) based on the work of Goodman et al. (1987) and Helmreich and Schaefer (1994) identifies six sets of variables that influence the process and performance of work groups. These variables are (1) the external or contextual conditions

Figure 8.1   Group Process Model

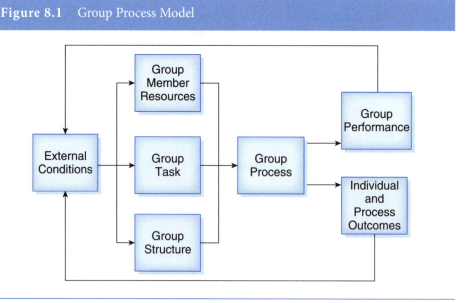

SOURCE: Based on Goodman, Ravlin, & Schminke (1987) and Helmreich & Schaefer (1994).

imposed on the group, (2) the resources of group members, (3) the structure of the group, (4) the group task, (5) the group process, and (6) the composition of the group.

Although international managers might be most concerned with the cultural composition and/or the geographic dispersion of the group, these factors cannot be understood in isolation and must be considered in the context of the dynamics of the group. Each of the six sets of variables that affect group processes and performance are discussed briefly in the following sections.

External Conditions

Part of group behavior is determined by the larger organization to which the group belongs (Friedlander, 1989). The strategy of the organization, the authority structures, and regulations employed to implement that strategy determine which groups in organizations get resources and dictate the type of behavior that receives rewards. Research indicates that contextual factors influence both the productivity of work groups and employee satisfaction with the group (Campion, Medsker, & Higgs, 1993). Furthermore, such organizational factors as firm strategy and human resource practices influence the impact of diversity in work groups (Jehn & Bezrukova, 2004). Obviously, large profitable organizations can provide more resources for any type of group that is consistent with the organizational strategy and culture. In addition, the composition of the group is dependent on the selection process of the organization, as group members must first be organization members. This selection process is critical in determining the skills, attitudes, values, and beliefs that organization members bring to work groups. And, of course, the geographic dispersion of the organization influences the manner in which work groups must interact (Leung & Peterson, 2010; Maznevski & Cudoba, 2000).

In recent years it has become more and more common for individuals to be members of multiple work groups in organizations. In some cases, an individual might be a member of as many as twelve teams at any one time (Zika-Viktorsson, Sundstrom, & Engwall, 2006). Both the number of work groups to which a person belongs and their diversity in terms of task, technologies, and locations has an influence on the ability of individuals to effectively engage with the group and to process information and learn from the group (O'Leary, Mortensen, & Woolley, 2011). The number and variety of group memberships can have competing effects on group productivity and learning.

Group Member Resources

Group members bring two types of resources to groups: personal attributes, including personality, values, and attitudes, and their skills and abilities, both technical and social. In general and as one might expect, member skills and abilities are positively related to group performance (Szilagyi & Wallace, 1987; Taggar, 2002).

No single personal attribute has been found to facilitate group performance, and little research has examined the relationship between personality and group dynamics (Hoyle & Crawford, 1994). However, some evidence suggests that the characteristics of individuals in groups influence the overall affective tone or climate of the group.

This, in turn, relates to the extent to which the group engages in prosocial behavior (George, 1990). Moreover, some research argues that personality variables can be powerful predictors of some group outcomes, such as innovation (Bunce & West, 1995). A group member's cultural profile is one task-related personal attribute, as discussed in this chapter.

Group Structure

As noted previously, work groups can be categorized as task forces, crews, or teams. Each of these structures shapes the behavior of group members by prescribing the norms, role expectations, and status relationships shared by group members. Of particular importance to the effectiveness of work groups are norms about the processes related to task performance (Goodman et al., 1987). These norms specify such things as what methods and channels of communication are important and the level of individual effort expected, and they also provide group members with explicit guidance as to how to accomplish the task.

Although all groups share the same types of norms, the norms for a particular group are unique. Group norms can come from explicit statements made by group members, critical incidents in the group's history, an early behavior that emerges and persists, and from other previous group situations (Feldman, 1984). Group members from different cultures can vary in the source of their normative beliefs of how groups should function because of differences in their prior group experience. The importance of norms compared to other sources of guidance that influence managers in groups also varies among countries in ways that are associated with cultural value dimensions (Smith, Peterson, & Schwartz, 2002). And, the ability of work groups to adjust their role structure to changes in the context of their task influences their performance (LePine, 2003).

Group member roles are affected by the conflict created in the process of role assignment (Moreland & Levine, 1982). This is the conflict created by differing opinions about who should assume a role or how it should be played. Some anecdotal evidence suggests that cultural difference in preferences for different roles in multicultural groups exists (Schneider & Barsoux, 1997). Generally, examinations of the effect of role conflict have indicated a negative relationship to group effectiveness (Jackson & Schuler, 1985). However, not all conflict within a group has negative results (Kirchmeyer & Cohen, 1992).

The effect of status systems in groups can be summarized in three categories. First is the effect of a person's status on his or her relationship with other group members, such as emerging as a leader (see Kelsey, 1998). Second is the effect of a group member's status on his or her evaluation by others. Third is the effect of status on a group member's self-esteem (see Chattopadhyay, George, & Lawrence, 2004). In general, group members with higher status are more influential in the group, are evaluated more positively, and have higher self-esteem than group members with lower status. And, as discussed ahead, cultural differences can influence individuals' perceived status and legitimacy in their group (see Ravlin et al., 2000).

Group Processes

Group processes are *how* groups achieve their outcomes (Weingart, 1997) and involve such things as focusing group effort, the dynamics that occur during group functioning, and the relationships among group members. Because groups form their own social systems, the outcomes of work groups are not the same as the sum of their individual members' efforts. When group processes such as communication patterns, decision processes, and conflict reactions cause a group to fail to meet its potential, it has suffered a process loss. When the efforts of the group exceed that of individual members, a process gain or synergy is experienced. This simple effect of group process is shown graphically in Figure 8.2.

Examples of process losses include *groupthink*, in which the norm for group consensus overrides the motivation to realistically appraise alternative courses of action (Janis, 1982), and *social loafing*, in which individuals reduce their effort on group tasks expecting that other members will do the work for them (Thomas & Fink, 1963). As discussed in more detail ahead, some process losses are dramatically influenced by cultural differences (Earley, 1989).

Group Processes Over Time

An additional element of group process is the change that groups go through over time. Early in the study of group process, Tuckman (1965) proposed that all groups go through five stages called *forming, storming, norming, performing,* and *adjourning.* In

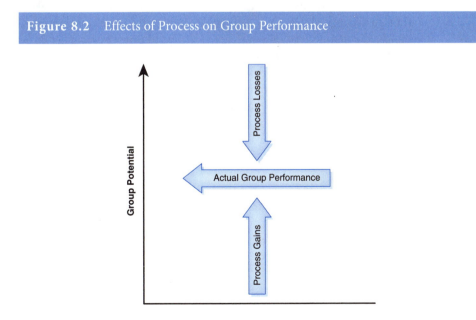

Figure 8.2   Effects of Process on Group Performance

the first or *forming* stage, group members just begin to think of themselves as part of a group and might be uncertain about the group and how they fit into it. In the second or so-called *storming* stage, the characteristics, attitudes, and expectations of individuals come into conflict with the structure of the group. In the third or *norming* stage, the group agrees on the expectations that specify the acceptable behavior (norms) of the group. In the fourth or *performing* stage, the efforts of the group shift to accomplishing the task at hand. As noted previously, some work groups, such as teams, would remain in this stage. Task forces and crews would proceed to the fifth or *adjourning* stage once the task was completed. Although this model of group development is informative, research suggests that groups do not necessarily proceed sequentially from one stage to the next and that several stages can occur at the same time (Gersick, 1988). In addition, groups can revert to prior stages.

For groups that have a deadline for the accomplishment of their task, another development model called the punctuated equilibrium model (Gersick, 1989) might be more helpful. In this group development model, the group sets its direction at the first meeting, and this pattern of behavior and approach to the task become firmly adhered to for the first one-half of the group's existence. Although group members might have alternative ideas about the group process, the group is often unable to act on these ideas. Despite the length of time the group has to complete the task, a transition seems to occur at about the midway point between the first meeting and the official deadline. At this point, the group seems to get a wake-up call and drops the previous patterns of behavior and perspectives in favor of a new direction and enhanced activity. Following the transition, another period of equilibrium ensues and the group focuses on implementing the direction set during the transition. At the final meeting of the group, a flurry of activity occurs as the group members press each other to make their contribution to accomplish the task. An issue in multicultural groups, however, is the well-established cultural variation in orientations toward time (Boyacigiller & Adler, 1991).

Finally, the virtual global teams, discussed ahead, seem to engage in specific patterns of temporal rhythms that involve face-to-face interactions interspersed with electronically mediated communication and telephone calls (Maznevski & Chudoba, 2000). While none of these patterns of interaction may be applicable to all work groups, in combination they provide some insight into the possible patterns of work group interaction.

Group Task

The nature of the tasks in which the work group is engaged influences both the processes and outcomes of the group (Goodman, 1986). Tasks relate not only to the end result of group activity but also specify such aspects of group processes as the degree and nature of interdependence of group members. Jackson (1992) provides a useful classification of group tasks into three primary types: clearly defined production tasks, cognitive or intellectual tasks, and creative idea generation and decision-making tasks. Production tasks require motor skills, and some objective standard of performance is assumed to exist. Intellectual tasks are problem-solving tasks with a correct answer, whereas decision-making tasks are involved with reaching consensus on the best solution to a problem. In simple routine production tasks, group processes, such as communication, are less important. Therefore, in this type of task, a work group with *potentially* high process losses might still be effective. However, the same group involved in a problem-solving task might suffer the negative effects of those more important process activities. Because intellective tasks (that is, tasks with objectively correct answers) rarely exist in organizations, this type of task has few implications for managers and is not discussed further.

Group Composition

Members of work groups might be similar or different on a number of different dimensions (e.g., gender, age, experience, nationality) important to the performance of the group. Although the focus in this chapter is the cultural composition of groups, research on other dimensions of similarity and difference can shed light on how group composition influences group processes and outcomes. Group composition can be classified as homogeneous on a particular dimension, heterogeneous on that dimension, or minority-majority. Minority-majority groups consist of groups in which one or a few members are different on the dimension of interest. A single U.S. person in a group of Japanese would be a minority-majority group on the dimension of nationality, whereas a group of all Japanese would be classified as homogeneous on that dimension, and a group with a variety of nationalities would be heterogeneous. Much research on the effect of group composition on work group outcomes has focused on a comparison of homogeneous and heterogeneous groups. Recently, there has been an emphasis on differentiating between surface level diversity (gender, ethnicity, etc.) and deep level diversity (values, beliefs, etc.) (e.g., Mohammed & Angell, 2004). Results of this comparison have been mixed. Heterogeneity in observable attributes is generally found to have a negative effect on affective outcomes, such as identification with the group and satisfaction (Mannix & Neale, 2005; Milliken & Martins, 1996). In addition, group heterogeneity on underlying attributes, such as skills and tenure in the organization, has a direct relationship to the level of process losses suffered by the group (Milliken & Martins, 1996; Steiner, 1972). However, group heterogeneity on task-related abilities and skills is often positively related to group performance on the tasks typically found in organizations (Jackson, 1992), particularly if group processes are carefully controlled (Mannix & Neale, 2005). In summary, heterogeneous work groups probably have a higher performance potential but also a higher tendency to suffer process losses. Also, different types of diversity may have different effects on group processes and performance (e.g., Mannix & Neale, 2005; Jehn, Northcraft, & Neale, 1999).

Research on the special case of minority-majority groups has tended to focus on the influence of minority members on the majority. For example, some research has found that minority members can influence the majority if they are consistent and persistent in their arguments (Nemeth, 1992). Other research suggests that by expressing alternative views, minority members can improve the decision making and performance of the group by increasing the group's attention to the process of decision making (Nemeth, 1992). However, minority members are slower to express their opinions, but this speed increases as the size of the minority grows (Bassili, 2003).

Culture's Influence on Work Groups

The general model of work group functioning described in this chapter makes it possible to examine the way in which culture influences work group processes and outcomes. While this influence is perhaps most apparent in the cultural composition of the work group, the organizational context in which the group functions, the work group structure, and the task in which the group is involved also influence how much cultural differences affect the work group. The cultural backgrounds of a work group's members affect the way they function through three general types of mechanisms:

   a. Cultural norms: the orientations of the specific cultures represented in the group toward the functioning of groups
   b. Cultural diversity: the number of different cultures represented in the group
   c. Relative cultural distance: the extent to which group members are culturally different from each other

These mechanisms are interrelated, but each affects the way groups operate in different ways.

Box 8.1 Culture Clash in the Cockpit

In a very famous case of drunk flying, Japan Airlines cargo flight 8054 carrying the pilot (a 53-year-old U.S. national), two co-pilots (both Japanese aged 31 and 35), two cargo handlers, and 65 beef cattle crashed shortly after take-off in Anchorage, Alaska, killing all on board. Postmortem analysis indicated the captain had a blood alcohol level of .29 percent (a U.S. driver with .08 percent is considered legally intoxicated). The captain's preflight behavior included staggering and slurring his words and was noticed by the driver who took the crew to the airport. The National Transportation Safety Board determined that the probable cause of the accident was "a stall that resulted from the pilot's control inputs aggravated by airframe icing while the pilot was under the influence of alcohol. Contributing to the cause of this accident was the failure of the other flight crew members to prevent the captain from attempting the flight." The cockpit voice recorder data showed that neither the first or second officer remarked about the captain's intoxication, nor did they try to deter him from controlling the aircraft. Subsequent investigation attributed the reluctance of the junior flight crew members to confront the captain to the fact that suggesting to the captain, their superior, that he delegate the takeoff to a junior crew member would have caused him to lose face.

SOURCE: Strauch (2010) and NTSB.

Cultural Norms

One of the most important influences on group effectiveness is the mix of cultural norms represented in the work group. Different cultures have very different orientations toward what is appropriate in terms of work group function and structure (Thomas et al., 1996). As noted in Box 8.1, these beliefs are not checked at the workplace door but spill over into the work environment. For example, many collectivist cultures believe that maintaining a sense of harmony is extremely important in interpersonal interactions. This contrasts dramatically with notions of constructive conflict and devil's advocacy popular in some individualist cultures, such as the United States. Cultural orientations such as individualism and collectivism have been shown to be related to the metaphors that individuals in different cultures used to describe their teams (Gibson & Zellmer-Bruhn, 2001). For example, metaphors in individualist cultures reflected clear team objectives and voluntary membership, such as sports teams, while metaphors in collectivist cultures emphasized a broad scope of activity and clear member roles, such as in families.

A number of studies support the idea that individuals bring such mental representations (metaphors or scripts) to the work group with which they interpret events, behaviors, expectations, and other group members. For example, research shows that group members initially base their actions on their previous experiences in other groups. In one study, members of new groups who previously developed norms for cooperation acted cooperatively in a subsequent similar situation (Bettenhausen & Murnighan, 1991). There is also evidence to suggest that people with different cultural orientations have different views of what are appropriate group processes. For example, the task-related norms of a group might be set based on the individual cultural backgrounds of group members (Hackman & Morris, 1978). In another example, individuals from a collectivist culture have been found to be less likely to engage in social loafing than were members from a more individualist culture (Earley, 1989). The reason that social loafing does not occur among collectivists is that they bring their norms for placing group goals ahead of their own interest to the work group situation. By contrast, the motivation for personal gain of individualists also carries over into the work group setting.

In summary, like other behavioral norms, the norms for interacting in a group can vary according to culture. Although the norms for any work group are unique, one of the bases for these norms in all groups is the individuals' previous group experience (Feldman, 1984). Therefore, in multicultural work groups, individuals from different cultures are likely to have very different ideas, at least initially, about how the work group should go about its task, how they should behave, and how they should interact with other group members.

Cultural Diversity

A second influence on work group effectiveness is the number of different cultures represented in the group—its cultural diversity. Cultural diversity has been shown to have both positive and negative effects on work group effectiveness (see Stahl, Maznevski, Voigt & Jonsen, 2010 for a review). Culturally diverse groups, particularly those acting face-to-face, are likely to suffer from increased process losses and have lower group performance than are homogeneous groups (Carte & Chidambaram, 2004; Hill, 1982; Staples & Zhao, 2006). These increased process losses result from the culturally different perceptions and communication patterns noted in previous chapters. Alternatively, because of the different perspectives of group members, cultural diversity should result in more creative and higher-quality group decisions (Earley & Mosakowski, 2000; Elron, 1997; McLeod, Lobel, & Cox, 1996; Thomas et al., 1996).

Another way in which cultural diversity affects group functioning is through the formation of subgroups within the task group. When group members fall into two, non-overlapping cultural categories, as opposed to many cultures, individuals sometimes identify more strongly with their cultural subgroup than with the task group as a whole. This causes cultural subgroup favoritism and negatively affects information flow across subgroup boundaries. In this case, it is not the overall amount of cultural diversity that affects group functioning but the extent to which the task group is divided along these so-called *faultlines* that affects group performance (Lau & Murnighan, 1998; 2005). This may explain, in part, why groups with either high or low cultural diversity seem to perform better than those with moderate amounts of diversity (Earley & Mosakowski, 2000).

The effect of process losses and gains is not consistent over the life of the group. Over time, culturally diverse groups achieve a reduction in process losses (Pelz, 1956; Watson, Kumar, & Michaelson, 1993). As groups age, members find ways of dealing with the problems of intercultural interaction, thus increasing the possibility that, given an appropriate task, they will demonstrate superior performance (Katz, 1982).

This can include the development of a *hybrid* team culture (Earley & Mosakowski, 2000) that emerges in similar fashion to the change of direction in Gersick's (1988) model of team development and that facilitates the performance of culturally diverse work groups. In this case, the norms of the hybrid culture override the conflicting norms brought to the group by individuals. In addition, over time, work groups have the opportunity to receive feedback about both individual and group processes (Watson, Johnson, & Merritt, 1998). This feedback can come from both inside and outside the work group and might be particularly useful to culturally diverse work groups that are trying to overcome the problems of cross-cultural interaction (Ayoko, Hartel, & Callen, 2002; Baba, Gluesing, Ratner, & Wagner, 2004; Thomas, 1999).

The effect of cultural diversity in the work group clearly has both positive and negative elements (Stahl, Maznevski, Voigt, & Jonsen, 2006; 2010). On the one hand, it has the potential to increase group performance through a greater variety of ideas and perspectives and an increased focus on group processes by members. On the other, the probability of increased process losses exists, but this negative effect is likely to diminish over time, particularly if process-related feedback is received.

Relative Cultural Distance

A third way in which the cultural composition of the group influences group effectiveness is the extent to which each individual in the group is culturally different from the other group members. Culturally different work group members are aware that they are different (Randel, 2003), and this awareness causes them to compare themselves to the other members of the group (Bochner & Ohsako, 1977; Bochner & Perks, 1971). Based on this comparison, they evaluate the appropriateness of their behavior and their status in the work group. If group members perceive their status in the group favorably, they are likely to participate more fully and to perceive the group more positively (Mullen, 1987; Mullen & Baumeister, 1987; Tajfel & Turner, 1986). For example, a study of multicultural work groups in Japan (Thomas et al., 1996) found that the extent to which individuals were culturally different from other group members affected their assessments of group cohesiveness and satisfaction with the group process.

The relative difference of individuals from other group members also influences the extent to which they identify with the task group versus their cultural group. And, in general, group members' willingness to participate depends on the salience of the task group identity versus that of their cultural group (e.g., Wit & Kerr, 2002). A common group identity seems to be important to group processes and outcomes (Salk & Brannen, 2000; Van der Zee, Atsma, & Brodbeck, 2004).

The extent to which group members differ from other members of the group affects their assessment of the level of conflict in the group and their willingness to express their ideas (Thomas, 1999). Greater cultural difference between an individual and the rest of the group makes it more likely that the individual's cultural norms for group behavior vary from those of the group. Also, relative cultural difference influences the extent to which individuals will be competent in the language or communication style of a multicultural group (Brett & Gelfand, 2006; Elron, Halevy, Ben-Ari, & Shamir, 2003). These differences can result in a lower expectation of a successful interaction with the other group members and a higher estimate of the effort required for achieving success. Individuals might be reluctant to invest high amounts of effort in interacting with other group members who are very different, because these interactions might be viewed as costing more in time and effort than the potential benefit (Thibaut & Kelley, 1959).

In summary, the influence of culture is evident through three related mechanisms. These are the culturally based norms that the group members bring to the work group situation, the cultural diversity or number of cultures in the group, and the degree of cultural difference of group members relative to the group. Each of these mechanisms has different effects on work group processes and outcomes.

Culture's Effect in Different Group Structures and Tasks

The nature of the task and the structure of the work group influence the extent to which the cultural composition of the work group affects its outcomes. Previously, group structures were classified as crews, task forces, or teams, and group tasks as production or creative idea generation and decision making. Both the structure of the work group and the task with which it is involved specify the nature of the relationships among work group members. Group tasks that allow little employee discretion, are not sensitive to variations among group members, and are not controlled by the group offer very limited opportunities for the characteristics of group members to influence outcomes (Goodman, 1986). Therefore, production tasks would generally offer less opportunity for the effects of cultural composition (either positive or negative) than would creative idea generation and decision-making tasks. Crews, task forces, and teams differ in terms of the importance of member composition to their functioning (Arrow & McGrath, 1995). Because the nature of the interaction of crews is through the tools that they use, who the members are as people is of little importance to the function of the group. For example, an airline copilot from one culture could replace another from a different culture on short notice with little effect on the routine operation of a flight deck crew. In contrast, the structure of a team makes it very sensitive to member differences. These groups require highly developed intermember relationships and are therefore very sensitive to cultural differences among group members. For task forces, group composition is more important than for crews but less important than for teams. Because task forces are temporary and project focused, member interactions are limited in both intensity and time. The influence of cultural composition in different group structures and tasks is depicted graphically in Figure 8.3.

In summary, both the types of group task and the group structure can affect the extent of influence that the cultural composition of the work group has on group outcomes. For example, a product development task force engaged in planning a product introduction to a foreign market might benefit substantially from having foreign nationals represented in the group. In this case, the national culture of group members might be viewed as a task-relevant skill that members bring to the group and that can be used to the advantage of the group. In contrast, the potential influence of cultural diversity among production workers in a vehicle assembly team is limited by the nature of the task. When this same group is involved in solving problems associated with designing the production process, as in quality-improvement teams, the

Figure 8.3   Effects of Cultural Composition on Different Tasks and Group Types

Task Type

Group Type	Decision Making	Production
Team	Very High	Moderate
Task Force	High	Low
Crew	Low	Very Low

opportunity for cultural differences to influence the group process (either positively or negatively) is enhanced.

Global Virtual Teams

A key underlying assumption about the discussion of work groups to this point is that they interact face-to-face. This might have been true for the majority of work groups in organizations in the recent past and may still be relevant for some work groups. However, one way in which many organizations are dealing with the challenges of globalization is by forming work groups with geographically dispersed structures (Greiner & Metes, 1995; MacDuffie, 2008). Called, variously, virtual teams, ad hoc networks, and electronically mediated groups (Gibson & Cohen, 2003), a key characteristic is that they interact primarily by electronic networks. Therefore, work group members can be separated by time, geography, and culture but also by work practices, organization, or technology. All of these elements can contribute to the degree of distance (*discontinuity*) between work group members (Chudoba, Wynn, Lu, & Watson-Manheim, 2005). These *virtual* teams can span the globe and are possible because of recent advances in computer and telecommunications technology (Leung & Peterson, 2010). Teams can use a variety of technologies, such as desktop videoconferencing, collaborative software systems, and Internet-Intranet systems. The proposed advantages of global virtual teams focus on the ability to choose the best group members regardless of geographic (MacDuffie, 2008; Townsend, DeMarie, & Hendrickson, 1998) or organizational (Maznevski & Chudoba, 2000) boundaries and also to allow knowledge workers to operate from remote locations (Cascio, 2000).

Teams in organizations that do not at some time interact through electronic media are increasingly rare (Bell & Kozlowski, 2000). It is therefore important to understand the special challenges that confront virtual teams. These challenges can be categorized in terms of communication, relationship building and conflict management, and task management (Jonsen, Maznevski, & Davison, 2012).

Communication

The electronic communication tools used by virtual teams differ in their media richness as communication channels (see Chapter 6). They provide a foundation for group work but do not truly replicate face-to-face interaction. And people seem to prefer face-to-face communication to electronic media for complex, innovative, subtle, or ambiguous messages (Allen & Hauptman, 1990; DeMeyer, 1993; Treviño, Lengel, & Daft, 1987). Communication using this type of technology takes place in an asynchronous manner with a lag between one message being sent and another received. Electronically mediated groups tend to form more slowly (Kraut, Egido, & Galegher, 1990) because of asynchronous communication, and the electronic media reduces the ability to sense the social presence of other group members. While this virtuality may improve the sharing of unique information, it seems to hinder the openness of sharing that is important to the effectiveness of virtual teams (Mesmer-Magnus, DeChurch, Jimenez-Rodriguez, Wildman, & Shuffler, 2011). However, it may be that the social information difficulties experienced because of electronic intermediation dissipate over time (Chidambaram, 1996) and the reliance on communication technology may itself impose more structure on the team (Guzzo & Dickson, 1996). A final important aspect of communication in virtual teams is that current technologies rely heavily on the written word and the language in use is most often English (Jonsen, Maznevski, & Schneider, 2011). This can facilitate communication by aiding those who are working in a second language and are conversationally weak. However, it does not eliminate the problems of second language use (see Chapter 6).

Relationship Building and Conflict Management

Good relationships among team members characterized by trust, respect, cooperation, and commitment are desirable in all teams. The ability to develop and maintain these relationships in virtual teams may be affected both by electronic intermediation and cultural diversity. Because of electronic intermediation there is a lack of *evidence* of cultural differences, including language differences that might make culture a somewhat less salient dimension in these groups (Jarvenpaa & Leidner, 1999). Some research indicates that these reductive effects of collaborative technologies are beneficial for culturally diverse teams in reducing the process losses from diversity (Carte & Chidambram, 2004; Staples & Zhao, 2006). For example, some studies have reported less conflict in virtual than in face-to-face teams (e.g., Mortensen & Hinds, 2001; Stahl, Maznevski, Voigt, & Jonsen, 2010). However, the lack of physical contact in these groups highlights the importance of identification with the team that is required for cohesion building (Fiol & O'Conner, 2005). The fact that members of virtual teams may have little in the way of shared context makes the development of team identity more difficult (Canella, Park, & Lee, 2008). Research indicates that a shared team identity moderates the effects of interpersonal conflict (Hinds & Mortensen, 2005). In combination, the characteristics typical of global virtual teams (electronic communication, cultural diversity, lack of onsite monitoring) decrease the salience of the work group identity and may result in team members withholding effort (Shapiro, Furts, Speitzer, Von Glinow, 2002). Regardless of cultural background, team members tend to report less confidence in their ability to work in virtual team environments than in face-to-face teams (Hardin, Fuller, & Davison, 2007).

Task Management

Different virtual team tasks require different strategies and processes. The degree of task interdependence and urgency influence the frequency of communication required (Maznevski & Chudoba, 2000). Highly interdependent and urgent tasks require more frequent interaction. The extent to which the task requires the exchange of tacit as opposed to explicit knowledge influences the characteristics of the interaction required among team members. Explicit knowledge is more easily transferred in the absence of shared background and experience (Nonaka & Takeuchi, 1995). The importance of defined roles, a clear task strategy, and explicit interaction norms is heightened in virtual teams. As opposed to face-to-face teams where these issues can be resolved on a continuous basis as team members interact, virtual teams have little opportunity to manage task processes in this way (Jonsen, Maznevski, & Davison, 2012). An important element is, of course, that the team members must be capable of using the technology involved in task management (Townsend et al., 1998). Research has consistently found that virtual teams take more time to complete their tasks than do face-to-face teams (Martins, Gilson, & Maynard, 2004). However, research findings about the effects of virtualness on the *quality* of team's decisions have been mixed. In some cases, virtual teams made more effective decisions or generated more unique ideas, while in others, very similar results for face-to-face and virtual teams have been found (see Martins, Gilson, & Maynard, 2004 for a review). These mixed findings may be due to moderators of virtual team performance, such as the team's task (as discussed previously) and the extent of performance monitoring provided by the interaction context (Aiello & Kolb, 1995). Additionally, opportunities for the influence of culturally based characteristics, such as differences in tolerance of ambiguity and explicitness (high- versus low-context) of communication styles, are apparent.

In summary, the use of electronic media allows firms to build work groups with optimum membership without regard for the restrictions of time and space. However, the ability of these work groups to work effectively requires overcoming the additional barriers presented by the discontinuity among group members and by electronic mediation. Global virtual teams seem to perform best when they use a coordination mechanism that accommodates both the time frames and interdependence required by the task, they have participation norms that allow the skills, abilities, and knowledge of group members to be leveraged, and they develop a strong group identity and trust among group members.

Organizational Context and Culturally Diverse Work Groups

Work groups are influenced by the larger organization of which they are a part. The dominant characteristics of the organization influence the types of goals and methods that are acceptable for work groups (Campion et al., 1993). In addition, management controls the resources required for work groups to be effective. Apart from the technological and geographic issues mentioned previously, key organizational factors that influence the effectiveness of work groups are the level of management support, the extent to which individual rewards come from the group, the status afforded the group, the amount of training provided to the group, and the extent to which the organization allows groups to be self-managed.

Management Support

It might seem obvious that the most effective work groups exist in organizations that provide high levels of organizational support, such as making sure the work groups have the materials and information necessary to achieve their goals. However, numerous examples exist of organizations setting challenging goals for work groups and then failing to provide adequate support (Hackman, 1991). The success of globally dispersed teams is likely to be greater when management has fostered an organizational culture that supports flexibility over control and an internal focus over an external focus (Kara & Zellmer-Bruhn, 2011). An additional element of support required for work groups composed of culturally diverse members is an organizational culture that supports diversity as indicated by an organizational culture that treats people of all cultures with respect (Cox, 1993) and has an integration and learning perspective (Ely & Thomas, 2001). Research with culturally diverse manufacturing teams indicates that the level of management support is positively related to the task performance of the work group and work group member attitudes, such as satisfaction with the group, group cohesiveness, commitment, and trust, and negatively related to the amount of conflict felt by group members (Thomas et al., 2000). With regard to global virtual teams, management support may be even more important in that the team rarely meets face-to-face and requires management to provide the information and reinforcement necessary to achieve their goals (Maznevski, Davison, & Jonsen, 2006).

Group-Level Rewards

The effect of rewards on individual performance is much better understood than the relationship between rewards and work group performance. Some research has suggested that a mix of individual and group rewards will be most effective with work groups, particularly the self-regulating variety (Pearce & Ravlin, 1987). More recently, however, others suggest that these hybrid reward systems can lead to lower individual effort and hence poor group performance (Wageman, 1995). One study of culturally diverse teams found that the extent to which individuals derived their rewards from the team was positively related to both team performance and team member attitudes (Thomas et al., 2000). However, these results must be treated with some caution based on what we know about preferences for reward allocation across cultures. For example, we know that individualists and collectivists are guided by different reward allocation norms (Leung & Bond, 1984). Individualists are typically more comfortable with rewards based on equity, in which rewards depend on the level of individual contribution. The norm for collectivists is more likely to involve equality of reward allocation in which all group members share equally in group rewards. And, as noted in Chapter 7, it is clear that more egalitarian societies have a preference for equality over equity in reward allocation (Fischer & Smith, 2003). The effectiveness of a particular reward allocation system is likely influenced by the cultural composition of the work group and the preferences of group members. For example, in egalitarian individualist cultures, making the ability to work well in a group a key component in an individual's performance review might be more acceptable than tying rewards more directly to work group performance.

Work Group Status

The argument that the status of a work group in the organization will influence its performance is based on the idea that being a member of a high-status group will increase members' feelings of self-worth and effectiveness. As in other groups, individuals are motivated to maintain and enhance their work groups and hence their own standing (Tajfel & Turner, 1986). The positive effect that high-group status has on the individual improves both individual and work group performance (Ravlin et al., 2000). Successful work groups get the recognition that signals to the rest of the organization that they are an important element of organizational success. However, the extent to which individuals from different cultures derive their self-esteem from work groups can vary considerably (Erez & Earley, 1993). For example, people from collectivist cultures are likely to identify more strongly with their cultural or family group than they are with a work group composed of relative strangers (Triandis, 1995). Therefore, the status of work groups might have a greater influence on the feelings of self-worth, confidence, group potency, and desire to work in the group for some cultures, such as individualists, as opposed to others, such as collectivists. However, affording work groups high status in the organization would seem to make sense in terms of making group membership desirable, regardless of culture.

Training

The concept that work group success requires training in interaction skills as well as technical skills is well established (Wagner, Hibbits, Rosenblatt, & Schulz, 1977). Often, however, managers seem to assume that employees automatically have the skills to be effective work group members (Hackman, 1991). The need for training in the specific electronic tools required for interaction in global virtual teams should be obvious. However, in situations in which all work group activities and tasks cannot be specified in advance and in which individuals can have different assumptions about how the work group should operate, training in interaction skills is especially important. Communication training has been found to be effective in improving interaction processes, trust, and commitment in virtual team environments (Warkentin & Beranek, 1999). Cross-cultural training has the objective of bringing the expectations of individuals from different cultural backgrounds in line with the reality of working in a multicultural context. The effectiveness of cross-cultural training programs on improving interpersonal interactions is documented in a number of studies (e.g., Black & Mendenhall, 1990) and recent research suggests that multicultural experience can have a super-additive effect on the performance of culturally diverse work groups (Tadmor et al., 2012).

Self-Management

The argument for self-managing work groups (teams) stems from the idea that the benefits of group work are related to the delegation of a substantial amount of authority to the work group or team (Barry, 1991; Pearce & Ravlin, 1987). However, if too much authority is delegated, work groups can charge off in inappropriate directions. Research on multicultural work groups has failed to show clear support for self-management as a determining factor in work group effectiveness (Thomas et al., 2000). Setting the direction for a work group might empower it, but dictating work processes and procedures can actually inhibit group performance. Alternatively, insufficient direction can result in work groups with an unclear sense of appropriate task-related processes. This may be particularly true of global virtual teams (Lurey & Raisingham, 2001; Maznevski et al., 2006). Recent research in a single culture has suggested that it is the extent to which work group members feel empowered rather than the degree of self-management that might be most important to group effectiveness (Kirkman & Rosen, 1999) and that empowerment stems from more than just the degree of self-management. In addition, other research (Ayoko et al., 2002; Baba et al., 2004; Thomas, 1999) argues that process-related feedback could be the key factor in determining if culturally diverse work groups overcome the process losses associated with diversity. Therefore, achieving an appropriate level and type of delegation for multicultural work groups can be a particularly difficult management task (see Kirkman & Shapiro, 1997).

Managing Multicultural Work Groups

Even if it were possible to determine the optimal cultural mix in a particular work group situation, it is unrealistic for managers to control the cultural composition of work groups. Instead, they must try to find ways to maximize the positive consequences of both homogeneity and diversity while minimizing the negative consequences of both (Jackson, 1992). The complexity of this endeavor suggests that there is not a universal prescription that can be applied to every multicultural work group. The following ideas are derived from our current knowledge about this management challenge.

Work Group Task and Structure

The research to date suggests that both the positive and negative effects of cultural diversity depend on how the work group is structured and the nature of the task. Work groups with high degrees of interpersonal interaction, such as teams, will be more susceptible to both the process losses and process gains produced by cultural differences among members. In addition, less structured tasks, such as creative problem solving and decision making, are more open to the influence of cultural differences than are highly structured and regulated-production tasks. For example, cultural differences might be masked on the production line only to become apparent in a weekly team meeting at which improvements in the production process are being discussed. In another example, airline flight deck crews might operate very similarly across cultures under routine conditions, but the influence of cultural differences becomes apparent when handling emergency situations (Merritt & Helmreich, 1996). Finally, some tasks may lend themselves better to virtual environment than others (Hollingshead, McGrath, & O'Conner, 1993), and an important element of group structure in the virtual environment is matching the communication channel to the task environment (Maznevski et al., 2006). Therefore, one avenue for intervention is matching the task and work group structure with other characteristics of the situation.

Broad Evaluation Criteria

Multicultural work groups should be evaluated in terms of group processes and individual outcomes as well as task accomplishment. The long-term effectiveness of a work group depends on its ability to help individuals meet their personal goals and to maintain group processes to facilitate performance. Multicultural work groups often take longer to reach their potential than do homogeneous work groups (Watson, Kumar, & Michaelson, 1993). Considering broad performance criteria means encouraging what has been called exploration activities as opposed to exploitation activities (Mannix & Neale, 2005). Exploration involves experimentation, innovation, and divergent thinking, while exploitation focuses on production, efficiency, and convergent thinking. Thus, taking advantage of the benefits of cultural diversity in teams may require a significant broadening of evaluation criteria.

Composition and Task Requirements

Multicultural work groups are very sensitive to the need for resources, including member resources. The guiding principle for work group organization should be to ensure that the work group has the task-related knowledge, skills, and abilities required to complete the group tasks (Hackman, 1987). These task-related requirements can also include culture, in that characteristics of specific culturally based knowledge and skills might be appropriate to certain tasks. For example, some research with Japanese teams found that when culturally based tacit knowledge or *in the bones expertise* was made explicit, greater gains were made in productivity and knowledge (Nonaka, 1994). And the cultural composition may allow culturally diverse groups to adapt to changing task contexts (LePine, 2003).

Common Purpose

Creating a shared sense of purpose among work group members can be especially important in multicultural work groups. The idea that groups with goals that transcend the individual differences of group members (superordinate goals) have better group processes is well established (Sherif, Harvey, White, Hood, & Sherif, 1961). Establishing this shared sense of purpose among individuals with different values, attitudes, and beliefs is challenging. It requires managers to understand and be sensitive to the values, attitudes, and beliefs of culturally different work group members. However, establishing these overarching goals can be an important way for managers to bridge cultural differences by focusing on commonalities, while allowing individuals to maintain their cultural distinctiveness (Mannix & Neale, 2005). The existence of common goals can also facilitate a positive work group identity, which is important to the functioning of work groups of all types but seems to be especially critical for global virtual teams (Martins et al., 2004).

Summary

This chapter explored the management challenge of effectively managing culturally diverse work groups and teams. The effective performance of work groups, in general, is affected by six sets of factors; the external or contextual conditions imposed on the group, the resources of group members, the structure of the group, the group task, the group process, and the composition of the group. Cultural diversity in work groups influences the group through three distinct but inter-related mechanisms of the cultural norms of group members, cultural diversity or the number of different cultures represented in the group, and the extent to which group members are culturally different from each other. In addition, the nature of the task and the structure of the group influence the extent to which the cultural composition of a group affects its processes and outcomes. One way in which many organizations are dealing with the challenges of globalization is by forming work groups with geographically dispersed structures that operate through electronic networks. These global virtual teams present the opportunity for selecting the best members without regard to location but also present an additional set of challenges. Their ability to work effectively depends on overcoming the additional barriers presented by the discontinuity among group members and by electronic mediation. Key organization factors that influence work group effectiveness are the level of management support, the extent to which individual rewards come from the group, the status afforded the group, the amount of training provided to the group, and the extent to which the organization empowers the group. In short, managing multicultural work groups involves trying to find ways to maximize the positive consequences of both homogeneity and diversity, while at the same time minimizing their negative consequences.

Questions for Discussion

1. How do you know if a work group is functioning well in an organization?

2. What effects do factors external to the work group have on its functioning?

3. Explain how the cultural composition of work groups affects the way they function.

4. How do the group task and the structure of the group influence the extent to which cultural composition has an effect in work groups?

5. Discuss the advantages and disadvantages of global virtual teams.

9

The Challenge of International Organizations: Structure and Culture

Globalization does not mean imposing homogeneous solutions in a pluralistic world. It means having a global vision and strategy, but it also means cultivating roots and individual identities.

Gucharan Das, former chairman and
managing director, Procter & Gamble, India

All organizations create structure to coordinate activities and control the actions of their members. However, the forms that organizations take both domestically and around the world vary considerably. This chapter reviews the management challenges presented by international organizations. International organizations are discussed both in terms of a universal logic to organizing and the influence of culture on organizational structure. First, the basic dimensions of organizational structure and design are described, and different schools of thought about explaining organizational structure are discussed. Then, the influence of culture and examples of cross-national variation in organizational forms are presented. A discussion of the MNO as a unique organizational form leads to consideration of its influence on managerial roles and the relationship of culturally different individuals to the firm. Finally, the shared perception of organizational work practices, called organizational culture, is discussed in terms of its functional and dysfunctional properties in international organizations.

Organizations

Organizations are social systems that are both intentionally structured to achieve goals and spontaneously develop apart from managerial intent. They are not independent of their surroundings but are open systems that continuously take inputs from the environment, such as raw materials, human resources, and ideas, transform them, and then exchange output with the environment in the form of products, services, or knowledge in return for more resources (Katz & Kahn, 1978). As systems of people, organizations must be coordinated through a differentiation of roles and a hierarchy of authority to achieve goals. This *structure* of the organization can be described by its degree of complexity, formalization, and centralization (Pugh, Hickson, Hinings, MacDonald, & Turner, 1963).

The complexity of an organization is the extent to which it is differentiated along three dimensions: horizontal, vertical, and spatial. *Horizontal differentiation* refers to the number of different types of jobs that exist in an organization. The greater the number of different occupations in an organization, the greater is its horizontal differentiation. *Vertical differentiation* refers to the number of levels in the hierarchy of the organization. *Spatial differentiation* refers to the extent to which the organization's physical facilities and personnel are geographically dispersed. Horizontal, vertical and spatial differentiation increase complexity, which increases the management challenges of organizations. The addition of geographic dispersion to all of the cultural and governmental challenges of international activities multiplies the other forms of complexity that international organizations face.

Formalization is the extent to which rules and procedures govern the activities of organization members. For example, the level of documentation for employee behavior is a good indicator of the formality of an organization. Formal organizations allow little discretion in the way people do their jobs. The degree of centralization in an organization is indicated by the extent to which decision making is concentrated at a single point. Among the most centralized organizations are small businesses in which almost all significant decisions are made by a single owner-manager. In decentralized organizations, decisions are pushed down and out through the organization. The three elements of organizational structure—complexity, formalization, and centralization—can be combined in a variety of ways.

Organizational Designs

A number of simple ways of thinking about organizations use metaphors, such as whether an organization is managed as though it is more like a machine or more like an organism (e.g., Burns & Stalker, 1961). A more refined perspective on the fundamentals of organizational forms is offered by Mintzberg (1983). He proposed that all organizations are composed of five essential parts. These are the operating core, the middle line, the support staff, the technostructure, and the strategic apex. According to Mintzberg, each of these parts is dominant in one of five basic types of organizational design as shown in Table 9.1

The *operating core* consists of the employees who perform the basic tasks related to the production of products and services. This part of the organization is dominant in a *professional bureaucracy*, which is populated by highly trained specialists. Examples include universities, museums, and hospitals. Consulting companies that rely heavily on highly trained and experienced individuals to provide services for international businesses sometimes have this structure. The *strategic apex* is composed of the top-level managers who have overall responsibility for the organization. In *simple* organizational structures, the strategic apex dominates. Simple structures are characteristic of entrepreneurial ventures, such as small import-export firms in which virtually everyone reports to one person. The direct supervision by this individual is the key coordinating mechanism. The *middle line* consists of those managers that connect the operating core to the strategic apex. Middle-line managers predominate in *divisional structures*, which are characterized by groups of semiautonomous units coordinated by a central headquarters. Many large multinationals that expect geographic division managers to make major decisions for their area are characteristic of this structure. The *technostructure* is composed of technical analysts, such as accountants and industrial

Table 9.1 Five Structural Configurations of Organizations		
Type of Structure	**Characteristics**	**Examples**
Simple	Little or no technostructure, few support staff, loose division of labor, minimal differentiation between units, informal	Small, entrepreneurial firms
Machine bureaucracy	Highly specialized routine operations, very formalized, large operating core, centralized decision making	Banks, government agencies
Professional bureaucracy	Decentralized, coordination by standardization of skills, operating core of highly trained professionals who have collective control over administration	Universities, hospitals
Divisional	Central headquarters oversees a set of somewhat autonomous divisions, typically large, mature organizations, limited parallel type of vertical decentralization	Multinationals, conglomerates
Adhocracy	Experts from different specialties formed into project teams, organic structure with little formalization, coordination by mutual adjustment	High-tech organizations

SOURCE: Adapted from Mintzberg (1980).

engineers, who have responsibility for formulating rules and procedures to standardize the organization. The influence of the technostructure is strongest in the type of design that Mintzberg calls the *machine bureaucracy.* Organizations that rely on standardized procedures and policies for coordination and control, such as banks and government departments, are characteristic of this design. Production organizations whose international strategy is largely to take advantage of global resources to limit production costs often have machine bureaucracy characteristics. *Support staffs* provide advice, internal consulting, and other indirect support services to the rest of the organization. The support staff is especially influential in an organizational form called an *adhocracy.* The adhocracy, like the professional bureaucracy, is composed of highly skilled professionals. However, this organizational design depends on mutual adjustment among professionals rather than the individual autonomous judgment of each professional to see that work is conducted effectively.

These five types of organizational designs represent a conceptual framework that can be used to understand the variety of organizational forms that exist. Management scholars have drawn on a number of logical approaches and some empirical research to suggest the circumstances in which a particular organization form tends to occur or when a particular form is likely to work best. These schools of thought tend to focus on a single aspect of the issue and use different logics and terminology. However, some reconciliation of the different points of view is possible (e.g., Astley & Van de Ven, 1983; Scott & Davis, 2006), and each perspective provides an insight into our contemporary understanding of international organizational forms.

Explaining Organizational Structure

Explanations for the existence of different organizational structures can be classified into four groups. Roughly in the order of their development, they are deterministic theories, contingency theories, ecological theories, and institutional theories. Both deterministic and contingency theories operate at the level of individual organizations, whereas ecological and institutional theories deal with populations or communities of organizations.

Deterministic Theory

The initial study of organizational structure focused on finding the one best way to organize. These approaches proposed that one factor or another was dominant in explaining the structural aspects of organizations. Significant are those that proposed technology, strategy, and size as determinants of structure.

Based on studies of English manufacturing firms, Woodward (1965) found that the three technological classifications of *unit production, mass production,* and *process production* explained the differences in structure she observed. The technology argument was later refined to include knowledge technology as well as production technology (Perrow, 1967). By classifying tasks by the number of exceptions encountered and how well defined were the methods available to find solutions to these exceptions, organizations could be classified as routine, craft, engineering, or nonroutine. Although the relationship between technology, in terms of routineness, and structure is not particularly strong, organizations composed of routine tasks tend to be more differentiated both horizontally and vertically (Hage & Aiken, 1969).

The origin of the theories about the relationship between strategy and structure lies in Alfred Chandler's study of the development of numerous large U.S. firms (Chandler, 1962). In essence, the argument is that as the strategy of the firm moves from a single product through vertical integration to product diversification, the firm must develop more complex and formal structures to coordinate activities. Over the years, the idea of what constitutes a strategy has matured (e.g., Miles & Snow, 1978; Porter, 1980). However, the basic premise of the relationship to structure remains. This view suggests that some optimal structure exists that reflects a particular strategy.

The argument for organization size as a determinant of organization structure has a long history, beginning with studies by Blau (1970) and also the Aston researchers (e.g., Pugh & Hickson, 1976). Although not without its critics (e.g., Argyris, 1972; Hall, Haas, & Johnson, 1967), size seems to be strongly related to at least some elements of structure. The greatest effect of size is on vertical differentiation (Mileti, Gillespie, & Haas, 1977). As organizations employ more people, they add more levels. The rate of increase in differentiation is initially rapid but decreases as the organization grows. In addition, increases in organizational size are related to increases in formalization but to decreases in centralization (Blau & Schoenherr, 1971). The logic is that as organizations grow, they substitute formal rules for direct supervision and the ability to centralize decision making effectively declines.

Contingency Theory

Deterministic theories are concerned only with factors internal to the organization. Contingency theories of organization developed because of the recognition that organizations, as open systems, interact with their environment. A popular definition of environment describes it as those institutions and forces that affect the organization but are outside of its control (Churchman, 1968). Therefore, it can include economic, political, legal, and social conditions, although management might not be concerned with all of these at any one time. Organizational environments are described in a variety of ways (e.g., Emery & Trist, 1965). Perhaps the most useful categorization is in terms of environmental uncertainty, because managers will try to reduce uncertainty in order to improve effectiveness (Dill, 1958). Simple static environments create less uncertainty for managers than do complex dynamic environments. The classic studies of Burns and Stalker (1961) and Lawrence and Lorsch (1967) supported the fundamental idea that managers adjust the organization structure to reduce environmental uncertainty. In general, simple static environments (low environmental uncertainty) give rise to organizations with high complexity, high formalization, and high centralization, whereas complex dynamic environments result in high uncertainty and give rise to organizations with low complexity, low formalization, and decentralization (Duncan, 1972). Although contingency theories allow for multiple causes (e.g., strategy, technology, size, environment; and more recently knowledge [Birkenshaw, Nobel, & Ridderstråle, 2002]) for an organization's structure, there is some question as to whether or not this approach reflects reality (Child, 1974). That is, if environments are increasingly complex and dynamic, most organizations should adopt a more organic structure. However, observation suggests a significant amount of complexity, formalization, and centralization in modern organizations. Even if one's view is restricted to Western cultures, the evidence for the relationship between contingency variables and organizational structure is mixed (Tayeb, 1987). Additionally, the assumption of a Western notion of rational choice (see Chapter 5) of structural forms creates some questions about the applicability of this approach in international contexts. Managers may be limited in their ability to understand and implement the organizational design they desire. Two alternatives to contingency theory that recognize the limits on manager rationality and control on organizational structure in international environments are ecological and institutional theories.

Ecological Theories

Ecological theories focus not on single organizations but on the structures of whole populations of organizations, such as industries (Westney, 1997). In this view, the environment determines organizational structure not through choice by managers but by selecting out those organizations that do not fit (Hannan & Freeman, 1977). Organizations are relatively inert and either die or are absorbed by other organizations as environmental conditions change (Hannan & Freeman, 1984). Managers are viewed as very limited in their ability to adapt their organizations' structures. This natural selection view of organizations suggests that environmental forces drive the evolution of corporate structures and that actions by managers have little effect (Astley & Van de Ven, 1983). Although the idea that managerial strategizing has little significance might be an unpalatable option for some, ecological theories serve to point out possible constraints on the ability of organizations to adapt and suggest reasons for inertia in organizational structures (Westney, 1997).

Institutional Theory

Institutional theory focuses on the ways that organizations in shared environments come to adopt structures viewed as appropriate and that are reinforced in interactions with other organizations (Westney, 1997). It explains the structural similarity (isomorphism) that exists across organizations. For example, commercial banks have a number of structural similarities, as do hospitals, as do universities. Fundamentally, institutional theory suggests that two factors influence organizational structure. The first is the effect of environmental agents (e.g., regulatory agencies, professional societies, consulting firms) in shaping the organization. The second are those processes within the firm that interpret certain externally validated structures as appropriate. DiMaggio and Powell (1983) defined three categories of environmental pressures toward institutional isomorphism:

- *Coercive* isomorphism: Patterns of organization are imposed on the firm by an outside authority, such as government.
- *Normative* isomorphism: Professional bodies promote "proper" organizational structure.
- *Mimetic* isomorphism: Organizations copy the structure of firms that have been successful in dealing with a particular environment.

Although institutional theory was not formulated with large MNCs that operate in multiple countries and industries in mind, it has been applied to the study of these international organizations (Rosenzweig & Singh, 1991). Large MNCs often span both countries and industries. Therefore, they can be subjected to competing isomorphic pressures in the different environments in which they operate (Westney, 1993). As discussed ahead, the structures of MNCs that straddle multiple environments reflect the necessity of accommodating these sometimes conflicting pressures (Westney, 1993). The approaches to understanding the structures of organizations described here differ both in terms of the role of managers and in the effect of environmental factors in determining structure. At one end of the continuum, managers make strategic choices regarding adapting the internal structure of the organization to the environment. At the other, managers have little influence, and forces in the external environment largely determine effective structures. The debate among organization theorists concerning the most appropriate approach to studying international organizations continues (Ghoshal, 1997). The view presented here is that although none of the perspectives is entirely satisfactory, they all identify important facets of the pressures and contingencies that face international organizations. As such, they provide a backdrop for examining the influence of culture on organizational forms.

Culture and Organizational Structure

A fundamental question concerning international organizational design is why organizations in different societies are alike in some respects and different in others. Reflecting on the organization theories presented previously, we can see why all organizations might share similar characteristics but also why cultural differences in organizational structures exist.

Culture-Free Perspective

One view is that the contingencies that affect organizations operate in a similar fashion across cultures. For organizations to be effective, the design of the organization must fit with their size, technology, and strategy, regardless of culture (Child, 1974, 1981; Hickson, Hinings, McMillan, & Schwitter, 1991). This so-called culture-free approach does not deny the existence of cultural differences; it just considers culture irrelevant. Research from the Aston studies, which over the course of two decades studied over 1,000 organizations in 14 (primarily western European) countries

(Hickson & Pugh, 1995), showed a very strong effect of size on organization structure in all countries studied (Hickson & McMillan, 1981). Regardless of country, larger organizations tended to be more formalized, specialized, and less centralized. Additional support for the culture-free contingency approach has been found in samples from the Middle and Far East (Donaldson, 1986). Despite this general pattern, some of the Aston studies showed country differences in the strength of the effects of size as well as in typical levels of some of these organization characteristics. For example, in one study Japanese firms were found to be more centralized and more formal than British firms (Azumi & McMillan, 1975). Also, size was found to have stronger effects on centralization in British than in German organizations, and he also found a tendency for German organizations to show higher centralization in general than British organizations (Child, 1981). Another study showed that technology had a smaller effect in Japanese than in U.S. organizations, and that Japanese organizations showed greater formal centralization but less centralization in practice than did U.S. organizations (Lincoln, Hanada & McBride, 1986).

The distinction between formal centralization and centralization in practice opens up an area for considering effects of culture that are not well represented in the Aston research. The Aston model implies that the specification of organization structure will have a direct effect on organization members and that the duties and roles implied by structure are not open to cultural interpretation (Smith & Bond, 1999). For example, centralization in the Aston model is indicated by who is *formally responsible* for making decisions in the organization, but it does not address the degree of consultation that *actually* occurs before the decision is announced. Also, while firms respond similarly to contingency variables, the means by which they do so has been found to be different and consistent with the cultural characteristics of the countries studied (Tayeb, 1987). Therefore, the *culture-free* perspective provides insight in terms of very general structural configurations. However, it is not entirely adequate to explain many of the differences observed in organizations across cultures. In addition, even if the structure of organizations appears objectively similar, the meaning that culturally different organization members give to the structure can be different and affect their behavior (Inzerilli & Laurent, 1983). These insights about cultural adaptations of organization structure arrangements are especially important for managers of MNCs to consider when assessing whether the rules, procedures, and hierarchical structures that they are accustomed to using at home will have the same implications in overseas subsidiaries.

Structural Variation Across Cultures

Alternatives to the culture-free perspective often rely on the effect of societal institutions, defined as the political, social, and legal ground rules of a society, and on national differences in organizational structures (Peng, 2002). Institutions are presented as a broader concept than culture, but include its influence. In this way culture has an indirect effect on the structure of organizations. A number of approaches that specify more direct mechanisms of cultural influence have been proposed (e.g.,

Gibson, 1994; Hofstede, 1991; Lachman, Nedd, & Hinings, 1994), and some empirical evidence supports a relationship between culture and organizational structure (e.g., Dunphy, 1987). Based on the definition of culture adopted in this book and the perspectives on general causes of organizational structure discussed previously, two mechanisms by which national culture influences organizational structure emerge. In the first case, organizational structure is seen as a manifestation or *symptom* of the management group's cultural background. The logical extensions of specific cultural value orientations include explicit organizational structure arrangements, but even more strongly, the way that these arrangements are put into practice. For example, in a high power distance culture, organizations would operate in a hierarchical and centralized way (Hofstede, 1980). Country differences in the sources of guidance on which managers rely most heavily suggests that the extent to which managers rely on rules (related to formalization) and on superiors (related to centralization) varies among countries in ways that are related to other culture dimension measures (Peterson & Smith, 2008). In the second case, national culture influences the extent to which different ways of organizing are accepted by the members of a society. Pressures from the organizational environment, which includes the cultural context, dictate the type of structure seen as correct or legitimate. For example, normative pressures influence the tendency of Chinese firms in Hong Kong to stay small and family owned (Chen, 1995).

Research directed at determining which of these perspectives is most powerful in explaining the relationship between culture and organizational structure has failed to find overwhelming support for any one perspective (Gibson, 1994; Peng 2002). As with the more general approaches to understanding differences in organizational structures, each mechanism can help capture the complexity of the relationship between national culture and organizational structure. Figure 9.1 presents a synthesis of the previous discussion of how culture might influence the design of organizations in different countries.

As shown in Figure 9.1, the contextual variables central to contingency approaches (e.g., size, technology, strategy) can account for the similarity in organizational structures found around the world. Through one path, differences in the organizational choices that managers make are guided by their culturally based value orientations. Managers are not necessarily aware of these subconscious influences and simply make choices about structure that feel correct. The more hierarchical organizational structures found in German organizations provides an example (Child & Kieser, 1979; Ruedi & Lawrence, 1970). This rigidity in organizational structures is consistent with dominant German value orientations. Likewise, the flat structure of firms in the Swedish automobile industry can be explained as a manifestation of egalitarian cultural values (Ellegard et al., 1992). Examinations of Japanese business organizations operating in the United States are also indicative of this mechanism for culture's influence. In one study, the structural characteristics of the U.S. organization (specialization specifically) varied with the number of Japanese nationals employed (Lincoln et al., 1978). In this case, the characteristic values of the Japanese manifested themselves in lower specialization.

Figure 9.1 Cultural Influence on Organizational Design

SOURCES: Adapted from Cullen (1999) and Gibson (1994).

The other avenue for cultural influence relies on environmental pressure to shape organizational structure. Organizational structure is less the product of conscious design than it is a reflection of the structures that society will accept as legitimate. Many of the pressures that society brings to bear on organizations emanate from the institutions (e.g., legal, political) of a society. However, the culture and the institutions of society are inevitably linked as they have evolved together over time.

Several examples of this approach exist. First, the Chinese family structure of business is an example of a structure that results in part because of isomorphic pressures. The Chinese family business centers on paternalism, which results in simple structures that restrict the focus to a single aspect of business (Chen, 1995). The societal characteristics of mutual obligation, familialism, and personal connections (*guanxi*) support the effectiveness of this organizational form (Wu, 1999).

Two organizational forms that have similar orientations to the family business but that reflect different societal pressures are the *keiretsu* in Japan and the *chaebol* in Korea. The Japanese *keiretsu* originated with the pre-World War II family-owned *zaibatsu*. These, in turn, had origins in the 19th century feudal-like aristocratic family systems, each of which predominated in a different region of Japan. Often the original *zaibatsu* family name survived, as in Mitsui, Mitsubishi, and Sumitomo. The modern *keiretsu*, although no longer family owned, is a complex network of interfirm networks consisting of a large number of industries, including a trading company (*sogo shosha*), and is usually anchored by a bank. Functioning like an extended family, the coordination and control is facilitated by reciprocal ownership and the focus is typically on long-term gains (Ghauri & Prasad, 1995). This organizational form, although sharing some characteristics with both Korean and Italian networks of firms, is a unique product of its national environment. The Korean *chaebol* are family dominated, multi-industry conglomerates, such as Hyundai, Samsung, Lucky-Goldstar, and Daewoo. They differ from *zaibatsu* in that they are heavily populated with family members, particularly in key positions, and are financed by the government (Steers, Shin, & Ungson, 1989). Although paternalistic and highly centralized like other family business, the *chaebol* is also a unique product of its environment. Korean society, through government policy, such as low-interest loans, tax rebates, and access to foreign currency, has favored the development of large-scale business. Therefore, the structure of the huge but still family-run Korean *chaebol* is the result of societal pressure for large firms or, in intuitionalism terms, coercive isomorphism.

A final example of environmental influence on organizational structure is the knitwear industry of the Modena region of Italy. In this region of Italy, a system of production called *putting out* that economists consider archaic and inefficient survives. In the putting-out system of organization, the manufacturer *puts out* raw materials to independent artisanal firms, who assemble the goods, often in their homes. In Modena, the putting-out system relies on small (less than nine workers on average), family-owned firms to cut, assemble, dye, press, and package knitwear, and results in high living standards and high organizational efficiency (Lazerson, 1995). The success of the system in modern Modena rests on the presence of cohesive family units, cooperative relationships, and an environment supportive of small, family-run firms. Centuries of societal engagement in cooperative endeavors, dating back to straw hat weaving in the 1600s, created a unique set of normative conditions that allow this type of enterprise to flourish (Putnam, 1993). The fit of these small firms with the traditions of family work in the region produced a unique and competitive organizational form.

The model presented in Figure 9.1 is a synthesis of several approaches to understanding organizational structure and seeks to account for both the similarities and differences in organizational structure that are observed in different national cultures. It recognizes the influence of contextual variables such as size, technology, and strategy on organizational design, which accounts for the many similarities. However, it also makes explicit two avenues for the influence of national culture. First, as managers make choices in organizational structure, they are influenced by deeply held values and beliefs that influence what seems normal in terms of organization. In addition, however, organizations are open systems influenced by pressures from the environment. The cultural context of the firm determines, at least in part, what types of organizational structures are viewed as appropriate by society.

Informal Organization

Informal organization refers to those elements of an organization that help to reduce individual variability in the behavior of organization members but is not reflected in a formal organization chart. In Chapter 2, the idea of a set of understandings, behaviors, and relationships that are shared by members of an organization, its *organizational culture*, was introduced. In that chapter, the important differences between organization culture as a set of shared norms associated with an organization and the more fundamental set of shared meanings associated with national culture was introduced. Here we recognize the influence on these informally shared assumptions that guide behavior in organizations and also discuss how these informal aspects of organizations may be linked to national culture.

Organizational culture produces both functional behaviors that contribute to the goals of the organization and dysfunctional behaviors that have negative effects. The main positive effects of organizational culture are to provide a sense of identity for the organization, which differentiates it from other organizations, and also a mechanism of socializing organization members into a way of doing things that is consistent with the goals of the organization. In this way, organization members develop a sense of commitment to the organization and its goals (Robbins, 1992). The negative effects of culture stem from the fact that organizational culture provides members with a set of behaviors that have served them well historically. Therefore a strong organizational culture can be a barrier to change in the organization and can also create conflict among organizational subcultures or when firms with different cultures merge.

Despite the long interest in organizational culture, there has been little systematic study of organizational cultures in different parts of the world. Those few studies that do exist tend to show differences in the descriptions of organizational cultures in different countries (Dedoussis, 2004; Denison, Haaland, & Goelzer, 2004; Sagiv, Schwartz, & Arieli, 2011). However, the dimensions along which organizational cultures are compared vary widely. Van den Berg and Wilderom (2004) suggest that organizational cultures can be defined along five dimensions of (1) autonomy, (2) external orientation, (3) interdepartmental coordination, (4) human resource orientation, and (5) improvement orientation.

Miriam Erez and her colleagues (e.g., Erez & Shokef, 2008) provide a perspective on the organizational cultures of multinational organizations that operate beyond their national cultures. She suggests that to some extent the forces of globalization are shaping the cultures of global organizations to be similar, at least on certain dimensions. New, shared meanings resulting from a global work context lead to similar organizational orientations toward such things as the nature of competition, response to uncertainty and change, acceptance of diversity, social responsibility, and a focus on people. The emergence of this so-called global work culture parallels the need for organizations to function in a global context. It is this organizational need that is discussed next.

Organizing in Multinational Organizations

Thus far in this chapter, our concern has been directed at understanding formal and informal organizations in different national cultures. However, MNOs operate across cultural boundaries and present a number of additional issues for international managers. The MNO is a single organization with a need to coordinate its operations across multiple environments.

Multinational Structures

The need for MNOs to coordinate and control operations across multiple environments led to several approaches to placing foreign activity within the broader organizational structure. The approach taken can depend on the location and type of foreign subsidiaries, the impact of international operations on corporate performance, and the path through which the firm's international operations have developed over time (e.g., Stopford &Wells, 1972). In addition, the preference for a particular method to integrate international operations can vary according to the firm's country of origin (Leksell, 1981; Marschan, 1996). Five ways of integrating international activity are common. The *international division* groups all international activities together in a single organizational unit and is more popular with U.S. than European MNOs (Daniels & Radebaugh, 1998). This structure has also been the initial choice of a significant number of firms as they expand internationally (Davis, 1992). The *product division* structure groups all units involved with like products together around the world. In this case, it is possible for foreign subsidiaries in the same country to have a different relationship to the firm depending on the product line. The *functional division* expands its domestic functional units into its foreign counterparts (e.g., Marketing Europe, Marketing North America, etc.) based on geography, whereas the *geographic division* structure groups all functional areas into geographic units (e.g., North American Division, European Division, etc.). As long as geographic divisions provide the investment returns or other output that headquarters seeks, these division managers typically have a great deal of autonomy, although modern communication technology can foster excessive micromanagement by headquarters (Leung & Peterson, 2010). In the *matrix* structure, each subsidiary reports to more than one group (product, geographic, or functional) for the purpose of integrating international operations with functional areas, product areas, or both. The popularity of this type of structure has waxed and waned as the advantages of integration versus the disadvantages of dual reporting were weighed against each other.

A popular and influential categorization of multinational organization types that builds on these five MNC types is provided by Bartlett and Ghoshal (1989), who consider the configuration of the organizations' capabilities, the role of overseas operations, and the development and diffusion of knowledge. This categorization is presented in Table 9.2. The clear implication presented by the typology shown in Table 9.2 is that any of these forms might be effective in differing contexts. As important, however, is that each organizational form has different implications for the role of managers (Bartlett & Ghoshal, 1989).

International Collaborative Alliances

A recently emerged international organizational form is that of collaborative alliances with foreign firms. These alliances typically take one of three forms: informal cooperative alliances, formal cooperative alliances, and international joint ventures (Lorange & Roos, 1992). The informal type of arrangement is usually limited in scope and has no contractual requirement. Formal arrangements typically require a contractual agreement and are often indicated by broader involvement. In addition, joint ventures are separate legal entities with joint ownership. A considerable literature has developed concerning these organizational forms, a complete discussion of which is outside the scope of this book (e.g., Beamish & Killing, 1997). However, consistent with the focus

Table 9.2　Categorization of MNOs

Organizational Characteristics	Multinational	Global	International	Transnational
Configuration of assets and capabilities	Decentralized and nationally self-sufficient	Centralized and globally scaled	Sources of core competencies centralized, others decentralized	Dispersed, interdependent, and specialized
Role of overseas operations	Sensing and exploiting local opportunities	Implementing parent company strategies	Adapting and leveraging parent company competencies	Differentiated contributions by national units to integrated worldwide operations
Development and diffusion of knowledge	Knowledge developed and retained within each unit	Knowledge developed and retained at the center	Knowledge developed at the center and transferred to overseas units	Knowledge developed jointly and shared worldwide

on organizational structure in this chapter, it is important to note that collaborative arrangements result in new structures, the form of which must be determined from the organizational preferences of the partners. Despite the trend toward this organizational form, most international alliances have a short duration, with as many as 70 percent of alliances failing to meet performance expectations (Geringer & Hebert, 1991). The most often cited reason for failure is incompatibility of the partners (Dacin, Hitt, & Levitas, 1997). However, when selecting a potential partner to a collaborative agreement, the focus of firms is typically on complementarity of task-related capabilities. A firm searches for partners with capabilities that it lacks itself. However, research indicates that such compatibility factors as the national culture of the partner, its organizational structure and culture, and past experience are as important to success as task-related criteria such as technical know-how, financial assets, and access to markets (Fey & Beamish, 2001; Geringer, 1988). Joint venture partners from different cultures also often differ with regard to the procedural legitimacy of such major functions as recruitment, performance appraisal, and training and development (Leung & Kwong, 2003). While both the national and organizational culture of firms can affect international joint venture performance, some research suggests that the more important factor is organizational culture (Pothukuchi et al., 2002). Recent research on international joint ventures also suggests post-joint venture formation processes that improve cultural understanding influence joint venture performance through establishing higher levels of trust (Brouthers & Bamossy, 2006). This suggests that the selection of partners and the formation of structure in the alliance is facilitated by an understanding of the culturally based assumptions and preferences of potential partners with regard to both the formal and informal organization.

International Mergers and Acquisitions

Another way in which new organizational forms are created is through the merger of firms or the acquisition of one firm by another. Inevitably the new organization that emerges differs from its predecessors, and this post-merger integration does not always achieve the desired results. The majority of firms that have acquired other firms seem to perform more poorly than non-acquiring firms (King, Dalton, Daily, & Covin, 2004). Increasingly, mergers and acquisitions occur across national and cultural boundaries with the attendant concern for the effect of cultural differences on the post-merger integration process (see Stahl, 2008). Cross-border M&As demand a "double-layered acculturation" (Barkema, Bell, & Pennings, 1996); as organizations must align both organizational and national cultures, one may conclude that they will be significantly more challenging than domestic M&As. Differences in national culture imply differences in commonly accepted norms, management styles, and prevalent practices, all of which can impede building a sense of shared identity or development of trust between the M&A partners. While a number of studies provide some support for the negative impact of culture differences between parties, there are also studies that reach an opposite conclusion and suggest that cultural distance is an asset rather than a liability. A key argument to support this line of reasoning is that, in addition to being a potential source of conflict, cultural difference can also be a source of value creation, as it provides access to potentially valuable capabilities, resources, and learning opportunities. Research suggests that national culture differences can promote learning especially when steps are taken to integrate the organizational culture of the acquired organization (Sarala & Vaara, 2010), such as temporarily assigning middle or supervisory level staff from headquarters to the acquired facility or sending supervisors in the acquired company to the headquarters company for training (Brannen & Peterson, 2009).

Cross-cultural comparison of mergers and acquisition have found cultural differences in preferences for types of integration process, control systems, and management practices by acquiring firms. For example, consistent with higher power distance and uncertainty avoidance, French acquiring firms tend to exercise greater control over acquired firms than do British or American firms, by managerial transfer and centralized control from headquarters (Calori, Lubatkin, & Very, 1994). Child, Faulkner, and Pitkethly (2001) characterized these preferences for different integration approaches as *Absorbers* (U.S. firms), *Imperialists* (French firms), and *Preservers* (Japanese firms). On the other side of the coin is evidence that integration approaches and practices need to be aligned with the cultural and institutional context in which the merger partner (target firm) operates (Stahl, 2008). For example, one study found that members of target firms in countries high on uncertainty avoidance responded negatively to high levels of integration (Morosini & Singh, 1994), and another found that employees of German, Canadian, and Singaporean firms reacted differently to an acquirer's integration approach and management practices (Stahl, Chua, & Pablo, 2003). In summary, it seems that acquirers have cultural-based preferences for approaches to integration, and targets have culturally based tendencies for the way they react to integration (Goulet & Schweiger, 2006).

In an integration of various perspectives on the effect of culture in mergers and acquisitions, Stahl (2008) suggests that culture affects the outcomes of mergers and acquisitions in two distinct and sometimes opposing ways. First, cultural differences can have an adverse effect on integration outcomes, such as the creation of positive attitudes toward the new organization, the emergence of a shared sense of identity, and the development of trust. However, cultural differences can also be a source of value creation by providing new and unique capabilities, resources, and learning opportunities. The influence of cultural differences seems to depend on the integration design chosen (ranging from total autonomy to total absorption) and on the use of *social* integration mechanisms, such as informal control, personnel rotation, training programs, and cross unit teams (Stahl, 2008).

When involved in international M&As, organizations have increased awareness of the importance of cultural issues for the integration process. They tend to pay much more attention to them and, subsequently, engage in culture integration more purposefully. However, there is no compelling evidence for a relationship (be it positive or negative) between cultural difference between M&A parties and post-M&A performance. Looking for such direct relationships may be too simplistic. A balanced perspective suggests that the outcomes of cross-border M&A depend not on whether the cultures are different but on the nature and extent of culture differences and, more importantly, on strategic intent, integration approach, and specific interventions chosen to manage the integration of the two entities across borders (see Stahl, 2008; Stahl, Pucik, Evans, & Mendenhall, 2004; Pucik, Björkman, Evans, & Stahl, 2011). What seems clear is that even in the most well thought out M&As, their ultimate success may depend on the ability to integrate across boundaries effectively (Stahl, 2008). However, what *integration* means may differ depending on the strategic intent underlying the M&A. As with multicultural teams (Chapter 8) the challenge is to maximize the benefits of cultural differences while minimizing negative effects.

MNO Subsidiary Structure

Regardless of the overall organizational form, the subunits of the MNO operate in distinct local environments, each with the type of isomorphic pressures noted earlier. This additional complexity has caused some researchers to suggest that the MNO is a unique organizational form and is best understood as a complex network of differentiated subsidiaries (Ghoshal & Bartlett, 1990). This idea shifts the fundamental emphasis from understanding the overall organizational structure to understanding the effects of firm and environmental characteristics on the foreign subsidiary (Roth, Schweiger, & Morrison, 1991). An idea helpful in understanding these effects is that the organizational structure and management practices of subsidiaries of the MNC are influenced by the opposing forces toward adaptation to the local environment (local responsiveness) and consistency within the organization (global integration) (e.g., Bartlett, 1986; Porter, 1986). According to Rosenzweig and Singh (1991), the pressures for consistency among subsidiaries in the international firm (global integration) stem from two factors: *organizational replication* and the *imperative for control.* Organizational replication is the tendency of the firm to duplicate, in new environments, existing structures and procedures that are effective. For example, Procter & Gamble initially designed each new foreign subsidiary to be an exact replica of the U.S. organization because of a belief that the same policies and procedures that were successful in the United States would work equally well overseas (Bartlett & Ghoshal, 1989). The imperative for control suggests that standardization of policies is used to reduce the complexity and uncertainty inherent in the control of international operations.

MNOs are confronted with additional complexity because of geographic and cultural differences among subsidiaries and between the subsidiary and headquarters. As noted previously, in new environments, the pressures for local adaptation derive from the social nature of organizations and hence their tendency to reflect the values, norms, and accepted practices of the societies in which they operate (Westney, 1993). The elements of organizational structure in the foreign subsidiaries of MNOs can be represented in terms of these dual pressures as shown in Figure 9.2.

As shown in Figure 9.2, the pressures for conformity to local norms and for internal consistency with the rest of the organization can vary from subsidiary to subsidiary. This results in a variety of structures across the organization. A complex pattern emerges with elements of foreign subsidiaries having various degrees of conformity to local demands and with the subsidiaries in different countries resembling each other to varying degrees. An important distinction of this approach

Figure 9.2   Variations in Structure Across Subsidiaries of a Multinational Enterprise

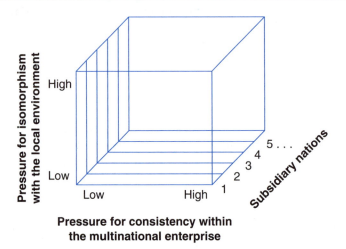

SOURCE: Adapted from Rosenzweig & Singh (1991).

to understanding organizational forms is that it recognizes that the influence of the environment on the MNO is not uniform across the subunits of the firm (Rosenzweig & Singh, 1991). Therefore, it explicitly recognizes the influence of national culture in defining the environment of the organization.

Relationship of the MNO to Its Members

Both the formal and informal structure of the organization influence the way in which organization members perceive their relationship to the organization. Formal organizational structure limits the choices that organization members have about how they perform their jobs and also constrain and place demands on their behavior (Chapter 1). The informal organization and its norms for behavior are a similarly powerful influence on organization members. Additionally, the perceptions that organization members have about their relationship to the firm are determined in part by its organizational characteristics. Two lenses have been used to examine the relationship of individuals to multinational organizations. These are the roles of managers and the psychological contract.

Managerial Roles in MNOs

The complexity of the global environment of multinational organizations emphasizes the key managerial roles of information exchange, coordination, information scanning, and control (Vora, 2008). Considering the structure of the MNO as a network of subunits that exists in a variety of environments and thus in terms of competing forces on the subsidiary raises additional issues about the role of the managers of the organization. Because of the *loose coupling* of subunits of the organization that results from this organizational form, much of the coordination and control shifts to individuals in positions that link the subunits (Bartlett & Ghoshal, 1989).

The managers of subsidiaries of MNOs, because they function across internal and external organizational boundaries, perform this linking function and occupy these unique boundary-spanning roles (Thomas, 1994). The subsidiary manager has membership in the two separate but related entities (the larger organization and the local operation). Each contains a distinctive set of role expectations, rules, and norms (Peterson & Smith, 2008). The subsidiary manager is, therefore, the recipient of expectations from both. In the international environment, the opposing pressures for local adaptation and global integration felt by the firm intensify these different role expectations. To the extent that role pressures of the senders differ, are contradictory, or are mutually exclusive, the manager will experience conflict about the appropriate role; and to the extent that these role pressures are incomplete, the manager will experience role ambiguity (Kahn, Wolfe, Quinn, Snoek, & Rosenthal, 1964). Conflicting expectations raise the possibility that subsidiary managers might have difficulty in accommodating both sets of role expectations. In extreme cases, these managers can *go native* and fail to consider the parent company's perspectives in the performance of their duties, or alternatively, can fail to consider local interests. Vora and Kostova (2007) suggest that the extent and manner in which managers identify both with the parent organization and the local subsidiary (dual organizational identification) can be predicted by the type of multinational structure (international, multinational, global, transnational) and country context. Managers can respond to these conflicting demands by attempting to alter the way in which they interact with their environment and thereby change their roles. The fact that managers attempt to alter the content of their jobs to make them less reactive and dependent on the demands of others is well documented (Sayles, 1964; Stewart, 1982) and some research suggests that this occurs in an international context (Delios & Björkman, 2000). For example, strong forces toward local adaptation might result in an emphasis in liaising with elements of the local environment as opposed to a focus on allocating resources within the organization.

Consistent with the fundamentals of cross-cultural interaction introduced in Chapter 4, in cases in which the expectations of the environment are conflicting or unclear, the emphasis that managers place on different roles can be more susceptible to cultural influence. Managers might rely on culturally based scripts to carry out their jobs when the organizational environment does not clearly indicate appropriate behavior. Research in international strategic alliances provides some support for the idea that managers have different expectations of their roles in an ambiguous context based on national culture (Cui, Ball, & Coyne, 2002). Researchers have addressed the nature of the relationship between culture and managerial-role characteristics. For example, in a 21-nation study, role conflict, role ambiguity, and role overload were found to be related to Hofstede's national scores on power distance, individualism, uncertainty avoidance, and masculinity (Peterson, Smith, Akande, et al., 1995). In the same study, perceived role stress was found to be more heavily influenced by national culture than by personal or organizational factors (Peterson et al., 1995). Responses to role stress were found to be influenced by national culture in a small number of studies. For example, research found that responses to role ambiguity differed for Chinese and Western managers (Smith, Peterson, & Wang, 1996). Chinese managers responded to this role stress by relying on rules and procedures, whereas Western managers were more likely to rely on their own training and experience. In addition, the relationship between role conflict and commitment was found to be different for Chinese and U.S. managers (Perrewe, Ralston, & Fernandez, 1995). Finally, the specific behaviors that are considered to be required by a particular role versus those behaviors considered to be *extra-role* also seem to be influenced by culture (Farh, Hackett, & Chen, 2008). Although research on this issue is limited, what is clear from these results is that in cases in which role expectations are conflicting or ambiguous, such as in the boundary-spanning roles of MNO managers, the national culture of the manager can influence how the role is perceived and how the manager responds. Culture should exert an even more pronounced influence under these conditions.

Cultural Differences in the Psychological Contract

The unique characteristics of multinational organizations serve as one indicator of what is expected of organization members and what they can expect in return. Because employers can never specify all the terms and conditions of the employment relationship, individuals supplement this information by forming what is called their psychological contract. The psychological contract consists of individual beliefs or perceptions concerning the terms of the exchange relationship between the individual and the organization (Rousseau, 1989). It can include beliefs about such things as performance requirements, job security, training, compensation, and career development. Organizations signal their commitments and obligations to the employee through such things as overt statements, expressions of organizational policy, and references to history or reputation. In addition, as noted in Chapter 6, the social context in which these messages are conveyed influences how they are perceived and recorded in memory. A key element of establishing employee expectations is the differentiation of roles and hierarchy of authority embodied in the organizational structure.

Psychological contracts involving the employment relationship have both transactional and relational elements, but they can differ in the extent to which they are transactional versus relational (Morrison & Robinson, 1997). Transactional aspects of contracts emphasize specific, short-term, monetary obligations, such as payment for services provided by employees. Contracts of this type require only limited involvement of the parties. Relational contracts, by contrast, emphasize broad, long-term, socioemotional obligations, such as commitment and loyalty. The psychological contract is fundamentally tied to how people view themselves. Because people in different cultures have very different conceptions of the self and the interdependence of themselves and others (Markus & Kitayama, 1991), cultural differences can influence how individuals perceive and manage the social exchange with their employer. Although psychological contracts appear to generally be increasingly transactional rather than relational, considerable variability in the specifics of psychological contracts around the world continue to exist (Schalk & Soeters, 2008).

In terms of the formulation of the psychological contract, we can predict that cultural differences will exist in terms of the extent to which social cues are important in defining the contract, the extent to which characteristics of the contract are shared among organization members, and the extent to which the contract with the employer is perceived as transactional or relational (Thomas, Au, & Ravlin, 2003). We expect individualists to have a more transactional perception of the relationship with their employer, whereas a collectivist's perception would be more relational. For example Thomas, Fitzsimmons, Ravlin, Au, Ekelund, and Barzanty (2010) found that the dominant form of the psychological contract in a country varied in a manner consistent with the cultural profile of countries based on the horizontal and vertical individualism and collectivism framework. Also, King and Bu (2005) found differences in beliefs about employer obligations among new IT recruits in China and the United States. Recent research has suggested that culture influences the form of an individual's psychological contract through fundamental beliefs about exchange in society, called exchange ideology (Ravlin, Liao, Morrell, Au, & Thomas, 2012).

In addition to influencing contract formation, cultural variability can influence what is perceived as a violation of the contract and how such violation develops (Kikul, Lester, & Belgio, 2004). Culture might also affect employee responses to violations in the psychological contract both directly and indirectly. That is, cultural norms can indicate appropriate responses to changes in the relationship with their employer. For example, the norm for the maintenance of harmony prevalent in some cultures would argue against voicing one's displeasure to a superior as a typical response.

A more indirect means of cultural influence might also exist in the way that individuals evaluate the nature of their relationship with their organization. The context of the situation, such as the availability of good job alternatives or their previous satisfaction with their job, can be evaluated differently. For example, Turnley and Feldman (1999) found that high-quality job alternatives promoted exit (leaving the organization) in response to psychological contract violations, but Thomas and Au (2002) found that national culture moderated the effect of quality of job alternatives on loyalty as a response to the more general situation of a decline in job satisfaction.

In summary, the multicultural nature of global organizations, coupled with the requirements of coping with a dynamic and complex environment, make it difficult for organizations to consistently and objectively specify the relationship with their employees. This increases the importance of understanding the perception of the relationship that culturally different employees might hold.

Summary

In this chapter, two challenges presented by international organizations were discussed. First, international managers must confront organizational structures that are both similar and different to their own when interacting with suppliers, competitors, and collaborators. Although all organizations can be defined in terms of their complexity, formalization, and centralization, a variety of organizational forms exist across industries and countries. Theoretical approaches, such as contingency, ecological, and institutional theories, have been formulated in order to explain organizational structure. Although none of these is adequate on its own to explain international organizations, they all provide insight into important contingencies and pressures faced by international firms. Some determinants of organizational structure can have a consistent relationship across cultures. For example, large organizations are consistently more formalized, specialized, and less centralized in all countries. However, culture influences organizational structure through its influence on the choices that managers make about organizational design and through the types of structures that societies view as legitimate.

Questions for Discussion

1. What are the fundamental characteristics through which the structure of any organization can be described?

2. Describe two mechanisms through which culture might have an influence on the structure of organizations.

3. Give examples of organizational structures that are specific to their cultural context.

4. Discuss the influence of culture in cross-border mergers, acquisitions, and joint ventures.

5. The relationship that individuals perceive with their organization is called their psychological contract. How does culture influence this relationship?

10

The Challenge of International Assignments

If you reject the food, ignore the customs, fear the religion and avoid the people, you might better stay at home.

—James Michener (1907–1997)

The increasing cultural diversity in the workforce of industrialized countries makes understanding cross-cultural interactions important for all managers. However, one of the most difficult situations in which to confront cultural differences is as a manager on temporary assignment in a foreign country. Understanding the special circumstances of employees sent overseas for temporary assignments (expatriates) has been a management concern since the rapid expansion of cross-border business activity that occurred after World War II. The trends toward staffing with local nationals or expatriates have varied over time, and companies are now considering a number of options to the traditional overseas posting (Shaffer, Kraimer, Chen, & Bolino, 2012). However, managers on temporary assignments overseas continue to play a very important role in managing today's global organizations (Skovbro & Worm, 2002; Thomas, 1994). For example, in 2012, 64 percent of international firms surveyed reported an increase in their expatriate population (Global Relocation Trends, 2012). The additional difficulties presented by overseas assignments combined with the often critically important nature of the expatriate role have made the experience of these employees of special interest and generated a significant amount of research.

In this chapter, the term *expatriate experience* is used to encompass both the experience of firms with staffing with expatriates and the experience of these employees with an overseas assignment. First, the firm's perspective on staffing with expatriates and its influence on employee selection is contrasted with the employee's decision to accept an overseas assignment. Then, common ways of determining whether an overseas experience is successful are explored. A significant volume of research has attempted to explain the success of overseas employees by examining individual, organizational, and environmental factors. An examination of this literature points to contradictions and paradoxes that suggest that an overseas assignment can be a double-edged sword from the perspective of both the employee and the firm.

The Role of Expatriates

The role that expatriates must take on is affected by the staffing strategy that the multinational organization (MNO) has for its foreign operations. The fundamental preferences of MNOs for a particular staffing strategy have been described as *poly-centric* (local foreign managers only), *ethnocentric* (home country managers predominate), *geocentric* (a mix of nationalities at home and abroad), or *regiocentric* (a mix of nationalities within regions) (Perlmutter, 1969; Heena & Perlmutter, 1979). Early research suggested that the use of expatriates (home country nationals) followed a cycle consistent with the stage of internationalization of the firm (Franko, 1973) discussed in Chapter 9. Expatriates predominated in top managerial jobs in early stages of internationalization, with the use of third-country national managers growing as the technology of the firm was disseminated among nations. This staffing pattern was found in both U.S. and European MNOs (Franko, 1973), but some research suggests that these patterns might have changed over time, and numerous other factors affecting the use of expatriates have been proposed (see Harzing, 2001). For example, one longitudinal study of the staffing patterns of 50 U.S. affiliates of a Japanese firm found, contradictory to the stage model suggested previously, a positive relationship between the company's international experience, its size, and the use of expatriates (Beechler & Iaquinto, 1994). In addition, other factors not related to the stage of internationalization, such as the task complexity of the affiliate and the cultural distance of the affiliate from headquarters, have also been found to be related to the use of expatriates (Boyacigiller, 1990). In a study showing support for both perspectives, Gong (2003) found that cultural distance increases the tendency for MNOs to use expatriates in overseas subsidiaries but that this tendency becomes weaker over time. Different staffing patterns can also exist in the foreign affiliates of firms with different countries of origin. For example, research has indicated that Japanese-owned firms have more expatriates in their foreign affiliates than their U.S. or European counterparts (e.g., Beechler, 1992; Harzing, 2001; Kopp, 1994; Peterson, Napier, & Won, 1995; Tung, 1981).

In summary, the staffing strategy of an MNO is affected by its stage of internationalization, its country of origin, the size and the task complexity of its foreign affiliates, and the cultural distance of the affiliate from headquarters. There are advantages and disadvantages for the firm associated with each of these strategies (Reiche & Harzing, 2011). Staffing strategy is important for cross-cultural management in part because it can influence the role expectations that the firm has for its overseas employees (Harzing, 2001; Thomas, 1998). The role expectations that organizations have for expatriates can vary considerably in the extent to which they emphasize coordination and control or boundary spanning (Thomas & Lazarova, 2013). For example, the greater numbers of expatriates in Japanese-owned firms might indicate that these firms rely more heavily on expatriates as means of managerial control (Baliga & Jaeger, 1984; Rosenzweig & Nohria, 1994). Expatriates can also act as cultural-boundary spanners to connect groups and resources throughout the organization or as language nodes upon return to headquarters by bridging different language groups (Marschan-Piekkari, Welch, & Welch, 1999).

Individual Staffing Decisions

Individual staffing decisions reflect the overall firm-level staffing strategy mentioned previously, whether or not this strategy is made explicit. However, some consistency across firms exists. An influential study of why firms might fill an overseas position with an expatriate suggested that firms transferred personnel internationally for one of three reasons: to fill a technical requirement, to develop the manager, or to develop the organization (Edstrom & Galbraith, 1977). Research indicates some generality in the use of expatriates, with British, German, Japanese, and U.S. firms all reporting that filling a technical requirement was the main reason for selecting expatriates (Peterson et al., 1995; Scullion, 1991). However, some variation might exist based on both the home country or host country culture and conditions. For example, New Zealand firms have been more likely to cite the development of the organization and the expatriate manager as the major reasons for using expatriates (Enderwick & Hodgson, 1993), and a survey of managers of U.S. firms in Korea found that the most important reason stated for staffing with a local national instead of an expatriate was the manager's lack of local knowledge (Park, Sun, & David, 1993).

In summary, the staffing strategy of MNOs affects the role that the employee is expected to fill while on the overseas assignment. This role is very likely to involve the use of his or her technical expertise or the exercise of managerial control over the foreign operation but can have a developmental or boundary spanning component. Although these roles seem fairly consistent across cultures, the nationality of the firm might influence both the strategy of the firm and the role expectation that it has for employees on a foreign assignment.

Selection of Managers for Overseas Assignments

Based on the reasons given by firms for sending a manager on an overseas assignment, it is not surprising that early research indicated that technical competence was the primary decision criterion used by firms in selecting employees for these assignments (e.g., Bormann, 1968; Hays, 1971; Howard, 1974; Ivancevich, 1969; Miller, 1975; Tung, 1981). Recent research indicates that little has changed in expatriate selection in recent years, with managerial performance in the domestic setting and technical competences continuing to lead the list of selection criteria (Anderson, 2005; Graf, 2004; Tye & Chen, 2005). The 2012 Global Relocation Trends Survey reported that for 55 percent of expatriate assignments the objective was to fill a managerial or technical skills gap (Global Relocation Trends, 2012). Other criteria that can have a substantial bearing on an employee's performance seem to be generally neglected. This overemphasis on technical competence as a selection criterion may result because high technical qualifications present a lower perceived risk of adverse consequences to the selecting manager (Miller, 1975). In addition, firms may place the most emphasis on selection criteria that are most easily measured, such as technical skills. Interestingly, host country organizations also view technical expertise as an important selection criterion for the expatriates assigned to them (Zeira & Banai, 1985). In addition, consistent with the discussion on decision making in Chapter 5, there seem to be some differences in selection criteria based on the nationality of the firm. For example, one study found that the ability to adapt was ranked as the most important selection criterion by Australian managers and by expatriates on assignment and was ranked second to technical competence by Asian managers (Stone, 1991). As is noted ahead in this chapter, the reliance on technical expertise as the most important selection criterion for success in an overseas assignment is probably not well founded.

Decision to Accept an Overseas Assignment

The pool of potential applicants available to the manager making a staffing decision is limited by a number of factors, including restrictions imposed by other organizational requirements and those imposed by the individuals themselves. One of these is the willingness and motivation of applicants to accept the overseas posting. Reasons for accepting an overseas posting run the gamut from personal development to financial gain. Early studies found that the motives of people from the United States for accepting an assignment were (a) a sense of vocation, (b) financial rewards, and (c) the desire to escape undesirable circumstances at home (Cleveland, Mangone, & Adams, 1960). Enhancing an international career remains a significant factor in the decision to accept an overseas posting (Stahl, Miller, & Tung, 2002). In addition, studies show that U.S. people accepting their first overseas assignment were more likely to be motivated by the opportunity to advance their career than were employees with previous international experience and that the willingness to relocate overseas was significantly related to the expatriate's focus on career advancement (Brett, Stroh, & Reilly, 1993; Miller & Cheng, 1978). And, more than for other types of assignments, the willingness to undertake an overseas posting is influenced by the willingness of the spouse to relocate (Konopaske, Robie, & Ivancevich, 2005). This willingness can also be influenced by the destination of the expatriate assignment. In the most recent Global Relocation Trends Survey (2012) organizations were asked which countries presented the most challenge for expatriates. The most difficult were China (16%), Brazil (9%), India (8%), Russia (6%), and the United States (4%). One study (Tharenou, 2003) suggested that individuals most likely to be receptive to an overseas assignment were people with high outcome expectancies (personal agency) and few family concerns, such as partner's employment and children's schooling (low barriers), and those who have worked in organizations with an international focus (opportunities).

Overall, research highlights the differing perspectives on an overseas assignment from the point of view of the firm and from that of the employee. Although firms tend to select expatriates based largely on technical requirements, the expatriates themselves are motivated primarily, at least on their first posting, by the opportunity for career advancement. And they are more concerned with family issues. It seems, therefore, that conflict between the expectations that firms have for an expatriate and the perceptions that expatriates have of their role is often built in at the outset of the experience.

Definitions of Success

Firms and their expatriate employees are concerned with the success of overseas assignments. However, whether an overseas assignment is viewed as a success or failure depends in part on the definition of success. These definitions vary widely; however, research in this area has focused primarily on three outcomes of the expatriate experience: turnover, adjustment, and task performance.

Turnover

The most frequently used measure of expatriate success (or failure) has been turnover, or more specifically, the premature return of expatriates to their home country (Black & Gregersen, 1990). Most often, this has been measured as the intent to remain on assignment for the time originally agreed upon. Reports that a very high percentage of expatriates failed to complete their initial overseas assignment were responsible for much of the research into the determinants of expatriates' success (Thomas, 1998). However, the exact rate of premature return from overseas assignments is difficult to pinpoint. Many firms do not keep track of this statistic, and academic research has reported widely varying figures. The 2010 Global Relocation Trends Survey reported that 7 percent of expatriates returned early and 7 percent of families returned early leaving expatriates behind (Global Relocation Trends, 2010). Turnover of expatriates is of special concern to firms because of the extra costs of maintaining these employees.

Adjustment

The second major focus of research on expatriate success has been the ability of the expatriate to overcome culture shock (Oberg, 1960) and adjust to the new environment. A psychological definition of adjustment is a condition consisting of a relationship with the environment in which needs are satisfied and the ability to meet physical and social demands exists (English, 1958). This overall adjustment was refined in later research to include three dimensions of adjustment (Black, Gregersen, & Mendenhall, 1992; Black, Mendenhall, & Oddou, 1991; Parker & McEvoy, 1993; Takeuchi & Hannon, 1996). Although this three-dimension model is not without its critics (see Thomas & Lazarova, 2006), the three dimensions of general living adjustment, work adjustment, and interaction adjustment seem to be influenced by somewhat different factors (Black & Gregersen, 1991a; Parker & McEvoy, 1993).

Figure 10.1 summarizes the proposed relationships between the three facets of adjustment and their individual, job, cultural, and nonwork antecedents. Noteworthy in this summary of relationships is that job characteristics are related primarily to work adjustment and that individual characteristics are related to all three facets of adjustment.

Much of the research on expatriate adjustment was based on an assumption of a cycle of adjustment to the foreign environment that follows a U-shaped pattern (Lysgaard, 1955). The model is extended to a W shape when repatriation is considered (Gullahorn & Gullahorn, 1963). This adjustment cycle is presented graphically in Figure 10.2. According to the model shown in Figure 10.2, expatriates progress at regular intervals through four phases of honeymoon, culture shock, adjustment, and finally, mastery. In the *honeymoon* stage, everything is new, exciting, and interesting and the new environment intrigues the expatriate in much the same way as if the expatriate were a tourist. At the

Figure 10.1   Framework of International Adjustment

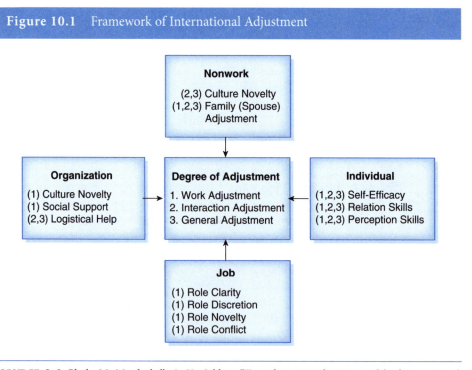

Figure 10.2 The U-Curve of Cross-Cultural Adjustment

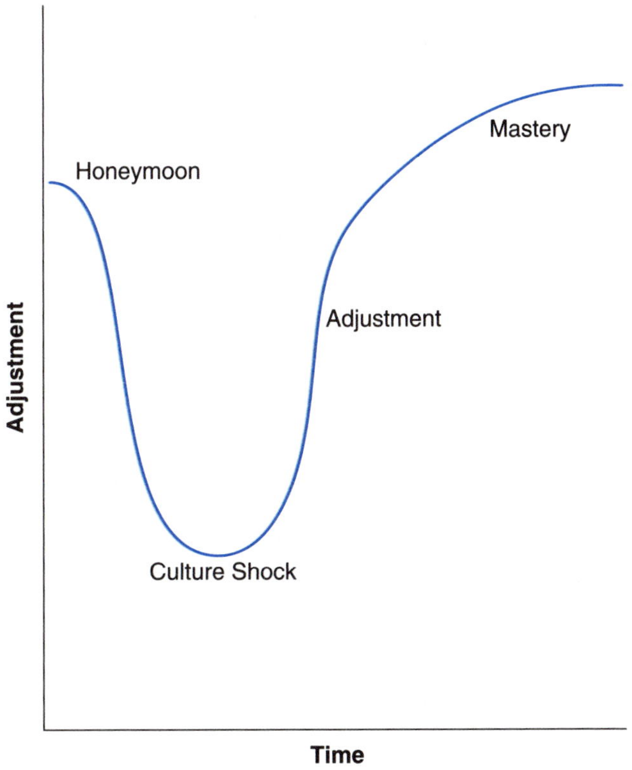

culture shock stage, the expatriate becomes frustrated and confused because the environment is not providing familiar cues. At the *adjustment* stage, the expatriate begins to understand cultural differences, learns the ways to get things done, and begins to settle into the rhythm of daily living in the foreign country. Eventually, the expatriate can achieve the *mastery* stage and become able to function in the new culture almost as well as at home. Not all expatriates achieve mastery in their new environment. Some return home early, whereas others complete their assignment but without really adjusting. Research supports the existence of such a model of adjustment (Black & Mendenhall, 1991). However, there is not overwhelming support for the generality of either the phases or the time parameters of the U-curve (Church, 1982). In addition, different patterns of adjustment in the work and nonwork environments as well as different adjustment patterns for expatriates and for their spouses have been found (Briody & Chrisman, 1991; Nicholson & Imaizumi, 1993). Despite the lack of strong empirical support, the idea that expatriates might go through some systematic and discernible pattern of adjustment remains an attractive notion from both an academic and a practical perspective.

Task Performance

Task performance is the third major indicator of expatriate success. A distinctive feature of the expatriate role is the requirement that expatriates meet the often-conflicting performance expectations of home office superiors and host nationals (Mendenhall & Oddou, 1985). Only very recently have researchers begun to examine the processes used to evaluate expatriate performance. In general, this research indicates that accurate appraisals of expatriate performance are difficult to obtain but might be facilitated by balancing the appraisals of home and host country raters, by increasing the frequency of appraisal (Gregersen, Hite, & Black, 1996), and by clarifying performance expectations (Martin & Bartol, 2003). However, to a large extent expatriate performance appraisals often tend to be extensions of systems developed for domestic purposes (Shih, Chiang, & Kim, 2005).

Adjustment–Performance Relationship

Much of the research on the expatriate experience has assumed a direct, positive relationship between the adjustment and the performance of expatriates (e.g., Mendenhall & Oddou, 1985). However, this relationship might be more complicated than has often been assumed. Research support for a positive relationship between adjustment and performance is somewhat equivocal (Lazarova & Thomas, 2012; Thomas & Lazarova, 2006). Some studies have found performance negatively related to expatriates' perceptions of the intensity of their adjustment to the new culture (Earley, 1987). However, other studies have found different effects depending on the facet of adjustment and the measure of performance used. The following are examples of these findings:

- Interaction and general adjustment were positively related to intent to stay on assignment, whereas no relationship was found for adjustment to work (Gregersen & Black, 1990).
- Work adjustment but not general adjustment or interaction adjustment was positively related to performance (Nicholson & Imaizumi, 1993).
- Work adjustment was positively related to performance, but general living adjustment was negatively related to performance, after work adjustment and interaction adjustment were controlled for (Parker & McEvoy, 1993).
- Performance and adjustment were predicted by different factors in a study of Japanese and U.S. managers (Clarke & Hammer, 1995).
- Interaction and work adjustment were related to task performance (Caligiuri, 1997).
- Self-reported adjustment was moderately related to self-reported performance (Shaffer, Harrison, Gregerson, Black, & Ferzandi, 2006).
- No relationship existed between adjustment and self-rated performance (Shay & Baack, 2004).

In summary, this evidence suggests that different facets of adjustment can affect the performance of employees on overseas assignment in different ways. The relationship also depends on how performance is assessed. In addition, some research suggests that the highest-performing individuals, at least in terms of their effectiveness in transferring skills and knowledge to host nationals, are also the most likely to experience severe culture shock (Kealey, 1989; Ruben & Kealey, 1979). Also, the high stress levels associated with adjustment may actually facilitate high performance in some individuals (Boswell, Olson-Buchanan, & LePine, 2004). Alternatively, expatriate adjustment may operate on job performance by improving job satisfaction and organizational commitment (Hechanova, Beehr, & Christiansen, 2003). Overall, the assumption that good adjustment leads *directly* to good performance is probably an oversimplification.

The different parties involved in the expatriate experience—the home country, the host country, and the expatriate—can have somewhat different expectations. In addition, the outcomes of an expatriate experience can vary widely. Therefore, the following multidimensional definition of success in an expatriate assignment has evolved (Caligiuri & Tung, 1999; Feldman & Thomas, 1992). An overseas assignment is successful if the individual

- meets the performance expectations of quality and quantity of both home country and host country superiors,
- develops and maintains satisfactory relationships with local nationals,
- acquires skills related to managing people of different cultures, and
- remains on assignment the agreed-upon length of time.

Factors Affecting Expatriate Success

In an effort to provide appropriate expatriate selection and training recommendations, a number of factors related to one measure or another of expatriate success have been examined. These include individual, organizational, and environmental variables. The following section describes the key research findings regarding the effects of these three categories of variables on outcomes of an overseas assignment.

Individual Factors

Similar to early leadership research, much of the early research on individual differences focused on the personality characteristics of people who were effective in overseas assignments (e.g., Cleveland et al., 1960; Guthrie & Zektrick, 1967; Mottram, 1963; Sewell & Davidson, 1956; Stein, 1966). Although recent research has found that personality characteristics are related to some expatriate outcomes (e.g., Caligiuri, 2000; Shaffer et al., 2006), the failure of empirical tests to establish consistent relationships between personality characteristics and measures of success, such as task performance, adjustment, and satisfaction, originally resulted in a shift in emphasis to the behavior of successful individuals or their social skills (Brein & David, 1971; Furnham & Bochner, 1986; Stening, 1979). Individuals who described themselves as being satisfied with and functioning well in a foreign culture identified the following behaviors or personal abilities considered important to their success:

- The ability to manage psychological stress
- The ability to communicate effectively
- The ability to establish interpersonal relationships (Abe & Wiseman, 1983; Hammer, 1987; Hammer, Gudykunst, & Wiseman, 1978)

In addition, some research sought the opinions of employees (U.S. people) overseas regarding critical success factors. Consistent among the studies was that family situation (lack of spouse adjustment) was mentioned as the factor most likely to be linked to expatriate failure (Hays, 1971, 1974; Tung, 1981). A study of expatriates of 26 different nationalities (Arthur & Bennett, 1995) identified five characteristics of individuals related to success. In order of importance to respondents, these were the following:

- Family situation
- Adaptability
- Job knowledge
- Relational ability
- Openness to other cultures

Clearly, a wide range of individual characteristics can potentially influence the success or failure of an expatriate experience. In addition, some evidence suggests that the importance of these factors might be cross-culturally consistent (Stahl, 1998). For example, personality as measured by the Big Five personality factors (extroversion, emotional stability, agreeableness, conscientiousness, and openness) seems to be as predictive of expatriate job performance as it is in a purely domestic setting (Mol, Born, Willemsen, & Van der Molen, 2005). Because of the difficulty involved in defining the prototypical expatriate, the classification of these individual differences into broad skill or behavior dimensions may be a more useful way to include individual characteristics in the evaluation of antecedents to success in an overseas assignment. However, even after more than 40 years of study there is no consensus as to which of the myriad skills are most important for expatriate effectiveness (Yamazaki & Kayes, 2004). Recently, it has been suggested (Thomas & Fitzsimmons, 2008) that developable attributes of individuals that have been shown to be related to effective cross-cultural interactions can be classified as informational, interpersonal, action, and analytical skills. However, the relative importance of these broad skill sets has not been established.

Demographics. In addition to individual differences noted previously, demographic characteristics of expatriates, such as age, tenure, educational level, and marital status, have all been found to influence the expatriate experience. The following is a summary of these research findings:

- The age of the expatriate has been found to be positively related to organizational commitment, work adjustment, and job satisfaction but negatively correlated with willingness to relocate, intent to leave, and general satisfaction.
- Tenure of expatriates has been found to be positively related to job satisfaction and negatively related to intent to leave.
- The education level of expatriates has been found to be negatively related to job satisfaction and commitment to the organization and positively related to general adjustment and interaction adjustment but not work adjustment.
- Married expatriates have been found to be more job satisfied and higher performers.
- The adjustment of the spouse or family is positively related to expatriate adjustment and negatively related to intent to leave. (Thomas, 1998)

The rationale for these effects has rarely been specified. Instead, it is assumed that demographic characteristics indicate underlying values, attitudes, and beliefs, which in turn relate to outcomes, sometimes perhaps because of social categorization by host nationals (see Mamman, 1995). The contribution of the effect of demographics alone to our understanding of the expatriate experience is somewhat limited. However, as shown ahead in this chapter, as indicators of life stage, career stage, and family situation in combination with organizational and environmental variables, they may prove somewhat more useful in explaining the expatriate experience.

Foreign Language Ability and Previous International Experience. Two individual factors with established linkages to expatriate success are the ability of the overseas employee to communicate in the host country language and previous international experience. Both foreign language fluency and prior overseas experience can be important to expatriate success. However, the particular elements of success to which these factors apply and the mechanisms through which they operate have not been clearly defined. For example, substantial support has been found for a positive relationship between foreign language fluency and the degree of interaction with host nationals and to a lesser extent with satisfaction, commitment, and adjustment (Church, 1982; Thomas & Fitzsimmons, 2008). Also, some support for a modest relationship between language fluency and expatriate performance has been reported (Mol et al., 2005). These effects might be based on the ability of expatriates to develop a so-called conversational currency (being able to make conversation about everyday things such as local sporting events) that can facilitate interactions with host nationals (Brein & David, 1971). However, several empirical studies suggest that foreign language skill is not necessarily an effective predictor of expatriate success (Benson, 1978). However, it may help expatriates form accurate expectations of their new cultural environment (Puck, Kittler, & Wright, 2008). It may not be language skill that is the critical factor but the willingness to communicate, which is of course facilitated by skill in the foreign language.

In considering previous overseas experience, it might be that the quality of international experience is as important as the amount in facilitating adjustment to another culture. Some studies have found that the amount of prior overseas experience was positively related to adjustment and to job satisfaction (Naumann, 1993; Parker & McEvoy, 1993; Takeuchi & Hannon, 1996). In addition, one study found that U.S. managers with prior experience abroad were more likely to use appropriate intercultural behaviors (Dunbar, 1992). However, other research suggests that previous overseas experience can be negatively related to some attitudes of expatriates, such as the amount of discretion they feel they have in performing their jobs (Black & Gregersen, 1990).

The intuitively appealing notion that foreign language fluency and previous overseas experience are positively related to expatriate success seems, at best, to be an oversimplification of the relationship. The likelihood is that the relationship between language fluency and expatriate effectiveness is not a linear one. For example, anecdotal evidence suggests that the returns for a small amount of foreign language knowledge (knowing a few words) are great but that to achieve substantial additional benefit, a significant degree of language fluency (the ability to develop conversational currency) is required. A similar relationship might be suggested for overseas experience, with the additional recognition that all overseas experiences are not identical, and the ability of individuals to learn from prior overseas experiences might be highly variable. In addition, the effects of these two factors are likely to be influenced by the amount of intercultural interaction required by the assignment, the degree of cultural novelty in the situation, or the level of the expatriate in the organization (Taylor & Napier, 1996).

Nationality of Expatriates. Early studies of foreign students (see Church, 1982, for a review) indicated that the nationality of the individual was important to adjustment to the foreign environment. However, the vast majority of research on overseas business experiences has been conducted with U.S. expatriates. Some research suggests that U.S. expatriates might have higher rates of premature return from their assignment than, for example, Europeans and Japanese (Tung, 1981) or New Zealanders (Enderwick & Hodgson, 1993). In addition, differences have been found in the cultural skill and knowledge and in job satisfaction reported by U.S. and German expatriates living in Japan (Dunbar, 1994) and in the self-perceived effectiveness of Japanese and U.S. expatriates in Thailand (Stening & Hammer, 1992). Other studies have shown that expatriates from different countries establish different kinds of social networks, which in turn influence their adjustment (Wang & Kanungo, 2004). These results suggest that the cultural background of the expatriates themselves as well as the characteristics of the foreign culture can influence some aspects of their overseas experience.

Gender of Expatriates. The possible effect of the gender of the expatriate manager has in recent years become a more important and recognizable issue. Twenty-five years ago, Adler (1987, p. 169) noted, "About the single most uncontroversial, incontrovert-ible statement to make about women in international management is that there are very few of them." Ten years later, about 14 percent of expatriates were female (Solo-mon, 1998), but only about 4 percent of top executives in international subsidiaries were women (Elron, 1997). True to the predictions made by Antal and Izraeli (1993), a shortage of qualified men, legal and social pressure for equal opportunity, the increasing familiarity with women in management positions, and the increasing ability of women to self-select for an overseas assignment because of changing company atti-tudes have resulted in a greater presence of women in the expatriate community. How-ever, the percentage of women expatriates seems to have plateaued at around 20 percent (Global Relocation Trends 2012), which is still lower than the percentage of women in management, 25 to 45 percent (Caligiuri & Lazarova, 2002).

A persistent barrier for women has been the reluctance of companies to send them overseas. An early survey of international personnel managers from 60 U.S. and Canadian companies concerning their perceptions of barriers to women expatriates is illuminating (Adler, 1984). Fifty-four percent indicated that their firm would hesitate to send women on an expatriate assignment. In order, the personnel managers listed the following reasons: foreigners' prejudice against women (72.7%), dual careers (69.1%), selection bias (53.8%), women not interested (24.5%), women unqualified (18.2%), and women not effective (5.6%). These results are consistent with other find-ings that top managers feel that women face significant resistance when seeking over-seas assignments (Thal & Cateora, 1979), that female international assignees and their immediate supervisors view the international experience of women very differently (Stroh, Varma, & Valy-Durbin, 2000), and that male decision makers may harbor a bias against selecting women (Chusmir & Frontczak, 1990).

In addressing the perceived reluctance of women to take an overseas assign-ment, a survey of 1,129 graduating MBAs from the United States, Canada, and Europe indicated that male and female MBA graduates were equally interested in international careers (Adler, 1986). Tung (1998) also reported no difference in men and women with regard to willingness to accept an overseas assignment. However, women may have low expectations of their opportunity for being selected and there-fore fail to actively pursue opportunities for overseas placement (Chusmir & Frontczak, 1990).

A central issue for women expatriates is the extent to which women actually face greater difficulty overseas than men. Surveys have generally indicated negative atti-tudes by local businesspeople toward women expatriates (Stone, 1991), discrimina-tion against them (Westwood & Leung, 1994), and a preference of overseas businesspeople for dealing with male executives (e.g., Izraeli, Banai, & Zeira, 1980). And Caligiuri and Tung (1999) found that women were less cross-culturally adjusted than men in countries with low female workforce participation and a low percentage of women managers. Compared to men, women are exposed to additional work and nonwork challenges, including the attitudes of local nationals toward working women but also family issues, such as child care and dual career conflicts (Caligiuri & Lazarova, 2002).

However, some research has suggested that being female can be an advantage overseas. Adler's (1987) survey of 52 women expatriates in Asia indicated the following: 42 percent felt that being female was an advantage, 22 percent found it irrelevant, 16 percent said that being female had both positive and negative effects, and 20 percent found it primarily negative. Anecdotal reports suggest that advantages can accrue to women expatriates because their small number increases visibility, they are afforded higher status because of their uniqueness, or they have better interpersonal skills than men (Adler, 1987; Taylor & Napier, 1996; Westwood & Leung, 1994). And some research has reported better interaction and work adjustment for women (Selmer & Leung, 2003). Recent empirical studies of gender and expatriate performance have found no difference between men and women on performance factors (Caligiuri & Tung, 1999) even in environments considered unfriendly to female managers (Sinangil & Ones, 2003).

Job and Organizational Factors

In addition to characteristics of individuals, aspects of the job and the organization are important to the expatriate experience. Consistent with the managerial role focus of this book, job-related factors can perhaps best be described in terms of role characteristics, such as novelty, ambiguity, discretion, conflict, and overload. In addition, the job level of the expatriate has an influence on the experience. Important organizational factors are the degree of training provided to the expatriate and, relatedly, the extent to which the expatriate has realistic prior knowledge about the assignment.

Expatriate Job Characteristics. The reason for examining the characteristics of the expatriate experience, in terms of role characteristics, stems from the idea that an expatriate assignment involves the adjustment to a new work role as well as to a new environment (Black, 1988). In general, these results suggest that, as might be expected, work role characteristics have an influence on the work adjustment of expatriates. Specifically, the amounts of ambiguity, novelty, and conflict in the expatriate's role all have a negative effect on adjustment to a new work role and on job satisfaction (Thomas, 1998). Not surprisingly, work adjustment is, in turn, positively related to the intent to remain on assignment (Black, 1990). A consistent finding is that the amount of discretion that expatriates have in conducting their role has a positive effect on their adjustment to their new work role and their intention to remain on assignment (Thomas, 1998). Although the main influence of characteristics of the job is on the expatriate's adjustment to the work of the new assignment, in some cases work role characteristics have shown some spillover effect on other facets of adjustment. Specifically, discretion in one's work role seems to facilitate general adjustment, and ambiguity and conflict in the role negatively affect both general adjustment and the ability to interact with host nationals (Thomas, 1998).

Job Level. The organizational level of job changers influences the types of strategies available to them to deal with the effects of moving to a new role and hence the probability of favorable outcomes (Feldman & Brett, 1983). For example, the organizational level of expatriates was found to be positively related to job satisfaction, intent to remain on assignment, and self-reports of performance (Thomas, 1998). However, higher-level expatriates have also been reported as having more trouble adjusting to new jobs, and some higher-level Japanese expatriates have more difficulty with interaction and general adjustment (Gregersen & Black, 1990; Takeuchi & Hannon, 1996). These results suggest that the organizational level of expatriates might also carry with it other factors, such as more challenging assignments, which may need to be considered in predicting the effect of organizational level on the expatriate experience.

In addition to characteristics of a specific overseas job, more general organizational characteristics have an influence on the expatriate experience. Key organizational factors that influence success include the amount of organizational support provided expatriates and their families, the extent to which the expatriate was provided with realistic information about the country and the assignment, and the amount of cross-cultural training provided. Of these factors, the amount of training has received the most attention.

Expatriate Training. The conventional wisdom regarding cross-cultural training of expatriates is that, although the positive effect of such training is well documented (e.g., Brislin, MacNab, & Nayani, 2008), firms often fail to provide training because they believe it is not effective or that there is insufficient time before departure. The failure of firms to provide extensive cross-cultural training is documented in studies in a number of different countries (e.g., Enderwick & Hodgson, 1993; Tung, 1981). The most recent Global Relocation Trends Survey (2012) reported that while 81 percent of firms surveyed provided preassignment cross-cultural training, only 37 percent of companies offered it for all assignments, and it was mandatory in only 24 percent of the firms that offered it. Broad support for a positive relationship between cross-cultural training and outcomes related to managerial effectiveness has been documented (Black & Mendenhall, 1990; Deshpande & Viswesvaran, 1992; Morris & Robie, 2001). Specifically, these reviews suggest that cross-cultural training is positively related to self-development (self-oriented skills, perceptual skills, and relational skills), adjustment, relationships with host nationals, and performance. Despite this general endorsement for the effectiveness of training, less is known about the effects of different training types, such as informational training, area studies, cultural-awareness training, and intercultural-skill training. In addition, questions remain regarding the appropriate timing (before departure vs. in country) of training. At what point in the expatriate experience is training most beneficial?

Figure 10.3 is derived from research by Black and Mendenhall (1989) and draws on social learning theory for guidance (Bandura, 1977). It suggests that the selection of training methods for a particular situation can be determined by referring to the degree of cultural novelty in the situation, the requirements for intercultural interaction with host nationals, and the degree of novelty in the job. The rationale presented in the model is that as the requirements of the situation become more demanding, the cross-cultural training required should move from more passive to more participative modes. Whereas fact-oriented training might suffice in situations with low cultural novelty, low interaction requirements, and low job novelty, more rigorous training, involving more analytical and experiential elements, is required for situations at the other end of the spectrum. Very little research has examined the effectiveness of different types of training. However, the few studies that have examined the effect of type of training have found that more rigorous experiential training has the best results (Brislin et al., 2008).

The idea that expatriate training might be delivered more effectively after the expatriates arrive in country is based on the notion that for training to be effective, it should be delivered when trainees are most motivated to learn (Grove & Torbion, 1985). Predeparture trainees may neither see the need for training nor have an adequate frame of reference for predeparture training to have the desired effect. The limited research that exists tends to support the idea that in-country (integrated) training is more effective than predeparture training in many instances (Eschbach,

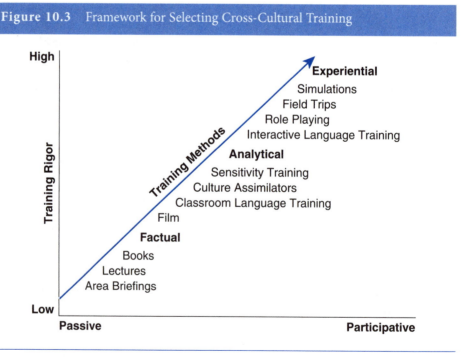

Figure 10.3   Framework for Selecting Cross-Cultural Training

SOURCE: J. S. Black & M. Mendenhall. *Human Resource Management* © 1989. Reprinted with permission of John Wiley & Sons.

Parker, & Stoeberl, 2001; Feldman & Bolino, 1999; Selmer, 2001). However, there are numerous factors that can moderate the effect of training type on effectiveness (Brislin et al., 2008).

Related to the issue of cross-cultural training is the expatriate's accurate or realistic conception of the situation to which the expatriate is moving. According to research regarding the realistic expectations of new jobs (e.g., Meglino & DeNisi, 1987), one might anticipate that realistic expectations by the expatriate would be related to positive outcomes. Accurate information about the environment provides the opportunity for expatriates to make adjustments in anticipation of environmental differences (Gullahorn & Gullahorn, 1963). For example, realistic expectations have been found to be positively related to expatriate adjustment and job satisfaction (Feldman & Tompson, 1993; Stroh, Dennis, & Cramer, 1994). Similarly, a positive relationship between expatriates' predeparture knowledge about the host country and all the facets of expatriate adjustment has been documented (Black, 1990), and the relevance of cross-cultural training has an impact on the extent to which expatriate expectations about the new culture are met (Caligiuri, Phillips, Lazarova, Tarique, & Bürgi, 2001). These results emphasize that the reduction of uncertainty is an important consideration in the overseas experience and therefore in cross-cultural training.

A third organizational factor that has been found to be related to elements of expatriate success, is the extent of the organizational support received by expatriates. For example, one measure of organizational support, the amount of contact (through visits to headquarters, letters, telexes) that expatriates have with the parent company, has been positively related to some facets of adjustment (Black, 1990). In addition, the level of company assistance has been found to be positively related to expatriate job satisfaction (Stroh et al., 1994) and, in a study of Australian expatriate spouses, also a significant predictor of psychological adjustment (DeCieri, Dowling, & Taylor, 1991). However, the effect of the level and nature of organizational support is complicated. For example, the support requirements of women (Caligiuri & Lazarova, 2002) and of dual-career couples (Harvey, 1997) are very different from those of male expatriates. In addition, the level of the expatriate's commitment to the organization determines, in part, the effectiveness of support programs (Guzzo, Noonan, & Elron, 1994). Therefore, it is an oversimplification to say that more organizational support is better. Support requirements seem to be related to the needs and expectations of each employee's situation.

Environmental Factors

In addition to job and organizational factors, other factors external to the expatriate and over which the expatriate has little control can influence the expatriate's success. Of these, both the novelty and toughness of the new culture and the amount of social support available have been the subjects of some research.

Cultural Novelty. The extent to which the host country culture is different from the expatriate's home culture is typically thought to make the adjustment process more difficult (Church, 1982; Mendenhall & Oddou, 1985). Studies of expatriates have found that cultural novelty is negatively related to interaction adjustment, general adjustment, and willingness to accept an assignment and positively related to social difficulty (Thomas, 1998). However, the research support for these negative effects of cultural novelty on outcomes is not universal. Positive relationships between cultural novelty and general adjustment (Black & Gregersen, 1991a; Parker & McEvoy, 1993) and to all three facets of adjustment for Japanese expatriates (Takeuchi & Hannon, 1996) are documented. Similarly, for Europeans on assignment in Europe, North America, and Asia, cultural novelty was found to be positively related to the level of intercultural interaction (Janssens, 1995). These contradictory findings suggest the possibility that cultural novelty can exert its influence differently depending on the characteristics of the individual and the situation. For example, environmental differences encountered by Japanese in the United States might result in their expectations about housing being exceeded, which in turn influences their perceptions of adjustment difficulties. Finally, it is entirely possible that adjusting to a similar culture is fraught with just as many problems as adjusting to a culturally distant one (O'Grady & Lane, 1996; Selmer, 2006). Subtle differences, though important, may be difficult to anticipate and thus prepare for.

Social Support. The logic behind the effect of social support on the expatriate experience is that being able to draw on social relationships provides a mechanism for dealing with the stress associated with an overseas assignment. Research generally supports the direct positive effect of social support from both host and home country nationals on the adjustment of expatriates (Thomas, 1998). However, some differences in the nature of the social support of expatriates and their spouses have been documented. For example, at least one study finds that expatriates derived their social support primarily from host country nationals, whereas spouses interacted primarily with home country nationals (Briody & Chrisman, 1991). Also, social support networks have been established around the fact that most accompanying partners were female. This can make male trailing spouses feel uncomfortable or disinterested in the activities of these groups. Male accompanying partners report being perceived as atypical by others in the host country, which can cause them to reexamine their identity, even if they themselves have no gender-role concerns (Harris, 2004).

Repatriation

It has long been recognized that reentry to one's home country after a long sojourn requires a process of adjustment similar to that of the initial transfer overseas (Gullahorn & Gullahorn, 1963). Additionally, repatriation is distinct, in both degree and kind, from other types of job-related geographic transfers (Black et al., 1992; Feldman & Thomas, 1992). First, the degree of novelty (e.g., cultural, organizational, job) is higher for a transfer between countries as compared to within a country. Second, in the repatriation situation, the individual is returning to his or her home country after a period of absence of typically two to five years for U.S. and British expatriates (Black & Gregersen, 1991b) and potentially longer for German or Japanese expatriates (Peterson et al., 1995). During this time, both the individual and the home country have undergone changes largely independent of each other. Unlike the domestic job changer, the repatriate is likely to be confronted with these changes simultaneously. In addition, for most expatriates the repatriate experience is qualitatively different from the expatriate experience. Most repatriates (80% according to Black & Gregersen, 1991b) are returning home from an assignment in a country of which they had little or no prior experience. Therefore, their prior knowledge and expectations about the country they are moving to are likely to be substantially different in the case of repatriation versus expatriation.

One of the earliest studies to directly examine repatriation adjustment found that for U.S. expatriates, repatriation adjustment was facilitated by such factors as the amount of clarity and discretion the expatriate had in the new role but negatively affected by the time spent overseas, social status, and housing conditions (Black & Gregersen, 1991b). These results were largely confirmed in a replication with a sample of 173 Japanese expatriates who had recently returned from a foreign assignment (Black, 1994). More recently, in a survey of 133 repatriates in 14 MNEs, Lazarova and Cerdin (2007) examined the availability and effectiveness of repatriation support practices. Table 10.1 shows the percentage of repatriates reporting the availability of each practice. Although the types of support practices varied widely, what seems fairly clear is that an integrated set of practices was required for successful repatriation (Lazarova & Cerdin, 2007).

Results of several studies suggest that factors that facilitate expatriate adjustment can in turn inhibit repatriation (Black, 1994; Black & Gregersen, 1991b; Poe, 2000; Stroh, Gregersen, & Black, 1998). For example, the improved housing conditions that most expatriates experience overseas might help them cope while there, but the drop in housing conditions on return has a negative effect. Likewise, the longer employees are overseas, the more difficult is their adjustment on return. Despite the difficulties associated with repatriation, organizations typically do not take an integrated approach to expatriation, failing to consider the longer-term career implications of the overseas experience (Stahl & Cerdin, 2004).

Outcomes of Overseas Assignments and Global Careers

Management development may be a key reason that an individual is sent on an overseas assignment, and personal development is an often reported outcome of overseas experience (Stahl et al., 2002). In fact, an overseas posting has the characteristics of what many believe to be the key elements of management development. That is the belief that people develop best through situations that challenge them (see Evans, Pucik & Barsoux, 2002). However, challenging assignments come with a risk of failure

Table 10.1 Availability of Repatriation Support Practices	
Practice	**Availability (%)**
Continuous communications with the home office	49.6
Communications with the home office about the details of the repatriation process	42.4
Career planning sessions	41.9
Guarantee/agreement outlining the type of position expatriates will be placed in upon repatriation	33.6
Lifestyle assistance and counseling on changes likely to occur in expatriates' lifestyles upon return	33.6
Predeparture briefings on what to expect during repatriation	31.1
Visible signs that the company values international experience	25.2
Financial counseling and financial/tax assistance	9.8
Mentoring programs while on assignment	8.9
Reorientation program about the changes in the company	8.1
Repatriation training seminars on the emotional response following repatriation	8.1
Mean availability (average across all practices)	26.6

SOURCE: Lazarova, M. B., & Cerdin J.-L. (2007). Revisiting repatriation concerns: Organizational support versus career and contextual influences. *Journal of International Business Studies, 38,* 404–429. © 2007. Reproduced with permission of Palgrave Macmillan.

and may need to be managed so that individuals learn to deal with situations outside their comfort zone but without disastrous results for the organization (McCall, 1998). Recent research supports the notion of the beneficial effects of overseas experience. Based on the idea that dealing with the dissonance that individuals experience when they are exposed to a different culture causes them to develop more complex cognitive structures (Tadmor & Tetlock, 2006), multicultural experience has been found to enhance individual creativity (Leung, Maddux, Galinsky, & Chiu, 2008) and even results in higher promotion rates and enhanced professional reputations (Tadmor, Galinsky & Maddux, 2012). The following quote from an individual having returned from an extended overseas assignment is indicative of the type of personal development that seems to take place:

> I have learned to look at the world around me with a childlike wonder and to drop any preconceived notions I may have been holding. I have learned that just because I have grown up indoctrinated by a certain set of rules regarding how relationships and society in general work, that does not make them universally true or right (Thomas & Inkson, 2008, p. 170).

The effect of an overseas assignment on the longer-term career of managers depends in part on how a person views his or her career. From a traditional "move up the career ladder" perspective, expatriate assignments do not seem to have positive effects on the development of one's career. Reports are common that expatriates are often neglected on their return, put in holding patterns, and not valued for their international experience by their firms (e.g., Adler, 1981; Feldman & Thomas, 1992; Harvey, 1989; Stahl & Cerdin, 2004; Tung, 1981). Adler (1981) reported that one out of four expatriates leave the firm upon reentry and that graduating MBAs (Adler, 1987) perceive an international assignment as a risky career move. Although an international assignment might facilitate an individual's movement to a higher career stage, in general expatriates have reported that their overseas assignment did not have a positive long-term effect on their career, that their firms do not take advantage of the skills they learned overseas, and that their assignments were better for their personal development than for their professional careers (Oddou & Mendenhall, 1991; Stahl, Miller, & Tung, 2002). However, the extent to which the expatriate assignment fits with employees' career plans influences the effectiveness of expatriates on assignment. For example, the extent to which the assignment is perceived as a promotion has been found to be positively related to the intention to remain on assignment (Birdseye & Hill, 1995). And, the expatriate's perception of a connection between the expatriate assignment and long-term career has been positively related to his or her performance on assignment (Feldman & Thomas, 1992) and with effective repatriation (Gomez-Meija & Balkin, 1987). Inadequate career advancement upon repatriation has been shown to be related to perceptions of underemployment among repatriates, which in turn lead to higher turnover intentions (Kraimer, Shaffer & Bolino, 2009). And, we have evidence that lack of career-related support is linked to repatriate intentions to leave their companies, such that career prospects after repatriation are positively related to retaining repatriates two and four years after their assignments have ended (Reiche, Kraimer, & Harzing, 2011).

Until recently, the study of global careers focused on the assignment of expatriates by multinational organizations. However, the nature of how people view their careers has been changing from an upward progression of job experiences to a more subjective sense of where one is going in one's work life (Schein, 1996). This change in careers perception (often called *boundaryless* careers [Arthur & Rousseau, 1996]) explains in part why individuals seek international assignments while also believing that they will not be rewarded for doing so (Thomas, 1998). While individuals recognize that an overseas assignment may not have a positive effect on their (external) career, they accept it because they view the experience as positive for their (internal career) personal and professional development (Stahl et al., 2002). This has also led to a recognition that personal and professional development need not be associated only with a traditional expatriate assignment but can also be gained through *self-initiated* overseas experiences (Inkson, Arthur, Pringle, & Barry, 1997; Suutari & Brewster, 2000). Thus, the nature of a career in the age of globalization is quite different from the past and requires that we consider an overseas assignment from the perspective of both the individual and the firm that employs him or her (Thomas, Lazarova, & Inkson, 2005).

Summary

In this chapter, the challenge of overseas assignments was presented from both the point of view of the firm and that of the individual expatriate. These employees are of special concern because of their often-critical role in bridging both organizational and cultural boundaries. Firms might decide to use expatriates for a variety of strategic or developmental reasons, and a significant amount of research identifies individual organizational and environmental factors that contribute to the success or failure of these managers. A review of these findings suggests that an overseas experience can have both positive and negative consequences, for both the individual and the firm. Managing these contradictory or paradoxical effects is a significant challenge for international managers. The following summarizes the most apparent of these contradictions.

The relationship between expatriate adjustment and performance on an international assignment has been assumed to be direct and positive, and this assumption underlies a great deal of research and practice. However, research does not indicate overwhelming support for this assumption. In fact, as stated previously, it seems possible that the highest-performing expatriates are those who experience the most severe culture shock and have the most difficult time adjusting (Thomas & Lazarova, 2006). The same characteristics that allow individuals to be effective overseas (e.g., others orientation, perceptual skills) can make it more stressful to adjust.

A second individual characteristic that has a paradoxical relationship to success on an international assignment is the family situation of the expatriate. Married expatriates adjust better than do single expatriates, and social support (potentially provided by the spouse in some cases) is important to overseas adjustment. However, substantial evidence suggests that the main reason for an expatriate's premature return home is the failure of his or her family (or spouse) to adjust. This apparent paradox suggests that the relationship between the expatriate's family situation and his or her effectiveness is likely to be much more complex than conceptualized to date.

A small but growing number of women are international assignees, but there continues to be a bias against selecting women for overseas assignments (Varma & Stroh, 2001). However, women expatriates are likely to be more highly educated and better prepared for international assignments than their male counterparts. In addition, women's management styles are more consistent with the relational and perceptual abilities that some authors suggest are required for overseas effectiveness (Davidson & Cooper, 1987; Freedman & Phillips, 1988; Napier & Taylor, 2002). As the presence of women in management roles in general and the expatriate role in particular increases, the need to understand the issues involved in placing women overseas will certainly increase.

The vast majority of expatriate research has studied U.S. nationals abroad. In the few studies involving other nationalities, cultural differences have had a sometimes contradictory effect on a variety of outcomes. For example, the reasons for staffing with expatriates, selection criteria for expatriates, failure rates as measured by premature return, relationship between adjustment and performance, and antecedents to organizational commitment all vary by nationality (Thomas, 1998).

Perhaps the most studied organizational factor related to the international assignments is the amount of cross-cultural training provided. The contradiction that cross-cultural training is effective but that firms fail to avail themselves of it is a long-standing issue. Although it seems clear that cross-cultural training can have very positive benefits, the effectiveness of training may have been oversimplified. Despite the suggestion that different approaches to cross-cultural training can be effective in different circumstances and questions about the different effects of predeparture and in-country training, these issues have not been fully examined. In addition, it would be naive to suggest that the quality of cross-cultural training was consistent across programs or that quality does not influence effectiveness.

The idea that the greater the differences between one's home and host country, the greater the adjustment difficulties has been supported in a number of studies. However, contradictory results suggest that cultural novelty can facilitate certain types of adjustment. The relationship of cultural novelty to the expatriate experience is clearly not as simple as it is often portrayed. It seems possible that a number of variables, such as the expectation that expatriates have about the foreign environment, might influence the relationship.

Firms tend to select individuals for overseas assignments based on the individual's ability to fill a technical requirement, with little regard for the effect on the individual's career. However, people accept overseas assignments primarily to advance their careers and are more effective and satisfied if they see the connection between the expatriate assignment and their long-term career plans. In addition, the clarity of the role expectations that the firm has for the individual has a significant positive relationship on the expatriate experience.

Individuals report considerable personal development along a wide range of skill and knowledge dimensions because of their overseas assignment. However, when they return to their home country, their newly won skills are rarely used, and the net effect of the overseas assignment is often described as having a neutral to negative effect on their long-term career. In addition, although it can take several years for an individual to become truly effective in an international assignment, longer tenure overseas results in more difficult repatriation. These effects raise considerable concern about the value of an international assignment for an individual's career and for the development of the firm.

Questions for Discussion

1. If expatriate managers are so expensive and so many of them fail to complete their assignment, why do firms continue to use them?

2. What is the main reason that expatriates fail on overseas assignment? What can be done about it?

3. If cross-cultural training is so effective, why don't firms generally provide training?

4. Why can repatriation adjustment be even more difficult than the adjustment required on expatriation?

5. What are some of the effects of an expatriate assignment on the individual? On his or her career?

The Challenge of Managing Across Cultures in the Future

Prediction is very difficult, especially about the future.

—Niels Bohr (1885–1962)

Twenty-five years ago the word *globalization* was rarely heard. Today its use evokes strong responses, both positive and negative. Proponents tout its benefits, whereas opponents see the destruction of indigenous aspects of developing countries. One thing is certain: it is an irreversible process. In the future managers must deal with the many additional layers of complexity that the changing environment of business brings to their jobs. They must learn to operate within the complex interplay between the various trends in the cultures of the world and the process of globalization (Kedia, 2006).

The Changing Environment of Business

Globalization is characterized by growing worldwide connections between organizations and their various constituencies, by rapid and discontinuous change, by growing numbers and diversity of actors involved in global activities, and by greater managerial complexity (Parker, 2005). Because organizations are open systems, managers must adapt structures and procedures to this environment. From the wide range of environmental issues, this chapter concentrates on four trends that set the stage for cross-cultural management in the future: the uneven development in the world, the increased influence of economies in transition, the continued influence of information and communication technology, and the growing pressure on the natural environment.

Uneven Development

The uneven economic development around the globe, as evidenced by the range in gross domestic product per capita and the Human Development Index, has numerous implications for policymakers and business people. These include the stimulation of economic growth in various regions, the ethnic tensions that parallel economic issues, the backlash against the United States and the exportation of U.S.-style capitalism and culture, and the extreme responses by terrorists (see Rosen, Digh, Singer, & Phillips, 2000). Although all these issues create a heightened sense of uncertainty in the business environment, perhaps the most significant effect of the differences in development from a cross-cultural management perspective has to do with the impact on the labor pool. Economic development within nations affects the availability of wage-earning jobs. About 28 percent of the world's workforce lives in countries with per capita incomes of less than US$2.00 a day. Eighty percent live on less than US$3,650 per year with the bottom of the pyramid anchored by the Democratic Republic of the Congo at US$231 GNP per capita. This compares to a 2011 GNP per capita of US$98,102 for Norway, US$60,642 for Australia, US$56,927 for Sweden, and US$48,442 for the United States (International Labour Organization, 2012; 2013). In developing countries, working hours are longer, part-time employment is high, and many people work several part-time jobs because of limited full-time employment. Additionally, few developing countries provide the type of social safety net enjoyed in the industrialized world, and workers are often subject to a variety of abuses on the job, including discrimination based on gender and the employment of child labor (Parker, 2005). Multinational enterprises create many of the jobs on which the domestic economies of developing countries are based and can therefore influence work lives in these countries (Hawken, 1993).

Uneven economic development is the second (after political issues) biggest influence on worldwide migration, with economic migrants crossing boundaries between developing and developed countries (Parker, 2005). These immigrants increase the diversity of the workforce and add to the managerial complexity of the firms that employ them. Additionally, policies that favor the migration of skilled workers raise issues about the so-called *brain drain* from less developed countries (Carr et al., 2005). Although the majority of economic migrants are men, there is a trend toward more women migrants (Parker, 2005).

Differences in the cost of labor between the developed and developing world are a major factor influencing the migration of jobs to countries where labor is cheap and abundant. Developing countries continue to experience an increase in employment, which had slowed following the financial crisis of 2008 through 2009. However, the labor markets in most countries have not recovered from the global crisis, which has led to an increase in poverty and inequality even in the advanced economies (International Labour Organization, 2012). Outsourcing of jobs can provide access to skills not available in the local labor pool. Although the first jobs to migrate are typically low-skilled manufacturing jobs, the trend is toward the migration of service and medium-skill jobs, such as those in call centers and payment processing centers. The final stage of job migration occurs when highly skilled professional and knowledge jobs are outsourced (see Parker, 2005). The effect is often that jobs designed for one type of cultural environment create management challenges in their new and often culturally different setting. A related trend is what might be called reverse migration that occurs because of economic liberalization. Traditional economic migration, which involves a permanent move from a developing to a developed country, is being replaced by migrants returning to their country of origin. This reverse migration has most often been seen with Chinese and Indian migrants and involves the high-tech sector or, more broadly, professional employees (Tung & Lazarova, 2006). Reverse migration can also occur as business conditions in a country shift from attractive to unattractive. For example, many Eastern Europeans who migrated to their more advanced EU neighbors after the EU enlargement in the early 2000s are returning home as the post 2008 global financial crisis worsened conditions in the EU (Dougherty, 2008).

Some argue that the creation of jobs anywhere aids overall economic development. However, Korten (1995) suggests that the global competition for jobs results in low-wage jobs being replaced by even lower-wage jobs, downward pressure is put on labor standards, and hiring cheap labor globally disrupts social contracts and cultural norms in the host country. Job migration in concert with the growing need for knowledge workers will increase the numbers of women in the workforce, particularly in developing countries, increase the average age of workers, particularly in the developed world, and increase the demand for people with higher levels of education worldwide (Parker, 2005).

Influence of Transition Economies

Following the collapse of the Berlin Wall in 1989, the final two decades of the last century saw a widespread decline in centrally planned economies in favor of market-based approaches. By the early 1990s, a country that was not a democracy or democratizing society but that held on to a highly regulated centrally planned economy was on the wrong side of history. The failure of state socialism has left only one viable economic ideology, and that is capitalism. The fall of state socialism had a ripple effect that was felt in the huge populations of China and the developing world. As these transition economies grow in importance on the global stage, multinational organizations (MNOs) and their managers will be confronted with the need to understand the legacy of state socialism that influences both organizations and managers (Napier & Thomas, 2004). Fundamental to economic transition is the replacement of one set of institutions that govern economic activity by another. Although managers in transition economies are heavily influenced by the external influences of the market, they must respond to new institutions that are acceptable in their own society (see Chapter 9). The exact end point of this institutional context is uncertain, but it will inevitably contain some vestiges of state socialism.

The fundamental institution in the power structure of the socialist countries was the single-party system (Kornai, 1992). Under state socialism, plans were fulfilled in large part according to state priority, and many countries rapidly industrialized. Many controls were used to achieve the central planning goals of avoiding overproduction, massive unemployment, and economic depression. Peng (2000) lists several of these controls and compares them to market practices:

- Firms are created by the state as opposed to by an entrepreneur.
- The state decides whether to liquidate firms as opposed to allowing a firm to survive or not on its own.
- Production goals are set by the state as opposed to by management.
- The state determines the allocation and distribution of products by matching users and producers as opposed to allowing the market to determine who buys what from whom.
- Decisions about prices, investment, technology development, and use are made by the state rather than by managers.
- Manager selection, promotion, and dismissal are done by the state as opposed to firm managers or directors.
- The state assigns workers to facilities and bases their pay on centrally determined wage rates rather than allowing firms to make these decisions.

A central belief of the socialist system was that a worker had a right to a job and its associated benefits (Lee, 1987). For example, in China factories approximated the institutions of societies, providing for all the workers' needs, such as food, housing, and hospitalization (Warner, 2002). These characteristics of socialist organizations created a psychological contract between employees and the firm that differed dramatically from the Western capitalist model. Employees under state socialism were encouraged to perceive their relationship with the organization in long-term socioemotional terms that included commitment and loyalty, consistent with the collective interest.

In addition to the institutional and organizational context of transition economies, two individual-level issues with regard to managers in these countries should be noted. First, managerial behavior is influenced by the extent to which managers have been exposed to formal management training. Although managers in transition economies often have exceptional educational backgrounds, their exposure to management education is highly variable (Napier & Thomas, 2004). There has been a boom in management education in transition economies (Child & Tse, 2001), but there is also cause to be pessimistic about the ability to deliver management education in societies where there is so much to learn and still political and social resistance to a market economy (Puffer, 1996). Second, the cultural profile of managers in these economies is likely to reflect hierarchical and collectivist value orientations that have been reinforced by the socialist system. For example, paternalistic management in these societies may have evolved because society fostered it. Child and Markóczy (1993, p. 617) suggest that defensive, conforming behavior will have been learned under a system where protection from censure and the securing of resources both depended on the maintenance of good personal relations with higher level officials and to some extent, with political organs within the enterprise itself.

Additional cultural effects that are an outcome of this juxtaposition of cultural values and institutional influences include learned helplessness in the control over rewards and punishments and a reluctance to take risks or stand out from the crowd. The following quote from a German manager working in Poland, reported by Napier and Thomas (2004, p. 135), is consistent with this influence:

> They called themselves *gray mice*. They didn't want to be noticed, just wanted to make the quota that came from central government and not to be noticed beyond that. They didn't want to expose themselves—if they stood out in good or bad ways—to the hardships that would come or to the secret police. They weren't risk takers, wanted to keep the old system and job for life approach.

At the same time, managers in transition economies are often sensitive to being treated as inferior by foreigners. As one Russian manager reported,

> At first, I personally was very depressed by the systematic approach of every-thing. . . . I thought it was completely crazy to create policies for everything. Some of them were written and repeated many times. They seemed to be so obvious to me that I thought: "What a nonsense! How can you even talk about it?" Often they were related to some organizational moments, like what time you come to work, what time you leave, how you should be dressed. And you think: "Do they take us for idiots?" (Napier & Thomas, 2004, p. 140)

Against the influence of globalization, managers in transition economies still exist in an environment that contains the remains of state socialism. As has been appropriately pointed out, new post socialist structures are built not *on* the ruins but *with* the ruins of communism. The legacy of socialism includes:

- Centralization and bureaucratic organization of power
- A drive for production quantity over quality
- Paternalistic behavior of superiors
- Soft budget constraints
- Weak responses to prices
- Mechanisms to compensate for chronic shortages
- A disregard for the external environment (Napier & Thomas, 2004)

In addition to operating in this different institutional context, managers in transition economies are likely to be highly educated, but not in Western market-oriented management; to have a cultural profile characterized by vertical collectivism; and to have come to management from a wide range of backgrounds. Thus, interacting effectively with managers and employees in transition economies carries with it unique challenges.

Information and Communication Technology

Information and communication technologies involve two main activities: processing information (e.g., storing, searching, and reproducing) and transmitting it from one location (or entity) to another. In the twenty-first century these technologies are a digital revolution that has created a platform for the free flow of information, ideas and knowledge around the globe. The Internet has become a global resource that is important to both the developed world as a business and social tool and the developing world as a passport to a more level playing field as well as to economic, social, and educational development. The percentage of individuals using the Internet and mobile phones continues to grow worldwide. By the end of 2011, 2.3 billion people were online and there were 6 billion mobile cellular subscriptions (International Telecommunications Union, 2012).

However, there remains a *digital divide* that separates those who are connected to the digital revolution in information and communications technology and those who have no access to the benefits of the new technologies. Information and communications technology services continue to be more affordable in developed as opposed to developing countries, but the cost of technology is decreasing (down 18% from 2008–2010) (International Telecommunications Union, 2012). As the cost of technology decreases, the developing world is making steady progress in coming online. And as the world's online population becomes more culturally diverse, the Internet will lose its U.S.-centric flavor and may over time be as generalized and invisible as today's electrical networks. The influence of the flow of high-quality and inexpensive information will be felt by firms and households both in the organization of work and in consumer behavior and by societies as they adjust to this influence.

Increasingly, the work environment relies on knowledge. The ability to take advantage of knowledge can be a strategic advantage for organizations (Senge, 1990) and a source of power for individuals in global organizations (Parker, 2005). Clearly, the ability to leverage the ever-expanding sea of knowledge on a global scale will be an important future management challenge. Information technology can become an equalizer in terms of access to knowledge and may also have an effect on work opportunities. For example, because of strong cultural norms, having a career and a family was impossible for Japanese women until some women began setting up Internet-intensive home businesses (Guth, 2000). Because of changing work methods, such as the virtual global teams discussed in Chapter 8, the most in-demand jobs 10 years from now probably do not even exist today. What's next is difficult to predict. Will human salespeople, travel agents, shop assistants, and even university professors be replaced? The possible long-term impact of such changes is only beginning to be analyzed.

Finally, the advent of nearly universal language translation capability, which is already beginning to appear on the Internet, has the potential for an even greater exchange of ideas than exists today. We can hope that the effect of this exchange will create an increased sense of global identity among the people of the world, as opposed to the confusion in identity predicted by some (Rosen et al., 2000).

Pressure on the Natural Environment

Because of globalization, it is increasingly obvious that activities in one part of the world affect organizations and individuals in other regions. Likewise, we have all become increasingly aware that the earth is a finite natural resource that must be shared by everyone. A recent study commissioned by the United Nations (involving 1,360 experts) concluded that in the second half of the 20th century, humans have changed the earth's ecosystems more rapidly and extensively than during any other time in human history (Hoffman & Bansal, 2011). Finally, it is becoming apparent that national governments are ill equipped to address global environmental issues alone (French, 2003), and large MNOs are more powerful than some governments. Therefore, there will be increasing pressure on the international manager of the future to be environmentally responsible.

The developing and developed worlds face different population challenges. In most industrialized countries, population growth began to approach zero in the 1970s (United Nations, 2006). Population decline means a reduction in the indigenous labor supply and an aging workforce. Until recently the low birthrates in the developed world were more than offset by high rates in developing countries (United Nations, 2006). Issues here include the ability to feed, house, and educate the growing population. Exacerbating the effects of differential population growth is that the relatively small populations of the developed world consume the majority of the world's resources.

The world's population growth combined with global economic development is placing increasing demands on the resources we all share, which some authors (Buck, 1998; Parker, 2005) call the *global commons*. Obviously such natural resources as air and water are shared by everyone, but the global commons can also include such things as the atmosphere, space, and even the Internet (Henderson, 1999). An example is the basic natural resource of water. Water shortages occur as population rises, caused not only by increased usage but also by human-made degradation such as industrial pollution and poor waste treatment. By some estimates, as many as 2 billion people could face water shortages by 2050, and this impact will be felt more strongly in the developing world (see Ward, 2002). Because national interests sometimes conflict with global water use standards, global organizations are becoming water system builders and managers almost by default (Parker, 2005). The self-interest of nations and individuals also affects the land on which the world's food is grown. For example, some reports suggest that a significant portion of the world's farmland is threatened by erosion, nutrient depletion, and increased salinity. The influence of global organizations on other aspects of the natural environment are perhaps more direct (see Parker, 2005). For example, despite the widespread use of electronic communication, global paper use continues to rise, and paper production requires vast amounts of timber. Additionally, globalization, travel, and trade are at least partly responsible for the approximately 50,000 species of plants and animals that disappear each year.

The approaches to dealing with the stress being placed on the natural environment by development are tremendously variable across countries and are potentially a result of the influence of national culture. Although it is rarely studied, some evidence suggests that culture is an important influence on a nation's performance regarding environmental sustainability. For example, the national-level cultural values of power distance and masculinity have been shown to be negatively related to country-level scores on the Environmental Sustainability Index of the World Economic Forum (Park, Russell, & Lee, 2007).

In summary, the industrialization that accompanies economic development increases the world's prosperity but also increases the potential for ecological disruption. Tensions between economic growth and environmental protection will continue to rise. Developing nations will not be able to imitate the consumption patterns of the developed world. But also, the lifestyles in the rich nations of the world will need to change. And maximization of profits will need to be replaced by the expansion of opportunities (Parker, 2005). For international managers, this means that organizations involved in global business will be expected to explicitly consider their role in preserving the natural environment. Relevant to this increasingly important role of international managers are three principles suggested by Bird and Smucker (2007) that managers must take into account when addressing the responsibility of international organizations in developing countries:

- An awareness of the cultural, historical, and institutional dynamics of the local community, which reflect the type of responsibilities expected of the organization and the limitations of any universal codes of conduct.
- The necessity of nonintimidating communication with local stakeholders that allows the organization to recognize and respond to local concerns in pursuit of its own objectives.
- The need for the firm's operations to safeguard and improve the social and economic assets of the local communities with regard to the inevitable disruptions that international business brings.

Thus, the fourth of our trends that influence the environment for international and cross-cultural management is the vested interest we all have in protecting the natural environment and the fact that this interest influences the role managers play. In this role, managers will increasingly find themselves engaged with the different values, attitudes, and assumptions about the natural environment that exist throughout the world.

The Adaptation of Organizations and People

The four trends with regard to the future environment of business set the stage for cross-cultural management in the future. In the following section, the adaptation that organizations and individuals might engage in with regard to these trends are discussed in terms of the cross-cultural management issues they present. Three categories of adjustment to our thinking about cross-cultural management are presented:

understanding the context of management in MNOs, the future of the organization of work, and the development of global managers.

The MNO Context

Cross-cultural management involves the interaction of culturally different people in the context of organizations. Often this occurs in MNOs, which are increasingly important players on the global stage. These issues are distinguished from other approaches to social interactions by their focus on the organizational context. And the defining quality of MNOs as a context for management is that they actively manage assets in several nations rather than only engaging in market transactions across national boundaries. MNOs include both businesses and nongovernment organizations, which must contend with societal differences in employee diversity, customers, competitors, and suppliers, as well as in economic and government institutions, that are of a far greater magnitude than in purely domestic organizations. MNOs have several distinctive characteristics, including high levels of organizational complexity and the need to transfer complex knowledge over distance. MNOs need numerous linkages to the diverse and dynamic external environment. The central question is exactly how this "multinational-ness" of the organizational context affects management over and above what happens in a purely domestic context (see Feldman, 1997).

According to Peterson and Thomas (2007), the MNO provides a context that can have a unique effect in any of three ways: (1) *frequency of occurrence*—extremes occur in a management factor (e.g., a manager's ties to the local environment), which makes its relationship with other factors more obvious in the MNO than in purely domestic organizations; (2) *functional relationships*—an extreme or set of extremes produces a moderator effect in the relationships between management activities (e.g., the moderating effect of cultural differences on the transfer of knowledge); and (3) *unique constructs*—something unusual or unique about the MNO context produces differences in a known management issue (e.g., global virtual teams). Understanding the ways in which the context of the multinational enterprise affects the roles of managers is important as organizations adapt to the trends in the business environment that affect management across cultures.

One way in which organizations are responding to the emerging environment of business is by adapting their organization structure. One of the most recent adaptations has been the formation of more loosely coupled organizational forms of strategic alliances, discussed in Chapter 9. The future of organizational structures as MNOs adapt to the emerging business environment is unclear. On one hand, as information technology becomes even more sophisticated and inexpensive, it is more convenient to delegate decision making at all organizational levels, resulting in flatter organizations. Not only is this more efficient, but it also has a liberating effect on the diverse individuals in the MNO (see Malone, 2004). On the other hand, hierarchical organizations may continue to persist (while adapting management strategies) because they provide individuals with a sense of identity, status, and belonging and can be efficient in managing complex tasks (see Leavitt, 2005). Regardless of the form taken by the

MNO, a continuing issue will be the establishment and maintenance of legitimacy by the MNO in the multiple cultural environments in which it must operate (Kostova & Zaheer, 1999).

In recent years, the development and dissemination of knowledge have taken center stage as a consideration in the global competitiveness of MNOs. The improvement of communication technology mentioned previously will undoubtedly influence how organizations manage the transfer of knowledge across borders, seen as critical to organizational design, renewal, and competitiveness (Leung & Peterson, 2011). In the past, the transfers of knowledge for the most part assumed that the transfer was from the parent to the local subsidiary. However, this transfer need not originate with the parent and can also involve transfer back to the parent or among foreign operations (called reverse transfer or *diffusion*) (Edwards & Tempel, 2010). The effectiveness of cross-border knowledge transfer is related not only to the type of knowledge being transferred (complex vs. simple, explicit vs. tacit, systematic vs. independent) but also to culturally based transaction patterns and the cognitive styles of individuals involved (Bhagat, Kedia, Harveston, & Triandis, 2002). The influence of culture on the ability to transfer knowledge may be most apparent in situations with large cultural differences, such as the transfer of management knowledge developed in a free market context to individuals and organizations in transition economies (e.g., May, Puffer, & McCarthy, 2005). Also, as knowledge is transferred it is often modified in some way or given different meaning as it moves to a new institutional and cultural context. In some cases, this modification or *hybridization* of the practice is planned and anticipated (Zhu & Dowling, 2002). However, in other cases the policy or practice is reinterpreted in unpredictable ways. In these cases the transferred knowledge takes on a new meaning as it moves from one sociocultural context to another and can be said to be *recontextualized* (Brannen, 2004). Recontextualization does not always conform to strategic intent. Positive recontextualizations may be a source of sustainable competitive advantage, but negative ones can come as an unwelcome shock.

A third management issue involving the MNO context is that new types of organizations are beginning to consider their multinational-ness. In particular, both peacekeeping and police organizations have recently begun to address the cultural diversity that exists both in the organization and in the populations being served. These types of organizations differ from their civilian counterparts in that they have frequent rotation of personnel and commanders and are imbued with a sense of urgency in addressing ad hoc problems (Elron, Halevy, Ben-Ari, & Shamir, 2003). However, they share the fact that their effectiveness is increasingly influenced by their ability to manage their culturally diverse workforce effectively and respond appropriately to culturally different external stakeholders (e.g., Tresch & Picciano, 2007). Finally, of course, failed cross-cultural interactions in these organizations can have the kind of dire consequences that end up being reported on the evening news.

A final contextual issue facing cross-cultural management in the future is the relationship between individuals and organizations across cultures. Framed in terms of the psychological contract in Chapter 9, the issues associated with the preferences individuals have for associating with organizations that have certain characteristics may take on even greater importance in the future. Recent research points in this direction. For example, one study in China found that fit with organizational characteristics combined with personality influenced the extent to which individuals were attracted to an organization (Turban, Lau, Ngo, Chow, & Si, 2001). And, another study found that collectivist's preference for organizations exhibiting a relational psychological contract was mediated by fundamental beliefs about social exchange (Thomas, Ravlin, Liao, Morrell & Au, in press). Collectivists have been found to be more committed when employed by an Asian organization as compared to an Australian organization (Parkes, Bochner & Schneider, 2001). However, other research has suggested that person-organization fit may not be as important in developing countries where such factors as high unemployment and norms that suppress the expression of individual preference are a significant factor (Nyambegera, Daniels, & Sparrow, 2001).

Although there may be questions about fit, the future will clearly require managers to understand the influence that the organizational characteristics of the MNO have on the quality of cross-cultural interactions within the organization (see Cooper, Doucet, & Pratt, 2007). This includes how the MNO context influences the relationship between host country nationals and expatriates, a topic that has only recently begun to be explored (Toh & DeNisi, 2007). Also, because the structure of MNOs involves entities in multiple contexts, it is possible, even likely, that individuals will identify with more than one organizational entity, such as with the parent and the subsidiary. This dual organizational identification, which can take different forms (distinct, compound, or nested) and can vary in magnitude, has profound implications for how individuals perceive and enact their roles in the organization (Vora & Kostova, 2007).

The Future of the Organization of Work

In addition to the influence that the changing environment for business will have at the organizational level of the MNO, these same forces will influence the way in which work is organized. Based on current trends, it is possible to identify several areas in which organizations are likely to need to adapt work practices. These involve the increased reliance on global virtual teams, the changing nature of overseas assignments, and work–family reconciliation issues.

One of the most obvious issues with regard to the organization of work is the continued widespread use of global virtual teams, discussed in Chapter 8. As discussed, teams that do not at some time interact through electronic media may largely cease to exist. And multinational enterprises increasingly rely on global virtual teams to overcome the boundaries of time and geography. The future of global virtual teams is closely tied to the developments in information and communication technology on which they rely. Questions can be asked about the nature of this influence as this technology comes closer and closer to replicating face-to-face interactions. For example, will the lack of social presence resulting from electronic intermediation be reduced, will language differences become more or less salient, and will conflict between culturally different team members be increased or reduced? In addition, a central issue in the global virtual teams of today is the extent to which team members identify with the team (Shapiro et al., 2002). These identity issues pose questions with regard to role perceptions and behavior similar to that of dual organizational identification, mentioned previously. As teams engage in problem solving across time, space, and cultures, the type and strength of their identification with the team as compared with other entities will increasingly be an issue of concern to managers. Finally, while global virtual teams are becoming increasingly common in organizations as they try to deal with the increased complexity of the competitive environment, the possibility of unintended negative consequences on employee well-being is just beginning to be recognized (Glazer, Kożusznik, & Shargo, 2012).

A second but related issue is the extent to which cultural differences influence individuals' perceived status within a work group or team and the status of the team in the organization. Both developments in information and communication technology and the increased opportunities for interaction with individuals from less developed and transition economies can be anticipated to influence perceptions of status differences of individuals within the group and of the group by others. Cultural differences in perceived status lead to differences in beliefs about the legitimacy of group participation and the nature of the status hierarchy of the group, which in turn affect the amount of conflict in the group (Ravlin et al., 2000). Additionally, group members may be more likely to identify with groups that enjoy high status, which in turn might focus team members' attention away from cultural differences and toward task accomplishment.

A third issue in the organization of work category is the changing nature of overseas assignments. Overseas assignments will also be discussed ahead from the individual perspective of global manager development. Here, however, the issue is the needs of the firm, particularly its need to capitalize on knowledge gained from overseas experience. Although the bulk of international assignees may remain in traditional overseas assignments, a growing trend in nonstandard overseas assignments is emerging (Global Relocation Trends, 2012). Nonstandard assignments include commuting overseas (typically on a weekly or biweekly basis), rotational (home-overseas-home) assignments, and contractual (short-term six- to 12-month) postings (Mayrhofer, Reichel, & Sparrow, 2012). The main reasons for this approach are cost reduction (expatriates are expensive) and employee immobility (often resulting from dual-career couples). However, advances in communication technology are also a factor, with some part of the assignment often conducted on a virtual basis. The issues associated with these nonstandard assignments are different from those of the traditional expatriate assignment and include family separation, travel stress, health issues, safety concerns, and inconsistent work demands (Welch & Worm, 2006).

An additional trend with regard to overseas assignments concerns the recognition that knowledge gained by expatriates overseas can be integrated into more effective business practice. The need for this knowledge in order to gain competitive advantage means the management of expatriates will be increasingly concerned with knowledge transfer by repatriates. A key issue is the retention of repatriates long enough for the transfer of knowledge to take place (Lazarova & Cerdin, 2007). Consistent with the transfer of knowledge across cultural boundaries discussed previously, both individual and organizational antecedents to effective knowledge transfer by repatriates have been proposed. These include the type of knowledge to be transferred, individual readiness to transfer the knowledge, the receptivity of the organization to international knowledge, and the intensity of the knowledge transfer mechanisms (see Lazarova & Tarique, 2005).

A final future consideration for cross-cultural management in the organization of work has to do with the widespread difficulties in reconciling work and family. Trends in both the developed and the developing world have made balancing work and family responsibilities a major concern for organizations with regard to recruitment, retention, and productivity (Poelmans, Maestro, & Greenhaus, 2013). Three areas of concern to international managers are apparent: the work–family issues associated with overseas assignments, the influence of different institutional arrangements around the world on reconciliation of work and family, and finally the role of culture in balancing work and family (Lazarova & Lowe, 2008). With regard to the expatriate experience, we have long known about the relationship of spousal adjustment to expatriate adjustment (see Chapter 10 and Bhaskar-Shrinivas, Harrison, Shaffer, & Luk, 2005). This and other expatriate research has focused largely on how family-related demands affect the expatriate's work performance rather than how work demands influence family (Lazarova & Lowe, 2008). The future will require a better understanding of how the demands of the expatriate assignment (and also nonstandard assignments discussed previously) influence work–family balance.

Cross-national differences in work–family reconciliation, both as a result of institutional differences and as a result of cultural differences, will be of concern to managers in the future. The most common institutional factors are government regulations and the presence of statutory family support arrangements. As regards culture, the question revolves around the extent to which culture influences the relationship between various work and family issues. For example, Spector et al., 2007 found that country cluster (Anglo versus Asia, Eastern Europe, and Latin America) moderated the relationship between work interference with family (WIF) and job satisfaction and turnover. And, it seems clear that the approach that governments and national institutions take toward the reconciliation of work and family affects the support provided by employers, and that value orientations such as individualism and collectivism moderate work–family relationships. However, little is known beyond these broad generalizations (Lazarova & Lowe, 2008).

The Development of Global Managers

The future managers who will be able to deal with the many additional layers of complexity that globalization brings to their jobs and who operate effectively within the complexity of the various trends in the cultures of the world will be different. They will be truly global managers, able to function effectively in a cross-cultural context. They will have competencies that allow them to compete in an increasingly competitive and multicultural world (Suutari, 2002). Three issues with regard to the development of global managers are presented here. These are the changing nature of international management careers, the development of skills and abilities related to effective inter-cultural interactions, and the role of bicultural individuals.

International Management Careers

Until recently, discussions about international management careers focused on select-ing and training managers for one-time expatriate assignments under the assumption that global competencies could best be developed through an overseas assignment. However, the idea of what constitutes a career has taken on new characteristics that broaden its applicability to global managers. As noted in Chapter 10, the way in which managers view their careers has shifted from a progression up the career ladder to a more subjective sense of what one does during one's working life. And the kinds of knowledge and competencies required of global managers can be developed by means other than company-sponsored overseas assignments (Inkson et al., 1997). These per-spectives, coupled with the recognition that global managers play a significant role in capitalizing on the knowledge that exists throughout the MNO, focus attention on how to best develop these global leaders. Concurrently, the characteristics of the interna-tional manager are changing (Thomas et al., 2005). Because of work–family issues and changing career expectations, the pool of candidates desiring a global career will be far different from the mid-career male expatriate of the past. First, the number of women on overseas assignment has been steadily increasing, and the willingness of women to have global careers is about the same as that of men (Caligiuri, Joshi, & Lazarova, 1999). Second, the number of dual-career partnerships is increasing (Harvey, Speier, & Novicevic, 1999). And third, international managers will increasingly include individu-als from places other than the United States and Western Europe. Thus, the global managers of the future are very likely to be female, part of a dual-career partnership, and from transition or developing countries. These differences will be particularly import-ant in terms of the effective cross-cultural interactions required of global managers. The focus of selection, training, and career development for the global manager of the future will need to be significantly different from that of the expatriate manager of the past.

Cross-Cultural Skills and Abilities

Interacting effectively with people from other cultures and behaving appropriately in a culturally novel context are indications of the cross-cultural skills and abilities needed by global managers. The characteristics of effective intercultural interaction in a management context can be summarized as

- *good personal adjustment,* indicated by feelings of contentment and well-being,
- development and maintenance of *good interpersonal relationships with culturally different others*, and
- the effective *completion of task-related goals.* (Thomas & Fitzsimmons, 2008)

Despite an assumption that there is consensus on the basic predictors of cross-cultural effectiveness, a recent review identified 73 different skills thought to predict managerial success in a cross-cultural context (Yamazaki & Kayes, 2004). These skills included a wide range of information, interpersonal, analytic, and behavioral skills. More than one cross-cultural trainer must have expressed concern about designing training processes focused on developing so many skills. The identification of the skills and abilities needed by global managers has focused on individual characteristics that were anecdotally reported to be associated with success (Hannigan, 1990), skills related to coping with the stress associated with working in or adjusting to a foreign culture (Black et al., 1991) or the development of cross-cultural skills (Hammer et al., 1978). The search for a universal skill set that is important to cross-cultural interactions is leading to the development of new models that predict intercultural effectiveness. They contain both general and culture-specific elements, but as opposed to concentrating on constituent elements, they focus on the ability to exhibit appropriate behavior. Examples of this type of model are Ting-Toomey's (1999) conceptualization of cross-cultural communication, models of cultural intelligence (e.g., Earley, 2002; Earley & Ang, 2003; Thomas, 2006; Thomas & Inkson, 2004), and the cognitive complexity that results from multicultural experience (Leung, Maddox, Galinsksy & Chiu, 2008; Tadmor & Tetlock, 2006; Tadmor, Hong, Chao, Wiruchnipawan, & Wang, 2012). They focus on how culture-specific experiences can be converted into general cognitive skills that can then be applied to new cross-cultural structures. The central component is provided by an analytic ability, variously called mindfulness, cultural metacognition, or integrative complexity that accomplishes this task. These models shift the focus from specific skills to a culture-general skill. Additionally, in order to reflect the demands of the changing environment of global managers and their changing characteristics, the most ambitious of these models take a system perspective. In this case, the interaction of various skills and abilities, facilitated by higher-level cognitive functions, results in the emergence of a unique ability that is not tied to a specific culture (see Thomas, Stahl, Ravlin, Perkerti, Maznevski, et al., 2006). The utility of these models in developing the cross-cultural skills needed by the global managers of the future awaits further development.

Biculturals

Cross-cultural management research typically assumes that individuals have only one cultural profile. However, given the changing patterns in the world's workforce, it is increasingly possible that more employees and managers will be bicultural. Biculturals have a dual pattern of identification, not with different organizational units, as discussed previously, but with different cultures. Bicultural individuals have a simultaneous awareness of being a member of (and sometimes an alien in) two cultures (LaFromboise, Coleman, & Gerton, 1993). They have more cognitively complex cultural representations than do monoculturals (Benet-Martínez, Lee, & Leu, 2006). Although it was once thought that individuals had to give up their identity with one culture in order to identify with a new one, it is increasingly clear that people can gain competence in more than one culture without losing their old cultural identity or having to choose one culture over the other (LaFromboise et al., 1993).

The ability of biculturals to operate within both cultures as a native (Fu, Chiu, Morris, & Young, 2007) raises interesting questions for cross-cultural management. For example, can the subconscious and nonvolitional way in which biculturals learn a new culture (Devos, 2006) be applied to developing global managers? Do biculturals possess unique skills and abilities that allow them to function more effectively in global business environments? For example, are they better able to cope with the potentially conflicting organizational identities imposed by the multinational enterprise? Also, can the way in which biculturals shift from one cultural context to the other (called cultural frame switching [Hong, Morris, Chiu, & Benet-Martínez, 2000]) help us understand how global managers can choose from a repertoire of behaviors to adapt appropriately to the cultural context (Molinsky, 2007; 2013)? Do the different ways in which individuals experience their biculturalism lead to different personal, social, and task outcomes in organizations (Fitzsimmons, 2013). Although interest by psychologists in biculturals is growing rapidly, the current state of knowledge about bicultural individuals provides as many questions as answers for cross-cultural management. However, the understanding of these individuals holds promise for a better understanding of effective cross-cultural interactions in organizational settings.

Summary

Based on an observation of current trends, this chapter has outlined some of the future challenges that cross-cultural managers will face. First, the environment of business is changing as a result of the irreversible forces of globalization. These changes are many but include the uneven development in the world, the increased influence of economies in transition, the continued influence of information and communication technology, and the growing pressure on the natural environment. An important implication of these changes is that the individuals with whom future managers interact are going to be influenced by and derive their identity from different contexts than in the past. In response to this changing environment, organizations and individual managers will need to adapt. Issues with regard to this adaptation were framed with regard to our understanding of the context of management in the multinational enterprise, the future of the organization of work, and the development of global managers. Again, a recurring theme in understanding the adaptation necessary to be effective in cross-cultural contexts is that it is important to understand both the sources and outcomes of different cultural and social identities.

As suggested by the quote that opened this chapter, predicting the challenges of cross-cultural management in the future is fraught with problems. The trends observed today are influenced by a complex set of factors, a change in any one of which could set the future spiraling off in an unpredictable direction. However, one thing seems clear: The discontinuous rates of change in the legal, political, economic, and cultural aspects of the environment of international management will continue to highlight the need to understand its cross-cultural aspects for the foreseeable future.

Questions for Discussion

1. How is uneven economic development likely to affect international management?

2. What are the special characteristics of transition economies?

3. Describe the implications of the rapid advancements in information and communications technology.

4. How does a concern for the natural environment affect cross-cultural management?

5. How do changes in the global environment affect the MNO context? How will this influence the organization of work apart from MNOs?

6. What does the future hold for the development of global managers?

References

Abe, H., & Wiseman, R. L. (1983). A cross-cultural confirmation of the dimensions of intercultural effectiveness. *International Journal of Intercultural Relations, 7,* 53–67.

Abelson, R. P. (1981). Psychological status of the script concept. *American Psychologist, 36,* 715–729.

Abrahamson, E., & Fairchild, G. (1999). Management fashion: Lifecycles, triggers, and collective learning processes. *Administrative Science Quarterly, 44,* 708–740.

Adair, W. L., Weingart, L., & Brett, J. M. (2007). The timing and function of offers in U.S. and Japanese negotiations. *Journal of Applied Psychology, 94,* 1056–1068.

Adams, J. S. (1965). Inequity in social exchange. In L. Berkowitz (Ed.), *Advances in experimental social psychology* (Vol. 2, pp. 267–299). New York: Academic Press.

Adler, N. J. (1981). Re-entry: Managing cross-cultural transitions. *Group and Organization Studies, 6,* 341–356.

Adler, N. J. (1983). Cross-cultural management research: The ostrich and the trend. *Academy of Management Review, 8,* 226–232.

Adler, N. J. (1984). Women in international management: Where are they? *California Management Review, 26,* 78–89.

Adler, N. J. (1986). Do MBAs want international careers? *International Journal of Intercultural Relations, 10,* 277–300.

Adler, N. J. (1987). Pacific Basin managers: A *gaijin,* not a woman. *Human Resource Management, 26,* 169–191.

Adler, N. J. (1997). *International dimensions of organizational behavior* (3rd ed.). Cincinnati, OH: South-Western.

Ah Chong, L. M., & Thomas. D. C. (1997). Leadership perceptions in cross-cultural context: Pacific Islanders and Pakeha in New Zealand. *Leadership Quarterly, 8*(3), 275–293.

Aharoni, Y. (1994). How small firms can achieve competitive advantage in an interdependent world. In T. Agmon & R. Drobnick (Eds.), *Small firms in global competition* (pp. 9–18). New York: Oxford University Press.

Aiello, J. R., & Kolb, K. J. (1995). Electronic performance monitoring and social context: Impact on productivity and stress. *Journal of Applied Psychology, 80,* 339–353.

Albright, L., Malloy, T. E., Dong, Q., Kenny, D. A., & Fang, X. (1997). Cross-cultural consensus in personality judgments. *Journal of Personality and Social Psychology, 73,* 270–280.

Alderfer, C. P. (1977). Group and intergroup relations. In J. R. Hackman & J. L. Suttle (Eds.), *Improving life at work* (pp. 227–296). Santa Monica, CA: Goodyear.

Aldrich, H., & Herker, D. (1977). Boundary spanning roles and organizational structure. *Academy of Management Review, 2,* 217–230.

Alexashin, Y., & Blenkinsopp, J. (2005). Changes in Russian managerial values: A test of the convergence hypothesis. *International Journal of Human Resource Management, 16,* 427–444.

Ali, A. J. (1990). Management theory in a transitional society: The Arab's experience. *International Studies of Management and Organization, 20,* 7–35.

Al-Kubaisy, A. (1985). A model in the administrative development of Arab Gulf countries. *The Arab Gulf, 17*(2), 29–48.

Allen, R. S., Takeda, M., & White, C. S. (2005). Cross-cultural equity sensitivity: A test of differences between the United States and Japan. *Journal of Managerial Psychology, 20*(8), 641–662.

Allen, T. J., & Hauptman, O. (1990). The substitution of communications technology for organizational structure in research and development. In J. Fulk & C. Stenfield (Eds.), *Organizations and communication technology* (pp. 275–294). Newbury Park, CA: Sage.

Allport, G. W. (1954). *The nature of prejudice.* Reading, MA: Addison-Wesley.

Almaney, A., & Ahwan, A. (1982). *Communicating with the Arabs.* Prospect Heights, IL: Waveland.

Alvesson, M. (2011). Organizational culture: Meaning, discourse and identity. In N. M. Ashkanasy, C. P. M. Wilderom, & M. F. Peterson (Eds.), *Handbook of Organizational Culture and Climate* (2nd ed.). Thousand Oaks, CA: Sage, pp. 11–28.

Al-Zahrani, S. S. A., & Kaplowitz, S. A. (1993). Attributional biases in individualist and collectivists cultures: A comparison of Americans with Saudis. *Social Psychology Quarterly, 56,* 223–233.

Andersen, P. A., & Bowman, L. (1985). *Positions of power: Nonverbal cues of status and dominance in organizational communication.* Paper presented at the annual convention of the International Communication Association, Honolulu, HI.

Anderson, B. A. (2005). Expatriate selection: Good management or good luck? *International Journal of Human Resource Management, 16,* 567–583.

Antal, A. B., & Izraeli, D. (1993). A global comparison of women in management: Women managers in their homelands and as expatriates. In E. A. Gagenson (Ed.), *Women in management: Trends, issues, and challenges in managerial diversity* (Vol. 4, pp. 206–223). Newbury Park, CA: Sage.

Argyle, M. (1988). *Bodily communication* (2nd ed.). London: Methuen.

Argyris, C. (1972). *The applicability of organizational sociology.* Cambridge UK: Cambridge University Press.

Aronoff, J., Woike, B. A., & Hyman, L. M. (1992). Which are the stimuli in facial displays of anger and happiness? *Journal of Personality and Social Psychology, 62,* 1050–1066.

Arrow, H., & McGrath, J. E. (1995). Membership dynamics in groups at work: A theoretical framework. *Research in Organizational Behavior, 17,* 373–411.

Arthur, M. B., & Rousseau, D. M. (Eds.). (1996). *The boundaryless career: A new employment principle for a new organizational era.* Boston: Cambridge University Press.

Arthur, W., & Bennett, W. (1995). The international assignee: The relative importance of factors perceived to contribute to success. *Personnel Psychology, 48,* 99–114.

Asch, S. (1951). Effects of group pressure on the modification and distortion of judgments. In H. Guetzkow (Ed.), *Groups, leadership and men* (pp. 177–190). Pittsburgh: Carnegie.

Ashmore, R. D., & Del Boca, F. K. (1981). Conceptual approaches to stereotypes and stereotyping. In D. L. Hamilton (Ed.), *Cognitive processes in stereotyping and intergroup behavior* (pp. 1–35). Hillsdale, NJ: Lawrence Erlbaum.

Astley, W. G., & Van de Ven, A. H. (1983). Central perspectives and debates in organization theory. *Administrative Science Quarterly, 28,* 245–273.

Au, K. Y. (1999). Intra-cultural variation: Evidence and implications for international business. *Journal of International Business Studies, 30,* 799–812.

Avolio, B. J., & Gardner, W. L. (2005). Authentic leadership development: Getting to the root of positive forms of leadership. *Leadership Quarterly, 16,* 315–338.

Aycan, Z. (2006). Paternalism: Towards conceptual refinement and operationalization. In K. S. Yang, K. K. Hwang, & U. Kim (Eds.), *Scientific advances in indigenous psychologies:*

Empirical, philosophical, and cultural contributions (pp. 445–466). London: Cambridge University Press.

Aycan, Z. (2008). Cross-cultural approaches to leadership. In P. B. Smith, M. F. Peterson, & D. C. Thomas (Eds.), *Handbook of cross-cultural management research* (pp. 219–238). Thousand Oaks, CA: Sage.

Ayman, R., & Chemers, M. M. (1983). Relationship of supervisory behavior ratings to work group effectiveness and subordinate satisfaction among Iranian managers. *Journal of Applied Psychology, 68*(2), 338–341.

Ayman, R., & Chemers, M. M. (1991). The effect of leadership match on subordinate satisfaction in Mexican organizations: Some moderating influences of self-monitoring. *Applied Psychology: An International Review, 40*(3), 299–314.

Ayoko, B. O., Hartel, C. E., & Callan, V. J. (2002). Resolving the puzzle of productive and destructive conflict in culturally heterogeneous workgroups: A communication accommodation theory approach. *International Journal of Conflict Management, 13*, 165–195.

Azumi, K., & McMillan, C. J. (1975). Culture and organization structure: A comparison of Japanese and British organizations. *International Studies of Management and Organization, 5*(1), 35–47.

Baba, M. L., Gluesing, J., Ratner, H., & Wagner, K. H. (2004). The contexts of knowing: Natural history of a globally distributed team. *Journal of Organizational Behavior, 25*, 547–587.

Bagby, J. (1957). Dominance in binocular rivalry in Mexico and the United States. *Journal of Abnormal and Social Psychology, 54*, 331–334.

Baliga, B. R., & Jaeger, A. M. (1984). Multinational corporations: Control systems and delegation issues. *Journal of International Business Studies, 15*(3), 25–40.

Bandura, A. (1977). *Social learning theory.* Englewood Cliffs, NJ: Prentice Hall.

Barkema, H. G., Bell, J. H. J., & Pennings, J. M. (1996). Foreign entry, cultural barriers, and learning. *Strategic Management Journal, 17*, 151–166.

Barlow, C. (1991). Tikanga whakaaro: *Key concepts in Maori culture.* Auckland, NZ: Oxford University Press.

Barnlund, D. C., & Araki, S. (1985). Intercultural encounters: The management of compliments by Japanese and Americans. *Journal of Cross-Cultural Psychology, 16*, 9–26.

Baron, J., & Miller, J. G. (2000). Limiting the scope of moral obligations to help: A cross-cultural investigation. *Journal of Cross-Cultural Psychology, 31*(6), 703–725.

Barraclough, R. A., Christophel, D. M., & McCroskey, J. C. (1988). Willingness to communicate: A cross-cultural investigation. *Communication Research Reports, 5*, 187–192.

Barrett, D. B., Kurian, G. T., & Johnson, T. M. (Eds.). (2001). *World Christian encyclopedia: A comparative survey of churches and religions.* New York: Oxford University Press.

Barry, D. (1991). Managing the bossless team: Lessons in distributed leadership. *Organizational Dynamics, 21*(1), 31–47.

Bartlett, C. (1986). Building and managing the transnational: The new organizational challenge. In M. Porter (Ed.), *Competition in global industries* (pp. 367–401). Boston: Harvard Business School Press.

Bartlett, C. A., & Ghoshal, S. (1989). *Managing across borders: The transnational solution.* Boston: Harvard Business School Press.

Bass, B. M. (1985). *Leadership and performance beyond expectation.* New York: Free Press.

Bass, B. M. (1990). *Bass and Stogdill's handbook of leadership: Theory, research and managerial applications* (3rd ed.). New York: Free Press.

Bass, B. M. (1991). *Is there universality in the full range model of leadership?* Paper presented at the National Academy of Management annual meeting, Miami, FL.

Bass, B., & Yokochi, N. (1991). Charisma among senior executives and the special case of Japanese CEOs. *Consulting Psychology Bulletin, 1*, 31–38.

Bass, B. M., Burger, P. C., Doktor, R., & Barrett, G. V. (1979). *Assessment of managers: An international comparison.* New York: Free Press.

Bassili, J. N. (2003). The minority slowness effect: Subtle inhibitions in the expression of views not shared by others. *Journal of Personality and Social Psychology, 84*(2), 261–276.

Bazerman, M. (1998). *Judgment in managerial decision making* (4th ed.). New York: John Wiley & Sons.

Beamish, P. B., & Killing, J. P. (Eds.). (1997). *Cooperative strategies.* San Francisco: New Lexington Press.

Beaver, W. (1995, March–April). Levis is leaving China. *Business Horizons,* pp. 35–40.

Beechler, S. (1992, November). International management control in multinational corporations: The case of Japanese consumer electronics firms in Asia. *OECD Economic Journal,* pp. 20–31.

Beechler, S. L., & Iaquinto, A. L. (1994). *A longitudinal study of staffing patterns in U.S. affiliates of Japanese transnational corporations.* Paper presented to the International Management Division of the Academy of Management, Dallas.

Beechler, S. L., & Pucik, V. (1989). The diffusion of American organizational theory in post war Japan. In C. A. B. Osigweh (Ed.), *Organizational science abroad: Constraints and perspectives* (pp. 119–134). New York: Plenum.

Bell, B. S., & Kozlowski, S. W. J. (2000). A typology of virtual teams. *Group & Organization Management, 27,* 14–49.

Bell, D. (1973). *The coming of post-industrial society.* New York: Basic Books.

Benet-Martínez, V., Lee, F., & Leu, J. (2006). Biculturalism and cognitive complexity: Expertise in cultural representations. *Journal of Cross-Cultural Psychology, 37,* 386–407.

Bennett, M. (1977). Testing management theories cross-culturally. *Journal of Applied Psychology, 62*(5), 578–581.

Bennis, W. (1984). The 4 competencies of leadership. *Training & Development Journal, 38*(8), 14–19.

Benson, P. G. (1978). Measuring cross-cultural adjustment: The problem of criteria. *International Journal of Intercultural Relations, 2*(1), 21–37.

Berger, P. L., & Luckman, T. (1966). *The social construction of reality: A treatise in the sociology of knowledge.* Garden City, NY: Doubleday.

Berlo, D. K. (1960). *The process of communication.* New York: Holt, Rinehart & Winston.

Berman, J. J., Murphy-Berman, V., & Singh, P. (1985). Cross-cultural similarities and differences in perceptions of fairness. *Journal of Cross-Cultural Psychology, 16,* 55–67.

Berry, J. W. (1969). On cross-cultural comparability. *International Journal of Psychology, 4,* 119–128.

Berry, J. W. (1989). Imposed etics–emics–derived etics: The operationalization of a compelling idea. *International Journal of Psychology, 24,* 721–735.

Berry, J. W. (1990). The role of psychology in ethnic studies. *Canadian Ethnic Studies, 22,* 8–21.

Berry, J. W. (1997). Immigration, acculturation, and adaptation. *Applied Psychology: An International Review, 46,* 5–34.

Bettenhausen, K. L., & Murnighan, J. K. (1991). The development of an intragroup norm and the effects of interpersonal and structural changes. *Administrative Science Quarterly, 36,* 20–35.

Bhagat, R. S., & McQuaid, S. J. (1982). Role of subjective culture in organizations: A review and directions for future research. *Journal of Applied Psychology, 67*(5), 653–685.

Bhagat, R. S., Kedia, B. L., Harveston, P. D., & Triandis, H. C. (2002). Cultural variations in the cross-border transfer of organizational knowledge: An integrative framework. *Academy of Management Review, 27,* 204–221.

Bhaskar-Shrinivas, P., Harrison, D. A., Shaffer, M. A., & Luk, D. M. (2005). Input-based and time-based models of international adjustment: Meta-analytic evidence and theoretical extensions. *Academy of Management Journal, 48*, 257–281.

Bhawuk, D. P. S., & Brislin, R. W. (1992). The measurement of intercultural sensitivity using the concepts of individualism and collectivism. *International Journal of Intercultural Relations, 16*, 413–436.

Bird, F., & Smucker, J. (2007). The social responsibilities of international business firms in developing areas. *Journal of Business Ethics, 73*, 1–9.

Birdseye, M., & Hill, J. S. (1995). Individual, organizational, and environmental influences on expatriate turnover tendencies: An empirical study. *Journal of International Business Studies, 26*, 787–813.

Birkenshaw, J., Nobel, R., & Ridderstråle, J. (2002). Knowledge as a contingency variable: Do the characteristics of knowledge predict organization structure? *Organization Science, 13*, 274–289.

Black, J. S. (1988). Work role transitions: A study of American expatriate managers in Japan. *Journal of International Business Studies, 19*, 277–294.

Black, J. S. (1990). Locus of control, social support, stress and adjustment in international transfers. *Asia Pacific Journal of Management, 7*, 1–29.

Black, J. S. (1994). *O Kaerinasai:* Factors related to Japanese repatriation adjustment. *Human Relations, 47*(12), 1489–1508.

Black, J. S., & Gregersen, H. B. (1990). Expectations, satisfaction and intention to leave of American expatriate managers in Japan. *International Journal of Intercultural Relations, 14*, 485–506.

Black, J. S., & Gregersen, H. B. (1991a). Antecedents to cross-cultural adjustment for expatriates in Pacific Rim assignments. *Human Relations, 44*, 497–515.

Black, J. S., & Gregersen, H. B. (1991b). When Yankee comes home: Factors related to expatriate and spouse repatriation adjustment. *Journal of International Business Studies, 21*(4), 671–694.

Black, J. S., & Mendenhall, M. (1989). A practical but theory-based framework for selecting cross-cultural training methods. *Human Resource Management, 28*, 511–539.

Black, J. S., & Mendenhall, M. (1990). Cross-cultural training effectiveness: A review and a theoretical framework for future research. *Academy of Management Review, 15*(1), 113–136.

Black, J. S., & Mendenhall, M. (1991). The U-curve adjustment hypothesis revisited: A review and theoretical framework. *Journal of International Business Studies, 22*, 225–247.

Black, J. S., Gregersen, H. B., & Mendenhall, M. E. (1992). Toward a theoretical framework of repatriation adjustment. *Journal of International Business Studies, 22*, 737–760.

Black, J. S., Mendenhall, M., & Oddou, G. (1991). Toward a comprehensive model of international adjustment: An integration of multiple theoretical perspectives. *Academy of Management Review, 16*, 291–317.

Blau, P. M. (1970). A formal theory of differentiation in organizations. *American Sociological Review, 35*, 201–218.

Blau, P. M., & Schoenherr, R. A. (1971). *The structure of organizations.* New York: Basic Books.

Bochner, S., & Ohsako, T. (1977). Ethnic role salience in racially homogeneous and heterogeneous societies. *Journal of Cross-Cultural Psychology, 8*, 477–492.

Bochner, S., & Perks, R. W. (1971). National role evocation as a function of cross-national interaction. *Journal of Cross-Cultural Psychology, 2*, 157–164.

Boisot, M., & Xing, G. L. (1992). The nature of managerial work in the Chinese enterprise reforms: A study of six directors. *Organization Studies, 13*(2), 161–184.

Bolino, M. C., & Turnley, W. H. (2008). Old faces, new places: Equity theory in cross-cultural contexts. *Journal of Organizational Behavior, 29*, 29–50.

Bond, M. H. (1985). Language as a carrier of ethnic stereotypes in Hong Kong. *Journal of Social Psychology, 125,* 53–62.

Bond, M. H., & Hwang, K. K. (1986). *The psychology of the Chinese people.* Hong Kong: Oxford University Press.

Bond, M. H., & King, A. Y. C. (1986). The social psychology of the Chinese people. In M. H. Bond (Ed.), *The psychology of the Chinese people* (pp. 213–264). Hong Kong: Oxford University Press.

Bond, M. H., & Yang, K. S. (1982). Ethnic affirmation versus cross-cultural accommodation: The variable impact of questionnaire language on Chinese bilinguals in Hong Kong. *Journal of Cross-Cultural Psychology, 12,* 169–181.

Bond, M. H., Leung, K., & Schwartz, S. (1992). Explaining choices in procedural and distributive justice across cultures. *International Journal of Psychology, 27*(2), 211–225.

Bond, M. H., Leung, K., Au, A., Tong, K.-K., de Carrasquel, S. R., Murakami, F., et al. (2004). Culture-level dimensions of social axioms and their correlates across 41 cultures. *Journal of Cross-Cultural Psychology, 35,* 548–570.

Bontempo, R., Lobel, S. A., & Triandis, H. C. (1990). Compliance and value internalization in Brazil and the U.S.: Effects of allocentrism and anonymity. *Journal of Cross-Cultural Psychology, 21,* 200–213.

Bonvillian, N. (1993). *Language, culture and communication: The meaning of messages.* Englewood Cliffs, NJ: Prentice Hall.

Borchert, D., & Stewart, E. (1986). *Exploring ethics.* New York: Macmillan.

Bormann, W. A. (1968). The problem with expatriate personnel and their selection in international enterprises. *Management International Review, 8*(4–5), 37–48.

Boski, P. (1991). Remaining a Pole or becoming a Canadian: National self-identity among Polish immigrants to Canada. *Journal of Applied Social Psychology, 21*(1), 41–77.

Boswell, W. R., Olson-Buchanan, J. B., & LePine, M. A. (2004). Relations between stress and work outcomes: The role of felt challenge, job control, and psychological strain. *Journal of Vocational Behavior, 64,* 165–181.

Bourhis, R. Y., Giles, H., Leyens, J. P., & Tajfel, H. (1979). Psycholinguistic distinctiveness: Language divergence in Belgium. In H. Giles & R. N. St. Clair (Eds.), *Language and social psychology.* Baltimore: University Park Press.

Bowers, D. G., & Seashore, S. E. (1966). Predicting organizational effectiveness with a four factor theory of leadership. *Administrative Science Quarterly, 11,* 238–263.

Boyacigiller, N. (1990). The role of expatriates in the management of interdependence, complexity and risk in multinational corporations. *Journal of International Business Studies, 21,* 357–381.

Boyacigiller, N. A., & Adler, N. J. (1991). The parochial dinosaur: Organizational science in a global context. *Academy of Management Review, 16*(2), 262–290.

Brannen, M. Y. (2004). When Mickey loses face: Recontextualization, semantic fit, and the semiotics of foreignness. *Academy of Management Review, 29,* 593–616.

Brannen, M. Y., & Peterson, M. F. (2009). Merging without alienating: Interventions promoting cross-cultural organizational integration and their limitations. *Journal of International Business Studies, 40*(3), 468–490.

Brein, D., & David, K. H. (1971). Intercultural communication and the adjustment of the sojourner. *Psychological Bulletin, 76,* 215–230.

Brenner, S. N., & Molander, E. A. (1977). Is the ethics of business changing? *Harvard Business Review, 55*(1), 57–71.

Brett, J., & Crotty, S. (2008). Culture and negotiation. In P. B. Smith, M. F. Peterson, & D. C. Thomas (Eds.), *Handbook of cross-cultural management research* (pp. 269–284). Thousand Oaks, CA: Sage.

Brett, J. M. (2001). *Negotiating globally*. San Francisco: Jossey-Bass.

Brett, J. M. (2007). *Negotiating globally*, 2nd ed. San Francisco: Jossey-Bass.

Brett, J. M., & Gelfand, M. J. (2006). A cultural analysis of the underlying assumptions of negotiation theory. In L. L. Thompson (Ed.), *Negotiation theory and research* (pp. 173–201). New York: Psychology Press.

Brett, J. M., & Okumura, T. (1998). Inter- and intracultural negotiation: U.S. and Japanese negotiators. *Academy of Management Journal, 41,* 495–510.

Brett, J. M., Stroh, L. K., & Reilly, A. H. (1993). Pulling up roots in the 1990s: Who's willing to relocate? *Journal of Organizational Behavior, 14,* 49–60.

Brett, J. M., Tinsley, C. H., Shapiro, D. L., & Okumura, T. (2007). Intervening in employee disputes: How and when will managers from China, Japan, and the U.S. act differently? *Management & Organization Review, 3*(2), 183–204.

Briody, E. K., & Chrisman, J. B. (1991). Cultural adaptation on overseas assignments. *Human Organization, 50*(3), 264–282.

Brislin, R. W. (1993). *Understanding cultures influence on behavior*. Fort Worth, TX: Harcourt Brace Jovanovich.

Brislin, R., MacNab, B., & Nayani, F. (2008). Cross-cultural training: Applications and research. In P. B. Smith, M. F. Peterson, & D. C. Thomas (Eds.), *Handbook of cross-cultural management research* (pp. 397–410). Thousand Oaks, CA: Sage.

Brouthers, K. D., & Bamossy, G. J. (2006). Post-formation processes in Eastern and Western European joint-ventures. *Journal of Management Studies, 43*(2), 203–229.

Brown, M. E., Treviño, L. K., & Harrison, D. A. (2005). Ethical leadership: A social learning theory perspective for construct development. *Organizational Behavior and Human Decision Processes, 97*(2), 117–134.

Bryant, J., & Law, D. (2004). *New Zealand's diaspora and overseas born population*. New Zealand Treasury Working Paper 04/13, Wellington, New Zealand.

Buck, S. (1998). *The global commons: An introduction*. Washington, DC: Island Press.

Bulmer, M., & Warwick, D. P. (1983). *Social research in developing countries*. New York: John Wiley & Sons.

Bunce, D., & West, M. A. (1995). Self perceptions and perceptions of group climate as predictors of individual innovation at work. *Applied Psychology: An International Review, 44*(3), 199–215.

Burns, T. (1978). *Leadership*. New York: Harper & Row.

Burns, T., & Stalker, C. M. (1961). *The management of innovation*. London: Tavistock.

Burris, C. T., Branscombe, N. R., & Jackson, L. M. (2000). For god and country: Religion and the endorsement of national self-stereotypes. *Journal of Cross-Cultural Psychology, 31*(4), 517–527.

Byrne, D. (1971). *The attraction paradigm*. New York: Academic Press.

Cairncross, F. (2001). *The death of distance*. Boston: Harvard Business School Press.

Caligiuri, P. (1997). Assessing expatriate success: Beyond just "being there." *New Approaches to Employee Management, 4,* 117–140.

Caligiuri, P., & Lazarova, M. (2002). A model for the influence of social interaction and social support on female expatriates' cross-cultural adjustment. *International Journal of Human Resource Management, 13,* 761–772.

Caligiuri, P., Phillips, J., Lazarova, M., Tarique, I., & Bürgi, P. (2001). The theory of met expectations applied to expatriate adjustment: The role of cross-cultural training. *International Journal of Human Resource Management, 12,* 357–372.

Caligiuri, P. M. (2000). The big five personality characteristics as predictors of expatriate's desire to terminate the assignment and supervisor-rated performance. *Personnel Psychology, 53,* 67–88.

Caligiuri, P. M., & Tung, R. L. (1999). Comparing the success of male and female expatriates from a US-based multinational company. *International Journal of Human Resource Management, 10,* 763–782.

Caligiuri, P. M., Joshi, A., & Lazarova, M. B. (1999). Factors influencing the adjustment of women on international assignment. *International Journal of Human Resource Management, 10,* 163–179.

Calori, R., Lubatkin, M., & Very, P. (1994). Control mechanism in cross-border acquisitions: An international comparison. *Organization Studies, 15*(3), 361–379.

Campion, M. A., Medsker, G. J., & Higgs, A. C. (1993). Relations between work group characteristics and effectiveness: Implications for designing effective work groups. *Personnel Psychology, 46,* 823–850.

Canella, A. A., Park, J., & Lee, H. (2008). Top management team functional background diversity and firm performance: Examining the roles of team member colocation and environmental uncertainty. *Academy of Management Journal, 51,* 768–784.

Carr, S. C., Inkson, K., & Thorn, K. (2005). From global careers to talent flow: Reinterpreting "brain drain." *Journal of World Business, 40,* 386–398.

Carte, T., & Chidambaram, L. (2004). A capabilities-based theory of technology deployment in diverse teams: Leapfrogging the pitfalls of diversity and leveraging its benefits with collaborative technology. *Journal of the Association for Information Systems, 5*(11–12), 448–471.

Cartwright, D., & Zander, A. (1968). Leadership and performance of group functions: Introduction. In D. Cartwright & A. Zander (Eds.), *Group dynamics: Theory and research* (3rd ed., pp. 301–307). New York: Harper and Row.

Cascio, W. F. (2000). Managing a virtual workplace. *Academy of Management Executive, 14,* 81–90.

Chan, D. K., Gelfand, M. L., Triandis, H. C., & Tzeng, O. (1996). Tightness and looseness revisited: Some preliminary analysis in Japan and the United States. *International Journal of Psychology, 31,* 1–12.

Chandler, A. D., Jr. (1962). *Strategy and structures: Chapters in the history of the industrial enterprise.* Cambridge: MIT Press.

Chattopadhyay, P., George, E., & Lawrence, S. A. (2004). Why does dissimilarity matter? Exploring self-categorization, self-enhancement, and uncertainty reduction. *Journal of Applied Psychology, 89,* 892–900.

Chen, C. C. (1995). New trends in reward allocation preferences: A Sino–U.S. comparison. *Academy of Management Journal, 38,* 408–428.

Chen, C. C., Chen, Y. R., & Xin, K. R. (2004). *Guanxi* practices and trust in management: A procedural justice perspective. *Organization Science, 15,* 200–209.

Chen, C., Meindl, J. R., & Hunt, R. (1997). Test effects of horizontal and vertical collectivism: A study of rewards allocation preferences in China. *Journal of Cross-Cultural Psychology, 28,* 44–70.

Chen, M. (1995). *Asian management systems: Chinese, Japanese, and Korean styles of business.* New York: Routledge.

Chidambaram, L. (1996). Relational development in computer-supported groups. *MIS Quarterly, 20,* 143–165.

Child, J. (1974, Summer). What determines organizational performance? The universals vs. the it all depends. *Organizational Dynamics, 3*(1), 2–18.

Child, J. (1981). Culture, contingency and capitalism in the cross-national study of organizations. In L. L. Cummings & B. M. Staw (Eds.), *Research in organizational behavior* (Vol. 3, pp. 303–365). Greenwich, CT: JAI.

Child, J., & Kieser, A. (1979). Organization and managerial roles in British and West German companies. In C. J. Lammers & D. J. Hickson (Eds.), *Organizations are alike and unlike* (pp. 251–271). London: Routledge and Kegan Paul.

Child, J., & Markóczy, L. (1993). Host-country managerial behavior and learning in Chinese and Hungarian joint ventures. *Journal of Management Studies, 4,* 611–631.

Child, J., & Tse, D. K. (2001). China's transition and its implication for international business. *Journal of International Business Studies, 32,* 5–21.

Child, J., Faulkner, D., & Pitkethly, R. (2001). *The management of international acquisitions.* Oxford, UK: Oxford University Press.

Chinese Culture Connection. (1987). Chinese values and the search for culture free dimensions of culture. *Journal of Cross-Cultural Psychology, 18*(2), 143–164.

Choi, I., & Nisbett, R. E. (2000). Cultural psychology of surprise: Holistic theories and recognition of contradiction. *Journal of Personality and Social Psychology, 79,* 890–905.

Choi, I., Dalal, R., Kim-Prieto, C., & Park, H. (2003). Culture and judgment of causal relevance. *Journal of Personality and Social Psychology, 84,* 46–59.

Choi, I., Nisbett, R. E., & Norenzayan, A. (1999). Causal attribution across cultures: Variation and universality. *Psychological Bulletin, 125,* 47–63.

Choran, I. (1969). *The manager of a small company.* (Unpublished master's thesis). McGill University, Montreal.

Christie, P. M. J., Kwon, I. W. G., Stoeberl, P. A., & Baumhart, R. (2003). A cross-cultural comparison of ethical attitudes of business managers: India, Korea and the United States. *Journal of Business Ethics, 46,* 263–287.

Chudoba, K. M., Wynn, E., Lu, M., & Watson-Manheim, M. B. (2005). How virtual are we? Measuring virtuality and understanding its impact in a global organization. *Information Systems Journal, 15,* 279–306.

Chung, K. H., & Lee, H. C. (1989). *Korean managerial dynamics.* Westport, CT: Greenwood.

Chung, K. H., Lee, H. C., & Jung, K. H. (1997). *Korean management: Global strategy and cultural transformation.* Berlin: de Gruyter.

Church, A. T. (1982). Sojourner adjustment. *Psychological Bulletin, 91*(3), 540–572.

Churchman, C. W. (1968). *The systems approach.* New York: Dell.

Chusmir, L. H., & Frontczak, N. T. (1990). International management opportunities for women: Women and men paint different pictures. *International Journal of Management, 7*(3), 295–301.

Clark, H. H., & Brennan, S. E. (1991). *Grounding in communication: Perspectives on socially shared communication.* Washington, DC: American Psychological Association.

Clarke, C., & Hammer, M. R. (1995). Predictors of Japanese and American managers job success, personal adjustment, and intercultural interaction effectiveness. *Management International Review, 35*(2), 153–170.

Cleveland, H., Mangone, G., & Adams, J. C. (1960). *The overseas Americans.* New York: McGraw-Hill.

Cohen, D. (2001). Cultural variation: Considerations and implications. *Psychological Bulletin, 127,* 451–471.

Colby, A., & Kohlberg, L. (1987). *The measurement of moral judgment.* Cambridge, MA: Cambridge University Press.

Colby, A., Kohlberg, L., Gibbs, J. C., & Lieberman, M. (1983). A longitudinal study of moral development. *Monographs of the Society for Research in Child Development, 48,* 1–124.

Cole, R. E. (1980). *Work, mobility, and participation: A comparative study of American and Japanese industry.* Berkeley: University of California Press.

Condon, J., & Yousef, F. (1975). *An introduction to intercultural communication.* Indianapolis: Bobbs-Merrill.

Conger, J. A., & Kanungo, R. (1987). Toward a behavioral theory of charismatic leadership in organizational settings. *Academy of Management Review, 12*, 637–647.

Conger, J. A., & Kanungo, R. (1988). *Charismatic leadership: The elusive factor in organizational effectiveness.* San Francisco: Jossey-Bass.

Cooke, R. A., & Szumal, J. L. (1993). Measuring shared beliefs and shared behavioral expectations in organizations: The reliability and validity of the Organizational Culture Inventory. *Psychological Reports, 72*, 1299–1330.

Cooke, R. A., & Szumal, J. L. (2000). Using the organizational culture inventory to understand the operating cultures of organizations. In N. M. Ashkanasy, C. P. M. Wilderom, & M. F. Peterson (Eds.), *Handbook of Organizational Culture and Climate* (pp. 147–162). Thousand Oaks, CA: Sage.

Cooper, D., Doucet, L., & Pratt, M. (2007). Understanding "appropriateness" in multinational organizations. *Journal of Organizational Behavior, 28,* 303–325.

Cox, T. (1993). *Cultural diversity in organizations: Theory, research & practice.* San Francisco: Berrett-Koehler.

Cui, C., Ball, D. F., & Coyne, J. (2002). Working effectively in strategic alliances through managerial fit between partners: Some evidence from Sino-British joint ventures and the implications for R & D professionals. *R & D Management, 32*(4), 343–357.

Cullen, J. B. (1999). *Multinational management: A strategic approach.* Cincinnati, OH: South-Western.

Cummings, T. G. (1978). Self-regulating work groups: A sociotechnical synthesis. *Academy of Management Review, 3*, 625–634.

Cushner, K., & Brislin, R. W. (1996). *Intercultural interactions: A practical guide.* Thousand Oaks, CA: Sage.

Dacin, M. T., Hitt, M. A., & Levitas, E. (1997). Selecting partners for successful international alliances: Examination of US and Korean firms. *Journal of World Business, 32*(1), 3–15.

D'Andrade, R. (1989). Cultural cognition. In M. I. Posner (Ed.), *Foundations of cognitive science* (pp. 795–830). Cambridge: MIT Press.

Daniels, J. D., & Radebaugh, L. H. (1998). *International business: Environments and operations* (8th ed.). Reading, MA: Addison-Wesley.

Darley, J. M., & Fazio, R. H. (1980). Expectancy confirmation processes arising in the social interaction sequence. *American Psychologist, 35*, 867–881.

Davidson, M., & Cooper, G. (1987). Female managers in Britain: A comparative perspective. *Human Resource Management, 26*(2), 217–242.

Davis, F. (1971). *Inside intuition: What we know about nonverbal communication.* New York: McGraw-Hill.

Davis, M. A., Johnson, N. B., & Ohmer, D. G. (1998). Issue-contingent effects on ethical decision making: A cross-cultural comparison. *Journal of Business Ethics, 17*, 373–389.

Davis, S. M. (1992). Managing and organizing multinational corporations. In C. A. Bartlett & S. Ghoshal (Eds.), *Transnational management* (pp. 607–620). Homewood, IL: Richard D. Irwin.

Dawes, R. M. (1980). Social dilemmas. *Annual Review of Psychology, 31,* 169–193.

Dawes, R. M. (1988). *Rational choice in an uncertain world.* New York: Harcourt Brace.

Dearborn, D. C., & Simon, H. A. (1958, June). Selective perception: A note on the departmental identification of executives. *Sociometry, 21*(2), 140–144.

DeCieri, H., Dowling, P. J., & Taylor, K. F. (1991). The psychological impact of expatriate relocation on partners. *International Journal of Human Resource Management, 2*(3), 377–414.

Dedoussis, E. (2004). A cross-cultural comparison of organizational cultures: Evidence from universities in the Arab world and Japan. *Cross-Cultural Management, 11*(1), 15–34.

Delios, A., & Björkman, I. (2000). Expatriate staffing in foreign subsidiaries of Japanese multinational corporations in the PRC and the United States. *International Journal of Human Resource Management, 11*(2), 278–293.

DeMeyer, A. (1993). Management of an international network of industrial R & D laboratories. *R & D Management, 23,* 109–120.

Den Hartog, D. N., Van Muijen, J. J., & Koopman, P. L. (1994, July). *Transactional versus transformational leadership: An analysis of the MLQ in the Netherlands.* Paper presented at the 23rd International Congress of Applied Psychology, Madrid, Spain.

Denison, D. R., Haaland, S., & Goelzer, P. (2004). Corporate culture and organizational effectiveness: Is Asia different from the rest of the world? *Organizational Dynamics, 33*(1), 98–109.

Denison, D., Xin, K., Guidroz, A. M., & Zhang, L. (2011). Corporate culture in Chinese organizations. In N. M. Ashkanasy, C. P. M. Wilderom, & M. F. Peterson (Eds.), *Handbook of Organizational Culture and Climate* (2nd ed., pp. 561–681). Thousand Oaks, CA: Sage.

DePaulo, B. M. (1992). Nonverbal behavior and self-presentation. *Psychological Bulletin, 111,* 230–243.

Deresky, H. (2006). *International management: Managing across borders and cultures.* Upper Saddle River, NJ: Pearson.

Der-Karabetian, A. (1992). World-mindedness and the nuclear threat: A multinational study. *Journal of Social Behavior and Personality, 7,* 293–308.

Desai, M., Fukuda-Parr, S., Johansson, C., & Sagasti, F. (2002). Measuring the technology achievement of nations and the capacity to participate in the network age. *Journal of Human Development, 3*(1), 95–122.

Deshpande, S. P., & Viswesvaran, C. (1992). Is cross-cultural training of expatriate managers effective: A meta-analysis. *International Journal of Intercultural Relations, 16,* 295–310.

Deutsch, M. (1975). Equity, equality, and need: What determines which value will be used as the basis of distributive justice? *Journal of Social Issues, 31,* 137–149.

Devos, T. (2006). Implicit bi-cultural identity among Mexican American and Asian American college students. *Cultural Diversity and Ethnic Minority Psychology, 12,* 381–402.

Diabiase, R., & Gunnoe, J. (2004). Gender and culture differences in touching behavior. *Journal of Social Psychology, 144,* 49–62.

Dickson, M. W., Castaño, N., Magomaeva, A., & Den Hartog, D. N. (2012). Conceptualizing leadership across cultures. *Journal of World Business, 47,* 483–492.

Dill, W. R. (1958). Environment as an influence on managerial autonomy. *Administrative Science Quarterly, 2,* 409–443.

DiMaggio, P. J., & Powell, W. W. (1983). The iron cage revisited: Institutional isomorphism and collective rationality in organizational fields. *American Sociological Review, 48,* 147–160.

Doi, T. (1973). *The anatomy of dependence.* New York: Harper & Row.

Doi, T. (1986). *The anatomy of self: The individual versus society.* Tokyo: Kodansha.

Doktor, R. H. (1990). Asian and American CEOs: A comparative study. *Organizational Dynamics, 19*(3), 46–56.

Doktor, R. H., Tung, R., & Von Glinow, M. (1991). Incorporating international dimensions in management theory building. *Academy of Management Review, 16*(2), 259–261.

Donaldson, L. (1986). Size and bureaucracy in East and West: A preliminary meta-analysis. In S. Clegg, D. C. Dunphy, & S. G. Redding (Eds.), *The enterprise and management in South-East Asia.* Hong Kong: Hong Kong University Centre for Asian Studies.

Donaldson, T. (1989). *The ethics of international business.* New York: Oxford University Press.

Donaldson, T. (1993). When in Rome, do . . . what? International business and cultural relativism. In P. M. Minus (Ed.), *The ethics of business in a global economy* (pp. 67–78). Boston: Kluwer Academic.

Donaldson, L. (2001). *The contingency theory of organizations.* Thousand Oaks, CA: Sage.

Donaldson, T., & Dunfee, T. W. (1994). Towards a unified conception of business ethics: Integrative social contracts theory. *Academy of Management Review, 19,* 252–284.

Doney, P. M., Cannon, J. P., & Mullen, M. R. (1998). Understanding the influence of national culture on the development of trust. *Academy of Management Review, 23,* 601–620.

Dorfman, P. W. (1996). International and cross-cultural leadership. In J. Punnitt & O. Shenkar (Eds.), *Handbook for international management research* (pp. 276–349). Cambridge, MA: Blackwell.

Dorfman, P. W. (2004). International and cross-cultural leadership research. In B. J. Punnett & O. Shenkar (Eds.), *Handbook for international management research* (2nd ed., pp. 267–349). Ann Arbor: University of Michigan Press.

Dorfman, P. W., & House, R. J. (2004). Cultural influences on organizational leadership: Literature review, theoretical rationale, and GLOBE project goals. In R. J. House, P. J. Hanges, M. Javidan, P. W. Dorfman, & V. Gupta (Eds.), *Culture, leadership, and organizations* (pp. 51–73). Thousand Oaks, CA: Sage.

Dorfman, P. W., & Howell, J. P. (1988). Dimensions of national culture and effective leadership patterns: Hofstede revisited. *Advances in International Comparative Management, 3,* 127–150.

Dorfman, P. W., Hanges, P. J., & Brodbeck, F. C. (2004). Leadership and cultural variation: The identification of culturally endorsed leadership profiles. In R. J. House, P. J. Hanges, M. Javidan, P. W. Dorfman, & V. Gupta (Eds.), *Culture, leadership, and organizations* (pp. 669–720). Thousand Oaks, CA: Sage.

Dougherty, C. (2008, June 26). Strong economy and labor shortages are luring polish immigrants back home. *New York Times.* Retrieved from http://www.nytimes.com/2008/2006/2026/world/europe/2026poles.html.

Drenth, P. J. D., & Wilpert, B. (1980). The role of "social contracts" in cross-cultural research. *International Review of Applied Psychology, 29*(3), 293–306.

Druckman, D., Benton, A. A., Ali, F., & Bagur, J. S. (1976). Cultural differences in bargaining behavior. *Journal of Conflict Resolution, 20,* 413–449.

Dubinsky, A. J., Kotabe, M., Lim, C. U., & Michaels, R. E. (1994). Differences in motivational perceptions among U.S., Japanese, and Korean sales personnel. *Journal of Business Research, 30,* 175–185.

Dunbar, E. (1992). Adjustment and satisfaction of expatriate U.S. personnel. *International Journal of Intercultural Relations, 16,* 1–16.

Dunbar, E. (1994). The German executive in the U.S. work and social environment: Exploring role demands. *International Journal of Intercultural Relations, 18,* 277–291.

Duncan, R. B. (1972). Characteristics of organizational environments and perceived environmental uncertainty. *Administrative Science Quarterly, 17*(3), 313–327.

Dunphy, D. (1987). Convergence/divergence: A temporal review of the Japanese enterprise and its management. *Academy of Management Review, 12,* 445–459.

Earley, P. C. (1987). Intercultural training for managers: A comparison of documentary and interpersonal methods. *Academy of Management Journal, 30*(4), 239–252.

Earley, P. C. (1989). Social loafing and collectivism: A comparison of the U.S. and the People's Republic of China. *Administrative Science Quarterly, 34,* 565–581.

Earley, P. C. (1999). Playing follow the leader: Status determining traits in relation to collective efficacy across cultures. *Organizational Behavior and Human Decision Processes, 80*(3), 192–212.

Earley, P. C. (2002). Redefining interactions across cultures and organizations: Moving forward with cultural intelligence. In B. Staw & R. M. Kramer (Eds.), *Research in Organizational Behavior, 24,* 271–299.

Earley, P. C., & Ang, S. (2003). *Cultural intelligence: Individual interactions across cultures.* Stanford, CA: Stanford University Press.

Earley, P. C., & Gibson, C. B. (1998). Taking stock in our progress on individualism collectivism: 100 years of solidarity and community. *Journal of Management, 24,* 265–304.

Earley, P. C., & Mosakowski, E. (2000). Creating hybrid team cultures: An empirical test of transnational team functioning. *Academy of Management Journal, 43*(1), 26–49.

Earley, P. C., & Singh, H. (1995). International and intercultural management research: What's next? *Academy of Management Journal, 38*(2), 327–340.

Echavarria, N. U., & Davis, D. D. (1994, July). *A test of Bass's model of transformational and transactional leadership in the Dominican Republic.* Paper presented at the 23rd International Congress of Applied Psychology, Madrid, Spain.

Eden, D. (1975). Intrinsic and extrinsic rewards and motives: Replications and extensions with kibbutz workers. *Journal of Applied Social Psychology, 5,* 348–361.

Edstrom, A., & Galbraith, J. R. (1977). Transfer of managers as a coordination and control strategy in multinational organizations. *Administrative Science Quarterly, 22,* 248–263.

Edwards, T., & Tempel, A. (2010). Explaining variation in reverse diffusion of HR practices: Evidence from the German and British subsidiaries of American multinationals. *Journal of World Business, 45,* 19–28.

Eisenberg, A. M., & Smith, R. R. (1971). *Nonverbal communication.* Indianapolis: Bobbs-Merrill.

Eisenhardt, S. N. (1973). *Tradition, change and modernity.* New York: John Wiley & Sons.

Ekman, P. W. (1982). *Emotion in the human face* (2nd ed.). Cambridge, UK: Cambridge University Press.

Ekman, P. W., Friesen, V., & Ellsworth, P. (1972). *Emotions in the human face: Guidelines for research and an integration of the findings.* Elmsford, NY: Pergamon.

Eldridge, J. E. T., & Crombie, A. D. (1974). *A sociology of organization.* London: Allen & Unwin.

Elkholy, A. A. (1981). The Arab American family. In C. H. Mindel & R. W. Hbenstein (Eds.), *Ethnic families in America: Patterns and variations* (pp. 145–162). New York: Elsevier.

Ellegard, K., Jonsson, D., Enstrom, T., Johansson, M., Medbo, L., & Johansson, B. (1992). Reflective production in the final assembly of motor vehicles: An emerging Swedish challenge. *International Journal of Operations and Production Management, 12*(7–8), 117–133.

Elliott, G. C., & Meeker, B. F. (1984). Modifiers of the equity effect: Group outcome and causes for individual performance. *Journal of Personality and Social Psychology, 46,* 586–597.

Ellis, S., Rogoff, B., & Cramer, C. C. (1981). Age segregation in children's social interactions. *Developmental Psychology, 17,* 399–407.

Ellsworth, P. C., & Carlsmith, J. M. (1973). Eye contact and gaze aversion in aggressive encounter. *Journal of Personality and Social Psychology, 33,* 117–122.

Elron, E. (1997). Top management teams within multinational corporations: Effects of cultural heterogeneity. *Leadership Quarterly, 8,* 393–412.

Elron, E., Halevy, N., Ben-Ari, E., & Shamir, B. (2003). Cooperation and coordination across cultures in the peacekeeping forces: Individual and organizational integrating mechanisms. In T. W. Britt & A. B. Adler (Eds.), *The psychology of the peacekeeper: Lessons from the field* (pp. 261–282). Westport, CT: Praeger.

Ely, R. J., & Thomas, D. A. (2001). Cultural diversity at work: The effects of diversity perspectives on work group processes and outcomes. *Administrative Science Quarterly, 46,* 229–273.

Emery, F. E., & Trist, E. L. (1965). The causal texture of organizational environments. *Human Relations, 17*(1), 21–32.

Enderwick, P., & Hodgson, D. (1993). Expatriate management practices of New Zealand businesses. *International Journal of Human Resource Management, 4,* 407–423.

Engholm, C. (1991). *When business east meets business west: The guide to practice & protocol in the Pacific Rim.* New York: John Wiley & Sons.

England, G. W. (1983). Japanese and American management: Theory Z and beyond. *Journal of International Business Studies, 14,* 131–141.

English, H. B. (1958). *A comprehensive dictionary of psychological and psychoanalytical terms.* New York: David McKay.

Erez, M. (1997). A culture-based model of work motivation. In P. C. Earley & M. Erez (Eds.), *New perspectives on international industrial/organizational psychology* (pp. 193–242). San Francisco: New Lexington Press.

Erez, M., & Earley, P. C. (1987). Comparative analysis of goal setting strategies across cultures. *Journal of Applied Psychology, 71,* 658–665.

Erez, M., & Earley, P. C. (1993). *Culture, self-identity and work.* New York: Oxford University Press.

Erez, M., & Shokef, E. (2008). The culture of global organizations. In P. B. Smith, M. F. Peterson, & D. C. Thomas (Eds.), *Handbook of cross-cultural management research* (pp. 285–300). Thousand Oaks, CA: Sage.

Eschbach, D. M., Parker, G. E., & Stoeberl, P. A. (2001). American repatriate employees' retrospective assessments of the effects of cross-cultural training on their adaptation to international assignments. *International Journal of Human Resource Management, 12,* 270–287.

Evans, P., Pucik, V., & Barsoux, J. L. (2002). *The global challenge: Frameworks for international human resource management.* New York, NY: McGraw-Hill.

Fadil, P. A., Williams, R. J., Limpaphayom, W., & Smatt, C. (2005). Equity or equality? A conceptual examination of the influence of individualism/collectivism on the cross-cultural application of equity theory. *Cross Cultural Management: An International Journal, 12*(4), 17–35.

Farh, J. L., Hackett, R., & Chen, Z. (2008). Organizational citizenship behavior in the global context. In P. B. Smith, M. F. Peterson, & D. C. Thomas (Eds.), *Handbook of cross-cultural management research* (pp. 165–184). Thousand Oaks, CA: Sage.

Farh, J.-L., Hackett. R. D., Liang, J. (2007). Individual-level cultural values as moderators of perceived organizational support-employee outcome relationships in China: Comparing the effects of power distance and traditionality. *Academy of Management Journal, 50*(3), 713–729.

Farnham, A. (1994, June 27). Global—or just globaloney? *Fortune,* pp. 97–100.

Feign, L. (1988). *The world of Lily Wong.* Hong Kong: Macmillan.

Feldman, D. C. (1976). A contingency theory of socialization. *Administrative Science Quarterly, 21,* 433–451.

Feldman, D. C. (1984). The development and enforcement of group norms. *Academy of Management Journal, 27,* 47–53.

Feldman, D. C. (1997). When does demonstrating a difference make a difference? An organizational behavior perspective on international management. In B. Toyne & D. Nigh (Eds.), *International business: An emerging vision* (pp. 446–466). Columbia: University of South Carolina Press.

Feldman, D. C., & Bolino, M. C. (1999). The impact of on-site mentoring on expatriate socialization: A structural equation modeling approach. *International Journal of Human Resource Management, 10,* 54–71.

Feldman, D. C., & Brett, J. M. (1983). Coping with new jobs: A comparative study of new hires and job changers. *Academy of Management Journal, 26,* 258–272.

Feldman, D. C., & Thomas, D. C. (1992). Career management issues facing expatriates. *Journal of International Business Studies, 23*, 271–293.

Feldman, D. C., & Tompson, H. B. (1993). Expatriation, repatriation, and domestic geographical relocation: An empirical investigation of adjustment to new job assignments. *Journal of International Business Studies, 24*(2), 507–529.

Ferner, A., Almond, P., & Colling, T. (2005). Institutional theory and the cross-national transfer of employment policy: The case of "workforce diversity" in US multinationals. *Journal of International Business Studies, 36*, 304–321.

Ferraro, G. P. (2006). *The cultural dimension of international business* (5th ed.). Englewood Cliffs, NJ: Prentice Hall.

Ferrell, O., & Fraedrich, J. (1994). *Business ethics: Ethical decision making and cases* (2nd ed.). Boston: Houghton Mifflin.

Festinger, L. (1957). *A theory of cognitive dissonance.* Stanford, CA: Stanford University Press.

Fey, C. F., & Beamish, P. W. (2001). Organizational climate similarity and performance: International joint ventures in Russia. *Organization Studies, 22*, 853–882.

Fiedler, F. E. (1966). The effect of leadership and cultural heterogeneity on group performance: A test of the contingency model. *Journal of Experimental Social Psychology, 2*, 237–264.

Fiedler, F. E. (1967). *A theory of leadership effectiveness.* New York: McGraw-Hill.

Fiol, C. M., & O'Connor, E. J. (2005). Identification in face-to-face, hybrid, and pure virtual teams: Untangling the contradictions. *Organization Science, 16*, 19–32.

Fischer, R., & Smith, P. B. (2003). Reward allocation and culture: A meta-analysis. *Journal of Cross-Cultural Psychology, 34*, 251–268.

Fischer, R., Smith, P. B., Richey, B., Ferreira, M. C., Assmar, E. M. L., Maes, J., et al. (2007). How do organizations allocate rewards? The predictive validity of national values, economic and organizational factors across six nations. *Journal of Cross-Cultural Psychology, 38*(1), 3–18.

Fischer, R., Vauclair, C.-M., Fontaine, J. R. J., Schwartz. S. H. (2010). Are individual-level and country-level value structures different? Testing Hofstede's legacy with the Schwartz value survey, *Journal of Cross-Cultural Psychology, 41*(2), 135–151.

Fiske, A. P. (1990). *Structures of social life: The four elementary forms of human relations.* New York: Free Press.

Fiske, S., & Taylor, S. (1984). *Social cognition.* Reading, MA: Addison-Wesley.

Fitzsimmons, S. R. (2013). Multicultural employees: A framework for understanding how they contribute to organizations. *Academy of Management Review, 38*(4), 491–502.

Fleishman, E. A. (1953). The description of supervisory behavior. *Personnel Psychology, 37*, 1–6.

Forgas, J. P., & Bond, M. H. (1985). Cultural influences on the perception of interaction episodes. *Personality and Social Psychology Bulletin, 11*, 75–85.

Francis, J. N. P. (1991). When in Rome? The effects of cultural adaptation on intercultural business negotiations. *Journal of International Business Studies, 22*(3), 403–428.

Franko, L. (1973). Who manages multinational enterprises? *Columbia Journal of World Business, 8*, 30–42.

Frederick, W. C. (1991). The moral authority of transnational corporate codes. *Journal of Business Ethics, 10*, 165–177.

Freedman, S., & Phillips, J. (1988). The changing nature of research on women at work. *Journal of Management, 14*(2), 231–251.

French, H. (2003). *Vanishing borders: Protecting the environment in the age of globalization.* New York: Norton Paperbacks.

French, J. R. P., Israel, J., & As, D. (1960). An experiment in a Norwegian factory: Interpersonal dimensions in decision-making. *Human Relations, 13*, 3–19.

Friedlander, F. (1989). The ecology of work groups. In J. W. Lorsch (Ed.), *Handbook of organizational behavior* (pp. 301–314). Englewood Cliffs, NJ: Prentice Hall.

Fritzsche, D. J., & Becker, H. (1984). Linking management behavior to ethical philosophy: An empirical investigation. *Academy of Management Journal, 27*(1), 166–175.

Fu, H., Morris, M. W., Lee, S., Chao, M., Chiu, C., & Hong, H. (2007). Epistemic motives and cultural conformity: Need for closure, culture and context as determinants of conflict judgments. *Journal of Personality and Social Psychology, 92*(2), 191–197.

Fu, J. H.-Y., Chiu, C.-Y., Morris, M. W., & Young, M. J. (2007). Spontaneous inferences from cultural cues. Varying responses of cultural insiders and outsiders. *Journal of Cross-Cultural Psychology, 38*, 58–75.

Furnham, A., & Bochner, S. (1986). *Culture shock: Psychological reactions to unfamiliar environments.* New York: Methuen.

Gabrielidis, C., Stephen, W. G., Ybarra, O., Dos Santos Pearson, V. M., & Villareal, L. (1997). Preferred styles of conflict resolution: Mexico and the United States. *Journal of Cross-Cultural Psychology, 28*(6), 661–677.

Gallois, C., & Callan, V. (1997). *Communication and culture: A guide for practice.* Chichester, UK: John Wiley & Sons.

Gannon, M. J., & Pillai, R. (2010). *Understanding global cultures* (4th ed.). Thousand Oaks, CA: Sage.

Gass, S. M., & Varonis, E. M. (1985). Variation in native speaker speech modification to non-native speakers. *Studies in Second Language Acquisition, 7*, 37–58.

Gelfand, M. J., & Cai, D. A. (2004). Cultural structuring of the social context of negotiation. In M. J. Gelfand & J. M. Brett (Eds.), *Handbook of negotiation and culture* (pp. 238–257). Palo Alto, CA: Stanford University Press.

Gelfand, M. J., & McCusker, C. (2002). Metaphor and the cultural construction of negotiation: A paradigm for research and practice. In M. J. Gannon & K. L. Newman (Eds.), *Handbook of cross-cultural management* (pp. 292–314). Malden, MA: Blackwell.

Gelfand, M. J., & Realo, A. (1999). Individualism–collectivism and accountability in intergroup negotiations. *Journal of Applied Psychology, 84*, 721–736.

Gelfand, M. J., Higgins, M., Nishii, L. H., Raver, J. L., Dominguez, A., Murakami, F., et al. (2002). Culture and egocentric perceptions of fairness in conflict and negotiation. *Journal of Applied Psychology, 87*, 833–856.

Gelfand, M. J., Leslie, L. M., & Fehr, Ryan (2008). To prosper, organizational psychology should . . . adopt a global perspective. *Journal of Organizational Behavior, 29*, 493–517.

Gelfand, M. J., Nishii, L. H., Holcombe, K. M., Dyer, N., Ohbuchi, K., & Fukuno, M. (2001). Cultural influences on cognitive representations of conflict: Interpretations of conflict episodes in the United States and Japan. *Journal of Applied Psychology, 86*, 1059–1074.

Gelfand, M. J., Raver, J. L., Nishii, L., Leslie, L. M., Lun, J., Lim, B. C., et al. (2011). Differences between tight and loose cultures: A 33-nation study. *Science, 332*(6033), 1100–1104.

George, J. M. (1990). Personality, affect, and behavior in groups. *Journal of Applied Psychology, 75*(2), 107–116.

Geringer, M. J. (1988, Summer). Partner selection criteria for developed country joint alliances. *Business Quarterly*, pp. 54–61.

Geringer, M. J., & Hebert, L. (1991). Measuring performance of international joint ventures. *Journal of International Business Studies, 22*(2), 249–264.

Gersick, C. J. G. (1988). Time and transition in work teams: Toward a new model of group development. *Academy of Management Journal, 31*, 9–41.

Gersick, C. J. G. (1989). Marking time: Predictable transitions in task groups. *Academy of Management Journal, 32*, 274–309.

Ghauri, P. N., & Prasad, S. B. (1995). A network approach to probing Asia's interfirm linkages. *Advances in International Comparative Management, 10*, 63–77.

Ghoshal, S. (1997). Of cakes, clothes, emperors, and obituaries. In B. Toyne & D. Nigh (Eds.), *International business: An emerging vision* (pp. 361–366). Columbia: University of South Carolina Press.

Ghoshal, S., & Bartlett, C. A. (1990). The multinational corporation as an interorganizational network. *Academy of Management Review, 15*, 603–625.

Gibbs, B. (1994). The effects of environment and technology on managerial roles. *Journal of Management, 20*(3), 581–604.

Gibson, C. B. (1994). The implications of national culture for organization structure: An investigation of three perspectives. *Advances in International Comparative Management, 9*, 3–38.

Gibson, C. B., & Cohen, S. G. (Eds.). (2003). *Virtual teams that work: Creating conditions for virtual team effectiveness.* San Francisco: Jossey-Bass.

Gibson, C. B., & Zellmer-Bruhn, M. E. (2001). Metaphors and meaning: An intercultural analysis of the concept of teamwork. *Administrative Science Quarterly, 46*, 274–303.

Giles, H., & Smith, P. (1979). Accommodation theory: Optimal levels of convergence. In H. Giles & R. N. St. Clair (Eds.), *Language and social psychology* (pp. 45–63). Baltimore: University Park Press.

Giles, H., Bourhis, R. Y., & Taylor, D. M. (1977). Toward a theory of language in ethnic group relations. In H. Giles (Ed.), *Language, ethnicity, and intergroup relations* (pp. 307–348). London: Academic Press.

Giles, H., Coupland, N., & Wiemann, J. M. (1992). Talk is cheap . . . but my word is my bond: Beliefs about talk. In K. Boulton & H. Kwok (Eds.), *Sociolinguistics today: Eastern and Western perspectives* (pp. 218–243). London: Routledge.

Gilovich, T., & Savitsky, K. (2002). Like goes with like: The role of representativeness in erroneous and pseudo-scientific beliefs. In T. Gilovich, D. Griffin, & D. Kahneman (Eds.), *Heuristics and biases: The psychology of intuitive judgment* (pp. 617–624). Cambridge, UK: Cambridge University Press.

Gioia, D. A., & Poole, P. P. (1984). Scripts in organizational behavior. *Academy of Management Review, 9*, 449–459.

Gironda, J., & Peterson, M. F. (in press). Interpersonal trust and within-nation regional e-commerce adoption. *European Journal of International Management.*

Glazer, S., Kożusznik, M. W., Shargo, I. A. (2012). Global virtual teams: A cure for—or a cause of—stress. *Research in Occupational Stress and Well-being, 10*, 213–266.

Glenn, E. S., Witmeyer, D., & Stevenson, K. A. (1977). Cultural styles of persuasion. *International Journal of Intercultural Relations, 1*, 52–66.

Global Commission on International Migration. (2005). *Migration in an interconnected world: New direction for action.* New York: Author.

Global Relocation Trends (2010). *Survey Report.* Woodbridge, IL: Brookfield GRS.

Global Relocation Trends (2012). *Survey Report.* Woodbridge, IL: Brookfield GRS.

Goldin, I., & Reinert, K. (2012). *Globalization for development: Meeting new challenges.* New York: Oxford University Press.

Goldstein, J. (1999). Emergence as a construct: History and issues. *Emergence, 1*, 49–72.

Gomez-Meija, L., & Balkin, D. (1987). The determinants of managerial satisfaction with the expatriation and repatriation process. *Journal of Management Development, 6*(1), 7–17.

Gong, Y. (2003). Toward a dynamic process model of staffing composition and subsidiary outcomes in multinational enterprise. *Journal of Management, 29*, 259–280.

Goodman, P. S. (1986). Impact of task and technology on group performance. In P. S. Goodman & Associates (Eds.), *Designing effective work groups* (pp. 120–167). San Francisco: Jossey-Bass.

Goodman, P. S., Ravlin, E. C., & Schminke, M. (1987). Understanding groups in organizations. In B. Staw & L. Cummings (Eds.), *Research in organizational behavior* (Vol. 9, pp. 124–128). Greenwich, CT: JAI.

Goulet, P. K., & Schweiger, D. M. (2006). Managing culture and human resources in mergers and acquisitions. In G. K. Stahl & I. Björkman (Eds.), *Handbook of research in international human resource management* (pp. 405–429). Cheltenham, UK: Edward Elgar.

Govindarajan, V., & Gupta, A. K. (2001). *The quest for global dominance: Transforming global presence into global competitive advantage*. San Francisco: Jossey-Bass.

Graen, G. (1976). Role-making processes within complex organizations. In M. D. Dunnett (Ed.), *Handbook of industrial and organizational psychology* (pp. 1201–1246). Chicago: Rand McNally.

Graf, A. (2004). Expatriate selection: An empirical study identifying significant skill profiles. *Thunderbird International Business Review, 46*, 667–685.

Graham, J. L. (1983, Spring/Summer). Brazilian, Japanese and American business negotiations. *Journal of International Business Studies*, 47–61.

Graham, J. L. (1985). The influence of culture on the process of business negotiations: An exploratory study. *Journal of International Business Studies, 16*, 81–96.

Graham, J. L. (1987). A theory of interorganizational negotiations. *Research in Marketing, 9*, 163–183.

Graham, J. L., Kim, D. K., Lin, C. Y., & Robinson, M. (1988). Buyer-seller negotiations around the Pacific Rim: Differences in fundamental exchange processes. *Journal of Consumer Research, 15*, 48–54.

Graham, J. L., Mintu, A. T., & Rodgers, W. (1994). Explorations of negotiation behaviors in ten foreign cultures using a model developed in the United States. *Management Science, 40*(1), 72–95.

Gray, I. (1987). *Henri Fayol's classic: General and industrial management*. Belmont, CA: Lake Publishers.

Greenleaf, R. K. (1970). *The servant as leader*. San Francisco, CA: Robert K. Greenleaf Center

Greenleaf, R. K. (1998). *The power of servant leadership*. San Francisco, CA: Robert K. Greenleaf Center.

Greer, C. R., & Stephens, G. K. (2001). Escalation of commitment: A comparison of differences between Mexican and U.S. decision-makers. *Journal of Management, 27*, 51–78.

Gregersen, H. B., & Black, J. S. (1990). A multifaceted approach to expatriate retention in international assignments. *Group and Organization Studies, 15*, 461–485.

Gregersen, H. B., Hite, J. M., & Black, J. S. (1996). Expatriate performance appraisal in U.S. multinational firms. *Journal of International Business Studies, 27*, 711–738.

Greiner, R., & Metes, G. (1995). *Going virtual*. Upper Saddle River, NJ: Prentice Hall.

Grove, C. L., & Torbion, I. (1985). A new conceptualization of intercultural adjustment and goals of training. *International Journal of Intercultural Relations, 9*, 205–233.

Gudykunst, W. B., Gao, G., & Franklyn-Stokes, A. (1996). Self-monitoring and concern for social appropriateness in China and England. In J. Pandey & D. Sinha (Eds.), *Asian contributions to cross-cultural psychology* (pp. 255–267). New Delhi, India: Sage.

Gudykunst, W. B., Ting-Toomey, S., & Chua, E. (1988). *Culture and interpersonal communication*. Newbury Park, CA: Sage.

Gullahorn, J. T., & Gullahorn, J. E. (1963). An extension of the U-curve hypothesis. *Journal of Social Issues, 19*, 33–47.

Gulliver, P. H. (1979). *Disputes and negotiations*. New York: Academic Press.

Guth, R. A. (2000, February 29). Net lets Japanese women join workforce at home. *The Wall Street Journal*, pp. B1, B20.

Guthrie, G. M., & Azores, F. M. (1968). Philippine interpersonal behavior patterns. *Ateneo de Manila University IPC Papers, 6*, 3–63.

Guthrie, G. M., & Zektrick, I. (1967). Predicting performance in the Peace Corps. *Journal of Social Psychology, 71,* 11–21.

Guzzo, R. A., & Dickson, M. W. (1996). Teams in organizations: Recent research on performance and effectiveness. *Annual Review of Psychology, 47,* 307–338.

Guzzo, R. A., Noonan, K. A., & Elron, E. (1994). Expatriate managers and the psychological contract. *Journal of Applied Psychology, 79,* 617–626.

Hackman, J. R. (1987). The design of work teams. In J. W. Lorsch (Ed.), *Handbook of organizational behavior* (pp. 312–342). Englewood Cliffs, NJ: Prentice Hall.

Hackman, J. R. (1991). *Groups that work (and those that don't).* San Francisco: Jossey-Bass.

Hackman, J. R., & Morris, C. G. (1978). Group process and group effectiveness: A reappraisal. In L. Berkowitz (Ed.), *Group process* (pp. 57–66). Reading, MA: Addison-Wesley.

Hackman, J. R., & Oldham, G. R. (1980). *Work redesign.* Reading, MA: Addison-Wesley.

Hage, J., & Aiken, M. (1969). Routine technology, social structure, and organizational goals. *Administrative Science Quarterly, 14,* 366–377.

Haire, M., Ghiselli, E. E., & Porter, L. W. (1966). *Management thinking: An international study.* New York: John Wiley & Sons.

Hale, J. R., & Fields, D. L. (2007). Exploring servant leadership across cultures: A study of followers in Ghana and the USA. *Leadership, 2,* 397–417.

Hales, C. P. (1986). What do managers do? A critical review of the evidence. *Journal of Management Studies, 23*(1), 88–115.

Hales, C., & Tamangani, Z. (1996). An investigation of the relationship between organizational structure, managerial role expectations and managers' work activities. *Journal of Management Studies, 33*(6), 731–756.

Hall, E. T. (1966). *The hidden dimension.* New York: Doubleday.

Hall, E. T. (1976). *Beyond culture.* New York: Doubleday.

Hall, E. T., & Hall, M. R. (1987). *Hidden differences.* New York: Doubleday.

Hall, R. H., Haas, J. E., & Johnson, N. J. (1967). Organizational size, complexity, and formalization. *Administrative Science Quarterly, 12,* 903–912.

Hallowell, A. I. (1955). *Culture and experience.* Philadelphia: University of Pennsylvania Press.

Hamaguchi, E. (1985). A contextual model of the Japanese: Toward a methodological innovation in Japan studies. *Journal of Japanese Studies, 11,* 289–321.

Hamilton, D. L. (1979). A cognitive-attributional analysis of stereotyping. In L. Berkowitz (Ed.), *Advances in experimental social psychology* (Vol. 12, pp. 53–84). New York: Academic Press.

Hammer, M. R. (1987). Behavioral dimensions of intercultural effectiveness: A replication and extension. *International Journal of Intercultural Relations, 11,* 65–87.

Hammer, M. R., Gudykunst, W. B., & Wiseman, R. L. (1978). Dimensions of intercultural effectiveness: An exploratory study. *International Journal of Intercultural Relations, 8,* 1–10.

Hannan, M. T., & Freeman, J. (1977). The population ecology of organizations. *American Journal of Sociology, 82,* 929–946.

Hannan, M. T., & Freeman, J. (1984). Structural inertia and organizational change. *American Sociological Review, 49,* 149–164.

Hannigan, T. P. (1990). Traits, attitudes, and skills that are related to intercultural effectiveness and their implications for cross-cultural training: A review of the literature. *International Journal of Intercultural Training, 14,* 89–111.

Hardin, A. M., Fuller, M. A., & Davison, R. M. (2007). I know I can, but can we? Culture and efficacy beliefs in global virtual teams. *Small Group Research, 38,* 130–155.

Harpaz, I. (1990). The importance of work goals: An international perspective. *Journal of International Business Studies, 21*(1), 75–93.

Harris, H. (2004). Global careers: Work-life issues and the adjustment of women international managers. *Journal of Management Development, 23*(9), 818–832.

Harvey, M. C. (1989). Repatriation of corporate executives: An empirical study. *Journal of International Business Studies, 20,* 131–144.

Harvey, M. C. (1997). Dual career expatriates: Expectations, adjustment and satisfaction with international relocation. *Journal of International Business Studies, 28,* 627–658.

Harvey, M., Speier, C., & Novicevic, M. M. (1999). The role of *inpatriation* in global staffing. *International Journal of Human Resource Management, 10,* 459–476.

Harzing, A. W. (2001). Who's in charge? An empirical study of executive staffing practices in foreign subsidiaries. *Human Resource Management, 40,* 139–158.

Hasegawa, T., & Gudykunst, W. B. (1998). Silence in Japan and the United States. *Journal of Cross-Cultural Psychology, 29,* 668–684.

Hawken, P. (1993). *The ecology of commerce.* New York: Harper Business.

Hays, R. D. (1971). Ascribed behavioral determinants of success–failure among U.S. expatriate managers. *Journal of International Business Studies, 2*(1), 40–46.

Hays, R. D. (1974). Expatriate selection: Insuring success and avoiding failure. *Journal of International Business Studies, 5*(1), 25–37.

Hechanova, R., Beehr, T. A., & Christiansen, N. D. (2003). Antecedents and consequences of employees' adjustment to overseas assignment: A meta-analytic review. *Applied Psychology: An International Review, 52,* 213–236.

Hecht, M. L., Andersen, P. A., & Ribeau, S. A. (1989). The cultural dimensions of nonverbal communication. In M. Kasante & W. B. Gudykunst (Eds.), *Handbook of international and intercultural communication* (pp. 163–185). Newbury Park, CA: Sage.

Heenan, D. A., & Perlmutter, H. V. (1979). *Multinational organizational development.* Reading, MA: Addison-Wesley.

Heine, S. J., & Lehman, D. R. (1995). Cultural variation in unrealistic optimism: Does the West feel more invulnerable than the East? *Journal of Personality and Social Psychology, 68,* 595–607.

Heller, F., & Wilpert, B. (1981). *Competence and power in managerial decision-making.* Chichester, UK: John Wiley & Sons.

Helmreich, R. L., & Schaefer, H. (1994). Team performance in the operating room. In M. S. Bogner (Ed.), *Human error in medicine* (pp. 225–253). Hillsdale, NJ: Lawrence Erlbaum.

Henderson, H. (1999). *Beyond globalization. Shaping a sustainable global economy.* West Hartford, CT: Kumarian.

Henley, N. M. (1977). *Body politics: Power, sex, and nonverbal communication.* Englewood Cliffs, NJ: Prentice Hall.

Hewstone, M. (1990). The "ultimate attribution error"? A review of the literature on intergroup causal attribution. *European Journal of Social Psychology, 20,* 614–623.

Hickson, D. J., & McMillan, (1981). *Organization and nation: The Aston programme IV.* Farnborough, UK: Gower.

Hickson, D. J., & Pugh, D. S. (1995). *Management worldwide: The impact of societal culture on organizations around the globe.* London: Penguin.

Hickson, D. J., Hinings, C. R., McMillan, C. J., & Schwitter, J. P. (1991). The culture-free context of organizational structure: A tri-national comparison. *Sociology, 8,* 59–80.

Hill, G. W. (1982). Group versus individual performance: Are *N*+1 heads better than one? *Psychological Bulletin, 91,* 517–539.

Hinds, P., & Mortensen, M. (2005). Understanding conflict in geographically distributed teams: The moderating effects of shared identity, shared context, and spontaneous communication. *Organizational Science, 16,* 290–307.

Hinkle, S., & Brown, R. (1990). Intergroup comparisons and social identity: Some links and lacunae. In D. Abrams & M. Hogg (Eds.), *Social identity theory: Constructive and critical advance.* Hemel Hempstead, UK: Harvester Wheatsheaf.

Hoerr, J. (1989, July 10). The payoff from teamwork. *Business Week,* pp. 55–62.

Hoffman, A. J., & Bansal, P. (2011). Retrospective, perspective and prospective: Introduction to the Oxford handbook on business and the natural environment. In P. Bansal & A. J. Hoffman (Eds.), *The Oxford handbook on business and the natural environment* (pp. 3–28). Oxford, UK: Oxford University Press.

Hofstede, G. (1980). *Culture's consequences: International differences in work related values.* Beverly Hills, CA: Sage.

Hofstede, G. (1983). The cultural relativity of organizational practices and theories. *Journal of International Business Studies, 14*(2), 75–89.

Hofstede, G. (1991). *Culture and organizations: Software of the mind.* London: McGraw-Hill.

Hofstede, G. (1993). Cultural constraints in management theories. *The Academy of Management Executive, 7,* 81–94.

Hofstede, G. (2001). *Culture's consequences: Comparing values, behaviors, institutions, and organizations across nations* (2nd ed.). Thousand Oaks, CA: Sage.

Hofstede, G. (2006). What did GLOBE really measure? Researchers' minds versus respondents' minds. *Journal of International Business Studies, 37,* 882–896.

Hofstede, G., & Bond, M. H. (1988). The Confucius connection: From cultural roots to economic growth. *Organization Dynamics, 16*(4), 5–21.

Hofstede, G., & McCrae, R. R. (2004). Personality and culture revisited: Linking traits and dimensions of culture. *Cross-Cultural Research, 38,* 52–88.

Hofstede, G., & Usunier, J. C. (1996). Hofstede's dimensions of culture and their influence on international business negotiations. In P. Ghauri & J. C. Usunier (Eds.), *International business negotiations* (pp. 119–129). Oxford, UK: Pergamon.

Hofstede, G., Hofstede, G. J., & Minkov, M. (2010) *Cultures and organizations: Software of the mind* (3rd ed.). New York: McGraw-Hill.

Hofstede, G., Neuijen, B., Ohayv, D. D., & Sanders, G. (1990). Measuring organizational cultures: A qualitative/quantitative study across twenty cases. *Administrative Science Quarterly, 35,* 286–316.

Hollingshead, A. B., McGrath, J. E., & O'Connor, K. M. (1993). Group task performance and communication technology: A longitudinal study of computer-mediated versus face-to-face work groups. *Small Group Research, 24,* 307–333.

Hong, Y. Y., Morris, M., Chiu, C. Y., & Benet-Martínez, V. (2000). Multicultural minds: A dynamic constructivist approach to culture and cognition. *American Psychologist, 55,* 709–720.

House, R. J. (1971). A path-goal theory of leader effectiveness. *Administrative Science Quarterly, 16,* 556–571.

House, R. J. (1977). A 1976 theory of charismatic leadership. In J. G. Hunt & L. L. Larson (Eds.), *Leadership: The cutting edge* (pp. 189–207). Carbondale: Southern Illinois University Press.

House, R. J. (1991). *The universality of charismatic leadership.* Paper presented at the National Academy of Management annual meeting, Miami, FL.

House, R. J., & Mitchell, T. R. (1974, Fall). Path-goal theory of leadership. *Contemporary Business, 3,* 81–98.

House, R. J., Hanges, P. J., Javidan, M., Dorfman, P. W., & Gupta, V. (2004). *Culture, leadership, and organizations: The GLOBE study of 62 societies.* Thousand Oaks, CA: Sage.

Howard, C. G. (1974, March–April). Model for the design of a selection program for multinational executives. *Public Personnel Management,* pp. 138–145.

Howard, G. (1991). Culture tales: A narrative approach to thinking, cross-cultural psychology and psychotherapy. *American Psychologist, 46,* 187–197.

Howell, J. P., & Dorfman, P. W. (1988). *A comparative study of leadership and its substitutes in a mixed cultural work settings.* Paper presented at the Western Academy of Management Meetings, Big Sky, MT.

Howell, J. P., Dorfman, P. W., & Kerr, S. (1986). Moderator variables in leadership research. *Academy of Management Review, 11*, 88–102.

Howell, J. P., Dorfman, P. W., Hibino, S., Lee, J. K., & Tate, U. (1994). *Leadership in Western and Asian countries: Commonalities and differences in effective leadership processes and substitutes across cultures.* Las Cruces: New Mexico State University, Center for Business Research.

Hoyle, R. H., & Crawford, A. M. (1994). Use of individual-level data to investigate group phenomena: Issues and strategies. *Small Group Research, 25*(4), 464–485.

Hui, C. H. (1990). Work attitudes, leadership styles, and managerial behaviors in different cultures. In R. W. Brislin (Ed.), *Cross-cultural research and methodology series: Vol. 14. Applied cross-cultural psychology* (pp. 186–208). Newbury Park, CA: Sage.

Hui, H. C., & Cheng, I. W. M. (1987). Effects of second language proficiency of speakers and listeners on person perception and behavioural intention: A study of Chinese bilinguals. *International Journal of Psychology, 22*, 421–430.

Hui, C. H., & Triandis, H. C. (1989). Effects of culture and response format on extreme response styles. *Journal of Cross-Cultural Psychology, 20*, 296–309.

Huismans, S. (1994). The impact of differences in religion on the relation between religiosity and values. In A. M. Bouvy, F. van de Vijver, P. Boski, & P. Schmitz (Eds.), *Journeys into cross-cultural psychology* (pp. 254–267). Lisse, The Netherlands: Swets & Zeitlinger.

Huntington, S. P. (1996). *The clash of civilizations and the remaking of the world order.* New York: Simon and Schuster.

Huo, Y. P., & Von Glinow, M. A. (1995). On transplanting human resource practices to China: A culture-driven approach. *International Journal of Manpower, 16*(9), 3–13.

Huo, Y. P., Huang, H. J., & Napier, N. K. (2002). Divergence or convergence: A cross-national comparison of personnel selection practices. *Human Resource Management, 41*(1), 31–44.

Huseman, R. C., Hatfield, J. D., & Miles, E. W. (1987). A new perspective on equity theory: The equity sensitivity construct. *Academy of Management Review, 12*(2), 222–234.

Husted, B. W. (2000). Toward a model of cross-cultural business ethics: The impact of individualism and collectivism on the ethical decision-making process. *Academy of Management Proceedings,* IM.

IDE Research Group. (1993). *Industrial democracy in Europe revisited.* New York: Oxford University Press.

Indvik, J. (1986). Path–goal theory of leadership: A meta-analysis. *Proceedings of the Academy of Management Meeting,* pp. 189–192.

Inglehart, R. (1977). *The silent revolution: Changing values and political styles among Western publics.* Princeton, NJ: Princeton University Press.

Inglehart, R. (1990). *Cultural shift in advanced industrial society.* Princeton, NJ: Princeton University Press.

Inglehart, R., & Baker, W. E. (2000). Modernization, cultural change, and the persistence of traditional values. *American Sociological Review, 65*, 19–51.

Inkeles, A., & Levinson, D. J. (1969). National character: The study of modal personality and sociocultural systems. In G. Lindzey & E. Aronson (Eds.), *Handbook of social psychology* (2nd. ed., Vol. 4, pp. 418–506). Reading, MA: Addison-Wesley.

Inkson, J. H. K., Arthur, M. B., Pringle, J., & Barry, S. (1997). Expatriate assignment versus overseas experience: Contrasting models of international human resource development. *Journal of World Business, 32*(4), 351–368.

International Labour Organization (2012). *World of work report: Better jobs for a better economy.* Geneva: Author.

International Labour Organization (2013). *Global employment trends: Recovering from a second jobs dip.* Geneva: Author.

International Telecommunications Union (2012). *ITU World Telecommunications Database*. New York: Author.

Inzerilli, G., & Laurent, A. (1983). Managerial views of organization structure in France and the USA. *International Studies of Management and Organization, 13*(1–2), 97–118.

Ivancevich, J. M. (1969, March). Selection of American managers for overseas assignments. *Personnel Journal,* 189–193.

Izard, C. (1991). *Human emotions* (2nd ed.). New York: Plenum.

Izraeli, D. (1988). Ethical beliefs and behavior among managers: A cross-cultural perspective. *Journal of Business Ethics, 7,* 263–271.

Izraeli, D. N., Banai, M., & Zeira, Y. (1980). Women expatriates in subsidiaries of multinational corporations. *California Management Review, 23*(1), 53–63.

Jackofsky, E. F., Slocum, J. W., Jr., & McQuaid, S. J. (1988). Cultural values and the CEO: Alluring companions? *The Academy of Management Executive, 2*(1), 39–49.

Jackson, S. E. (1992). Team composition in organizational settings: Issues in managing an increasingly diverse work force. In S. Worchel, W. Wood, & J. A. Simpson (Eds.), *Group process and productivity* (pp. 138–173). Newbury Park, CA: Sage.

Jackson, S. E., & Schuler, R. S. (1985). A meta-analysis and conceptual critique of research on role ambiguity and role conflict in work settings. *Organizational Behavior and Human Decision Processes, 36,* 16–78.

Jackson, T. (2000). Making ethical judgments: A cross-cultural management study. *Asia-Pacific Journal of Management, 17,* 443–472.

Janis, I. L. (1982). *Groupthink.* Boston: Houghton Mifflin.

Janis, I. L., & Mann, L. (1977). *Decision making.* New York: Free Press.

Janssens, M. (1995). Intercultural interaction: A burden on international managers? *Journal of Organizational Behavior, 16,* 155–167.

Jarillo, J. (1988). On strategic networks. *Strategic Management Journal, 9,* 31–41.

Jarvenpaa, S., & Leidner, D. (1999). Communication and trust in global virtual teams. *Organization Science, 10,* 791–815.

Javidan, M., House, R. J., Dorfman, P. W., Hanges, P. J., & Sully de Luque, M. S. (2006). Conceptualizing and measuring cultures and their consequences: A comparative review of GLOBE's and Hofstede's approaches. *Journal of International Business Studies, 37,* 897–914.

Jehn, K. A., & Bezrukova, K. (2004). A field study of group diversity, workgroup context, and performance. *Journal of Organizational Behavior, 25,* 703–729.

Jehn, K. A., Northcraft, G. B., & Neale, M. A. (1999). Why differences make a difference: A field study of diversity, conflict and performance in work groups. *Administrative Science Quarterly, 44,* 238–251.

Jensen, J. V. (1982). Perspective on nonverbal intercultural communication. In L. A. Samovar & R. E. Porter (Eds.), *Intercultural communication: A reader* (pp. 260–276). Belmont, CA: Wadsworth.

Johnston, W. B. (1991). Global workforce 2000: The new world labor market. *Harvard Business Review, 69,* 115–127.

Joiner, T. A. (2001). The influence of national culture and organizational culture alignment on job stress and performance: evidence from Greece. *Journal of Managerial Psychology, 16*(3), 229–242.

Jonsen, K., Maznevski, M., & Davison, S. C. (2012). Global virtual team dynamics and effectiveness. In G. K. Stahl, I. Björkman, & S. Morris (Eds.), *Handbook of research in international human resource management* (2nd ed., pp. 363–392). Cheltenham, UK: Edward Elgar.

Jonsen, K., Maznevski, M., & Schneider, S, (2011). Diversity and its not so diverse literature: A international perspective. *International Journal of Cross Cultural Management, 11,* 35–62.

Kahl, J. A. (1968). *The measurement of modernism: A study of values in Brazil and Mexico.* Austin: University of Texas Press.

Kahn, R., Wolfe, D., Quinn, R., Snoek, J., & Rosenthal, R. (1964). *Organizational stress: Studies in role conflict and ambiguity.* New York: John Wiley & Sons.

Kahneman, D. (2011). *Thinking, fast and slow.* Doubleday Canada.

Kakar, S. (1971). Authority patterns and subordinate behavior in Indian organizations. *Administrative Science Quarterly, 16,* 298–307.

Kandel, D. B. (1978). Similarity in real-life adolescent friendship pairs. *Journal of Personality and Social Psychology, 36,* 306–312.

Kara, A., & Peterson, M. F. (2012). The dynamic societal cultural milieu of organizations: Origins, maintenance and change. In L. Tihanyi, T. M. Devinney, & T. Pedersen (Eds.), *Institutional Theory in International Business and Management: Advances in International Management* (Vol. 25). Bingley, UK: Emerald Group Publishing.

Kara, A., & Zellmer-Bruhn, M. (2011). The role of organizational culture and underlying ideologies in the success of globally distributed teams. In N. M. Ashkanasy, C. P. M. Wilderom, & M. F. Peterson (Eds.), *Handbook of Organizational Culture and Climate* (2nd ed., pp. 538–560). Thousand Oaks, CA: Sage.

Katriel, T. (1986). *Talking straight: Dugri speech in Israeli Sabra culture.* Cambridge, UK: Cambridge University Press.

Katz, D., & Braly, K. W. (1933). Verbal stereotypes and racial prejudice. *Journal of Abnormal and Social Psychology, 28,* 280–290.

Katz, D., & Kahn, R. L. (1978). *The social psychology of organizations.* New York: John Wiley & Sons.

Katz, R. (1982). The effects of group longevity on project communication and performance. *Administrative Science Quarterly, 27,* 81–104.

Kavanaugh, K. H. (1991). Invisibility and selective avoidance: Gender and ethnicity in psychiatry and psychiatric nursing staff interaction. *Culture, Medicine and Psychiatry, 15*(2), 245–274.

Kayany, J. M., Wotring, C. E., & Forrest, E. J. (1996). Relational control and interactive media choice in technology-mediated communication situations. *Human Communication Research, 22,* 371–398.

Kealey, D. J. (1989). A study of cross-cultural effectiveness: Theoretical issues, practical applications. *International Journal of Intercultural Relations, 13,* 387–428.

Kedia, B. L. (2006). Globalization and the future of international management education. *Journal of International Management, 12,* 242–245.

Kelley, H. H. (1972). Attribution in social interaction. In E. E. Jones, D. E. Kanouse, H. H. Kelley, R. E. Nisbett, S. Valins, & B. Weiner (Eds.), *Attribution: Perceiving the causes of behavior* (pp. 1–26). Morristown, NJ: General Learning Press.

Kelsey, B. (1998). The dynamics of multicultural groups: Ethnicity as a determinant of leadership. *Small Group Research, 29,* 602–623.

Kenis, I. (1977). A cross-cultural study of personality and leadership. *Group and Organization Studies, 2*(1), 49–60.

Kerr, C., Dunlop, J. T., Harbison, F. H., & Myers, C. A. (1960). *Industrialism and industrial man: The problems of labor and management in economic growth.* London: Heinemann.

Kerr, S., & Jermier, J. M. (1978). Substitutes for leadership: Their meaning and measurement. *Organizational Behavior and Human Performance, 22,* 375–403.

Khadra, B. (1990). The prophetic-caliphal model of leadership: An empirical study. *International Studies of Management and Organization, 20*(3), 37–51.

Kickul, J., Lester, S. W., & Belgio, E. (2004). Attitudinal and behavioral outcomes of psychological contract breach: A cross-cultural comparison of the United States and Hong Kong Chinese. *International Journal of Cross Cultural Management, 4,* 229–252.

Kim, H. S., & Drolet, A. (2003). Choice and self-expression: A cultural analysis of variety seeking. *Journal of Personality and Social Psychology, 85*, 373–382.

Kim, K. I., Park, H. J., & Suzuki, N. (1990). Reward allocations in the United States, Japan, and Korea: A comparison of individualistic and collectivistic cultures. *Academy of Management Journal, 33*(1), 188–198.

Kim, M. S. (1994). Cross-cultural comparisons of the perceived importance of interactive constraints. *Human Communication Research, 21*, 128–151.

King, D. R., Dalton, D. R., Daily, C. M., & Covin, J. G. (2004). Meta-analysis of post-acquisition performance: Indications of unidentified moderators. *Strategic Management Journal, 25*(2), 187–200.

King, R. C., & Bu, N. (2005). Perceptions of the mutual obligations between employees and employers: A comparative study of new generation IT professionals in China and the United States. *International Journal of Human Resource Management, 16*(1), 46–64.

Kirchmeyer, C., & Cohen, A. (1992). Multicultural groups: Their performance and reactions with constructive conflict. *Group & Organization Management, 17*(2), 153–170.

Kirkman, B., & Law, K. (2005). International management research in AMJ: Our past, present and future. *Academy of Management Journal, 48*, 377–386.

Kirkman, B. L., & Rosen, B. (1999). Beyond self-management. Antecedents and consequences of team empowerment. *Academy of Management Journal, 42*(1), 58–74.

Kirkman, B. L., & Shapiro, D. L. (1997). The impact of cultural values on employee resistance to teams: Toward a model of globalized self-managing work team effectiveness. *Academy of Management Review, 22*(3), 730–757.

Kirkman, B. L., Lowe, K. B., & Gibson, C.B. (2006). A quarter century of *Culture's Consequences*: A review of empirical research incorporating Hofstede's cultural values framework. *Journal of International Business Studies, 37*, 285–320.

Kitayama, S., & Ishii, K. (2002). Word and voice: Spontaneous attention to emotional utterances in two languages. *Cognition & Emotion, 16*, 29–59.

Kitayama, S., & Uskul, A. K. (2011). Culture, mind and the brain: Current evidence and future directions. *Annual Review of Psychology, 62*, 419–449.

Kleinke, C. L. (1986). Gaze and eye contact: A research review. *Psychological Bulletin, 100*, 78–100.

Kluckhohn, C. (1961). Universal categories of culture. In F. W. Moore (Ed.), *Readings in cross-cultural methodology* (pp. 89–105). Cambridge, MA: Harvard University.

Kluckhohn, C., & Strodtbeck, K. (1961). *Variations in value orientations.* Westport, CT: Greenwood.

Knapp, M. L., & Hall, J. A. (2002). *Nonverbal communication in human interaction.* Belmont, CA: Wadsworth/Thomson Learning.

Knoke, W. (1996). *Bad new world.* New York: Kodansha International.

Kogut, B. (1989). A note on global strategy. *Strategic Management Journal, 10*, 383–389.

Kogut, B., & Singh, H. (1988). The effect of national culture on the choice of entry mode. *Journal of International Business Studies, 19*(3), 411–432.

Koh, W. L. (1990). *An empirical validation of the theory of transformational leadership in secondary schools in Singapore* (Unpublished doctoral dissertation). University of Oregon, Eugene.

Kohlberg, L. (1984). *Philosophy of moral development.* New York: Harper & Row.

Konopaske, R., Robie, C., & Ivancevich, J. M. (2005). A preliminary model of spouse influence on managerial global assignment willingness. *International Journal of Human Resource Management, 16*, 405–426.

Kopp, R. (1994). International human resource policies and practices in Japanese, European, and United States multinationals. *Human Resources Management, 33*, 581–599.

Kornai, J. (1992). *The socialist system: The political economy of communism.* Princeton, NJ: Princeton University Press.

Korten, D. C. (1995). *When corporations rule the world.* San Francisco: Berrett-Koehler.

Kosic, A., Kruglanski, A. W., Pierro, A., & Mannetti, L. (2004). The social cognition of immigrants' acculturation: Effects of the need for closure and the reference group at entry. *Journal of Personality and Social Psychology, 86,* 798–813.

Kostova, T., & Zaheer, S. (1999). Organizational legitimacy under conditions of complexity: The case of the multinational enterprise. *Academy of Management Review, 24,* 64–81.

Kraimer, M. L., Shaffer, M. A., & Bolino, M. C. (2009). The influence of expatriate and repatriate experiences on career advancement and repatriate retention. *Human Resource Management, 48*(1), 27–47.

Kraut, R. E., Egido, C., & Galegher, J. (1990). Patterns of contact and communication in scientific research collaborations. In J. Galegher, R. E. Kraut, & C. Egido (Eds.), *Intellectual teamwork: Social and technological foundations of cooperative work* (pp. 23–62). Hillsdale, NJ: Lawrence Erlbaum.

Kroeber, A. L., & Kluckhohn, F. (1952). Culture: A critical review of concepts and definitions. In *Peabody Museum papers* (Vol. 47, No. 1). Cambridge, MA: Harvard University Press.

Lachman, R., Nedd, A., & Hinings, B. (1994). Analyzing cross-national management and organizations: A theoretical framework. *Management Science, 40*(1), 40–55.

LaFromboise, T., Coleman, H., & Gerton, J. (1993). Psychological impacts of biculturalism: Evidence and theory. *Psychological Bulletin, 114,* 395–412.

Lalonde, R. N., & Cameron, J. E. (1993). An intergroup perspective on immigrant acculturation with a focus on collective strategies. *International Journal of Psychology, 28,* 57–74.

Lau, D. C., & Murnighan, J. K. (1998). Demographic diversity and faultlines: The compositional dynamics of organizational groups. *Academy of Management Review, 23,* 325–340.

Lau, D. C., & Murnighan, J. K. (2005). Interactions within groups and sub-groups: The effects of demographic faultlines. *Academy of Management Journal, 48,* 645–659.

Lawler, E. E., III, Mohrman, S. A., & Ledford, G. E., Jr. (1992). *Employee involvement and total quality management: Practices and results in* Fortune *1000 companies.* San Francisco: Jossey-Bass.

Lawrence, P., & Lorsch, J. (1967). Differentiation and integration in complex organizations. *Administrative Science Quarterly, 12,* 1–47.

Lawrence, P. R. (1987). Historical development of organizational behavior. In J. W. Lorsch (Ed.), *Handbook of organizational behavior* (pp. 1–9). Englewood Cliffs, NJ: Prentice Hall.

Lazarova, M. B., & Cerdin, J.-L. (2007). Revisiting repatriation concerns: Organizational support versus career and contextual influences. *Journal of International Business Studies, 38,* 404–429.

Lazarova, M. B., & Lowe, M. (2008). Work and family: Research in cross-national and international contexts. In P. B. Smith, M. F. Peterson, & D. C. Thomas (Eds.), *Handbook of cross-cultural management research* (pp. 185–200). Thousand Oaks, CA: Sage.

Lazarova, M. B., & Tarique, I. (2005). Knowledge transfer upon repatriation. *Journal of World Business, 40*(4), 361–373.

Lazarova, M. B., & Thomas, D. C. (2012). Expatriate adjustment and performance revisited. In G. Stahl & I. Björkman (Eds.), *Handbook of Research in International Human Resource Management* (pp. 271–292). Cheltenham, UK: Edward Elgar.

Lazerson, M. (1995). A new phoenix? Modern putting-out in the Modena knitwear industry. *Administrative Science Quarterly, 40,* 34–59.

Leavitt, H. J. (2005). *Top down: Why hierarchies are here to stay and how to manage them more effectively.* Boston: Harvard Business School Press.

Lee, C. M., & Gudykunst, W. B. (2001). Attraction in interethnic interactions. *International Journal of Intercultural Relations, 25,* 373–387.

Lee, P. N. (1987). *Industrial management and economic reform in China 1949–1984.* New York: Oxford University Press.

Lee, Y.-T., & Duenas, G. (1995). Stereotype accuracy in multicultural business. In *Stereotype accuracy: Toward appreciating group differences.* Washington, DC: American Psychological Association.

Leifer, R., & Huber, G. (1977). Relations among perceived environmental uncertainty, organizational structure, and boundary spanning behavior. *Administrative Science Quarterly, 22,* 235–247.

Leksell, L. (1981). *Headquarter-subsidiary relationships in multinational corporations.* Stockholm: Stockholm School of Economics.

Lenartowicz, T., & Johnson, J. P. (2003). A cross-national assessment of the values of Latin American managers: Contrasting hues or shades of gray? *Journal of International Business Studies, 34,* 266–281.

LePine, J. A. (2003). Team adaptation and postchange performance: Effects of team composition in team members' cognitive ability and personality. *Journal of Applied Psychology, 88,* 27–39.

Leung, A. K., Maddux, W. M., Galinksy, A. D., & Chiu, C. Y. (2008). Multicultural experience enhances creativity: The when and how. *American Psychologist, 63,* 169–181.

Leung, K. (1987). Some determinants of reactions to procedural models of conflict resolution: A cross-national study. *Journal of Personality and Social Psychology, 53*(5), 898–908.

Leung, K. (1997). Negotiation and reward allocation across cultures. In P. C. Earley & M. Erez (Eds.), *New perspectives on international industrial/organizational psychology* (pp. 650–675). San Francisco: Jossey-Bass.

Leung, K. (2008). Methods and measurement in cross cultural management. In Peter B. Smith, M. F. Peterson, & D. C. Thomas (Eds.), *Handbook of Cross-Cultural Management Research* (pp. 59–73). Thousand Oaks, CA: Sage.

Leung, K., & Bond, M. H. (1982). How Chinese and Americans reward task-related contributions: A preliminary study. *Psychology, 25,* 32–39.

Leung, K., & Bond, M. H. (1984). The impact of cultural collectivism on reward allocation. *Journal of Personality and Social Psychology, 47,* 793–804.

Leung, K., & Kwong, J. Y. Y. (2003). Human resource management practice in international joint ventures in mainland China: A justice analysis. *Human Resource Management Review, 13,* 85–105.

Leung, K., & Lind, E. A. (1986). Procedural justice and culture: Effects of culture, gender, and investigator status on procedural preferences. *Journal of Personality and Social Psychology, 50*(6), 1134–1140.

Leung, K., & Peterson, M. F. (2011). Managing a globally distributed workforce: Social and international issues. In S. Zedeck, H. Aguinis, W. F. Casio, M. J. Gelfand, K. Leung, S. K. Parker, & J. Zhou (Ed.), *APA Handbook of Industrial-Organizational Psychology* (Vol. 3, pp. 771–805). Washington, DC: American Psychological Association.

Leung, K., & Wu, P.-G. (1990). Dispute processing: A cross-cultural analysis. In R. Brislin (Ed.), *Applied cross-cultural psychology* (Vol. 14, pp. 209–231). Newbury Park, CA: Sage.

Leung, K., Bond, M. H., & Schwartz, S. H. (1995). How to explain cross-cultural differences: Values, valences and expectancies? *Asian Journal of Psychology, 1,* 70–75.

Leung, K., Bond, M. H., de Carrasquel, S. R., Muñoz, C., Hernández, M. A., Murakami, F., et al. (2002). Social axioms: The search for universal dimensions of general beliefs about how the world functions. *Journal of Cross-Cultural Psychology, 33,* 286–302.

Levenson, R. W., Ekman, P., Heider, K., & Friesen, W. V. (1992). Emotion and autonomic nervous system activity in the Minangkabau of West Sumatra. *Journal of Personality and Social Psychology, 62,* 972–988.

Levine, D. N. (1985). *The flight from ambiguity.* Chicago: University of Chicago Press.

Levine, R. V., Norenzayan, A., & Philbrick, K. (2001). Cross-cultural differences in helping strangers. *Journal of Cross-Cultural Psychology, 32,* 543–560.

Li, H. Z. (1994). *Inter- and intra-cultural information transmission.* (Unpublished doctoral dissertation), University of Victoria, B.C, Canada.

Liker, J. K., Fruin, W. M., & Adler, P. S. (1999). Bringing Japanese management systems to the United States: Transplantation or transformation? In J. K. Liker, W. M. Fruin, & P. S. Adler (Eds.), *Remade in America: Transplanting and transforming Japanese management systems* (pp. 3–5). New York: Oxford University Press.

Lincoln, J. R., Olson, J., & Hanada, M. (1978). Cultural effects of organizational structures: The case of Japanese firms in the United States. *American Sociological Review, 43,* 829–847.

Lincoln, J. R., & Miller, J. (1979). Work and friendship ties in organizations: A comparative analysis of related networks. *Administrative Science Quarterly, 24,* 181–199.

Lincoln, J. R., Hanada, M., & McBride, K. (1986). Organization structures in Japanese and U.S. manufacturing. *Administrative Science Quarterly, 31,* 338–364.

Linville, P. W., & Jones, E. E. (1980). Polarized appraisals of out-group members. *Journal of Personality and Social Psychology, 38*(5), 689–703.

Linville, P. W., Fischer, O. W., & Salovey, P. (1989). Perceived distributions of the characteristics of in-group and out-group members: Empirical evidence and a computer simulation. *Journal of Personality and Social Psychology, 57,* 165–188.

Little, K. B. (1968). Cultural variations in social schemata. *Journal of Personality and Social Psychology, 10,* 1–7.

Liu, I. (1986). Chinese cognition. In M. H. Bond (Ed.), *The psychology of the Chinese people* (pp. 73–105). New York: Oxford University Press.

Liu, M. (2009). The intrapersonal and interpersonal effects of anger in negotiation strategies: A cross-cultural investigation. *Human Communication Research, 35,* 148–169.

Liu, L. A., Friedman, R., Barry, B., Gelfand, M. J., & Zhang, Z.-X. (2012). The dynamics of consensus building in intracultural and intercultural negotiations. *Administrative Science Quarterly, 57,* 269–304.

Locke, E. A. (1996). Motivation through conscious goal setting. *Applied and Preventative Psychology, 5,* 117–124.

Locke, E. A., & Latham, G. P. (1984). *Goal setting: A motivational technique that works.* Englewood, Cliffs, NJ: Prentice Hall.

Locke, E. A., & Latham, G. P. (1990). *A theory of goal setting and task performance.* Englewood Cliffs, NJ: Prentice Hall.

Locke, E. A., & Schweiger, D. M. (1979). Participation in decision making: One more look. In B. M. Staw (Ed.), *Research in organizational behavior* (Vol. 1, pp. 169–339). Greenwich, CT: JAI.

Loh, T. W. C. (1993). *Responses to compliments across languages and cultures: A comparative study of British and Hong Kong Chinese* (Research Rep. No. 30). Hong Kong: City University of Hong Kong.

Loher, B. T., Noe, R. A., Moeller, N. L., & Fitzgerald, M. P. (1980). A meta-analysis of the relation of job characteristics to job satisfaction. *Journal of Applied Psychology, 65,* 280–289.

Lorange, P., & Roos, J. (1992). *Strategic alliances.* Cambridge, MA: Blackwell.

Lord, R., & Maher, K. J. (1991). *Leadership and information processing: Linking perceptions and performance.* Boston: Unwin-Everyman.

Lord, R. G., & Kernan, M. C. (1987). Scripts as determinants of purposeful behavior in organizations. *Academy of Management Review, 12*, 265–277.

Lord, R. G., Foti, R. J., & DeVader, C. L. (1984). A test of leadership categorization theory: Internal structure, information processing, and leadership perceptions. *Organizational Behavior and Human Performance, 34*, 343–378.

Lurey, J. S., & Raisingham, M. S. (2001). An empirical study of best practices in virtual teams. *Information and Management, 38*, 523–544.

Lydon, J. E., Jamieson, E. W., & Zanna, M. P. (1988). Interpersonal similarity and the social and intellectual dimensions of first impressions. *Social Cognition, 6*(4), 269–286.

Lysgaard, S. (1955). Adjustment in a foreign society: Norwegian Fulbright grantees visiting the United States. *International Social Science Bulletin, 7*, 45–51.

Ma, Z., & Jaeger, A. M. (2010). A comparative study of the influence of assertiveness on negotiation outcomes in Canada and China. *Cross Cultural management: An International Journal, 17*, 333–346.

MacDuffie, J. P. (2008). HRM and distributed work: Managing people across distances. In J. P. Walsh & A. P. Brief (Eds.), *The Academy of Management Annals* (Vol. 1, pp. 549–616). New York: Lawrence Erlbaum.

Malinowski, B. (1939; repr.1944). The functional theory. In *A scientific theory of culture and other essays* (pp. 146–176). Chapel Hill: University of North Carolina Press.

Malone, T. W. (2004). *The future of work: How the new order of business will shape your organization, your management style, your life.* Boston: Harvard Business School Press.

Mamman, A. (1995). Socio-biographical antecedents of intercultural effectiveness: The neglected factors. *British Journal of Management, 6*, 97–114.

Mann, L., Burnett, P., Radford, M., & Ford, S. (1997). The Melbourne decision making questionnaire: An instrument for measuring patterns for coping with decisional conflict. *Journal of Behavioral Decision Making, 10*, 1–19.

Mannix, E., & Neale, M. A. (2005). What difference makes a difference? The promise and reality of diverse teams in organizations. *Psychological Science in the Public Interest, 6*(2), 31–55.

March, J., & Simon, H. (1958). *Organizations.* New York: John Wiley & Sons.

Marginson, S. (2011). Higher education in East Asia and Singapore: Rise of the Confucian model. *Higher Education, 61*, 587–611.

Markus, H. R. (1977). Self-schemata and processing information about the self. *Journal of Personality and Social Psychology, 35*, 63–78.

Markus, H. R., & Kitayama, S. (1991). Culture and the self: Implications for cognition, emotion, and motivation. *Psychological Review, 98*(2), 224–253.

Markus, H. R., & Zajonc, R. B. (1985). The cognitive perspective in social psychology. In G. Lindzey & E. Aronson (Eds.), *Handbook of social psychology* (Vol. 1, pp. 139–230). New York: Random House.

Marschan, R. (1996). *New structural forms and inter-unit communication in multinationals.* Helsinki: Helsinki School of Economics.

Marschan-Piekkari, R., Welch, D., & Welch, L. (1999). Adopting a common corporate language: IHRM implications. *The International Journal of Human Resource Management, 10*(3), 377–390.

Martin, D. C., & Bartol, K. M. (2003). Factors influencing expatriate performance appraisal system success: An organizational perspective. *Journal of International Management, 9*, 115–132.

Martins, L. L., Gilson, L. L., & Maynard, M. T. (2004). Virtual teams: What do we know and where do we go from here? *Journal of Management, 30*, 805–835.

Maslow, A. H. (1954). *Motivation and personality.* New York: Harper & Row.

Matsui, T., & Terai, I. (1979). A cross-cultural study of the validity of expectancy theory of work motivation. *Journal of Applied Psychology, 60*(2), 263–265.

Matsumoto, D., & Kudoh, T. (1993). American-Japanese cultural differences in attributions of personality based on smiles. *Journal of Nonverbal Behavior, 17,* 231–244.

Matsumoto, D., & Willingham, B. (2006). The thrill of victory and the agony of defeat: Spontaneous expressions of medal winners of the 2004 Athens Olympics games. *Journal of Personality and Social Psychology, 91,* 568–581.

Maxwell, G., & Schmitt, D. R. (1975). *Cooperation: An experimental analysis.* New York: Academic Press.

May, R. C., Puffer, S. M., & McCarthy, D. J. (2005). Transferring management knowledge to Russia: A culturally based approach. *Academy of Management Executive, 19*(2), 24–35.

Mayer, D., & Cava, A. (1993). Ethics and the gender equality dilemma for U.S. multinationals. *Journal of Business Ethics, 12,* 701–708.

Mayrhofer, W., Reichel, A., & Sparrow, P. (2012). Alternative forms of international working. In G. K. Stahl, I. Björkman, & S. Morris (Eds.), *Handbook of research in international human resource management* (2nd ed., pp. 293–320). Northampton, MA: Edward Elgar.

Maznevski, M. L., & Athanassiou, N. A. (2006). Guest editors' introduction to the focused issue: A new direction for global teams research. *Management International Review, 46,* 631–645.

Maznevski, M. L., & Chudoba, K. M. (2000). Bridging space over time: Global virtual team dynamics and effectiveness. *Organization Studies, 11*(5), 473–492.

Maznevski, M. L., Davison, S. C., & Jonsen, K. (2006). Global virtual team dynamics and effectiveness. In G. K. Stahl & I. Björkman (Eds.), *Handbook of international human resource management* (pp. 364–384). Cheltenham, UK: Edward Elgar.

Maznevski, M. L., DiStefano, J. J., & Nason, S. W. (1993, October). *The cultural perspectives questionnaire: Summary of results using CPQ3.* Paper presented at the annual meeting of the Academy of International Business, Kihei, HI.

Maznevski, M. L., DiStefano, J. J., Gomez, C. B., Noorderhaven, N. G., & Wu, P.-C. (2002). Cultural dimensions at the individual level of analysis: The cultural orientations framework. *International Journal of Cross-Cultural Management, 2,* 275–295.

McCall, J. B., & Warrington, M. B. (1990). *Marketing by agreement: A cross-cultural approach to business negotiations* (2nd ed.). Chichester, UK: John Wiley & Sons.

McCall, M. W. (1998). *High fliers: Developing the next generation of global leaders.* Boston, MA: Harvard Business School Press.

McCarthy, A., Lee, K., Itakura, S., & Muir, D. W. (2006). Cultural display rules drive eye gaze during thinking. *Journal of Cross-Cultural Psychology, 37,* 717–722.

McClelland, D. C. (1961). *The achieving society.* Princeton, NJ: Van Nostrand.

McGuire, W. J., & Padawer-Singer, A. (1976). Trait salience in the spontaneous self-concept. *Journal of Personality and Social Psychology, 33,* 743–754.

McLeod, P. L., Lobel, S. A., & Cox, T. H. (1996). Ethnic diversity and creativity in small groups. *Small Group Research, 27*(2), 248–264.

McSweeney, B. (2009). Dynamic diversity: Variety and variation within countries. *Organization Studies, 30,* 933–957.

Mead, M. (1937). *Cooperation and competition among primitive peoples.* New York: McGraw-Hill.

Meaning of Work International Research Team. (1987). *The meaning of working: An international view.* New York: Academic Press.

Meglino, B. M., & DeNisi, A. (1987). Realistic job previews: Some thoughts on their more effective use in managing the flow of human resources. *Human Resource Planning, 10,* 157–167.

Mendenhall, M., & Oddou, G. (1985). The dimensions of expatriate acculturation: A review. *Academy of Management Review, 10,* 39–47.

Mendenhall, M. E., Punnett, B. J., & Ricks, D. (1995). *Global management.* Cambridge, MA: Blackwell.

Merritt, A. C., & Helmreich, R. L. (1996). Human factors on the flight deck. *Journal of Cross-Cultural Psychology, 27,* 5–24.

Mesmer-Magnus, J. R., DeChurch, L. A., Jimenez-Rodriguez, M., Wildman, J., & Shuffler, M. (2011). A meta-analytic investigation of virtuality and information sharing in teams. *Organizational Behavior and Human Decision Processes, 115,* 214–225.

Mezias, S., Chen, Y. R., & Murphy, P. (1999). Toto, I don't think we're in Kansas anymore: Some footnotes to cross cultural research. *Journal of Management Inquiry, 8,* 323–333.

Miles, R. E., & Snow, C. C. (1978). *Organizational strategy, structure, and process.* New York: McGraw-Hill.

Mileti, D. S., Gillespie, D. F., & Haas, J. E. (1977, September). Size and structure in complex organizations. *Social Forces,* pp. 208–217.

Mill, J. (1863). *Utilitarianism.* Indianapolis: Bobbs-Merrill.

Miller, E. L. (1975). The job satisfaction of expatriate American managers: A function of regional location and previous work experience. *Journal of International Business Studies, 6*(2), 65–73.

Miller, E. L., & Cheng, J. (1978). A closer look at the decision to accept an overseas position. *Management International Review, 18,* 25–33.

Miller, G. A. (1956). The magical number seven plus or minus two. Some limits on our capacity for processing information. *Psychological Review, 63,* 81–97.

Miller, J. G. (1984). Culture and the development of everyday social explanation. *Journal of Personality and Social Psychology, 67,* 961–978.

Miller, J. G. (1994). Cultural diversity in the morality of caring: Individually oriented versus duty-oriented interpersonal codes. *Cross-Cultural Research, 28,* 3–39.

Miller, J. G., Bersoff, D. M., & Harwood, R. L. (1990). Perceptions of social responsibilities in India and the United States: Moral imperatives or personal decisions. *Journal of Personality and Social Psychology, 58,* 33–47.

Miller, L. (1995). Two aspects of Japanese and American co-worker interaction: Giving instructions and creating rapport. *Journal of Applied Behavioral Science, 2,* 212–221.

Milliken, F. J., & Martins, L. L. (1996). Searching for common threads: Understanding the multiple effects of diversity in organizational groups. *Academy of Management Review, 21*(2), 402–433.

Minkov, M., & Hofstede, G. (2012). Hofstede's fifth dimension: New evidence from the World Values Survey. *Journal of Cross Cultural Psychology, 43,* 3–14.

Mintzberg, H. (1973). *The nature of managerial work.* New York: Harper & Row.

Mintzberg, H. (1980). Structure in 5's: A synthesis of the research on organization design. *Management Science, 26,* 322–341.

Mintzberg, H. (1983). *Structuring in fives: Designing effective organizations.* Englewood Cliffs, NJ: Prentice Hall.

Misumi, J. (1984). Decision making in Japanese groups and organizations. In B. Wilpert & A. Sorge (Eds.), *International perspectives on organizational democracy* (pp. 92–123). New York: Wiley.

Misumi, J. (1985). *The behavioral science of leadership: An interdisciplinary Japanese research program.* Ann Arbor: University of Michigan Press.

Misumi, J., & Peterson, M. F. (1985). The performance-maintenance theory of leadership: Review of a Japanese research program. *Administrative Science Quarterly, 30,* 198–223.

Misumi, J., & Peterson, M. F. (1987). Supervision and leadership. In B. M. Bass, P. J. D. Drenth, & P. Weissenberg (Eds.), *Advances in organizational psychology: An international review* (pp. 220–231). Newbury Park, CA: Sage.

Mittal, R., & Dorfman, P. W. (2012). Servant leadership across cultures. *Journal of World Business, 47,* 555–570.

Mohammed, S., & Angell, L. C. (2004). Surface- and deep-level diversity in workgroups: Examining the moderating effects of team orientation and team process on relationship conflict. *Journal of Organizational Behavior, 25,* 1015–1039.

Mol, S. T., Born, M. P., Willemsen, M. E., & Van der Molen, H. T. (2005). Predicting expatriate job performance for selection purposes: A quantitative review. *Journal of Cross-Cultural Psychology, 35*(5), 590–620.

Molinsky, A. (2007). Cross-cultural code switching: The psychological challenges of adapting behavior in foreign cultural interactions. *Academy of Management Review, 32,* 622–640.

Molinsky, A. L. (2013). The psychological process of cultural retooling. *Academy of Management Journal, 56,* 683–710.

Molinsky, A. L., Krabbenhoft, M. A., Ambady, N., & Choi, Y. S. (2005). Cracking the nonverbal code: Intercultural competence and gesture recognition across cultures. *Journal of Cross-Cultural Psychology, 36,* 380–395.

Montagu, A. (1972). *Touching: The human significance of the skin.* New York: Harper & Row.

Moreland, R. L., & Levine, J. M. (1982). Socialization in small groups: Temporal changes in individual-group relations. *Advances in Experimental Social Psychology, 15,* 137–192.

Morosini, P., & Singh, H. (1994). Post-cross-border acquisitions: Implementing "national culture compatible" strategies to improve performance. *European Management Journal, 4,* 390–400.

Morris, D., Collett, P., Marsh, P., & O'Shaugnessy, M. (1979). *Gestures: Their origins and distribution.* Briarcliff Manor, NY: Stein & Day.

Morris, M. W., & Peng, K. (1994). Culture and cause: Chinese attributions for social and physical events. *Journal of Personality and Social Psychology, 67,* 949–971.

Morris, M., & Robie, C. (2001). A meta-analysis of the effects of cross-cultural training on expatriate performance and adjustment. *International Journal of Training and Development, 5*(2), 112–125.

Morrison, E. W., & Robinson, S. L. (1997). When employees feel betrayed: A model of how psychological contract violation develops. *Academy of Management Review, 22,* 226–256.

Morrison, T., Conaway, W. A., & Borden, G. A. (1994). *Kiss, bow, or shake hands: How to do business in sixty countries.* Holbrook, MA: Bob Adams.

Morsbach, H. (1982). Aspects of nonverbal communication in Japan. In L. A. Samovar & R. E. Porter (Eds.), *Intercultural communication: A reader* (pp. 300–316). Belmont, CA: Wadsworth.

Mortensen, M., & Hinds, P. J. (2001). Conflict and shared identity in geographically distributed teams. *International Journal of Conflict Management, 12,* 212–238.

Mottram, R. (Ed.). (1963). *The selection of personnel for international service.* New York: World Federation for Mental Health.

Mueller, S. L., & Clarke, L. D. (1998). Political economic context and sensitivity to equity: Differences between the United Sates and the transition economies of Central and Eastern Europe. *Academy of Management Journal, 41,* 319–329.

Mullen, B. (1987). Self-attention theory: The effects of group composition on the individual. In B. Mullen & G. R. Goethals (Eds.), *Theories of group behaviour* (pp. 125–146). New York: Springer-Verlag.

Mullen, B., & Baumeister, R. F. (1987). Groups effects on self-attention and performance: Social loafing, social facilitation, and social impairment. In C. Hendrick (Ed.), *Review of personality and social psychology* (pp. 189–206). Newbury Park, CA: Sage.

Naisbitt, J. (1994). *Global paradox.* New York: William Morrow.

Naisbitt, J., & Aburdene, P. (1990). *Megatrends 2000: Ten new directions for the 1990s.* New York: Avon.

Nakane, C. (1970). *Japanese society.* Berkeley: University of California Press.

Napier, N. K., & Taylor, S. (2002). Experiences of women professionals abroad: Comparisons across Japan, China, and Turkey. *International Journal of Human Resource Management, 13*, 837–851.

Napier, N. K., & Thomas, D. C. (2001). Some things you may not have learned in graduate school: A rough guide to collecting primary data overseas. In B. Toyne, Z. Martinez, & R. Menger (Eds.), *International business scholarship: Mastering intellectual, institutional, and research design challenges* (pp. 180–197). Westport, CT: Quorum.

Napier, N. K., & Thomas, D. C. (2004). *Managing relationships in transition economies.* New York: Praeger.

Natlandsmyr, J. H., & Rognes, J. (1995). Culture, behavior and negotiation outcomes: A comparative and cross-cultural study of Mexican and Norwegian negotiators. *The International Journal of Conflict Management, 6*(1), 5–29.

Naumann, E. (1993). Organizational predictors of expatriate job satisfaction. *Journal of International Business Studies, 24*, 61–80.

Neale, M. A., & Northcraft, G. B. (1991). Behavioral negotiation theory: A framework for conceptualizing dyadic bargaining. In L. L. Cummings & B. M. Staw (Eds.), *Research in organizational behavior* (Vol. 13, pp. 147–190). Greenwich, CT: JAI.

Neeley, T. (2012, May). Global business speaks English: Why you need a language strategy now. *Harvard Business Review,* pp. 117–124.

Nelson, G. L., El Bakary, W., & Al Batal, M. (1993). Egyptian and American compliments: A cross-cultural study. *International Journal of Intercultural Relations, 17*, 293–314.

Nemeth, C. J. (1992). Minority dissent as a stimulant to group performance. In S. Worchel, W. Wood, & J. A. Simpson (Eds.), *Group process and productivity* (pp. 95–111). Newbury Park, CA: Sage.

Nicholson, N., & Imaizumi, A. (1993). The adjustment of Japanese expatriates to living and working in Britain. *British Journal of Management, 4*, 119–134.

Niles, F. S. (1999). Toward a cross-cultural understanding of work-related beliefs. *Human Relations, 52*(7), 855–867.

Nisbett, R. E., Peng, K., Choi, I., & Norenzayan, A. (2001). Culture and systems of thought: Holistic versus analytic cognition. *Psychological Review, 108*, 291–310.

Nollen, P. (1984). *Non-verbal communication and marital interaction.* Elmsford, NY: Pergamon.

Nonaka, I. (1994). A dynamic theory of knowledge creation. *Organization Science, 5*(1), 14–38.

Nonaka, I., & Takeuchi, H. (1995). *The knowledge-creating company: How Japanese companies foster creativity and innovation for competitive advantage.* London: Oxford University Press.

Nyambegera, S. M., Daniels, K., & Sparrow, P. (2001). Why fit doesn't always matter: The impact of HRM and cultural fit on job involvement of Kenyan employees. *Applied Psychology, 50*(1), 109–140.

Oberg, K. (1960). Cultural shock: Adjustment to new cultural environments. *Practical Anthropology, 7*, 177–182.

O'Connell, M. S., Lord, R. G., & O'Connell, M. K. (1990). *An empirical comparison of Japanese and American leadership prototypes: Implications for overseas assignment of managers.* Paper presented at the 1990 meeting of the Academy of Management, San Francisco, CA.

Oddou, G. R., & Mendenhall, M. (1991). Succession planning for the 21st century: How well are we grooming our future business leaders? *Business Horizons, 34,* 26–34.

OECD. (2007). *OECD factbook 2007: Economic, environmental and social statistics.* Paris: Author.

O'Fallon, M. J., & Butterfield, K. D. (2005). A review of the empirical ethical decision-making literature: 1996–2003. *Journal of Business Ethics, 59,* 375–413.

Offerman, L. R., & Gowing, M. K. (1990). Organizations of the future: Changes and challenges. *American Psychologist, 45,* 95–108.

O'Grady, S., & Lane, H. W. (1996). The psychic distance paradox. *Journal of International Business Studies, 27,* 309–333.

O'Leary, M. B., Mortensen, M., & Woolley, A. W. (2011). Multiple team membership: A theoretical model of its effects on productivity and learning for individuals and teams. *Academy of Management Review, 36,* 461–478.

Onglatco, M. L. U. (1988). *Japanese quality control circles: Features, effects and problems.* Tokyo: Asian Productivity Center.

Ordóñez, L. D., Schweitzer, M. E., Galinsky, A. D., & Bazerman, M. H. (2009). Goals gone wild: The systematic side effects of overprescribing goal setting. *The Academy of Management Perspectives, 23*(1), 6–16.

Osland, J. S., & Bird, A. (2000). Beyond sophisticated stereotypes: Cultural sensemaking in context. *Academy of Management Executive, 14,* 65–79.

Osland, J. S., & Osland, A. (2001). Mastering international qualitative research. In B. Toyne, Z. Martinez, & R. Menger (Eds.), *International business scholarship: Mastering intellectual, institutional, and research design challenges* (pp. 198–214). Westport, CT: Quorum.

Ouchi, W. (1981). *Theory Z: How American business can meet the Japanese challenge.* Reading, MA: Addison-Wesley.

Ouchi, W. (1984). *The M-form society.* Reading, MA: Addison-Wesley.

Padilla, A., & Perez. W. (2003). Acculturation, social identity, and social cognition: A new perspective. *Hispanic Journal of Behavioral Sciences, 25,* 110–122.

Park, H., Russell, C., & Lee, J. (2007). National culture and environmental sustainability: A cross-cultural analysis. *Journal of Economics and Finance, 31*(1), 104–121.

Park, H., Sun, D. H., & David, J. M. (1993). Local manager selection for U.S. firms in Korea. *Multinational Business Review, 1*(2), 57–65.

Parker, B. (2005). *Introduction to globalization and business: Relationships and responsibilities.* London: Sage.

Parker, B., & McEvoy, G. M. (1993). Initial examination of a model of intercultural adjustment. *International Journal of Intercultural Relations, 17,* 355–379.

Parkes, L. P., Bochner, S., & Schneider, S. K. (2001). Person-organization fit across cultures: An empirical investigation of individualism and collectivism. *Applied Psychology, 50,* 81–108.

Parsons, T., & Shils, E. A. (1951). *Toward a general theory of action.* Cambridge, MA: Harvard University Press.

Patterson, M. L. (1991). A functional approach to nonverbal exchange. In R. S. Feldman & B. Rime (Eds.), *Fundamentals of nonverbal behavior* (pp. 458–495). New York: Cambridge University Press.

Pearce, J. A., & Ravlin, E. C. (1987). The design and activation of self-regulating work groups. *Human Relations, 11,* 751–782.

Pekerti, A. A. (2001). *Influence of culture on communication: An empirical test and theoretical refinement of the high- and low-context dimension.* (Unpublished doctoral dissertation). University of Auckland, NZ.

Pekerti, A. A., & Sendjaya, S. (2010). Exploring servant leadership across cultures: Comparative study in Australia and Indonesia. *International Journal of Human Resource Management, 21,* 754–780.

Pellegrini, E. K., & Scandura, T. A. (2007). Paternalistic leadership: A review and agenda for future research. *Academy of Management Best Paper Proceedings,* pp. 1–6.

Pellegrini, E. K., Scandura, T. A., & Jayaraman, V. (2010). Cross-cultural generalizability of paternalistic leadership: An expansion of leader member exchange theory. *Group & Organization Management, 35,* 391–420.

Pelto, P. J. (1968, April). The difference between tight and loose societies. *Transaction,* pp. 37–40.

Pelz, D. C. (1956). Some social factors related to performance in a research organization. *Administrative Science Quarterly, 1,* 310–325.

Peng, M. W. (2000). *Business strategies in transition economies.* Thousand Oaks, CA: Sage.

Peng, M. W. (2002). Cultures, institutions, and strategic choices: Toward an institutional perspective on business strategy. In M. J. Gannon & K. L. Newman (Eds.), *Handbook of cross-cultural management* (pp. 52–66). Oxford, UK: Blackwell.

Peng, T. K., & Peterson, M. F. (1993). The concepts of etic/emic and their applications in cross-cultural management research. *Chinese Management Association Journal of Management Science, 10*(1), 131–155.

Peng, T. K., Peterson. M. F., & Shyi, Y. P. (1991). Quantitative methods in cross national management research: Trends and equivalence issues. *Journal of Organizational Behavior, 12,* 87–107.

Penn, W., & Collier, B. (1985). Current research in moral development as a decision support system. *Journal of Business Ethics, 4,* 131–136.

Perlmutter, H. (1969). The tortuous evolution of the multinational corporation. *Columbia Journal of World Business, 4,* 9–18.

Perrewe, P. L., Ralston, D. A., & Fernandez, D. R. (1995). A model depicting the relations among perceived stressors, role conflict and organizational commitment: A comparative analysis of Hong Kong and the United States. *Asia Pacific Journal of Management, 12*(2), 1–21.

Perrow, C. (1967). A framework for the comparative analysis of organizations. *American Sociological Review, 32*(2), 194–208.

Peterson, M. F. (1988). PM theory in Japan and China: What's in it for the United States? *Organizational Dynamics, 16,* 22–38.

Peterson, M. F. (2001). International collaboration in organizational behavior research. *Journal of Organizational Behavior, 22,* 59–81.

Peterson, M. F. (2004). Culture, leadership and organizations: The GLOBE study of 62 societies [Book review]. *Administrative Science Quarterly, 49,* 641–647.

Peterson, M. F. (2007). The heritage of cross cultural management research: Implications for the Hofstede chair in cultural diversity. *International Journal of Cross Cultural Management, 7*(3), 359–378.

Peterson, M. F. (2009). Cross-cultural comparative studies and problems of coordinating international research teams. In D. A. Buchanan and A. Bryman (Eds.), *Handbook of organizational research methods* (pp. 328–345). London: Sage.

Peterson, M. F. (2011). International themes in organizational culture research. In N. M. Ashkanasy, C. P. M. Wilderom, & M. F. Peterson (Eds.), *Handbook of organizational culture and climate* (2nd ed., pp. 483–493). Thousand Oaks, CA: Sage.

Peterson, M. F., & Hunt, J. G. (1997). International perspectives on international leadership. *Leadership Quarterly, 8*, 203–232.

Peterson, M. F., & Smith, P. B. (1997). Does national culture or ambient temperature explain cross-national differences in role stress? No sweat! *Academy of Management Journal, 40*, 930–946.

Peterson, M. F., & Smith, P. B. (2008). Social structures and processes in cross cultural management. In P. B. Smith, M. F. Peterson, & D. C. Thomas (Eds.), *Handbook of cross-cultural management research* (pp. 35–58). Thousand Oaks, CA: Sage.

Peterson, M. F., & Soendergaard, M. (2011). Traditions and transitions in quantitative societal culture research in organization studies. *Organization Studies, 32*(11), 1539–1558.

Peterson, M. F., & Thomas, D. C. (2007). Organizational behavior in multinational organizations. *Journal of Organizational Behavior, 28*, 262–279.

Peterson, M. F., & van Iterson, A. (in press). Differences in work goals among regions of the Netherlands and Germany: Functional, institutional and critical event influences. *International Journal of Human Resource Management.*

Peterson, M. F., & Wood, R. E. (2008). Cognitive structures and processes in cross-cultural management. In P. B. Smith, M. F. Peterson, & D. C. Thomas (Eds.), *Handbook of cross-cultural management research* (pp. 15–34). Thousand Oaks, CA: Sage.

Peterson, M. F., Brannen, M. Y., & Smith, P. B. (1994). Japanese and U.S. leadership: Issues in current research. In *Advances in international comparative management* (Vol. 9, pp. 57–82). Greenwich, CT: JAI.

Peterson, M. F., Smith, P. B., & Tayeb, M. H. (1993). Development and use of English version of Japanese PM leadership measures in electronics plants. *Journal of Organizational Behavior, 14*, 251–267.

Peterson, M. F., Smith, P. B., Akande, A., Ayestaran, S., Bochner, S., Callan, V., et al. (1995). Role conflict, ambiguity, and overload: A 21-nation study. *Academy of Management Journal, 38*(2), 429–452.

Peterson, M. F., Thomason, S. J., Althouse, N., Athanassiou, N., Curri, G., Konopaske, R., et al. (2010). Social structures and personal values that predict e-mail use: An international comparative study. *Journal of Global Information Management, 18*(2), 57–84.

Peterson, R. A., & Jolibert, A. J. P. (1995). A meta-analysis of country of origin effects. *Journal of International Business Studies, 26*, 883–900.

Peterson, R. B. (1993). Future directions in international comparative management research. In D. Wong-Reiger & F. Reiger (Eds.), *International management research: Looking to the future* (pp. 13–25). New York: de Gruyter.

Peterson, R. B., Napier, N., & Won, S. (1995). *Expatriate management: The differential role of national multinational corporation ownership.* Paper presented at the annual meeting of the Academy of International Business, Seoul, Korea.

Pettigrew, T. F. (1979). The ultimate attribution error: Extending Allport's cognitive analysis of prejudice. *Personality and Social Psychology Bulletin, 5*, 461–476.

Phatak, A., & Habib, M. (1998). How should managers treat ethics in international business? *Thunderbird International Business Review, 40*(2), 101–117.

Pinker, S. (1994). *The language instinct.* London: Penguin.

Pittman, J. (1994). *Voice in social interaction: An interdisciplinary approach.* Thousand Oaks, CA: Sage.

Poe, A. C. (2000). Welcome back. *HR Magazine, 45*(3), 94–105.

Poelmans, S., Maestro, M. L. H., & Greenhaus, J. (2013). *Expanding the boundaries of work-family research: A vision for the future.* Basingstoke, UK: Palgrave Macmillan UK.

Porat, A. (1970). Cross-cultural differences in resolving union management conflict through negotiation. *Journal of Applied Psychology, 54,* 441–451.

Porter, L. W., & Lawler, E. E. (1968). *Managerial attitudes and performance.* Homewood, IL: Irwin.

Porter, M. E. (1980). *Competitive strategy.* New York: Free Press.

Porter, M. E. (1986). Changing patterns of international competition. *California Management Review, 28*(2), 9–40.

Pothukuchi, V., Damanpour, F., Choi, J., Chen, C. C., & Park, S. H. (2002). National and organizational culture differences and international joint venture performance. *Journal of International Business Studies, 33,* 243–266.

Privatization. (1997, March). *Economist,* p. 143.

Prothro, E. T. (1955). Arab–American differences in the judgment of written messages. *Journal of Social Psychology, 42,* 3–11.

Pucik, V., Björkman, I., Evans, P., and Stahl, G. (2011). Human resource management in cross-border mergers and acquisitions. In A. W. Harzing and A. H. Pinnington (Eds.), *International human resource management* (3rd ed., pp. 119–152). London: Sage.

Puck, J. F., Kittler, M. G., & Wright, C. (2008). Does it really work? Re-assessing the impact of pre-departure cross-cultural training on expatriate adjustment. *The International Journal of Human Resource Management, 19,* 2182–2197.

Puffer, S. (1996). *Business and management in Russia.* Cheltenham, UK: Edward Elgar.

Puffer, S. (1994). Understanding the bear: A portrait of Russian business leaders. *Academy of Management Perspectives, 8,* 41–54.

Pugh, D. S., & Hickson, D. J. (1976). *Organizational structure in its context: The Aston programme I.* Farnborough, UK: Gower.

Pugh, D. S., Hickson, D. J., Hinings, C. R., MacDonald, K. M., & Turner, C. (1963). Dimensions of organization structure. *Administrative Science Quarterly, 13,* 65–105.

Putnam, R. (1993). *Making democracy work: Civic traditions in modern Italy.* Princeton, NJ: Princeton University Press.

Pye, L. (1982). *Chinese commercial negotiating style.* Cambridge, MA: Oelgeschlager.

Radford, M. H. B., Mann, L., Ohta, Y., & Nakane, Y. (1989). Individual decision making behavior and personality: A preliminary study using a Japanese university sample. *Japanese Journal of Experimental Social Psychology, 28,* 115–122.

Radford, M. H. B., Mann, L., Ohta, Y., & Nakane, Y. (1991). Differences between Australian and Japanese students in reported use of decision processes. *International Journal of Psychology, 26,* 284–297.

Ralston, D. A. (1993). Differences in managerial values: A study of the U.S., Hong Kong, and PRC managers. *Journal of International Business Studies, 24*(2), 249–275.

Ralston, D. A., Egri, C., Reynaud, E., Srinivasan, N., Furrer, O., Brock, D., et al. (2011). A 21st century assessment of values across the global workplace. *Journal of Business Ethics, 104*(4), 1–31.

Ralston, D. A., Holt, D. H., Terpstra, R. H., & Yu, K. (1997). The impact of national culture and economic ideology on managerial work values: A study of the United States, Russia, Japan, and China. *Journal of International Business Studies, 28*(1), 177–207.

Randel, A. E. (2003). The salience of culture in multinational teams and its relation to team citizenship behavior. *International Journal of Cross-Cultural Management, 3,* 27–44.

Rao, A., & Hashimoto, K. (1996). Intercultural influence: A study of Japanese expatriate managers in Canada. *Journal of International Business Studies, 27,* 443–466.

Ravlin, E. C., Liao, Y., Morrell, D. L., Au, K., & Thomas D. C. (2012). Collectivist orientation and the psychological contract: Mediating effects of creditor ideology. *Journal of International Business Studies, 43,* 772–782.

Ravlin, E. C., Thomas, D. C., & Ilsev, A. (2000). Beliefs about values, status, and legitimacy in multicultural groups. In P. C. Earley & H. Singh (Eds.), *Innovations in international and cross-cultural management* (pp. 17–51). Thousands Oaks, CA: Sage.

Redding, S. G., Norman, A., & Schlander, A. (1994). The nature of individual attachment to the organization: A review of East Asian variations. In H. C. Triandis (Ed.), *Handbook of industrial/ organizational psychology* (2nd ed., Vol. 4, pp. 647–688). Palo Alto, CA: Consulting Psychologists Press.

Reiche, B. S., & Harzing, A.-W. (2011). International assignments. In A.-W. Harzing, & A. Pinnington (Eds.), *International human resource management* (3rd ed., pp. 187–226). London, UK: Sage.

Reiche, B. S., Kraimer, M., & Harzing, A.-W. (2011). Why do international assignees stay? *Journal of International Business Studies, 42,* 521–544.

Renard, M. K., Tracy, K. B., Ostrow, M. H., & Chah, D. (1997). Cultural differences in equity sensitivity: A comparison between US and Korean subjects. *International Journal of Management, 14,* 476–489.

Renesch, J. (Ed.). (1992). *New traditions in business.* San Francisco: Berrett-Koehler.

Rest, J. R. (1994). Background: Theory and research. In J. R. Rest & D. Narváez (Eds.), *Moral Development in the Professions: Psychology and Applied Ethics* (pp. 1–26). Hillsdale, NJ: Lawrence Erlbaum.

Ricks, D. A. (1993). *Blunders in international business.* Cambridge, MA: Blackwell.

Robbins, S. P. (1992). *Essentials of organizational behavior* (3rd ed.). Englewood Cliffs, NJ: Prentice Hall.

Robertson, C., & Fadil, P. A. (1999). Ethical decision making in multinational organizations: A culture-based model. *Journal of Business Ethics, 19,* 385–392.

Robertson, R. (1995). Glocalization: Time-space and homogeneity-heterogeneity. In M. Featherstone, S. Lash, & R. Robertson (Eds.), *Global modernities* (pp. 25–44). London: Sage.

Robinson, R. D. (1984). *The internationalization of business: An introduction.* Chicago: Dryden.

Rohner, R. (1984). Toward a conception of culture for cross-cultural psychology. *Journal of Cross-Cultural Psychology, 15,* 111–138.

Rokeach M. (1968). A theory of organization and change within value-attitude systems. *Journal of Social Issues, 24,* 13–33.

Rokeach, M. (1973). *The nature of human values.* New York: Free Press.

Ronen, S. (1986). *Comparative and multinational management.* New York: John Wiley & Sons.

Rosen, R., Digh, P., Singer, M., & Phillips, C. (2000). *Global literacies: Lessons on business leadership and national cultures.* New York: Simon & Schuster.

Rosenzweig, P. M., & Nohria, N. (1994). Influences on human resource management practices in multinational corporations. *Journal of International Business Studies, 25,* 229–251.

Rosenzweig, P. M., & Singh, J. V. (1991). Organizational environments and the multinational enterprise. *Academy of Management Review, 16*(2), 340–361.

Rosette, A. S., Brett, J. M., Barsness, Z., & Lytle, A. L. (2012). When cultures clash electronically: The impact of e-mail and social norms on negotiation behavior and outcomes. *Journal of Cross Cultural Psychology, 43,* 628–643.

Ross, L. (1977). The intuitive psychologist and his shortcomings. In L. Berkowitz (Ed.), *Advances in experimental social psychology* (Vol. 10, pp. 173–220). New York: Academic Press.

Ross, S., & Shortreed, I. M. (1990). Japanese foreigner talk: Convergence or divergence. *Journal of Asian Pacific Communication, 1,* 134–145.

Roth, K., Schweiger, D., & Morrison, A. J. (1991). Global strategy implementation at the business unit level: Operational capabilities and administrative mechanisms. *Journal of International Business Studies, 22*, 369–402.

Rotter, J. B. (1966). Generalized expectancies for internal versus external control of reinforcement. *Psychological Monographs: General and Applied, 80*(1), 609.

Rousseau, D. M. (1989). Psychological and implied contracts in organizations. *Employee Responsibilities and Rights Journal, 2*, 121–139.

Rozin, P. (1998). Evolution and development of brains and cultures. In M. Gazzaniga & J. Altman (Eds.), *Brain and mind* (pp. 111–123). Strasbourg, France: Human Frontier Science Program.

Ruben, B. D., & Kealey, D. J. (1979). Behavioral assessment of communication competency and the prediction of cross-cultural adaptation. *International Journal of Intercultural Relations, 3*, 15–47.

Rubin, E. (1915). *Synsoplevede figurer* [Visual figures]. Copenhagen: Gyldendalske Boghandel.

Ruedi, A., & Lawrence, P. R. (1970). Organization in two cultures. In J. W. Lorsch & P. R. Lawrence (Eds.), *Studies in organizational design* (pp. 54–83). Homewood, IL: Irwin.

Rusbult, C. E., Insko, C. A., & Lin, Y.-H. W. (1993). Seniority-based reward allocation in the US and Taiwan. *Social Psychology Quarterly, 58*, 13–30.

Rushton, J. P. (1989). Genetic similarity, human altruism, and group selection. *Behavioral and Brain Sciences, 12*, 503–559.

"Russia's state sell off: 'It's sink or swim time.'" (1994, July 7). *Business Week,* p. 46.

Russo, J. E., & Shoemaker, P. J. H. (1989). *Decision traps.* New York: Doubleday.

Ryan, A. M., McFarland, L., Baron, H., & Page, R. (1999). An international look at selection practices: Nation and culture as explanations of variability in practice. *Personnel Psychology, 52*(2), 359–391.

Sack, R. (1973). The impact of education on individual modernity in Tunisia. *International Journal of Comparative Sociology, 14*, 245–272.

Sackmann, S. (2011). Culture and performance. In N. M. Ashkanasy, C. P. M. Wilderom, & M. F. Peterson (Eds.), *Handbook of organizational culture and climate* (2nd ed., pp. 188–224). Thousand Oaks, CA: Sage.

Sackmann, S. A., & Phillips, M. E. (2004). Contextual influences on cultural research: Shifting assumptions for new workplace realities. *International Journal of Cross Cultural Management, 4*, 370–390.

Sagiv, L., & Schwartz, S. H. (1995). Value priorities and readiness for out-group social contact. *Journal of Personality and Social Psychology, 69*, 437–448.

Sagiv, L., & Schwartz, S. H. (2000). A new look at national culture: Illustrative applications to role stress and managerial behavior. In N. N. Ashkanasy, C. Wilderom, & M. F. Peterson (Eds.), *The handbook of organizational culture and climate* (pp. 417–435). Thousand Oaks, CA: Sage.

Sagiv L., Schwartz, S. H., Arieli, S. (2011). Personal values, national culture and organizations: Insights applying the Schwartz value framework. In N. M. Ashkanasy, C. P. M. Wilderom, & M. F. Peterson (Eds.), *The handbook of organizational culture and climate* (2nd ed. pp. 515–537). Newbury Park, CA: Sage

Salacuse, J. (1991). *Making global deals.* Boston: Houghton Mifflin.

Salancik, G. R., & Pfeffer, J. (1978). A social information processing approach to job attitudes and task design. *Administrative Science Quarterly, 23,* 224–253.

Salk, J. E., & Brannen, M. Y. (2000). National culture, networks and individual influence in a multinational management team. *Academy of Management Journal, 43*, 191–202.

Sanchez-Burks, J., Lee, F., Choi, I., Nisbett, R., Zhao, S., & Koo, J. (2003). Conversing across cultures: East–West communication styles in work and nonwork contexts. *Journal of Personality and Social Psychology, 85*, 363–372.

Sanderson, S. W., & Hayes, R. H. (1990). Mexico: Opening ahead of Eastern Europe. *Harvard Business Review, 68*, 32–43.

Sarala, R., & Vaara, E. (2010). Cultural differences, convergence and crossvergence as explanations of knowledge transfer in international acquisitions. *Journal of International Business Studies, 41*, 1365–1390.

Sayles, L. R. (1964). *Managerial behavior.* New York: McGraw-Hill.

Schalk, R., & Soeters, J. (2008). Psychological contracts around the globe: Cultural agreements and disagreements. *HCCMR*, pp. 117–134.

Schein, E. (1996). Career anchors revisited: Implications for career development in the 21st century. *Academy of Management Executive, 10*(4), 80–88.

Schein, E. H. (1985). *Organizational culture and leadership.* San Francisco: Jossey-Bass.

Scherer, K. R. (1979). Personality markers in speech. In K. R. Scherer & H. Giles (Eds.), *Social markers in speech* (pp. 147–209). Cambridge, UK: Cambridge University Press.

Schneider, B., Ehrhart, M. G., & Macey, W. H. (2011). Organizational climate research: Achievements and the road ahead. In N. M. Ashkanasy, C. P. M. Wilderom, & M. F. Peterson (Eds.), *The handbook of organizational culture and climate* (2nd ed., pp. 29–49). Thousand Oaks, CA: Sage.

Schneider, S. C., & Barsoux, J. L. (1997). *Managing across cultures.* London: Prentice Hall Europe.

Schön, D. A. (1993). Generative metaphor: A perspective on problem-setting in social policy. In A. Ortony (Ed.), *Metaphor and thought* (pp. 137–163). Cambridge, UK: Cambridge University Press.

Schramm, W. (1980). How communication works. In S. B. Weinberg (Ed.), *Message: A reader in human communication* (pp. 51–63). New York: Random House.

Schriesheim, C. A., & Kerr, S. (1977). Theories and measures of leadership: A critical appraisal. In J. C. Hunt & L. L. Larson (Eds.), *Leadership: The cutting edge* (pp. 9–44). Carbondale: Southern Illinois University Press.

Schuster, B., Fosterlung, F., & Weiner, B. (1989). Perceiving the causes of success and failure. *Journal of Cross-Cultural Psychology, 20*(2), 191–213.

Schwartz, S. H. (1992). Universals in the content and structure of values: Theoretical advances and empirical tests in 20 countries. In M. P. Zanna (Ed.), *Advances in experimental social psychology* (pp. 1–65). San Diego, CA: Academic Press.

Schwartz, S. H. (1994). Beyond individualism/collectivism: New dimensions of values. In U. Kim, H. C. Triandis, C. Kağitçibasi, S. C. Choi, & G. Yoon (Eds.), *Individualism and collectivism: Theory, applications, and methods* (pp. 85–119). Thousand Oaks, CA: Sage.

Schwartz, S. H. (2009). Culture matters: National value cultures, sources and consequences. In C. Y. Chiu, Y. Y. Hong, S. Shavitt, & R. S. Wyer Jr. (Eds.), *Understanding culture: Theory, research, and application* (pp. 127–150). New York: Psychology Press.

Schwartz, S. H., & Bilsky, W. (1990). Toward a universal psychological structure of human values. *Journal of Personality and Social Psychology, 53*, 550–562.

Schwartz, S. H., & Sagie, G. (2000). Value consensus and importance: A cross national study. *Journal of Cross-Cultural Psychology, 31*(4), 465–497.

Scott, W. R., & Davis, G. F. (2006). *Organizations and organizing: Rational, natural and open systems perspectives.* London: Pearson Publishing.

Scullion, H. (1991, November). Why companies prefer to use expatriates. *Personnel Management,* pp. 32–35.

Selmer, J. (2001). Expatriate selection: Back to basics? *International Journal of Human Resource Management, 12,* 1219–1233.

Selmer, J. (2006). Cultural novelty and adjustment: Western business expatriates in China. *International Journal of Human Resource Management, 17,* 1209–1222.

Selmer, J., & Leung, A. S. M. (2003). International adjustment of female vs. male business expatriates. *International Journal of Human Resource Management, 14*(7), 1117–1131.

Semnani-Azad, Z., Alair, W. L. (2011). The display of "dominant" nonverbal cues in negotiation: The role of culture & gender. *International Negotiation, 16,* 451–479.

Senge, P. (1990). *The fifth discipline: The art and practice of the learning organization.* New York: Doubleday.

Sewell, W. H., & Davidson, O. M. (1956). The adjustment of Scandinavian students. *Journal of Social Issues, 12,* 9–19.

Shaffer, M. A., Harrison, D. A., Gregerson, H., Black, J. S., & Ferzandi, L. A. (2006). You can take it with you: Individual differences and expatriate effectiveness. *Journal of Applied Psychology, 91,* 109–125.

Shaffer, M., Kraimer, M., Chen, Y.-P., & Bolino, M. C. (2012). Choices, challenges, and career consequences of global work experiences: A review and future agenda. *Journal of Management, 38*(4), 1282–1327.

Shapiro, D. L., Furts, S. A., Spreitzer, G. M., & Von Glinow, M. A. (2002). Transnational teams in the electronic age: Are team identity and high performance at risk? *Journal of Organizational Behavior, 23,* 455–467.

Shaw, J. B. (1990). A cognitive categorization model for the study of intercultural management. *Academy of Management Review, 15*(4), 626–645.

Shaw, W. (1996). *Business ethics* (2nd ed.). Belmont, CA: Wadsworth.

Shay, J. P., & Baack, S. (2004). Expatriate assignment, adjustment and effectiveness: An empirical examination of the big picture. *Journal of International Business Studies, 35,* 216–232.

Sherif, M., Harvey, O. J., White, B. J., Hood, W. R., & Sherif, C. W. (1961). *Intergroup conflict and cooperation.* Norman, OK: Institute of Group Relations.

Shih, H. A., Chiang, Y. H., & Kim, I. S. (2005). Expatriate performance management from MNEs of different national origins. *International Journal of Manpower, 26*(2), 157–176.

Shimoda, K., Argyle, M., & Ricci-Bitti, P. (1984). The intercultural recognition of emotional expressions by three national racial groups: English, Italian, and Japanese. *European Journal of Social Psychology, 8*(2), 169–179.

Shuter, R. (1977). A field study of non-verbal communication in Germany, Italy and the United States. *Communication Monographs, 44*(3), 298–305.

Sidanius, J. (1993). The psychology of group conflict and the dynamics of oppression: A social dominance perspective. In S. Iyenger & W. McGuire (Eds.), *Explorations in political psychology* (pp. 183–219). Durham, NC: Duke University Press.

Simon, H. A. (1955). A behavioral model of rational choice. *Quarterly Journal of Economics, 69,* 129–138.

Sinangil, H. K., & Ones, D. S. (2003). Gender differences in expatriate performance. *Applied Psychology: An International Review, 52,* 461–475.

Singelis, T. M., & Brown, W. J. (1995). Culture, self, and collectivist communication: Linking culture to individual behavior. *Human Communication Research, 21,* 354–389.

Skovbro, C., & Worm, V. (2002). Mailing the myths of international assignment. *European Business Forum, 11,* 70–72.

Smircich, L. (1983). Concepts of culture in organizational analysis. *Administrative Science Quarterly, 28,* 339–358.

Smircich, L., & Calas, M. B. (1986). Organizational culture: A critical assessment. *Annual Review of Sociology, 2,* 228–263.

Smith, P. B. (2004). Acquiescent response bias as an aspect of cultural communication style. *Journal of Cross-Cultural Psychology, 35*(1), 50–61.

Smith, P. B. (2008). Indigenous aspects of management. In P. B. Smith, M. F. Peterson & D. C. Thomas (Eds.), *Handbook of cross-cultural management research* (pp. 319–332). Thousand Oaks, CA: Sage.

Smith, P. B., & Bond, M. H. (1999). *Social psychology across cultures.* Boston: Allyn & Bacon.

Smith, P. B., & Peterson, M. F. (1988). *Leadership, organizations and culture: An event management model.* London: Sage.

Smith, P. B., & Peterson, M. F. (1994). *Leadership in event management: A cross-cultural survey based upon middle managers from 25 nations.* Paper presented at the 23rd International Congress of Applied Psychology, Madrid, Spain.

Smith, P. B., Bond, M. H., & Kağitçibasi, C. (2006). *Understanding social psychology across cultures: Living and working in a changing world.* London: Sage.

Smith, P. B., Dugan, S., & Trompenaars, F. (1996). National culture and the values of organizational employees: A dimensional analysis across 43 nations. *Journal of Cross-Cultural Psychology, 27*(2), 231–264.

Smith, P. B., Fischer, R., Vignoles, V. L., & Bond, M. H. (2013). *Understanding social psychology across cultures: Engaging with others in a changing world* (2nd ed.). Thousand Oaks, CA: Sage.

Smith, P. B., Misumi, J., Tayeb, M., Peterson, M., & Bond, M. (1989). On the generality of leadership styles across cultures. *Journal of Occupational Psychology, 62,* 97–109.

Smith, P. B., Peterson, M. F., & Schwartz, S. (2002). Cultural values, sources of guidance and their relevance to managerial behavior: A 47 nation study. *Journal of Cross Cultural Psychology, 33*(1), 188–208.

Smith, P. B., Peterson, M. F., & Wang, Z. M. (1996). The manager as mediator of alternative meanings: A pilot study from China, the USA and U.K. *Journal of International Business Studies, 27*(1), 115–137.

Smith, P. B., Peterson, M. F., Bond, M., & Misumi, J. (1992). Leader style and leader behavior in individualist and collectivist cultures. In S. Iwawaki, Y. Kashima, & K. Leung (Eds.), *Innovations in cross-cultural psychology* (pp. 76–85). Amsterdam: Swets & Zeitlinger.

Smith, P. B., Peterson, M. F., Thomason, S. P., and the Event Meaning Management Research Group (2011). National culture as a moderator of the relationship between leaders' use of guidance sources and how well work events are handled. *Journal of Cross Cultural Psychology, 42*(6), 1103–1123.

Smith, P. B., Trompenaars, F., & Dugan, S. (1995). The Rotter locus of control scale in 43 countries: A test of cultural relativity. *International Journal of Psychology, 30,* 377–400.

Snarey, J. R. (1985). Cross-cultural universality of social–moral development: A critical review of Kohlbergian research. *Psychological Bulletin, 97,* 202–232.

Snyder, M. (1981). On the self-perpetuating nature of social stereotypes. In D. L. Hamilton (Ed.), *Cognitive processes in stereotyping and intergroup behavior* (pp. 183–212). Hillsdale, NJ: Lawrence Erlbaum.

Solomon, C. M. (1998, May). Women expats: Shattering myths. *Workforce,* pp. 5–10.

Spector, P. E., Allen, T. D., Poelmans, S. A., Lapierre, L. M., Cooper, C. L., & 18 others (2007). Cross-national differences in relationships of work demands, job satisfaction, and turnover intentions with work-family conflict. *Personnel Psychology, 60*(4), 805–835.

Spicer, A., Dunfee, T. W., & Bailey, W. J. (2004). Does national context matter in ethical decision making? An empirical test of integrative social contracts theory. *Academy of Management Journal, 47,* 610–620.

Spina, R. R., Ji, L.-J., Guo, T., Zhang, Z., Li, Y., & Fabrigar, L. (2010). Cultural differences in the representativeness heuristic: Expecting a correspondence in magnitude between cause and effect. *Personality and Psychology Bulletin, 36,* 583–597.

Stahl, G. K. (1998). *Internationaler einsatz von führungskäften* [International transfer of managers]. Munich: Oldenbourg.

Stahl, G. K. (2008). The cultural dynamics of mergers and acquisitions. In P. B. Smith, M. F. Peterson, & D. C. Thomas (Eds.), *Handbook of cross-cultural management research* (pp. 431–448). Thousand Oaks, CA: Sage.

Stahl, G. K., & Cerdin, J.-L. (2004). Global careers in French and German multinational corporations. *Journal of Management Development, 23,* 885–902.

Stahl, G. K., Chua, C. H., & Pablo, A. L. (2003). Trust following acquisitions: A three country comparative study of employee reactions to takeovers. *Academy of Management Best Paper Proceedings,* N1–N6.

Stahl, G. K., Maznevski, M. L., Voigt, A., & Jonsen, K. (2010). Unraveling the effects of cultural diversity in teams: A meta-analysis of research on multicultural groups. *Journal of International Business Studies, 41,* 690–709.

Stahl, G. K., Maznevski, M., Voigt, A., & Jonsen, K. (2006). *Unraveling the diversity-performance link in multicultural teams: A meta-analysis of studies on the impact of cultural diversity in teams.* Paper presented to the annual meeting of the Academy of Management, Atlanta, GA.

Stahl, G. K., Miller, E., & Tung, R. (2002). Toward the boundaryless career: A closer look at the career concept and the perceived implications for an international assignment. *Journal of World Business, 37,* 216–227.

Stahl, G. K., Pucik, V., Evans, P., & Mendenhall, M. E. (2004). Human resource management in cross-border mergers and acquisitions. In A.-W. Harzing & J. V. Ruysseveldt (Eds.), *International Human Resource Management* (2nd ed., pp. 89–114). London: Sage.

Staples, D. S., & Zhao, L. (2006). The effects of cultural diversity in virtual teams versus face-to-face teams. *Group Decision and Negotiation, 15,* 389–406.

Steers, R. M., & Sánchez-Runde, C. J. (2002). Culture, motivation, and work behavior. In M. J. Gannon & K. L. Newman (Eds.), *Handbook of cross-cultural management* (pp. 190–216). Oxford, UK: Blackwell.

Steers, R. M., Shin, Y. K., & Ungson, G. R. (1989). *The* chaebol. New York: Harper-Business.

Stein, M. I. (1966). *Volunteers for peace.* New York: John Wiley & Sons.

Steiner, I. D. (1972). *Group process and productivity.* New York: Academic Press.

Stening, B. W. (1979). Problems in cross-cultural contact: A literature review. *International Journal of Intercultural Relations, 3,* 269–313.

Stening, B. W., & Hammer, M. R. (1992). Cultural baggage and the adaptation of expatriate Japanese managers. *Management International Review, 32*(1), 77–89.

Stewart, R. (1982). *Choices for the manager.* Englewood Cliffs, NJ: Prentice Hall.

Stewart, R., Barsoux, J. L., Kieser, A., Ganter, H. D., & Walgenbach, P. (1994). *Managing in Britain and Germany.* Basingstoke, UK: Macmillan.

Stiglitz, J. E. (2007). *Making globalization work.* New York: Norton.

Stiglitz, J. E. (2008). Making globalization work—the 2006 Geary lecture. *The Economic and Social Review, 39,* 171–190.

Stogdill, R. M. (1948). Personal factors associated with leadership: A survey of the literature. *The Journal of Psychology: Interdisciplinary and Applied, 25,* 35–71.

Stone, R. J. (1991). Expatriate selection and failure. *Human Resource Planning, 29*(1), 9–17.

Stopford, J. M., & Wells, L. T. (1972). *Strategy and structure in multinational enterprise.* New York: Basic Books.

Strauch, B. (2010). Can cultural differences lead to accidents? Team cultural differences and sociotechnical systems operations. *Human Factors, 52,* 246–263.

Stroh, L. K., Dennis, L. E., & Cramer, T. C. (1994). Predictors of expatriate adjustment. *International Journal of Organizational Analysis, 2,* 176–192.

Stroh, L. K., Gregersen, H. B., & Black, J. S. (1998). Closing the gap: Expectations versus reality among expatriates. *Journal of World Business, 33*(2), 111–124.

Stroh, L. K., Varma, A., & Valy-Durbin, S. J. (2000). Why are women left at home: Are they unwilling to go on international assignment? *Journal of World Business, 35*(3), 241–255.

Sullivan, J. (1997). Theory development in international business research: The decline of culture. In B. Toyne & D. Nigh (Eds.), *International business: An emerging vision* (pp. 380–395). Columbia: University of South Carolina Press.

Sumner, W. G. (1940). *Folkways.* Boston: Ginn.

Sussman, N., & Rosenfeld, H. (1982). Influence of culture, language and sex on conversational distance. *Journal of Personality and Social Psychology, 42,* 66–74.

Suutari, V. (2002). Global leader development: An emerging research agenda. *Career Development International, 7,* 218–233.

Suutari, V., & Brewster, C. (2000). Making their own way: International experience through self-initiated foreign assignments. *Journal of World Business, 35*(4), 417–436.

Sweeney, E., & Hua, Z. (2010). Accommodating toward your audience: Do native speakers of English know how to accommodate their communication strategies toward non-native speakers of English? *Journal of Business Communication, 47,* 477–504.

Szilagyi, A. D., & Wallace, M. J., Jr. (1987). *Organizational behavior and performance* (4th ed.). Glenview, IL: Scott, Foresman.

Tabuchi, H. (2011, May 20). Head of Japanese utility steps down after nuclear crisis. *The NY Times.* http://www.nytimes.com/2011/05/21/business/global/21iht-tepco21.html?page wanted=all&_r=0

Tadmor, C. T., & Tetlock, P. E. (2006). Biculturalism: A model of the effects of second-culture exposure on acculturation and integrative complexity. *Journal of Cross-Cultural Psychology, 37,* 1733–190.

Tadmor, C. T., Galinsky, A. D., & Maddux, W. M. (2012). Getting the most out of living abroad: Biculturalism and integrative complexity as key drivers of creative and professional success. *Journal of Personality and Social Psychology, 103,* 520–542.

Tadmor, C. T., Hong. Y-y., Chao, M. M., Wiruchnipawan, F., & Wang, W. (2012). Multicultural experiences reduce intergroup bias through epistemic unfreezing. *Journal of Personality and Social Psychology, 103,* 750–772.

Tadmor, C. T., Satterstrom, P., Jang, S., & Polzer, J. T. (2012). Beyond individual creativity: The superadditive benefits of multicultural experience for collective creativity in culturally diverse teams. *Journal of Cross-Cultural Psychology, 43,* 384–392.

Taggar, S. (2002). Creativity and group ability to utilize creative resources: A multilevel model. *Academy of Management Journal, 45,* 315–330.

Tajfel, H. (1981). *Human groups and social categories.* Cambridge, UK: Cambridge University Press.

Tajfel, H. (1982). Social psychology of intergroup relations. *Annual Review of Psychology, 33,* 1–39.

Tajfel, H., & Turner, J. C. (1986). The social identity theory of intergroup behaviour. In S. Worchel & W. G. Wood (Eds.), *Psychology of intergroup relations* (pp. 7–24). Chicago: Nelson-Hall.

Takeuchi, R., & Hannon, J. M. (1996). *The antecedents of adjustment for Japanese expatriates in the United States.* Paper presented to the annual meeting of the Academy of International Business, Banff, Canada.

Tang, L., & Koveos, P. E. (2008). A framework to update Hofstede's cultural value indices: Economic dynamics and institutional stability. *Journal of International Business Studies, 39*(6), 1045–1063.

Taras, V., Kirkman, B. L., & Steel, P. (2010). Examining the impact of Culture's Consequences: A three-decade, multilevel, meta-analytic review of Hofstede's cultural value dimensions. *Journal of Applied Psychology, 95,* 405–539.

Tayeb, M. (1987). Contingency theory and culture: A study of matched English and the Indian manufacturing firms. *Organization Studies, 8*(3), 241–261.

Taylor, D. M., & Jaggi, V. (1974). Ethnocentrism and causal attribution in a South Indian context. *Journal of Cross-Cultural Psychology, 5,* 162–171.

Taylor, F. W. (1911). *The principles of scientific management.* New York: Harper & Row.

Taylor, S. (1981). A categorization approach to stereotyping. In D. Hamilton (Ed.), *Cognitive processes in stereotyping and intergroup behavior* (pp. 83–114). Hillsdale, NJ: Lawrence Erlbaum.

Taylor, S. E. (1989). *Positive illusions.* New York: Basic Books.

Taylor, S., & Napier, N. (1996). Working in Japan: Lessons from women expatriates. *Sloan Management Review, 37,* 76–84.

Taylor, W. (1991, March–April). The logic of global business: An interview with ABB's Percy Barnevik. *Harvard Business Review,* 91–105.

Terpstra, V., & David, K. (1985). *The cultural environment of international business.* Dallas: South-Western Publishing.

Thal, N. L., & Cateora, P. R. (1979). Opportunities for women in international business. *Business Horizons, 22*(6), 21–27.

Tharenou, P. (2003). The initial development of receptivity to working abroad: Self-initiated international work opportunities in young graduate employees. *Journal of Occupational and Organizational Psychology, 76,* 489–508.

Thibaut, J. W., & Kelley, H. H. (1959). *The social psychology of groups.* New York: John Wiley & Sons.

Thomas, A. (1996). A call for research in forgotten locations. In B. J. Punnett & O. Shenkar (Eds.), *Handbook for international management research* (pp. 485–506). Cambridge, MA: Blackwell.

Thomas, D. C. (1992). *Subordinates' responses to cultural adaptation by managers: The effect of stereotypic expectation.* (Unpublished doctoral dissertation). The University of South Carolina, Columbia.

Thomas, D. C. (1994). The boundary-spanning role of expatriates in the multinational corporation. *Advances in International Comparative Management, 9,* 145–170.

Thomas, D. C. (1998). The expatriate experience: A critical review and synthesis. *Advances in International Comparative Management, 12,* 237–273.

Thomas, D. C. (1999). Cultural diversity and work group effectiveness: An experimental study. *Journal of Cross-Cultural Psychology, 30*(3), 242–263.

Thomas, D. C. (2006). Domain and development of cultural intelligence: The importance of mindfulness. *Group & Organization Management, 31,* 78–99.

Thomas, D. C., & Au, K. (2002). The effect of cultural differences on the behavioral response to low job satisfaction. *Journal of International Business Studies, 33*(2), 1–18.

Thomas, D. C., & Fitzsimmons, S. R. (2008). Cross-cultural skills and abilities: From communication competence to cultural intelligence. In P. B. Smith, M. F. Peterson, & D. C. Thomas (Eds.), *Handbook of cross-cultural management research* (pp. 201–218). Thousand Oaks, CA: Sage.

Thomas, D. C., & Inkson, K. (2004). *Cultural intelligence: People skills for global business.* San Francisco: Berrett-Koehler.

Thomas, D. C., & Inkson, K. (2008). *Cultural intelligence: Living and working globally.* San Francisco, CA: Berrett-Koehler.

Thomas, D. C., & Lazarova, M. B. (2006). Expatriate adjustment and performance: A critical review. In G. H. Stahl & I. Björkman (Eds.), *Handbook of research in international human resource management* (pp. 247–264). Cheltenham, UK: Edward Elgar.

Thomas, D. C., & Lazorva, M. B. (2013). *Essentials of international human resource management: Managing people globally.* Thousand Oaks, CA: Sage.

Thomas, D. C., & Ravlin, E. C. (1995). Responses of employees to cultural adaptation by a foreign manager. *Journal of Applied Psychology, 80,* 133–146.

Thomas, D. C., Au, K., & Ravlin, E. C. (2003). Cultural variation and the psychological contract. *Journal of Organizational Behavior, 24,* 451–471.

Thomas, D. C., Fitzsimmons, S. R., Ravlin, E. C., Au, K. Y., Ekelund B. Z., & Barzanty, C. (2010). Psychological contracts across cultures. *Organization Studies, 31*(12), 1–22.

Thomas, D. C., Lazarova, M. B., & Inkson, K. (2005). Global careers: New phenomenon or new perspectives? *Journal of World Business, 40,* 340–347.

Thomas, D. C., Ravlin, E. C., & Barry, D. (2000). Creating effective multicultural teams. *University of Auckland Business Review, 2*(1), 10–25.

Thomas, D. C., Ravlin, E. C., & Wallace, A. W. (1996). Cultural diversity in work teams. *Research in the Sociology of Organizations, 14,* 1–13.

Thomas, D. C., Ravlin, E. C., Liao, Y., Morrell, D. L., and Au, K. Y. (in press). Collectivist values, exchange ideology and psychological contract preference. *Management International Review.*

Thomas, D. C., Stahl, G., Ravlin, E. C., Pekerti, A., Maznevski, M., Lazarova, M. B., et al. (2006, August). *Cultural intelligence: Domain and assessment.* Paper presented to the International Association of Cross-Cultural Psychology Congress, Spetses, Greece.

Thomas, E. J., & Fink, C. F. (1963). Effects of group size. *Psychological Bulletin, 60,* 371–384.

Thorne, L., & Saunders, S. B. (2002). The socio-cultural embeddedness of individuals' ethical reasoning in organizations (cross-cultural ethics). *Journal of Business Ethics, 35,* 1–14.

Thurow, L. (1984). Revitalizing American industry: Managing in a competitive world economy. *California Management Review, 27*(1), 9–41.

Ting-Toomey, S. (1999). *Communicating across cultures.* New York: Guilford.

Tinsley, C. (1998). Models of conflict resolution in Japanese, German, and American cultures. *Journal of Applied Psychology, 83*(6), 316–323.

Tinsley, C. H., & Pillutla, M. M. (1998). Negotiating in the United States and Hong Kong. *Journal of International Business Studies, 29,* 711–728.

Toh, S. M., & DeNisi, A. S. (2007). Host country nationals as socializing agents: A social identity approach. *Journal of Organizational Behavior, 28,* 281–301.

Torrence, E. P. (1980). Lessons about giftedness and creativity from a nation of 115 million achievers. *Gifted Child Quarterly, 24,* 10–14.

Townsend, A. M., DeMarie, S. M., & Hendrickson, A. R. (1998). Virtual teams: Technology and the workplace of the future. *Academy of Management Executive, 12,* 17–29.

Trafimow, D., & Finlay, K. A. (1996). The importance of subjective norms for a minority of people: Between-subjects and within-subjects analyses. *Personality and Social Psychology Bulletin, 60,* 820–828.

Tresch, T. S., & Picciano, N. (2007, March). *Effectiveness within NATO's multicultural military operations.* Paper presented to the conference on Cultural Challenges in Military Operations, NATO Defense College, Rome.

Treviño, L. K. (1986). Ethical decision making in organizations. *Academy of Management Review, 11,* 601–617.

Treviño, L. K., Lengel, R. H., & Daft, R. L. (1987). Media symbolism, media richness, and media choice in organizations. A symbolic interactionist perspective. *Communication Research, 14*, 553–574.

Treviño, L. K., Weaver, G. R., & Reynolds, S. J. (2006). Behavioral ethics in organizations: A review. *Journal of Management, 32*(6), 951–990.

Triandis, H. C. (1972). *The analysis of subjective culture.* New York: John Wiley & Sons.

Triandis, H. C. (1978). Some universals of social behavior. *Personality and Social Psychology Bulletin, 4*, 1–16.

Triandis, H. C. (1989). Cross-cultural studies of individualism and collectivism. In J. Berman (Ed.), *Nebraska symposium on motivation* (pp. 41–133). Lincoln: University of Nebraska Press.

Triandis, H. C. (1993). The contingency model in cross-cultural perspective. In M. M. Chemers & R. Ayman (Eds.), *Leadership theory and research: Perspectives and directions* (pp. 167–188). San Diego, CA: Academic Press.

Triandis, H. C. (1994). *Culture and social behavior.* New York: McGraw-Hill.

Triandis, H. C. (1995). *Individualism and collectivism.* Boulder, CO: Westview.

Triandis, H. C., & Suh, E. M. (2002). Cultural influences on personality. *Annual Review of Psychology, 53*, 133–160.

Triandis, H. C., Marin, G., Lisansky, J., & Betancourt, H. (1984). *Simpatia* as a cultural script for Hispanics. *Journal of Personality and Social Psychology, 47*, 1363–1375.

Trist, E. L. (1981). *The evolution of a socio-technical system.* Toronto: Quality of Working Life Center.

Trompenaars, F. (1993). *Riding the waves of culture.* Burr Ridge, IL: Irwin.

Trope, Y. (1986). Identification and inferential processes in dispositional attribution. *Psychological Review, 93*, 239–257.

Tscheulin, D. (1973). Leader behaviors in German industry. *Journal of Applied Psychology, 57*, 28–31.

Tse, D. K., Francis, J., & Walls, J. (1994). Cultural differences in conducting intra- and inter-cultural negotiations: A Sino-Canadian comparison. *Journal of International Business Studies, 25*(3), 537–555.

Tuckman, B. W. (1965). Developmental sequence in small groups. *Psychological Bulletin, 63*(6), 384–399.

Tung, R. L. (1981). Selection and training of personnel for overseas assignments. *Columbia Journal of World Business, 16*, 68–78.

Tung, R. L. (1984). *Business negotiations with the Japanese.* Lexington, MA: Lexington Books.

Tung, R. L. (1988). Toward a conceptual paradigm of international business negotiations. *Advances in International Comparative Management, 3*, 203–219.

Tung, R. L. (1998). A contingency framework of selection and training of expatriates revisited. *Human Resource Management Review, 8*(1), 23–37.

Tung, R. L., & Lazarova, M. (2006). Brain drain versus brain gain: An exploratory study of ex-host country nationals in Central and East Europe. *International Journal of Human Resource Management, 17*(11), 1853–1872.

Turban, D. B., Lau, C. M., Ngo, H. Y., Chow, I. H. S., & Si, S. X. (2001). Organizational attractiveness of firms in the People's Republic of China: A person-organization fit perspective. *Journal of Applied Psychology, 86*, 194–206.

Turner, J. C. (1987). *Rediscovering the social group.* Oxford, UK: Blackwell.

Turnley, W. H., & Feldman, D. C. (1999). The impact of psychological contract violations on exit, voice, loyalty and neglect. *Human Relations, 52*, 895–922.

Tversky, A., & Kahneman, D. (1973). Availability: A heuristic for judging frequency and probability. *Cognitive Psychology, 5*, 207–232.

Tversky, A., & Kahneman, D. (1974). Judgment under uncertainty: Heuristics and biases. *Science, 185*, 1124–1131.

Tversky, A., & Kahneman, D. (1982). Judgments of and by representativeness. In D. Kahneman, P. Slovic & A. Tversky (Eds.), *Judgment under uncertainty: Heuristics and biases*. Cambridge, UK: Cambridge University Press.

Tye, M. G., & Chen, P. Y. (2005). Selection of expatriates: Decision making models used by HR professionals. *Human Resource Planning, 28*(4), 15–20.

UN Conference on Trade and Development. (1999). *World investment report.* New York: United Nations.

UN Conference on Trade and Development. (2005). *World investment report.* New York: United Nations.

UN Conference on Trade and Development. (2013). *World investment report.* New York: United Nations.

United Nations. (2000). *Report of the high-level panel of experts on information and communication technology.* New York: Author.

United Nations. (2006). *World population prospects: The 2006 revision.* http://www.un.org/esa/population/publications/wpp2006/ wpp2006.htm

United Nations Conference on Trade and Development (UNCTAD), *Inward and outward foreign direct investment flows, annual, 1970–2012.* Retrieved from UNCSTADSTAT website: http://unctadstat.unctad.org/TableViewer/tableView.aspx?ReportId=88

Usunier, J. C. (1996). Cultural aspects of international business negotiations. In P. Ghauri & J. C. Usunier (Eds.), *International business negotiations* (pp. 91–118). Oxford, UK: Pergamon.

Usunier, J. C. (1998). *International and cross-cultural management research.* London: Sage.

van den Berg, P. T., & Wilderom, C. P. M. (2004). Defining, measuring, and comparing organizational cultures. *Applied Psychology: An International Review, 53*, 570–582.

van der Vegt, G. S., van de Vliert, E., & Huang, X. (2005). Location level links between diversity and innovative climate depend on national power distance. *Academy of Management Journal, 48*, 1171–1182.

van der Zee, K., Atsma, N., & Brodbeck, F. (2004). The influence of social identity and personality on outcomes of cultural diversity in teams. *Journal of Cross-Cultural Psychology, 35*, 283–303.

van de Vijver, F., & Leung, K. (1997). *Methods and data analysis for cross-cultural research.* Thousand Oaks, CA: Sage.

Varma, A., & Stroh, L. K. (2001). The impact of same sex LMX dyads on performance evaluations. *Human Resource Management, 12*, 84–95.

Vora, D. (2008). Managerial roles in the international context. In P. B. Smith, M. F. Peterson, & D. C. Thomas (Eds.), *Handbook of cross-cultural management research* (pp. 411–430). Thousand Oaks, CA: Sage.

Vora, D., & Kostova, T. (2007). A model of dual identification in the context of the multinational enterprise. *Journal of Organizational Behavior, 28*, 327–350.

Vroom, V. H. (1964). *Work and motivation.* New York: John Wiley & Sons.

Wageman, R. (1995). Interdependence and group effectiveness. *Administrative Science Quarterly, 40*, 145–180.

Wagner, H., Hibbits, N., Rosenblatt, R. D., & Schulz, R. (1977). *Team training and evaluation strategies: State of the art* (Technical report no. 771-1). Alexandria, VA: Human Resources Research Organization.

Wang, K., Hoosain, R., Lee, T. M. C., Meng, Y., Fu, J., & Yang, R. (2006). Perception of six basic emotional facial expressions by the Chinese. *Journal of Cross-Cultural Psychology, 37*, 623–629.

Wang, X., & Kanungo, R. N. (2004). Nationality, social network and psychological well being: Expatriates in China. *International Journal of Human Resource Management, 15,* 775–793.

Ward, D. R. (2002). *Water wars: Drought, flood, folly and the politics of thirst.* New York: Riverhead.

Warkentin, M. E., & Beranek, P. M. (1999). Training to improve virtual team communication. *Information Systems Journal, 9,* 271–289.

Warner, M. (Ed.). (2002). *Studies on the Chinese economy.* New York: St. Martin's Press.

Warren, W., Black, S., & Rangsit, S. (Eds.). (1985). *Thailand.* Englewood Cliffs, NJ: Prentice Hall.

Watson, J. L. (Ed.). (1997). *Golden arches east: McDonald's in east Asia.* Stanford, CA: Stanford University Press.

Watson, O. M. (1970). *Proxemic behavior: A cross cultural study.* The Hague, Netherlands: Mouton.

Watson, O. M., & Graves, T. D. (1966). Quantitative research in proxemic behavior. *American Anthropologist, 68,* 971–985.

Watson, W. E., Johnson, L., & Merritt, D. (1998). Team orientation, self orientation, and diversity in task groups. *Group and Organization Management, 23*(2), 161–188.

Watson, W. E., Kumar, K., & Michaelson, L. K. (1993). Cultural diversity's impact on interaction process and performance: Comparing homogeneous and diverse task groups. *Academy of Management Journal, 36*(3), 590–602.

Webber, R. H. (1969). Convergence or divergence? *Columbia Journal of World Business, 3,* 75–83.

Weick, K. E. (1974). *Henry Mintzberg, The nature of managerial work* [Book review]. *Administrative Science Quarterly, 19,* 111–118.

Weingart, L. R. (1997). How did they do that? The ways and means of studying group processes. *Research in Organizational Behavior, 19,* 189–239.

Weiss, S. E. (1993). Analysis of complex negotiations in international business: The RBC perspective. *Organization Science, 2,* 269–300.

Welch, D. E., & Worm, V. (2006). International business travelers: A challenge for IHRM. In G. H. Stahl & I. Björkman (Eds.), *Handbook of research in international human resource management* (pp. 283–301). Cheltenham, UK: Edward Elgar.

West, G. R. B., & Bocarnea, M. (2008). *Servant leadership and organizational outcomes: Relationships in United States and Filippino higher educational settings.* Paper presented at the Servant Leadership Roundtable at Regent University, Virginia Beach, VA.

Westney, D. E. (1993). Institutionalization theory and the multinational corporation. In S. Ghoshal & E. Westney (Eds.), *Organization theory and the multinational corporation* (pp. 53–76). New York: St. Martin's Press.

Westney, D. E. (1997). Organization theory perspectives and international business. In B. Toyne & D. Nigh (Eds.), *International business: An emerging vision* (pp. 296–312). Columbia: University of South Carolina Press.

Westwood, R. I., & Leung, S. M. (1994). The female expatriate manager experience: Coping with gender and culture. *International Studies of Management and Organization, 24,* 64–85.

Wheeler, K. G. (2002). Cultural values in relation to equity sensitivity within and across cultures. *Journal of Managerial Psychology, 17*(7), 612–627.

Whitehill, A. M., & Takezawa, S. (1978). Workplace harmony: Another Japanese "miracle"? *Columbia Journal of World Business, 13*(3), 25–39.

Whorf, B. L. (1956). A linguistic consideration of thinking in primitive communities. In J. B. Carroll (Ed.), *Language, thought and reality: Selected readings of Benjamin Lee Whorf* (pp. 65–86). Cambridge: MIT Press.

Wiemann, J., Chen, V., & Giles, H. (1986). *Beliefs about talk and silence in a cultural context.* Paper presented to the Speech Communication Association, Chicago, Illinois.

Wilder, D. A. (1978). Perceiving persons as a group: Effects on attribution of causality and beliefs. *Social Psychology, 41*(1), 13–23.

Wilder, D. A. (1986). Social categorization: Implications for creation and reduction of intergroup bias. In L. Berkowitz (Ed.), *Advances in experimental social psychology* (Vol. 19, pp. 291–355). New York: Academic Press.

Williams, A., Dobson, P., & Walters, M. (1993). *Changing cultures: New organizational approaches.* London: Institute of Personnel Management.

Williams, A., Garrett, P., & Tennant, R. (2004). Young adults' perceptions of communication with peers and adolescents. In S. H. Ng, C. N. Candlin, & C. Y. Chiu (Eds.), *Language matter: Communication, identity, and culture* (pp. 111–136). Hong Kong: City University of Hong Kong Press.

Wit, A. P., & Kerr, N. L. (2002). "Me versus just us versus us all" categorization and cooperation in nested social dilemmas. *Journal of Personality and Social Psychology, 83,* 616–637.

Witkin, H. A., & Goodenough, D. R. (1977). Field dependence and interpersonal behavior. *Psychological Bulletin, 84,* 661–689.

Wood, D. J. (1991). Corporate social performance revisited. *Academy of Management Review, 16,* 693–718.

Woodward, J. (1965). *Industrial organization: Theory and practice.* London: Oxford University Press.

World almanac and book of facts. (2006). New York: The New York World Telegram.

World Bank (n.d.). *GDP (annual %).* http://data.worldbank.org/indicator/NY.GDP.PCAP.CD

World Trade Organization. (2013). Regional trade agreements. http://www.wto.org/english/tratop_e/region_e/region_e.htm

World Trade Organization. (1999). *WTO annual report.* Geneva: Author.

World Trade Organization. (2005). *WTO annual report.* Geneva: Author.

World Trade Organization. (2013). *WTO annual report.* Geneva: Author.

Wright, G. N., & Phillips, L. D. (1980). Cultural variation in probabilistic thinking: An alternative way of dealing with uncertainty. *International Journal of Psychology, 15,* 239–257.

Wu, L. (1999). Guanxi: *A cross-cultural comparative study.* (Unpublished doctoral dissertation). University of Auckland, NZ.

Yamada, A.-M., & Singelis, T. M. (1999). Biculturalism and self-construal. *International Journal of Intercultural Relations, 23,* 697–709.

Yamaguchi, S. (2004). Further clarification of the concept of *amae* in relation to attachment and dependence. *Human Development, 47,* 28–33.

Yamazaki, Y., & Kayes, D. C. (2004). An experiential learning approach to cross-cultural learning: A review and integration of competencies for successful expatriate adaptation. *Academy of Management Learning & Education, 3,* 362–379.

Yang, K. S. (1988). Will societal modernization eventually eliminate cross-cultural psychological difference? In M. H. Bond (Ed.), *The cross-cultural challenge to social psychology* (pp. 67–85). Newbury Park, CA: Sage.

Yates, J. F., Lee, J. W., & Shinotsuka, H. (1996). Beliefs about overconfidence, including its cross-national variation. *Organizational Behavior and Human Decision Processes, 65,* 138–147.

Yates, J. F., Zhu, Y., Ronis, D. L., Wang, D., Shinostsuka, H., & Toda, M. (1989). Probability judgment accuracy: China, Japan and the United States. *Organizational Behavior and Human Decision Processes, 43,* 147–171.

Yukl, G. (1989). *Leadership in organizations* (2nd ed.). Englewood Cliffs, NJ: Prentice Hall.

Yukl, G. (1994a). *Leadership in organizations* (3rd ed.). Upper Saddle River, NJ: Prentice Hall.

Yukl, G. (1994b). A retrospective on Robert House's 1976 theory of charismatic leadership and recent revisions. *Leadership Quarterly, 4*(3–4), 367–373.

Yukl, G., & Van Fleet, D. (1992). Theory and research on leadership in organizations. In *Handbook of industrial and organizational psychology* (pp. 147–197). Palo Alto, CA: Consulting Psychology Press.

Zaheer, S., Schomaker, M. S., & Nachum, L. (2012). Distance without direction: Restoring credibility to a much-loved construct. *Journal of International Business Studies, 43,* 18–27.

Zander, L., Mockaitis, A. I., Harzing, A-W., Baldueza, J., Barner-Rasmussen, W., Barzantny, C., et al. (2011). Standardization and contextualization: A study of language and leadership across 17 countries. *Journal of World Business, 45,* 296–304.

Zeira, Y., & Banai, M. (1985). Selection of expatriate managers in MNCs: The host environment point of view. *International Studies of Management and Organization, 15*(1), 33–51.

Zenger, T. R., & Lawrence, B. S. (1989). Organizational demography: The differential effects of age and tenure on technical communication. *Academy of Management Journal, 32,* 353–376.

Zhu, C. J., Dowling, P. J. (2002). Staffing practices in transition: Some empirical evidence from China. *The International Journal of Human Resource Management, 13*(4), 569–597.

Zhuang, J., Thomas, S., & Miller, D. L. (2005). Examining culture's effect on whistle-blowing and peer reporting. *Business & Society, 44*(4), 462–486.

Zika-Viktorsson, A., Sundstrom, P., & Engwall, M. (2006). Project overload: An exploratory study of work and management in multi-project settings. *International Journal of Project Management, 24I,* 385–394.

Zimbardo, P. G. (1977). *Shyness: What it is and what we can do about it.* Reading, MA: Addison-Wesley.

Name Index

Subject Index

About the Authors

David C. Thomas (PhD, University of South Carolina) is currently Professor of International Business in the Australian School of Business, University of New South Wales, Australia. He is the author of nine books, including most recently *Essentials of International Human Resource Management: Managing People Globally* from SAGE Publications (with Mila B. Lazarova) and the best selling *Cultural Intelligence: People Skills for Global Business,* published by Berrett-Koehler Publishers (with Kerr Inkson). In addition, he has recently edited (with Peter B. Smith and Mark F. Peterson) the *Handbook of Cross-Cultural Management Research* from SAGE Publications. His research on cross-cultural interactions in organizational settings has appeared in numerous journals. He is Area Editor for the *Journal of International Business Studies* and also serves on the editorial boards of the *Journal of World Business, Journal of Organizational Behavior,* and *European Journal of Cross-Cultural Competence and Management.*

His previous academic postings have included positions at the Pennsylvania State University, the University of Auckland, New Zealand, where he was also Director of the Master of International Business Program, and Simon Fraser University, Canada. He has held visiting positions at the Chinese University of Hong Kong, the University of Hawaii, Massey University, New Zealand, ESCEM, Tours, France, and Koç University, Istanbul, Turkey. In addition to teaching at both the undergraduate and the postgraduate level, Dr. Thomas has developed executive education programs in Australia, New Zealand, Canada, and the United States and has served as a consultant to a number of multinational firms and government agencies in New Zealand and Canada. When not writing or teaching he can most likely be found sailing on Sydney harbor.

Mark F. Peterson (PhD, University of Michigan) is Professor of International Management at Florida Atlantic University and holds the Hofstede Chair in Cultural Diversity at Maastricht University. He has published over 110 articles and chapters, and five books. The articles have appeared in major management and international management journals such as *Administrative Science Quarterly*, the *Academy of Management Journal*, the *Journal of International Business Studies*, the *Journal of Organizational Behavior, Leadership Quarterly, Human Relations, Organization Studies,* and *Organization Science.* He has also contributed international management themes to the basic social science literature through chapters in the *Annual Review of Psychology*, the *Communication Yearbook*, the *Handbook of Industrial and Organizational Psychology,* and *Research in the Sociology of Organizations.* He is an Associate Editor for the *Journal of Organizational Behavior* and a Consulting Editor for the *Journal of International Business Studies.* He and Michael Soendergaard are currently editing a focused issue of *Management International Review* about national and other cultural boundaries.

His previous positions have been at Wayne State University, the University of Miami, and Texas Tech University. He has had visiting positions supported by Fulbright Fellowships to Osaka University and McMaster University, and he held the John R. Galvin Chair at the Fletcher School of Law and Diplomacy at Tufts University. He has also had visiting positions at the University of Pennsylvania and Aarhus University. Along with Mikael Soendergaard, Geert Hofstede, Michael Minkov, Gert Jan Hofstede, and others, he teaches an annual summer Ph.D. master class in cross cultural management at various locations in Europe. When at his home in Boca Raton in Florida, he spends his weekends tending to a collection of orchids and making orchid hybrids.

SAGE researchmethods

The essential online tool for researchers from the world's leading methods publisher

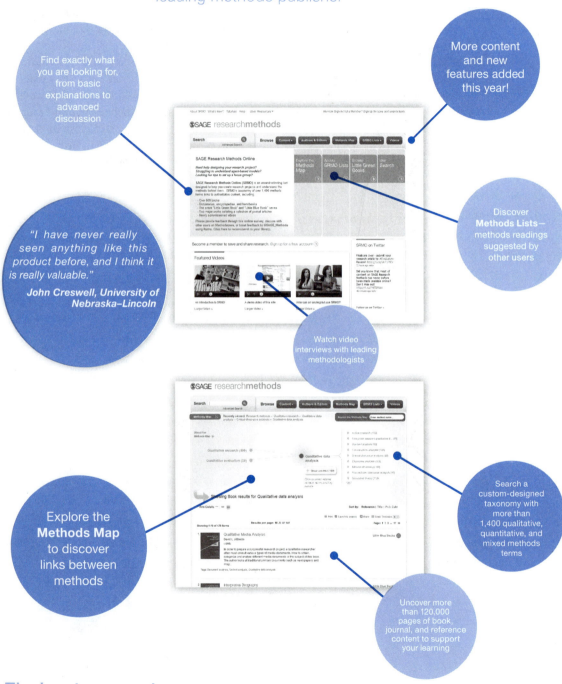

Find exactly what you are looking for, from basic explanations to advanced discussion

More content and new features added this year!

"I have never really seen anything like this product before, and I think it is really valuable."

John Creswell, University of Nebraska–Lincoln

Discover **Methods Lists**— methods readings suggested by other users

Watch video interviews with leading methodologists

Explore the **Methods Map** to discover links between methods

Search a custom-designed taxonomy with more than 1,400 qualitative, quantitative, and mixed methods terms

Uncover more than 120,000 pages of book, journal, and reference content to support your learning

Find out more at
www.sageresearchmethods.com